BEYOND ETHNICITY

Narratives of Conversion, 31
Am. pluralism, 38

Black   Piri Thomas   "Savior" (1972)

BEYOND ETHNICITY
Consent and Descent
in American Culture

WERNER SOLLORS

New York   Oxford
OXFORD UNIVERSITY PRESS
1986

12262578
DLC

8·25·87 jM

Oxford University Press

Oxford   New York   Toronto
Delhi   Bombay   Calcutta   Madras   Karachi
Petaling Jaya   Singapore   Hong Kong   Tokyo
Nairobi   Dar es Salaam   Cape Town
Melbourne   Auckland

and associated companies in
Beirut   Berlin   Ibadan   Nicosia

Published by Oxford University Press, Inc.,
200 Madison Avenue, New York, New York 10016

Oxford is a registered trademark of Oxford University Press

Library of Congress Cataloging in Publication Data

Sollors, Werner
Beyond Ethnicity

Bibliography: p.
Includes index
1. American literature—History and criticism   2. American
literature—Minority authors   3. Ethnicity
4. Literature and society   5. Minorities—United States
6. National characteristics—American   7. United
States—Civilization   8. United States—Emigration and
immigration   9. United States—Popular culture
10. United States—Race relations
ISBN 0-19-503694-8

Printing (last digit):   9 8 7 6 5 4 3 2 1

Printed in the United States of America

For My Mother with Love and Gratitude,
To the Memory of My Father,
And for David

For we are like tree trunks in the snow. In appearance they lie sleekly and
a light push should be enough to set them rolling. No, it can't be done, for
they are firmly wedded to the ground. But see, even that is only appearance.
—Franz Kafka, "The Trees,"
trans. Willa and Edwin Muir

Acknowledgments
and Prefatory Remarks

The undertaking of this project has met with much encouragement and support from numerous individuals and several institutions. Among the many teachers, friends, colleagues, copanelists, correspondents, students, critics, and helpers-without-responsibility-for-my-shortcomings, the following were most important to me: Daniel Aaron, Harold Abramson, Quentin Anderson, Nathan Austern, Sacvan Bercovitch, Warner Berthoff, William Boelhower, Robert Bone, Ursula Brumm, Carla Cappetti, Jules Chametzky, Abner Cohen, Donald Cunnigen, Mary Dearborn, Kathleen Diffley, Morris Dickstein, Janet Dolgin, Ann Douglas, Emory Elliott, Everett Emerson, James Engell, Geneviève Fabre, Thomas Ferraro, Philip Fisher, Fritz Fleischmann, Winfried Fluck, Joyce Flynn, Hans Galinsky, Herbert Gans, Cristina Giorcelli, Philip Gleason, Milton Gordon, Victor Greene, Olaf Hansen, Billy Joe Harris, Michael Hoenisch, Nathan Huggins, Everett Hughes, Michael Kramer, Karl Kroeber, Hans-Joachim Lang, Lawrence Levine, Christoph Lohmann, Agostino Lombardo, Glenn Loury, John Lowe, Richard McCoy, Elizabeth McKinsey, Jerre Mangione, Leo Marx, Martin Meisel, Sheldon Meyer, Geraldine Murphy, Albert Murray, Charles Nichols, Michael O'Friel, Ann Orlov, Berndt Ostendorf, Orm Øverland, Orlando Patterson, Tom Pearson, David Perkins, Joel Porte, Joseph Ridgely, David Riesman, Peter Rose, Jesper Rosenmeier, Paul Royster, Viola Sachs, Jack Salzman, Joseph Schoepp, Henry Shapiro, James Shenton, Mark Silk, Henry Nash Smith, Otto Sonntag, Leo Srole, Judith Steinsapir, the late Warren Susman, Thomas Tanselle, Alan Trachtenberg, Thomas Underwood, Gabriele Weber-Jaric, Lynn Weiss, Cornel West, Virginia Yans, and Rafia Zafar.

Harvard University, Columbia University, and the John F. Kennedy-Institut of the Freie Universität Berlin have given me institutional help throughout the years. The project was started in 1977–78 when I was an Andrew W. Mellon faculty fellow at Harvard and wrote the entry on literature for the *Harvard Encyclopedia of American*

Ethnic Groups. The John Simon Guggenheim Memorial Foundation and the Deutsche Forschungsgemeinschaft permitted me to pursue my research during academic leaves; and the Columbia University Council for Research in the Humanities supported the project for a summer. Finally, for me, as a German, to teach American literature and Afro-American Studies to American students has been a special sort of continuous inspiration.

I have followed some formal guidelines that need a word of explanation. The traditional methods of indicating sources are cumbersome for readers, and the listing at the end of the book of works consulted for a chapter is insufficient for the scholar. I have therefore decided to use a modified version of the new Modern Language Association style sheet in conjunction with traditional social science citations. This means that sources are indicated by differing combinations of author, brief title, year, and page in parentheses throughout the text. All full titles and dates appear at the end in the bibliography, which is organized alphabetically by author. (Unless otherwise indicated, all translations into English are mine.) In order to emphasize the importance of biblical allusions to the language of American ethnicity, biblical references are identified in brackets throughout the book. The first chapter explains my inclusive use of the term "ethnicity." I have made no attempt to aim for representativeness by ethnic groups.

Some of my conclusions have appeared previously, and I have here used sections, arguments, and examples from essays and reviews published in *American Quarterly* (1981 by the Trustees of the University of Pennsylvania), *American Studies in the Teaching of English, Appalachian Journal, Harvard Encyclopedia of American Ethnic Groups,* ed. Stephan Thernstrom, Ann Orlov, and Oscar Handlin (Cambridge, Mass.: Harvard University Press © 1980, by the President and Fellows of Harvard College), *In Their Own Words, Journal of American History,* Rob Kroes's *The American Identity,* MELUS, *Newsletter of the Intellectual History Group* (NYU Institute for the Humanities), *Prospects, Queen City Heritage* (by the Cincinnati Historical Society), *Letterature d'America,* and *Studies in American Indian Literature.* The following copyrighted materials by other copyright holders are reprinted by permission:

Texts: From *New Writing from the Philippines,* ed. Leonard Caspar. Copyright 1966 Syracuse University Press. Reprinted by permission of the author.

From "Otherness" by Diana Chang. Copyright 1974 by Diana Chang. Reprinted by permission of the author.

From *The Penal Colony* by Franz Kafka, trans. Willa and Edwin Muir. Copyright 1948, 1976 by Schocken Books. Reprinted by permission of Schocken Books Inc. and Secker and Warburg, Ltd.

From *Up Stream* by Ludwig Lewisohn. Copyright 1922 by Boni and Liveright. Reprinted by permission of Liveright Publishing Corporation.

From *Collected Poems* by Vachel Lindsay. Copyright 1917 by Macmillan Publishing Company, renewed 1945 by Mamie T. Wheless. Reprinted with permission of Macmillan Publishing Company.

From *Chicago Poems* by Carl Sandburg. Copyright 1916 by Holt, Rinehart and Winston, 1944 by Carl Sandburg. Reprinted by permission of Harcourt Brace Jovanovich Inc.

From *Collected Poems, 1940–1978* by Karl Shapiro. Copyright 1942 and renewed 1970 by Karl J. Shapiro. Reprinted with permission of Random House, Inc.

From *Have Come, Am Here* by José García Villa. Copyright 1942, renewed 1969 by José García Villa. Reprinted by permission of Viking Penguin Inc.

From *Harlem Gallery* by Melvin B. Tolson. Copyright 1965 and reprinted with the permission of Twayne Publishers, a division of G. K. Hall & Co., Boston.

From "Transcontinental" by Richard Wright. Copyright 1935 Richard Wright. By permission of Ellen Wright.

Illustrations: William Hamilton, "Are *we* ethnic?" from *The New Yorker* © 1972. Chrystal Herne and Walker Whiteside in *The Melting-Pot*, John Brougham as Metamora, Cartoon of Edwin Forrest, *Harper's Weekly Supplement*, 29 July 1876, and Po-ca-hon-tas with permission of Harvard Theatre Collection. Photograph of Thomas Crawford, *The Dying Indian Chief*, courtesy of The New-York Historical Society, New York City.

W.S.

Contents

BEYOND ETHNICITY

Introduction

Picture to yourself ... a society which comprises all the nations of the world—English, French, German: people differing from one another in language, in beliefs, in opinions; in a word a society possessing no roots, no memories, no prejudices, no routine, no common ideas, no national character, yet with a happiness a hundred times greater than our own.... What is the connecting link between these so different elements? How are they welded into one people?

—Alexis de Tocqueville

[B]eing an American is not something to be inherited so much as something to be achieved.

—Perry Miller

In an early essay of the genre, "What is American about America?" the Boston Brahmin and Harvard English professor Barrett Wendell tried to explore the nature of the "national character of America." One of the central texts he chose (after arguing that the first Puritan settlers were already "American") was an excerpt from a reply, probably written by John Cotton, to an inquiry by Lord Say, Lord Brooke, and "other Persons of quality." The English noblemen had asked, according to Wendell, "whether, in case they should emigrate to New England with their families, their descendants could be assured of the sort of distinction which persons of quality would enjoy in the mother country" (*Liberty* 28). Here is the official reply, which Wendell considered "characteristically American":

> Hereditary honors both nature and scripture doth acknowledge (Eccles.... [10:17]) but hereditary authority and power standeth only by the civil laws of some commonwealths, and yet, even amongst them, the authority and power of the father is no where communicated, together with his honors, unto all his posterity. Where God blesseth any branch of any noble or generous family, with a spirit and gifts fit for government, it would be a taking of God's name in vain to put such a talent under a bushel, and a sin against the honor of magistracy to neglect such in our public elections. But if God

should not delight to furnish some of their posterity with gifts fit for magistracy, we should expose them rather to reproach and prejudice, and the commonwealth with them, than exalt them to honor, if we should call them forth, when God doth not, to public authority. (Hutchinson, *History* 412)

One could probably assemble a whole bookshelf full of answers to similar requests by European noblemen and dignitaries, but I shall be content here with one more—very prominent—reply to another such inquiry. It is a letter dated June 4, 1819, in which John Quincy Adams answered Mr. Morris de Furstenwaerther's question whether German emigrants might expect, as an incentive, special favors or privileges in America. In his reply, Adams reminded German emigrants that they

come to a life of independence, but to a life of labor—and, if they cannot accommodate themselves to the character, moral, political, and physical, of this country, with all its compensating balances of good and evil, the Atlantic is always open to them to return to the land of their nativity and their fathers. To one thing they must make up their minds, or they will be disappointed in every expectation of happiness as Americans. They must cast off the European skin, never to resume it. They must look forward to their posterity rather than backward to their ancestors; they must be sure that whatever their own feelings may be, those of their children will cling to the prejudices of this country. . . . (Rischin, *Immigration* 47; see Hansen, *Atlantic* 96)

These two passages, both consciously written or quoted to invoke the "character . . . of this country,"—may seem to be of little immediate interest to readers concerned with American ethnicity, yet they are of central importance to the way ethnicity is symbolized in America. When Wendell discussed the excerpt, he pointed out that Cotton "knew all the while, as everybody knows, that the grace of God is not apt to descend hereditarily in prolonged family lines" (*Liberty* 69). Wendell saw at the core of "the American national character" a denial of legitimacy and privilege based exclusively on descent. The excerpt from Adams, which was included in a recent reader on immigration, expresses the classic American idea of the newcomers' rebirth into a forward-looking culture of consent. Cotton and Adams accepted the importance of descent; yet both also rejected it as an exclusive category in structuring a commonwealth. This tension between the rejection of hereditary old-world hierarchies (embodied by the European nobility) and the vision of a new people of diverse nativities united in the fair pursuit of happiness marks the course that American ideology has steered between descent and consent. It is this conflict which is at the root of the ambiguity surrounding the very terminology of American ethnic interaction.

Amused by the imaginative ways in which American historians have avoided using terms such as "imperialism," Robin Winks spoke of "semantic safety-valves" to which scholars resort (Kroes 145). The world of American group interaction is discussed with a whole arsenal of such safety valves, terms which are both ambiguous and elusive. Trying to grasp one concept, we are led to another; and as we are focusing on that, to yet another one. The feeling is reminiscent of grabbing a balloon filled with water: just as our grip tightens, the substance escapes. Terms like "ethnicity," "melting pot," "intermarriage," "regionalism," and "generation" are all used in a dazzling variety of elusive ways. They squush this way and that depending on how hard we squeeze the balloon.

The historian Frederick Jackson Turner's work is representative for many, as it provides us with numerous instances of heavily charged terms which are loosely arranged around his central metaphor of the frontier and offered as answers. In his famous collection *The Frontier in American History* (1920), one can read such resonant sentences as the following:

> In the crucible of the frontier the immigrants were Americanized, liberated, and fused into a mixed race, English in neither nationality nor characteristics. (23)

> The middle region {between New England and South} ... had a wide mixture of nationalities, a varied society, the mixed town and county system of local government, a varied economic life, many religious sects. In short, it was a region mediating between New England and the South and the East and the West. It represented that composite nationality which the contemporary United States exhibits, that juxtaposition of non-English groups occupying a valley or a little settlement, and presenting reflections of the map of Europe in their variety. It was democratic and nonsectional if not national; "easy, tolerant, and contented;" rooted strongly in material prosperity. It was typical of the modern United States. (27–28)

In such instances the idea of an American crucible, the mental map of the mediating region, and the distinction between "regional" and "sectional" are not explanatory categories but only vague metaphors.

In order to avoid such semantic safety valves, I am here trying to approach some of the most heavily charged terms head-on. In doing so, I rely on, and develop, a less overtaxed terminology which takes the conflict between contractual and hereditary, self-made and ances-

tral, definitions of American identity—between *consent* and *descent*—
as the central drama in American culture. Consent and descent are
terms which allow me to approach and question the whole maze of
American ethnicity and culture. They are relatively neutral though
by no means natural terms. Descent relations are those defined by
anthropologists as relations of "substance" (by blood or nature); consent relations describe those of "law" or "marriage." Descent language
emphasizes our positions as heirs, our hereditary qualities, liabilities,
and entitlements; consent language stresses our abilities as mature
free agents and "architects of our fates" to choose our spouses, our
destinies, and our political systems. As Wendell accurately perceived,
an attack on the system of hereditary privilege has American over-
tones; and modern, democratic political and family relations are
described in terms of the consent of the governed, the age of consent,
or consenting adults. We could rephrase Tocqueville's question and
ask: How can consent (and consensus) be achieved in a country
whose citizens are of such heterogeneous descent? And how can dissent be articulated without falling back on myths of descent?

Focusing on the tensions between consent and descent relations
permits us to look at American culture anew, including even its
familiar and ambiguous semantic safety valves. This enables us to
make some new connections between Puritan typology and immigration, regeneration sermons and debates about the melting pot, or
wedding imagery in church membership and American citizenship.
Most striking in a great variety of American texts are the persistent
attempts to construct a sense of natural family cohesion in the new
world, especially with the help of naturalizing codes and concepts
such as "love" and "generations." The conflicts between descent and
consent in American literature thus can tell us much about the creation of an American culture out of diverse pre-American pasts.

The literature customarily filed under labels such as immigration,
race, regionalism, and ethnicity provides a unique testing ground for
exceptionalist interpretations of America. If North American literature and culture are, indeed, dramatically different from European
and other old- and new-world counterparts, then we can investigate
the Americanness of American art in different ways. We may, as Barrett Wendell, Perry Miller, Ursula Brumm, and Sacvan Bercovitch
have done, date the origins of a characteristically American sense of
selfhood to the transformation of old-world into new-world traits
that took place in Puritan New England; we may also, as Quentin
Anderson and Richard Poirier have done, ascribe to Emersonian
transcendentalism the crucial role of shaping a typically American,

all-absorbing self; or we may think of other historical moments such as the American Revolution, the Civil War, or World War I as having given birth to a uniquely American cultural idiom. But whenever it was that America was born or came of age, in all the instances mentioned we may also look at the writings of and about people who were descended from diverse backgrounds but were, or consented to become, Americans. This way we may learn something about how Americanness is achieved, at the point of its emergence, and how it is established again and again as newcomers and outsiders are socialized into the culture—a process which inevitably seems to revitalize the culture at the same time. Works of ethnic literature—written by, about, or for persons who perceived themselves, or were perceived by others, as members of ethnic groups—may thus be read not only as expressions of mediation between cultures but also as handbooks of socialization into the codes of Americanness.

A cartoon published in the *New Yorker* in 1956 showed an exotic chieftain addressing a group of young males from his tribe with the words "Young men, you've now reached the age when it is essential that you know the rites and rituals, the customs and taboos of our island. Rather than go into them at detail, however, I'm simply going to present each of you with a copy of this excellent book by Margaret Mead." This cartoon functions in a revealingly double-edged way. Of course, we all know that this is not the way "Coming of Age" works in Samoa, but at the same time, books published in America do reveal some of the socializing rituals that initiate newcomers into an American identity. From Crèvecoeur's *Letters from an American Farmer* (1782) to Rølvaag's *Giants in the Earth* (1927), ethnic literature has provided Americans with a grammar of new world imagery and conduct. These writings have complemented popular culture in providing newcomers, outsiders, and insiders with the often complicated mental constructions of American codes. At times these codes may be contentless and merely contrastive definitions *against* an old world. With the help of such procedures America appears as the "un-Europe" characterized by negative catalogs as the land without kings, bishops, or medieval castles. Among more specifically defined codes are suggestive images of exodus and deliverance, newness and rebirth, melting pot and romantic love, jeremiads against establishment figures and lost generations—all of which, most important, contribute to the construction of new forms of symbolic kinship among people who are not blood relatives. Ethnic literature may thus be read as part of that body of cultural products which tells American initiates and neophytes about, and reminds elders of, "the rites and rituals, the customs and taboos of this country," rituals many of which were first developed by English immigrants of the seventeenth century. In this sense ethnic literature provides us with the central codes of Americanness.

Though it is often regarded as a very minor adjunct to great American mainstream writing, ethnic literature is, as several readers pointed out in the past, prototypically American literature. In *The Cultural Approach to History* (1940), Caroline Ware argued for a broad ethnic interpretation of America: "Immigrants and the children of immigrants *are* the American people. Their culture *is* American culture, not merely a contributor to American culture" (87). In his famous introduction to *The Uprooted* (1951), Oscar Handlin echoed: "Once I thought to write a history of the immigrants in America. Then I discovered that the immigrants *were* American history" (3). John F. Kennedy's *A Nation of Immigrants* (1964) popularized this way of looking at America *as* immigration. As did Frederick Jackson Turner, Ware, Handlin, and Kennedy placed a great rhetorical emphasis on migration. Following this emphasis one is sometimes persuaded to view slaves rather euphemistically as newcomers among others and to ignore Indians or to reinterpret them as "America's earliest immigrants." Yet despite such crucial shortcomings, the gist of these pronouncements is right; and it is well worth it to interpret America not narrowly as immigration but more broadly as ethnic diversity and include the pre-Columbian inhabitants of the continent, the kidnapped Africans and their descendants, and the Chicanos of the Southwest—though they, too, are not classic immigrants. As the Bureau of the Census pamphlet "We, the Mexican Americans" put it: "The United States Came to Us" (Simmen 46).

It has perhaps become obvious already that in order to answer Tocqueville's question with the help of literature, I use the term "literature" in a broad sense—to include *New Yorker* cartoons and works of history. In the course of the argument, I shall refer to some nationally and some internationally recognized American writers (the two are not always identical) as well as to phonograph records, movies, comics, songs, paintings and illustrations, essays, plays, sermons, poems, and many B novels. My selection of texts is thus a very broad one, ranging from Cotton Mather to *Young Frankenstein*, from Crèvecoeur to James Weldon Johnson's *Autobiography of an Ex-Colored Man*, from "The Son of Alknomook" to Horace Kallen's *Culture and Democracy in the United States*, and from John Brougham's burlesques to *Liquid Sky*. Rather than adhere to any canonization—be it mainstream or ethnic—I shall look at what I find fascinating in American culture, from well known to completely unknown, from authentic to unambiguously fake ethnic, and from complicated modernist to squarely melodramatic specimens of the culture.

Sociologists, historians, and literary critics have, of course, written about literature and ethnicity for a long time. The boundaries between disciplines, however, have sometimes had detrimental effects on some previous efforts of this sort.[1] Ethnicity specialists sometimes tend to misread literature or misinterpret it as direct social and historical evidence, whereas literary critics in many cases have stayed away from newer sociological and anthropological approaches to ethnicity.

Theorists of ethnicity have customarily drawn on literary examples in order to illustrate their theses—much as Bachofen drew on Aeschylus, Freud on Sophocles, or Marx on Eugène Sue's *Mysteries of Paris*. The Chicago sociologist Robert Park, for example, viewed "moral dichotomy and conflict" as probable characteristics "of every immigrant during the period of transition, when old habits are being discarded and new ones are not yet formed. It is inevitably a period of inner turmoil and intense self-consciousness." In order to flesh out this theory, which Park developed in his landmark essay "Human Migration and the Marginal Man" (1928), he referred to American Jewish autobiographies as "different versions of the same story—the story of the marginal man" and specifically mentioned Ludwig Lewisohn's *Up Stream* (1922): "Lewisohn's restless wavering between the warm security of the ghetto, which he has abandoned, and the cold freedom of the outer world, in which he is not yet quite at home, is typical" (Park 355). Perceptive and plausible though Park's thesis is, his literary witness Lewisohn—as we shall see in the chapter entitled "The Ethics of Wholesome Provincialism"—never dwelled in any ghetto, warm or otherwise. Even when the literary evidence is not so overtly misread, there are some problems with the way in which literature is viewed by the more theoretical analysts. Richard Wright's fiction, for example, is frequently invoked in sociological accounts of the ghetto. Yet it is—precisely in its depiction of psychological alienation and cultural deprivation—the partial product of Wright's immersion into Chicago school of sociology readings (Fabre 232). Such uses of literature as social evidence may be circular.[2]

My interest is not in the raw data of the so-called ethnic experience, but in the mental formations and cultural constructions (the codes, beliefs, rites, and rituals) which were developed in America in order to make sense of ethnicity and immigration in a melting-pot culture. These formations are palpable in imaginative literature of the most diverse ethnic provenance as well as in nonfiction, including academic discussions of the field. When Horace Kallen wrote that we cannot change our grandfathers, he was telling a *story*—even though he was telling it in the form of nonfiction. I shall pay special attention to such stories, whether told by writers or scholars, by ministers or essayists, in order to lay bare the lens through which fictional literature, historiography, and social sciences perceive consent and descent.

Perhaps the most popular literary text discussed by social scientists and immigration historians is Israel Zangwill's *The Melting-Pot* (1909), a play which has rarely if ever been read as literature. And yet, as we shall see in the melting-pot chapter, the social critics who take this play as the point of departure for an attack on the social concept which it supposedly embodies often go on to paraphrase the play's contagious rhetoric in their own predictions. One yearns for better ways in which literary and historical-sociological methodologies might be combined in order to illuminate the conflict between consent and descent as it operates in American culture.

I shall here try to draw on more recent conceptualizations of kinship and ethnicity, most especially those by Fredrik Barth, Abner Cohen, George Devereux, Herbert Gans, Ulf Hannerz, Orlando Patterson, David Schneider, and others, and look at the ways in which symbolic ethnicity and a sense of natural kinship that weld Americans into one people were *created*. For this purpose I shall take the liberty of reading all texts as if they were literature. This procedure allows me to look at Handlin's *Uprooted* as "the epic story of the great migrations that made the American people" (the book's subtitle) in the tradition of Cotton Mather's Vergilian format in the *Magnalia Christi Americana* (1702). Similarly, this approach might permit us to place Nathan Glazer and Daniel Patrick Moynihan's *Beyond the Melting Pot* or Michael Novak's *Rise of the Unmeltable Ethnics* in the tradition of community-scolding, yet community-building, American sermons: these and many other books could be profitably interpreted in the framework of Sacvan Bercovitch's study *The American Jeremiad* as they move from social critique to prophecy and promise.

When we turn to literary criticism devoted to ethnic literature, we encounter a different weakness. Sociologists may often overestimate and even exoticize literature (in the narrow sense of belles lettres) as supreme evidence while underestimating their own reliance on literary devices and story-telling techniques. Literary critics, on the other hand, tend to be either uninterested in anything but the leading American writers or unaware of the newer thinking on ethnicity. Although in 1972 the annual bibliography *American Literary Scholarship* called for a moratorium on further publications about, for example, William Faulkner's overinterpreted story "A Rose for Emily" (114), the publication machinery continues to churn out the most intensely interpreted texts again and again (see *American Literary Scholarship 1976*, 137; *1979*, 154). The selection of mainstream texts sometimes reveals the critics' anxiety about the value of American literature vis-à-vis British literature. American critics who do turn to other texts, studied under such romantic categories as "forgotten voices," the "outnumbered," and "the proud people," may feel so brave for simply touching these works and questions that they are sometimes contented to document them bibliographically or to "celebrate" their mere existence. With some important exceptions, scholarship of American ethnic writing has shown comparatively little theoretical interest in American-made ethnicity. Literary critics easily succumb to the danger of resorting to an implicit "good vibes" methodology (which approaches ethnic literature with well-intentioned optimism, though sometimes with moral indignation as its underpinning), grounding close readings of texts on static notions of descent and on primordial, organicist, sometimes even biological—but in all cases largely unquestioned—concepts of ethnic-group membership.

Literary critics have seldom fully appreciated their texts in the context of newer theories of ethnicity. Instead of understanding their texts as codes for a socialization into ethnic groups and into America, readers have overemphasized and exaggerated the (frequently exoticized) ethnic particularity of the works—even if they were published in English by major American publishing houses. The literature is often read and evaluated against an elusive concept of authenticity, and the question of who is entitled to interpret the literature is given undue emphasis. The belief is widespread among critics who stress descent at the expense of consent that only biological insiders can understand and explicate the literature of race and ethnicity. Published by Grove Press in 1965, *The Autobiography of Malcolm X* may appear to be a very American book to an innocent reader from abroad, who might be impressed by the classic account of a powerfully modern Augustinian conversion experience; yet Richard Gilman claimed some years ago that white American readers could not possibly understand or review this American book and suggested a general moratorium on white critics reviewing black writers (Bigsby 36-49).

Illustrating the influence black literary debates of the 1960s exerted on ethnics of the 1970s, this belief in ethnic exclusivity has proliferated into the various ethnic provinces of America, where it has been rephrased in different ethnic guises. At a professional panel in 1976, for example, a specialist in ethnic literature proclaimed:

> Even though I am hurt that Mario Puzo had to write a novel as potentially defaming to Italian Americans as *The Godfather*, I admit that every page of it touches me in a way that *Tom Sawyer* could never do. ... For me, *The Godfather* is not ethnic literature. It is simply literature—but remember who is saying this. I am, myself, an ethnic and, even more specifically, an ethnic of the group that Puzo is writing about. ... The novel is no more ethnic than the food I eat at home. As far as I am concerned, the Thanksgiving turkey with its cranberry sauce is ethnic and baked lasagna is not.

This attitude is quite common in ethnic studies today. It is based on the assumption that experience is first and foremost ethnic. Critics should practice cultural relativism and stick to their own turfs (based, of course, on descent), since an unbridgeable gulf separates Americans of different ethnic backgrounds and most especially all white Anglo-Saxon Protestants (acronymically known as WASPs) from all non-WASPs. As evidence for his own entitlement, this same lecturer also used the sentence "she called herself Kay Adams" from the novel which he—ethnic insider that he is—knew was a "word-for-word translation ... of the Italian *chiamarsi* which means not 'to call oneself' but simply 'to be named.'" And he concluded in his speech, which the ethnic journal *MELUS* considered worth reprinting in its spring 1977 issue: "I can only conjecture how readers not familiar with this Italian expression are interpreting the passage. Perhaps they find in it some doubt that the girl's name is really Kay Adams" (2–4).

When the lecture was delivered at the Hilton Hotel in New York City, a professor from Italy pointed out that he thought of *The Godfather* as a very American book, closer to Mark Twain than the lecturer believed. (And this was still before Puzo wrote the screenplay for the ultimate immigrant saga, *Superman—The Movie*.) One could also say to the Italian-American *Godfather* critic that recipes for lasagna are as generally available in American cookbooks as are those for turkey; that many languages (among them French and Russian) know the reflexive "calling oneself" in the sense of "being named"; or that, by the lecturer's own logic, one might assume that Italian-Americans might have difficulties understanding the first sentence of

Melville's *Moby-Dick*. One could furthermore indicate that the professor's rhetoric was more deeply influenced by black-white interaction in the 1960s than by any Italian tradition, and that he himself drew freely on Alex Haley's *Roots* without perceiving an analogous problem there. ... But all these objections would not go to the heart of the matter.

The heart of the matter is that in the present climate consent-conscious Americans are willing to perceive ethnic distinctions—differentiations which they seemingly base exclusively on descent, no matter how far removed and how artificially selected and constructed— as powerful and as crucial; and that writers and critics pander to that expectation. "You will never understand me. Don't you understand?"—is the gesture with which cultural interaction seems to function; and even the smallest symbols of ethnic differentiation ("she called herself Kay Adams") are exaggerated out of proportion to represent major cultural differences, differences that are believed to defy comparison or scrutiny. "Call me Ishmael" is ethnic for *Godfather*-Americans, basta! But a French surname doesn't make me an expert on Beaujolais; and critics should not give in to such demands for biological insiderism. Taken to its radical conclusion, such a position really assumes that there is no shared history and no human empathy, that you have your history and I have mine—in which case it becomes quite pointless to give lectures on ethnic literature. Agnes Heller recently reminded anthropologists that "no culture is absolutely hermetically sealed to all others" (272). This is, of course, even more true of the intricately interrelated ethnic and regional cultures in the United States. In the *American Scholar* (1976) Quentin Anderson described the self-authenticated values of American individuals who are, "socially speaking, reduced to units—with skylights" on their heads (417); the relativist position of ethnic insiderism uses ethnicity similarly to aggrandize and to wrap a cloak of legitimacy and authenticity around the speaker who invokes it.

Ironically, the very popularity of defiant ethnic revivalism and exclusivism in the United States suggests a widespread backdrop of assimilation against which it takes place (Higham 198; *HEAEG* 50, 150). The process works only in a context where values, assumptions, and rhetoric are shared. You do not approach an enemy army pointing out that they have no understanding of the subtle way in which you use a reflexive verb. In an article in *Center Magazine* (July/August 1974), Nathan Huggins observed: "Despite what one may suspect, an Afro-American and the grandson of a Polish immigrant will be able to take more for granted between themselves than the former could

with a Nigerian or the latter with a Warsaw worker" (56). It is, ironically, because Americans take so much for granted among themselves that they can dramatize their differences comfortably. Ethnicity
is thus constantly being invented anew in contemporary America.[3]

The dominant assumption among serious scholars who study ethnic literary history is that such history can best be written by separating the groups that produced literature in the United States. The
published results of this procedure are the readers and compendiums
made up of random essays on groups of ethnic writers who have little
in common except so-called ethnic roots; meanwhile, obvious and
important literary and cultural connections are obfuscated. The con-
tours of an ethnic literary history are beginning to emerge which
views writers primarily, if not exclusively, as members of various ethnic and gender groups. How an Italian-American academic picks up
an Afro-American militant gesture from the 1960s and uses it for his
own ends is not subjected to scrutiny. Instead, in the context of ethnic literary history, F. Scott Fitzgerald, whom Malcolm Cowley once
described as an Irishman in disguise (*Situation* 153), drifts away from
Ernest Hemingway (Anglo-American) and Gertrude Stein (Jewish-
American, women's literature) and moves closer to his fellow Irishman Finley Peter Dunne—with whom, of course, he has otherwise
little in common. A student interested in American poetry of the
1950s may find the following directions in ethnic literary
bibliographies:

> Allen Ginsberg—see Jewish-American literature
> Jack Kerouac—see Franco-American literature, French-Canadian
>   literature
> Frank O'Hara—see Irish-American literature, gay writers
> LeRoi Jones—see Afro-American literature
> Diane DiPrima—see Italian-American literature, women's literature.

Taken exclusively, what is often called the ethnic perspective—the
total emphasis on a writer's *descent*—all but annihilates art movements such as the Beat Generation or New York poetry and can do
little with a magazine of the late 1950s which contains all of these
writers side by side.

I would like to take the Beat Generation of this example (as it was
recently studied by Nathan Austern), or the Lost Generation of the
previous one, as a model for American literature as a whole. If anything, ethnic literary history ought to *increase* our understanding of
the cultural interplays and contacts among writers of different backgrounds, the cultural mergers and secessions that took place in Amer-

ica, all of which can be accomplished only if the categorization of writers as members of ethnic groups is understood to be a very partial, temporal, and insufficient characterization at best. If we want to apply temporal ethnic distinctions to a fuller interpretation of American culture (which a study of the Beat Generation that totally ignored descent and overemphasized *consent* would also miss), we have to develop a terminology that goes beyond the organicist imagery of roots and can come to terms with the pervasiveness and inventiveness of syncretism. Seen this way, the very assertion of the ethnic dimensions of American culture can be understood as part of the rites and rituals of this land, as an expression of a persistent conflict between consent and descent in America. Whether they know it or not, writers and literary historians participate in the delineation of this conflict. And the rhetoric in which this conflict is experienced and expressed may well be the "connecting link" that Tocqueville was looking for: the symbolic construction of American kinship has helped to weld Americans of diverse origins into one people, even if the code at times requires the exaggeration of differences.

In an article entitled "Symbolic Representation and the Urban Milieu" (1957–58), Richard Wohl and Anselm Strauss argued that "the complexity of the city calls for verbal management" (523), for symbolic representation ranging from the bird's-eye view to the personification, from "hymns of revulsion" to "paeans of praise or devotion" (529). These symbolic representations provide a sense of order and organization—even when they are highly unflattering. Their observation is equally applicable to ethnicity and ethnic groups which exist as abstract, complex, unfathomable units in constant need of symbolic representation.

I shall attempt to describe these symbolizations, and I shall act as if I lived in a universe in which anything can be compared and in which disciplinary boundaries are a challenge—never insurmountable walls—to readers. I shall furthermore assume that historical forces operate across the board, even though they may appear in particular ethnic emanations, creating such phenomena of trans-ethnic importance as the Beat Generation.

A good illustration of literature as such a cultural code is provided by the carefully detailed ethnic rooms which appear in American writing as obvious maps for characters and readers. A good example from the mid-nineteenth century appears in Emil Klauprecht's novel *Cincinnati; oder, Geheimnisse des Westens* (1853–54)—which is, incidentally, also full of hymns of revulsion toward the Queen City of the

West; it is the meticulously detailed description of the Hotel Dumas, frequented by free colored travelers.

> In the bar as well as in the men's and women's parlors we find all the comforts of larger hotels. The walls are adorned with portraits of liberty's martyr Ogee, of steadfast and heroic L'Ouverture, of witty Friedrich Douglass, and with historical pictures representing the liberation of the slaves in the West Indies, the attack by the Negro nobleman Cinqez on the captain and cook of the slave ship *Amistad*, scenes from *Othello*, and other subjects.

In this American hotel, where customers discuss the same political topics as guests in other hotels, difference is symbolically constructed by the images which convey a special sense of peoplehood to frequenters of the Hotel Dumas, the very name of which

> is taken from the fecund French novelist Alexander Dumas, whom the colored population recognizes with pride as a racial comrade; this often reminds them bitterly that in this land of human rights even the matador of the Western romance shops would be generally despised on account of his skin color and his woolly hair. (2:49–50)

Although the colored Cincinnatians could hardly forget their identity, the hotel surrounded them with community-building imagery. What was programmatically absent, however, was a national symbol, an absence that was in itself a symbolic statement.

Immigrants of the twentieth century often imagined symbolic objects and surroundings that would represent the conflicting realms of new country and old. In *Sommerløv* (1903), for example, the Danish-American minister Adam Dan pictured the Danish and the American flags on the Fourth of July:

> Danish cross, and stars and stripes,
> both beloved the same,
> remind us where we built our home
> and from whence we came. (Skårdal 295)

An ethnic flag is similarly combined with the American colors in many ethnic-group photographs of the World War I era and, in a rather elaborate surrounding, in Michael Gold's *Jews without Money* (1930): "At one end of the room," Moscowitz's wine cellar on Rivington Street,

> under a big American flag, hung a chromo showing Roosevelt charging up San Juan Hill. At the other end hung a Jewish Zionist flag — blue and white bars and star of David. It draped a crayon portrait of

Dr. Theodore Herzl, the Zionist leader, with his pale, proud face, black beard and burning eyes. (81)

Calogero's saloon in the Italian-American Rochester of Jerre Mangione's childhood is decorated in comparably paradoxical fashion. Mangione wrote in *Mount Allegro* (1942):

> What fascinated me most about the saloon was the art work on the huge mirror behind the bar. There I got my first glimpse of the Bay of Naples and Mount Vesuvius. The volcano was in scarlet red and the bay in dazzling blue, and the whole scene was set in a tremendous gold frame on which were glued wooden roses. On the bay were a large number of sailboats, with their sails bent in opposite directions, so that it appeared as though the wind were blowing from two directions at the same time. A pure ribbon was draped over the top of the frame, and on it was printed in Italian, "See Naples and Die."
>
> Above the whole thing an Italian flag was entwined with an American one, between a calendar reproduction of "September Morn" and a sign with rhinestone letters which read, "Home Sweet Home." (169-70)

Such rooms often have an ethnic and an American wall. In more recent writing the pattern continues, though the nature of the American and ethnic symbols may change. In the stage directions to his play *The Chickencoop Chinaman*, Frank Chin described the apartment of the Japanese-American dentist Kenji in the "Oakland" ghetto of Pittsburgh: "The walls are covered with posters of black country, blues and jazz musicians that clash with the few Japanese prints and art objects" (Chin, *Aiiieeeee!* 55). This set may be representative of a whole group of new immigrant intellectuals and writers whose Americanization has taken place through contact with Afro-American culture. Though the opposition of symbols is somewhat different in this example, it dramatizes the same antithesis between American and ethnic symbols: though conflict is what we are supposed to think of in these rooms, we may also look at these rooms through Herbert Gans's perspective and see popular objects used in the service of creating a sense of symbolic ethnicity—while leveling ethnicity and American identity to such parallel symbols as flags or portraits. As George Devereux showed in his seminal essay "Antagonistic Acculturation" (1943), even ethnic protest may have assimilative effects. In contemporary America ethnic revivalists who want to defy assimilation often adopt black American styles rather than white ones—which makes cultural sense, though it does little to support claims for authentically indigenous ethnic styles.

The time has come for American ethnic literary studies to rethink ethnicity theory and for social scientists and historians to understand literary and rhetorical patterns in a new way, even in their own works. Such new openness may also aid teachers of ethnic literature, inspire students of American culture (there are many paper and the-sis topics here), and provide Americans and non-Americans with new ways to understand the new world.

I am quite aware that—although I think of my subject and my texts as products of modern history—I shall attempt to work com-paratively and to lay bare mental structures, which might create the false impression of an unhistorical, merely structurally oriented inter-est. My defense lies again in the image of the balloon. If I tried to discuss my subject by narrowing it down, for example, to "Consent and Descent in American Culture: The Case of the Chicago South Side Writers' Workshop from 1925 to 1934," I might be in better company with currently practicing ethnic historians. However, with such a procedure I would have lost the wider view, and I might have felt tempted to structure such a study along melodramatic lines— against the previous period from which the workshop liberated itself or against North Side attempts to co-opt the imaginary venture. In the present, admittedly large scope of the book, what Orlando Pat-terson called the "beast" of ethnicity (*Chauvinism* 10–11) has no exit. Thus the book can avoid denouncing periods and ethnic groups or vilifying Puritans, the second generation, modernization, or—the most favored scapegoat in the field—the melting pot. It is the whole balloon that I am after.

This book investigates the origins and ambiguities of the term "ethnicity" and illustrates some of the newer theories (Chapter 1); describes the importance of New England's typological vision for the emergence of different peoplehoods in America (Chapter 2); dis-cusses the melting pot in some unusual contexts (Chapter 3); surveys the strange rhetorical conjunction of melancholy Indian and family drama in American popular culture (Chapter 4) and pursues devel-opmental lines from Indian to urban motifs (Interlude); looks at and interprets some tales of consent and descent (Chapter 5); develops some mental maps of the idealism of group-affiliation thinking (Chapter 6); attempts to get closer to the mysteries of generational counting and ancestor constructing in America (Chapter 7); and, finally, considers some formal implications of writing on themes of ethnicity (Chapter 8).

In his discussion of conversions, William James described experiencing a "wide field" of consciousness, when he wrote in *The Varieties of Religious Experience* (1902):

> Usually when we have a wide field we rejoice, for we then see masses of truth together, and often get glimpses of relations which we divine rather than see, for they shoot beyond the field into still remoter regions of objectivity, regions which we seem rather to be about to perceive than to perceive actually. (231)

This experience can come about in many different ways, among them, by reading. As Malcolm X wrote in the chapter entitled "Saved" in his autobiography, "reading had changed forever the course of my life" (179). I had many such experiences in the years of researching and writing this book, and often felt that Jamesian excitement of suddenly seeing masses of truth together. This happened, for example, when I detected melting-pot rhetoric in biblical commentaries on "partition walls," when I found an anonymous Swedish immigrant who called America his bride and Sweden his mother, when Royce's Aristotelian construction of "wholesome provincialism" became a key to so many confusing texts on regionalism and ethnicity, or when theoretical essays on generations gave me the feeling that I had been blind when I had used the term so naively earlier.

I can only hope that I shall be able to convey here and there some of this excitement to a reader whose eyes might halt on a passage in this book—and who might then see a wider field and look at literature (and life) in a new light. I would be happy if the way I have learned to look at consent and descent in America could prove useful to some readers or, better still, turn out to be just a bit contagious even to readers initially skeptical.

CHAPTER ONE

Beyond Ethnicity

Identification with an ethnic group is a source of values, instincts, ideas, and perceptions that throw original light on the meaning of America.
—Michael Novak

No one quite knows what ethnicity means: that is why it's so useful a term.
—Irving Howe

"Beyond the Melting Pot" was more than the title of a book by Nathan Glazer and Daniel Patrick Moynihan. Its publication in 1963 marked the end of an era. It paved the way for the revival of American ethnic identification in the 1960s and 1970s when attacks on the melting pot became the battle cry of "unmeltable ethnics" who admonished their audiences to pay attention to ethnicity and to give up the assimilationist hope that ethnicity was going to disappear. Following Milton Gordon's lead (*Human* 68), social scientists have described the more traditional scholarly attitudes toward ethnicity as "expectancies," and the expectation was that it was going to vanish. Gordon used the term "liberal expectancy" in order to characterize the sociologists' assessment that under modern, urban, and industrial conditions ethnic affiliations were going to yield to more universalist identifications. Thus Talcott Parsons wrote in *The Negro American* (1966) that

> the universalistic norms of society have applied more and more widely. This has been true of all the main bases of particularistic solidarity, ethnicity, religion, regionalism, state's rights and class. ... Today, more than ever before, we are witnessing an acceleration in the emancipation of individuals of all categories from these diffuse particularistic solidarities. (739)

In the introduction to their influential collection *Ethnicity: Theory and Experience* (1975), Nathan Glazer and Daniel Patrick Moynihan added the term "radical expectancy" in order to describe the belief that "class circumstances would become the main line of division between people, erasing the earlier lines of tribe, language, religion, and national origin, and that thereafter these *class* divisions would themselves, after revolution, disappear" (7). One could add a third, religious expectancy, according to which ethnicity was going to yield to an exclusively religious identification. According to Will Herberg, this country was a "triple melting pot," so that Americans would ulti-mately make the salient distinctions among *Protestant-Catholic-Jew* (1955) rather than among diverse ethnic groups.

According to some of the current literature, none of the expectan-cies came true. Parsons himself argued in 1975 that "full assimilation, in the sense that ethnic identification has virtually disappeared and become absorbed within the single category of 'American,' is very little the case" (Glazer, *Ethnicity* 64). In *Ethnic Diversity in Catholic America* (1973), Harold Abramson shattered the triple-melting-pot theory and showed that ethnic distinctions do matter even within religious groupings. And while the radical expectancy continues to find substantiation and support, scholars now regard ethnicity as much more than an uncomplicated way station toward, or simple camouflage of, class.

The Roots of Ethnicity

Ethnicity truly was in vogue in the 1970s, and new primordialist and even old biological interpretations of the power of descent affiliations became fashionable again. Andrew Greeley, Michael Novak, and, most recently, Pierre van den Berghe have stressed ethnicity as a pro-found and persistent "sociobiological" force, as a seemingly natural power which keeps us in thrall. According to Novak's *Rise of the Unmeltable Ethnics* (1972), descent is crucial in shaping character:

> Emotions, instincts, memory, imagination, passions, and ways of per-ceiving are passed on to us in ways we do not choose, and in ways so thick with life that they lie far beyond the power of consciousness (let alone of analytic and verbal reason). (xxviii)

Even Christopher Lasch has recently come out to advocate "roots," "ancient ties," and the like (*Democracy*, October 1981).

In the 1970s, "ethnicity" was still perceived as a new word that sent scholars to their dictionaries. "In recent years," Gunnar Myrdal wrote in a special ethnicity issue of *Center Magazine* (July-August 1974), "books and articles have appeared stressing 'ethnicity'—a word I do not find in my dictionary" (28). The coauthors of *Beyond the Melting*

Pot, Nathan Glazer and Daniel Patrick Moynihan, who have certainly *stressed* ethnicity consulted a better dictionary and reported their findings in the introduction to their 1975 *Ethnicity* collection:

> Ethnicity seems to be a new term. In the sense in which we use it—the character or quality of an ethnic group—it does not appear in the 1933 edition of the *Oxford English Dictionary*, but it makes its appearance in the 1972 Supplement, where the first usage recorded is that of David Riesman in 1953. (1)

The Riesman essay in question appeared in the context of a debate about McCarthyism, loyalty, and intellectual freedom. In response to Archibald MacLeish, who had drawn a dim picture of the limitations imposed upon intellectual freedom in McCarthyist America, Riesman made "Some Observations on Intellectual Freedom," in the course of which he guardedly affirmed the continued existence of liberty in America. Riesman resorts three times to the discussion of ethnic group life and, in the third instance, uses the word "ethnicity."

Riesman's *American Scholar* essay first calls attention to ethnic victims in America's past, a past he feels MacLeish idealized: "If ... a rough toleration has at times been maintained within our country ... , fears and hatreds have found outlets against Indians, Mexicans, Spaniards and Japanese ... " (12). Far from sharing MacLeish's apocalyptic views, however, Riesman, in his second ethnic reference, sees "our ethnic diversity, our regional and religious pluralism" (14) as a safeguard against the possibilities of fascism in the United States. What was bad in America's past as ethnic hatred and what is good in America's present as antitotalitarian diversity becomes, in Riesman's third and most significant reference, a source of strength and tension which, according to Riesman, outweighs concerns for power struggles and antagonisms between "the people" and "bosses":

> There is a tendency for the older "class struggles," rooted in clear hierarchical antagonisms, to be replaced by a new sort of warfare: the groups who, by reason of rural or small-town location, ethnicity, or other parochialism, feel threatened by the better educated upper-middle-class people (though often less wealthy and politically powerful) who follow or create the modern movements in science, art, literature, and opinion generally. (15)

The term "ethnicity" appears here in the context of a shift from a concern for power relationships to an interest in the contradiction between modernized, de-ethnicized intellectuals and artists and parochial, regional, ethnic sentiment (Murphy chap. 1). While responding to MacLeish's outcry that radical dissent and a leftist perspective were endangered in McCarthyist America, Riesman argued, in fact, that the very basis of what appeared as "witch hunts" to some intellectuals was to be found not in power relationships but in a struggle between intellectual urbanity and artistic modernity on the one hand and parochial ethnicity and small-town identity on the other. The very term "ethnicity" seemed to support an interpretation of America as a country beyond class struggles.

What is striking, however, is that in the article Riesman uses the word "ethnicity" without any self-consciousness and without a hint of semantic innovation. In 1977 Riesman reacted with surprise to the suggestion that he invented "ethnicity." After an elaborate search for the origins of the word—an appropriate enterprise in the ethnic field that inspires so many people to turn to origins in ancestor-hunting— I found the apparently first occurrences of "ethnicity" in W. Lloyd Warner's *Yankee City Series*, the well-known, five-volume community study of Newburyport, Massachusetts, which began to appear in 1941. In the first volume, entitled *The Social Life of a Modern Community*, the coauthors, Warner and Paul Lunt, dedicated one chapter to the ten ethnic groups of Yankee City which they correlate to their system of six classes: "(1) Native, or Yankee; (2) Irish; (3) French (French Canadian); (4) Jewish; (5) Italian; (6) Armenian; (7) Greek; (8) Polish; (9) Russian; and (10) Negro." Warner and Lunt defined the term "ethnic" as it relates to those groups:

> These groups, with the exception of the first, we have called "ethnics." The term "ethnic," as used in this study, does not refer simply to foreign birth. Rather, it has a wider meaning. An individual was classified as belonging to a specific ethnic group if (1) he considered himself or was considered by the Yankee City community as a member of the group, and (2) if he participated in the activities of the group. (211)

Returning to this statement a few pages later, Warner and Lunt rephrased their definition and stated that "the concept of ethnicity is not based simply on place of birth" (220). There was the word! In the second volume, *The Status System of a Modern Community* (1942), Warner and Lunt used the noun "ethnicity" several times (5, 66), often in parallel constructions with other nouns, and sometimes even in quotation marks. For example:

> ... we shall look upon "ethnicity" as one of the several characteristics which modify the social system and are modified by it. The other characteristics to be considered are age, sex, and religion. (73)

This is the Kunta Kinte of ethnicity scholarship! As the excerpts may have shown, however, Warner's new word has carried a confusing and contradictory legacy.

Are Yankees Ethnic?

On the one hand, Warner's "ethnicity" was an inclusive category, parallel to age, sex, religion, or class, by which every inhabitant of Newburyport could be classified. On the other hand, it was an abstraction that described all inhabitants except "the natives, or Yankees." "Are we ethnic?"—as the *New Yorker* put it in a cartoon of 1972 (illustration 1) depicting a white middle-class family in an elegant dining room—is the question Yankees or WASPs have had to ask themselves many times since then, and without getting just one universally accepted answer.

Two conflicting uses of "ethnic" and "ethnicity" have remained in the air. According to Everett and Helen Hughes "we are all ethnic" (*Where* 7), and in E. K. Francis's terminology of 1947 "not only the French-Canadians or the Pennsylvania Dutch would be ethnic groups but also the French of France or the Irish of Ireland" (395). But this universalist and inclusive use is in frequent conflict with the

DRAWING BY HAMILTON; © 1972 THE NEW YORKER MAGAZINE, INC.

"Are <u>we</u> ethnic?"

Illustration 1.

other use of the word, which excludes dominant groups and thus establishes an "ethnicity minus one." It may be absurd, as Harold Abramson has argued, to except white Anglo-Saxon Protestant Americans from the category of ethnicity (*Diversity* 9), and yet it is a widespread practice to define ethnicity as otherness. The contrastive terminology of ethnicity thus reveals a point of view which changes according to the speaker who uses it: for example, for some Americans eating turkey and reading Hawthorne appear to be more "ethnic" than eating lasagna and reading Puzo.

As Everett Hughes suggested in a personal letter in 1977, the association of the ethnic with the other is not made in some languages: "In Greece the national bank is the ethnic bank. In this country ethnic banks cannot be the national bank. ..." Yet precisely the Greek etymological roots of "ethnicity" have something to do with Warner's confusion. To say it in the simplest and clearest terms, an ethnic, etymologically speaking, is a *goy*. The Greek word *ethnikos*, from which the English "ethnic" and "ethnicity" are derived, meant "gentile," "heathen." Going back to the noun *ethnos*, the word was used to refer not just to people in general but also to "others." In English usage the meaning shifted from "non-Israelite" (in the Greek translation of the Bible the word *ethnikos* was used to render the Hebrew *goyim*) to "non-Christian." Thus the word retained its quality of defining another people contrastively, and often negatively. In the Christianized context the word "ethnic" (sometimes spelled "hethnic") recurred, from the fourteenth to the nineteenth century, in the sense of "heathen." Only in the mid-nineteenth century did the more familiar meaning of "ethnic" as "peculiar to a race or nation" reemerge. However, the English language has retained the pagan memory of "ethnic," often secularized in the sense of ethnic as other, as nonstandard, or, in America, as not fully American. This connotation gives the opposition of ethnic and American the additional religious dimension of the contrast between heathens and chosen people. No wonder that there is popular hesitation to accept the inclusive use of ethnicity. The relationship between ethnicity and American identity in this respect parallels that of pagan superstition and true religion. It is in this sense that the word "ethnicity" is once recorded in 1772, an instance listed as "obsolete and rare" in the *Oxford English Dictionary*: "NUGENT tr. *Hist. Friar Gerund*. I. 332 From the curling spume of Egean waves fabulous ethnicity feigned Venus their idolatress conceived."

Ethnic scholars like to poke around in etymology so that this instance of a religiocentric denigration of classical mythology as "fabulous ethnicity" has not gone by unnoticed. Yet the implications of the etymology are brushed aside when Glazer and Moynihan remark how very different the old and new meanings of ethnicity are (*Ethnicity* 1), or when Joshua Fishman writes that "in modern American usage the term seems to avoid much of the sense of paganism or heathenism implicit in its etymology" ("Language" 43 n. 1). Yet, as we have seen, in Warner's novel use of the word "ethnicity" the double sense of universal, inclusive peoplehood (shared by all Americans) and of exclusive otherness (separating ethnics from Yankee or mainstream culture) lives on.

To use another category from Warner's stratification story, some confusions about ethnicity might be illustrated by imagining that the English language had only one word for sex and for masculinity ("mexinity"?) and that femininity could at times be discussed as part of this term (sex) and at other times be defined as its negative contrast (masculinity). Fortunately, we don't have "mexinity," and much as some Americans may oppose ascriptive sexual identities, they are generally born as boys and girls. Yet we do have ethnicity as peoplehood and as otherness in a country where the phrase "ethnics all!" can be heard as a battle cry for diversity in unity.

We Are Not like Them

American culture is full of examples of the fusion of ethnicity and otherness. The Puritan uses of the word "ethnic" are instructive. William Ames, who went to Holland as a prominent English Puritan and never migrated to America, was so central a figure for New England that Perry Miller called him "the father of the New England church polity" (*Errand* 58). In 1643 Ames saw dancing as a "defiling of that dignity, which ought to be kept by all Christians," and noted that "graver Ethnicks" danced with hired prostitutes (Ziff, *Puritanism* 20). In 1702 Cotton Mather wrote that the "custom of preaching at *funerals* may seem *ethnical* in its original" (*Magnalia* 1:447). Both examples show the affinities of ethnics and heathens; and interestingly, both occur in discussions of the right code of *conduct*. Bad conduct on the terms of the community that is being established is labeled nonsacred and pagan. One can almost hear the Pharisee's sigh "God, I thank thee, that I am not as other men are, extortioners, unjust, adulterers, or even as this publican" {Luke 18:11}. In other words: thank God I am not ethnic!

Ethnic theorists have often dwelled on the antithetical nature of ethnicity. In ethnic name-calling the tendency persists, as George

Murdock argued in Seligman's *Encyclopedia of the Social Sciences*, that a people

> usually calls itself either by a flattering name or by a term signifying simply "men," "men of men," "first men," or "people." Aliens, on the other hand, are regarded as something less than men; they are styled "barbarians" or are known by some derogatory term corresponding to such modern American ethnic tags as "bohunk," "chink," "dago," "frog," "greaser," "nigger," "sheeny," and "wop." (Murdock 613)

As Agnes Heller writes, what "is now called 'ethnocentrism' is the natural attitude of all cultures toward alien ones" ("Can Cultures" 271). Such antithetical definitions not only are noticeable in the modern world (or among American ethnic writers and critics) but were also undertaken by American Indians. Thus, although it has become de rigueur in ethnic criticism to refer to the original inhabitants of the American continent as "Native Americans" in order to avoid the, not slur, but misnomer "Indians," the various Indian nations have followed the human pattern of calling themselves "people" and calling others less flattering things. The name Kiowa means "real or principal people" (Sumner, *Folkways* 14); Lenno-Lenapes are "original men" (Schoolcraft, *Indians* 256) and Algonquins "people of the other side." The name Apache means "enemy" in Zuñi. According to Keith Wilbur, the Algonquian meaning of other Indian names is striking: Iroquois "real adders," Mingo "treacherous," Mohawk "cannibals or cowards," and Pequot "destroyers" (*New England* 75). Many names are frozen curses.

   In his introduction to *Ethnic Groups and Boundaries* (1969), Fredrik Barth sees the essence of ethnicity in such (mental, cultural, social, moral, aesthetic, and not necessarily territorial) boundary-constructing processes which function as cultural markers between groups. For Barth it is "the ethnic *boundary* that defines the group, not the cultural stuff that it encloses" (15). "If a group maintains its identity when members interact with others, this entails criteria for determining membership and ways of signalling membership and exclusion" (15). Previous anthropologists (and, we might add, historians, sociologists, and literary critics) tended to think about ethnicity "in terms of different peoples, with different histories and cultures, coming together and accommodating themselves to each other"; instead, Barth suggests, we should "ask ourselves what is needed to make ethnic distinctions *emerge* in an area." With a statement that runs against the grain of much ethnic historiography, Barth argues that

> when one traces the history of an ethnic group through time, one is *not* simultaneously, in the same sense, tracing the history of "a culture": the elements of the present culture of that ethnic group have

not sprung from the particular set that constituted the group's culture at a previous time, whereas the group has a continual organizational existence with boundaries (criteria of membership) that despite modifications have marked off a continuing unit. (38)

Barth's focus on *boundaries* may appear scandalously heretical to some, but it does suggest plausible interpretations of the polyethnic United States. (Barth uses "polyethnic" instead of the more common Graeco-Roman mixture "multi-ethnic"—to maintain boundaries in etymology?) Barth's theory can easily accommodate the observation that ethnic groups in the United States have relatively little cultural differentiation, that the cultural *content* of ethnicity (the stuff that Barth's boundaries enclose) is largely interchangeable and rarely historically authenticated.

From such a perspective, contrastive strategies—naming and name-calling among them—become the most important thing about ethnicity. The process of rhetorical boundary construction is certainly pervasive in the literature, and we shall have many occasions to draw on Barth. A series of recent slurs, often hurled by some ingroup speakers against people who threaten the fixity of mental boundaries based on race, scolded blacks as Oreos, Asians as bananas, Indians as apples, and Chicanos as coconuts—all with the structurally identical criticism "they're white inside!" The warning had no specific cultural content but served as an interchangeable exhortation to maintain boundaries.

George Devereux has also investigated the contrastive and dissociative nature of ethnic behavior that is not actually prompted by any ethnic tradition but by the attempt to thwart a nonethnic otherness. In his contribution to de Vos's *Ethnic Identity* (1975), an essay richly interspersed with examples from classical literature, Devereux wrote that

the moment A insists on being only and ostentatiously an X, 24 hours a day, all those aspects of his behavior which cannot be correlated with his ethnic identity are deprived of any organizing and stabilizing framework. ... As a result, there tends to appear, side by side with what little structuring of his behavior his ethnic identity ("being an X") provides—even when it is asserted mainly dissociatively ("not being a Y")—a logically untenable and operationally fraudulent incorporation into the ethnic identity of ideologies based on principles which are, in essence, not only non-ethnic, but outright anti-ethnic. (66–67)

Devereux convincingly located the fascist potential of ethnic movements in this reduction of complex authentic identity to contrastive one-dimensionality in the name of ethnicity: "If one is nothing but a Spartan, a capitalist, a proletarian, or a Buddhist, one is next door to being nothing and therefore even to not being at all" (68). Although these sinister implications of ethnicity do underlie much American ethnic theory, they are not always spelled out that clearly.

In his superb essay "The Revolt against Americanism" (1970), Fred Matthews pointed out that

> for American intellectuals, folk romanticism tended to lead not to hatred of "outsiders" and a lust to purge them from the nation, but rather to a sense of guilt about their own society's exploitation of the strangers, and to the desire to protect them from the aggressive majority. In the American context, alienated romanticism created not xenophobia but xenophilia. (9)

While non-American observers may find it difficult to understand the positive charge given to expressions such as "ethnic purity" in the United States or the way in which ethnicity is sometimes considered the most harmless and nondivisive thing, American intellectuals have often invoked or kindled the life of ethnic nuclei in the hope that this would *reduce* ethnic friction. The negative antithesis against "them" is thus sometimes balanced by a positive charge given to "them."

In a Christian context, nobody wants to be a Pharisee, and ethnic writers who oppose America critically often draw on this knowledge. As the example of the Pharisee's prayer suggests, the negative separation from publican otherness is subject to New Testament injunction. The process may thus be inverted and give way to a more or less overt admiration for the other. The new motto is: If only we could be like them! When Cotton Mather described the Algonquian Indians in his "Life of John Eliot" (1702), he was torn between a contempt for their "barbarous" way of living and an admiration for their "extraordinary Ease in Childbirth" (Miller, *Puritans* 505). The strategy of inversion reached a high point with "romantic racialism" (Fredrickson 97–129) in the first half of the nineteenth century and has continued strongly since then. Thus, Harriet Beecher Stowe maintained in *Uncle Tom's Cabin* (1852) that Negroes make better Christians than whites do and predicted that "they will exhibit the highest form of the peculiarly *Christian* life" (2:259). Stowe's Anglo-Saxons, on the other hand, were a "cool, logical, and practical" race. They should remember, Stowe wrote in *The Key to Uncle Tom's Cabin* (1853), that God gave the Bible "to them in the fervent language and with the glowing imagery of the more susceptible and passionate Oriental races" (46). To Harriet Beecher Stowe, Jews and Africans were closer to the spirit of the Bible than Anglo-Saxons who had fallen into the place of Pharisaic concern for the letter of the law. In one of James Fenimore Cooper's last novels, *The Oak Openings* (1858), the Indians are seen as "the chosen people of the Great Spirit, and will one day be received back to his favor. Would that I were one of them, only enlightened by the words of the New Testament" (Fiedler, *Love* 199). The popular novel *The Fair Puritan* (1844–45) described the inversion exactly in the terms of Christ's parable when Frank Forrester (i.e., William Herbert) compared the slave woman Tituba favorably with Whalley, her Puritan master: "There was ... more of the true, the lowly, and the grateful spirit of the Christian, in that poor, overtasked, despised, scourged heathen, than in her haughty master, who like the pharisee blessed God that he was not as other men are" (Bell, *Hawthorne* 95). White Christians are thus often cast as hypocrites and Pharisees while so-called heathens, hethnics, or ethnics take the place of the truly chosen ones.

This tendency to use ethnicity as a positively charged antithesis has persisted, with some transformations, into the twentieth century, though, along the way, the word "Christian" may have been replaced by "American" or simply by "happy." In her anthology *The American Equation* (1971), Katharine Newman referred to modern exoticizations of other ethnic groups as "the attractive alternative." One of the examples she included in her collection is the second-generation Swedish-American Carl Sandburg's poem "Happiness":

> I asked professors who teach the meaning of life to tell me what is happiness.
> And I went to famous executives who boss the work of thousands of men.
> They all shook their heads and gave me a smile as though I was trying to fool with them.
> And then one Sunday afternoon I wandered out along the Desplaines river
> And I saw a crowd of Hungarians under the trees with their women and children and a keg of beer and accordion. (143)

Sandburg's redemptive Hungarian immigrants, characteristically contrasted with executives and professors (the next best thing to Pharisees in the modern world), are virtually interchangeable with the many other ethnic groups that appear through this idealized vision from the outside. Lincoln Steffens's and Jack Kerouac's Mexicans and Sherwood Anderson's and Norman Mailer's blacks are similarly idealized. Ralph Ellison wittily describes champions of the "Aren't-Negroes-Wonderful?" school who

> impute to Negroes sentiments, attitudes and insights which, as a group living under certain definite social conditions, Negroes could not humanly possess. It is the identical mechanism which William Empson identifies in literature as "pastoral." (*Shadow* 97)

Sandburg's only prerequisite seemed to be that he as an author could not be of Hungarian descent in order to cast his happy, pastoral, publican picnickers in that glorious way. As the Italian-American example of the introduction suggests, however, self-exoticization, too—or to speak with Ellison, pastoralization of the in-group—has become part of a familiar cultural scenario. Many ethnic writers in America, from Hjalmar Hjorth Boyesen to Ludwig Lewisohn, were professors, who may sometimes be especially eager to prove that they are not Pharisees at all and thus give us their own ethnic insiders' lowdown as "hip" people of the spirit. Also, let us not forget that in America *all* writers can view themselves romantically as members of some out-group so that combining the strategy of outsiderism and self-exoticization can be quite contagious. In America, casting oneself as an outsider may in fact be considered a dominant cultural trait. For example, Edward Hoagland in 1981 ironically but half seriously described his own predicament in the *New York Times Book Review*:

> I had arrived in New York from humble origins. That is, I was a WASP with an Ivy League education and a lawyer for a father at a time (a decade after Bellow's debut) when it was important for a young writer in the city to be an "ethnic" whose father was a bartender and to have gone to City College. My prep schoolmate John McPhee and college classmate John Updike both needed to write twice as many books twice as well to gather an acclaim at all equivalent to what they would have won much more quickly if they had not been WASP's from the Ivy League. ("Job" 36-37)

A case of literary reverse discrimination or a con game? If we are all other—and this plea makes Hoagland other by inverting the inversion—then we may also explore the otherness in ourselves, which is the theme of many American autobiographical conversion stories.

I Am Absolutely Other

Narratives of conversions, from criminal to social hero, from Pharisee to publican, from ethnic to American, or from shallow assimilationist

to reborn ethnic, have enjoyed much popularity. The affinities of ethnicity and heathendom are focused most clearly in these transformation stories that often carry the "from ... to" formula openly in
their titles. The list of transformation stories describing changes in
place, status, and personality includes Mary Antin, *From Plotzk to Boston* (1899), Edward Steiner, *From Alien to Citizen* (1914), Michael
Pupin, *From Immigrant to Inventor* (1923), and Richard Bartholdt,
From Steerage to Congress (1930).

"The Edward Bok of whom I have written," the Dutch immigrant
editor of *Women's Wear Daily* wrote in his *Americanization* (1920),

> has passed out of my being as completely as if he had never been
> there, save for the records and files on my library shelves. It is easy,
> therefore, for me to write of him as a personality apart: in fact, I could
> not depict him from any other point of view. To write of him in the
> first person, as if he were myself, is impossible, for he is not. (viii)

This is a strong polarization, characteristic of the many Sauls who
became Pauls in their Damascus of America. In *The Autobiography of
Malcolm X* (1965), the author describes his old self through the eyes
of a girlfriend's grandmother:

> What could she have thought of me in my zoot and conk and orange
> shoes? She'd have done us all a favor if she had run screaming for
> the police. If something looked as I did then ever came knocking at
> my door today, asking to see one of my four daughters, I know I
> would explode. (65)

Later, Malcolm X describes the process of his conversion.

> I remember how ... reading the Bible in the Norfolk Prison Colony
> library, I came upon, then I read, over and over, how Paul on the
> road to Damascus, upon hearing the voice of Christ, was so smitten
> that he was knocked off his horse, in a daze [see Acts 9:1–16]. I do
> not now, and I did not then, liken myself to Paul. But I do under-
> stand his experience. (163)

Though Malcolm X follows the Christian conversion pattern, his is,
of course, a conversion away from American assimilation and toward
the black nationalism of Elijah Muhammad's Nation of Islam.

"I was born, I have lived, and I have been made over. Is it not time
to write my life's story? I am just as much out of the way as if I were
dead, for I am absolutely other than the person whose story I have
to tell." This is the classic phrase from the beginning of Mary Antin's
immigrant autobiography, *The Promised Land* (1912). Antin, too,
reflected the narrator's distance from her old self, which she had left

behind in a rebirth experience in the grammatical distinction between first and third person: ". . . I can regard my earlier self as a separate being, and make it a subject of study" (xii). Sometimes there is a heathenish dimension to the past, to any past, in American writing, and a sacred dimension to the future in America.

The antithetical strategy of us against them, or old me against new me, is flexible and can be charged with different political meanings. Yet it remains noteworthy that the distinction between a sacred and a heathenish side was made by American writers of the most diverse ancestries, whether they sided with the saving grace of the American future and proclaimed themselves "Reborn in the Promised Land" (Ifkovic 111–208), or embraced the adversary ethnicity of a heathenish past and wished that they could simply say "Goodbye Columbus." The most familiar form of America blues is the curse upon Columbus, as it appears in Abraham Cahan's *Yekl* (66), in Israel Zangwill's *Melting-Pot* (24), and, in Pietro Di Donato's *Christ in Concrete*, as Nazone's specifically Italian-American disappointment: "Discovered by an Italian—named from Italian—But oh, that I may leave this land of disillusion!" (271).

Since the 1960s the sacred side of the antithesis has increasingly been the ethnic one. In contemporary usage ethnicity has largely been transformed from a heathenish liability into a sacred asset, from a trait to be overcome in a conversion and rebirth experience to a very desirable identity feature to be achieved through yet another regeneration. "I think," the Afro-American writer LeRoi Jones/ Amiri Baraka told Jules Feiffer in an open letter in 1961, "that if perhaps there were more Judeo-Americans and a few less bland, cultureless, middle-headed AMERICANS, this country might still be a great one" (*Home* 67). Yet, fortunately, and Hoagland's complaint notwithstanding, every American is now considered a potential ethnic. Michael Novak made descent at least partly a matter of choice (or consent) when he wrote: "Given a grandparent or two, one chooses to shape one's consciousness by one history rather than another" (*Rise* 56). I met two American-born brothers, one of whom identified himself as German-American while the other one opted for a Franco-American identity. If this form of voluntary or multiple-choice ethnicity is possible, then what is the *substance* of ethnicity in America?

The Content of Ethnicity

In a beautifully positivistic exercise which was included in Glazer and Moynihan's *Ethnicity* reader and in Andrew Greeley's own *Ethnicity in the United States* (1974), Greeley and William McCready set out to measure the differences in "trust," "fatalism," "authoritarianism," "anxiety," "conformity," "moralistic" (*sic*) and "independence for children" among Anglo-Saxon, Irish, and Italian respondents. Asking questions such as "How frequently do you find yourself anxious or worrying about something?" (to measure "anxiety") or "Do you think most people can be trusted?" (to measure, yes, "trust"), the researchers found out that, indeed, the "knowledge of the cultural heritage of an immigrant group helps us understand its present behavior" and that this behavior is often different from what we would expect. While the "Italians turn out to be less fatalistic than the Irish," the "Irish are, despite our hypothesis, significantly less 'anxious' and 'authoritarian,' and more 'trusting'" than the Anglo-Saxons. However, the most important statement appears in a footnote. "Ought one to be concerned about the possibility," Greeley and McCready ask their readers (after having just given them all the data about Anglo-Saxon/Irish differences),

> that the Irish may be more "cute" (to use their word) in answering questions than other respondents? May it be possible that among the cultural traits that have survived the immigration is the facility at blarney, which has been defined as the capacity never to mean what one says and never to say what one means? Anyone who has attempted to get a straight answer when wandering through the west of Ireland must be at least alive to this possibility. (Glazer, *Ethnicity* 216–17)

We know where we stand: however much we measure ethnic content, we have to rely on the unfathomable and on our own experience in order to make sense of these "empirical" findings. (One is reminded of Heinrich Heine's mocking dissertation proposal in which he set out to prove that the feet of the ladies of Göttingen were not as large as university gossip had it; after an elaborate prospectus which included a chapter on feet in the ancient world and an excursus on elephants, Heine added that he was going to append some empirical footprints of actual ladies to his completed thesis if only he could find large enough sheets of paper.) Greeley might next try to measure the veracity of the lying Cretans. His empirical machinery measures nothing here, and it is our consent definition of what constitutes Irishness that defines its supposedly empirically measurable content.

Herbert Gans pointed to a more general problem in measuring ethnic identity when he wrote in the foreword to Neil Sandberg's

Ethnic Identity (1974): "Attitude studies probably overstate interest in ethnicity, if only because it is easier for a respondent to say that he or she favors participating in Polish life than to actually do so" (vii). This challenges not only the question of content but the very assertion that there is a new and strong concern for ethnicity in post-melting-pot America. In his important work on symbolic ethnicity, Gans has also called attention to the ways in which modern ethnic identification works by external symbols rather than by continual activities that make demands upon people who define themselves as "ethnic."

Glazer and Moynihan, too, apparently disagreed with Greeley's sense of cultural differences among different ethnics when they wrote in the introduction to their reader that "the cultural *content* of each ethnic group, in the United States, seems to have become very similar to that of others, but the emotional significance of attachments to the ethnic group seems to persist" (*Ethnicity* 8). American ethnicity, then, is a matter not of content but of the importance that individuals ascribe to it, including, of course, scholars and intellectuals. James Patterson similarly argued in the *American Anthropologist* (1979) that American social scientists studying ethnic groups in America "tend to see relatively minor deviations from the American norm in the ethnic group as major cultural differences" (104). Talcott Parsons, whose turnabout from the 1960s to the 1970s we have already witnessed, maintained in his contribution to Glazer and Moynihan's *Ethnicity* that "however strongly affirmative these ethnic affiliations are, the ethnic status is conspicuously devoid of 'social content'" (65).

Parsons' own transformation and his new theory (which he developed from David Schneider's work) give us ample evidence that his shift was a change in *emphasis* only. By 1975 Parsons had come to stress the "optional and voluntary component of ethnic identification" and to say that the "marks of identity are in a very important sense 'empty symbols' . . . . [The] symbolization of ethnic identification is primarily focused on style of life distinctiveness within the larger framework of much more nearly uniform American social structure" (65). In other words, the universalistic norms of Parsons' earlier position have continued to apply more and more widely; however, their emanation has taken an increasingly particularistic and ethnic shape. Whereas Novak seemed to think that a specter was going around in America, the specter of ethnicity, Glazer, in the *Ethnicity* introduction, argued along Parsons' lines that under modern conditions these groups have in fact become "ghost nations" (8)—an expression that Maxine Hong Kingston might appreciate. Are ethnics merely Americans who are separated from each other by the same culture? If so, then the word "ethnicity" certainly is not helpful, since it seems to be associated more strongly with the belief in measurable differences by descent and thus obstructs a clear understanding of the newer theories.

Race and Ethnicity

To compound problems, there is another important line of disagreement concerning race and ethnicity. On the one hand, Harold Abramson argued that although "race is the most salient ethnic factor, it is still only one of the dimensions of the larger cultural and historical phenomenon of ethnicity" (*Diversity* 175). This position was shared by Milton Gordon and many contributors to Glazer and Moynihan's *Ethnicity* and to the *Harvard Encyclopedia of American Ethnic Groups* (1980; henceforth *HEAEG*), edited by Stephan Thernstrom, Ann Orlov, and Oscar Handlin. On the other hand, M. G. Smith (1982) would rather side with Pierre van den Berghe's *Race and Racism* (1967) and consider race a special "objective" category that cannot be meaningfully discussed under the heading "ethnicity" (Smith, "Ethnicity" 10).

I have here sided with Abramson's universalist interpretation according to which ethnicity includes dominant groups and in which race, while sometimes facilitating external identification, is merely one aspect of ethnicity. I have three reasons for doing so. First, the interpretation of the rites and rituals of culturally dominant groups sometimes provides the matrix for the emergence of divergent group identities. The ethnic system of Newburyport is as incomplete without Anglo-Americans as without Afro-Americans; it is also less easily comprehensible, even though some Yankees may resent being put into an ethnic category. Second, the discussions of ethnicity and the production of ethnic literature in the United States have been so strongly affected by Afro-Americans, and so actively and directly influenced by them since World War II, that an omission of the Afro-American tradition in a discussion of ethnic culture in America would create a very serious gap in our reflections. In fact, the very emergence of the stress on ethnicity and the unmeltable ethnics was directly influenced by the black civil rights movement and strengthened by its radicalization in the 1960s, as the examples of the *Godfather* critic and Frank Chin's Japanese-American ethnic room illustrate. Finally, I am interested in the processes of group formation and in the naturalization of group relationships (so well typified by Novak's prose) and have found examples from Puritan New England and Afro-America crucial to an understanding of these processes among other groups in America. The term "ethnicity" here is thus a broadly conceived term.

This choice does not represent an attempt to gloss over the special legacy of slavery and racism in America. Slavery has posed a special problem to interpretations of America and poses a special problem to our enterprise. In the terms of Fredrik Barth, slavery is not just a boundary but one of the most extreme forms of social boundaries constructed between people who considered themselves full human beings and cast others into the category that Orlando Patterson has forcefully described as "social death." When American historians today discuss slavery, they encounter the problem that it contradicts so many of their generalizations of American life. As the most recent debates have shown, historians are still searching for a moral and theoretical framework within which slavery can be understood and indicted.

America is a country which, from the times of Cotton Mather to the present, has placed great emphasis on consent at the expense of descent definitions. The widely shared public bias against hereditary privilege—which Wendell detected in John Cotton's argument—has strongly favored *achieved* rather than *ascribed* identity, and supported "self-determination" and "independence" from ancestral, parental, and external definitions. Yet precisely the same cultural framework had room for, and needed, slavery, even years after most old-world countries had abolished it. And later this supposedly consent-focused culture also *produced*—not inherited—segregation, one of the most sharply formulated systems of descent-based discrimination in the nineteenth and twentieth centuries. Other mixed societies with a historical background as new-world slaveholding countries—such as Brazil and Cuba—generally placed much less emphasis on cultural consent than did the United States. Still, in their definitions of racial groups the Latin Americans were much more presentist and "consentist" than their big northern neighbor, whose segregationist codes had only two categories. For North American lawyers there was only a pure-white category and its negation—black—which was constituted by the famous "one drop" rule, even if that one drop had to be traced way back in the descent line. One can view the emergence of legalized segregation in a country of consent as a paradox, especially since so many nineteenth-century Afro-Americans had developed a new-world sense of peoplehood which was quite congruent with American consent patterns. Yet one may also ask whether the two systems of widely shared consent bias and severe de jure discrimination of totally descent-defined groups were not intimately interrelated. In the essay "Caste, Racism, and 'Stratification'," Louis Dumont persuasively argued that

> racism fulfills an old function under a new form. It is as if it were representing in an egalitarian society a resurgence of what was differently and more directly and naturally expressed in a hierarchical society. (Dolgin, *Symbolic* 84)

The concepts of the self-made man and of Jim Crow had their origins in the same culture at about the same time, whereas aristocratic societies had no need for either. At the same time when consent language began to speak of the accident of one's birth, there were certain forms of descent which were considered to be of the greatest determining power. It was not the hereditary privilege of aristocratic blue blood but the culturally constructed supposed liability of black blood that mattered most in the United States. Belief in consent has coexisted with countervailing rigidities which were exceptional even in an international context and in comparison with countries that were much less enthusiastic about the ideals of the Enlightenment.

Nineteenth-century critics of the status quo were especially perceptive to this paradox and formulated it again and again as hypocrisy. Melville once described the paradoxes of American republicanism allegorically with the following inscription over the arch of the "tutelary deity of Vivenza": "In-this-re-publi-can-land-all-men-are-born-free-and-equal," to which is added, in smaller print, "Except-the-tribe-of-Hamo" (*Mardi* 2:224). The force of much antislavery agitation, and later of antisegregationist and civil rights writing as well as of much Afro-American writing in general, rested on this perception of hypocrisy.

The categorical separation of race and ethnicity too easily lends itself to false generalizations about America. As John Higham has shown, theorists of American pluralism have often excluded blacks from their concepts, which are therefore only partially valid for America (*Send* 208). Furthermore, before the rise of the word "ethnicity," the word "race" was widely used to refer to larger and smaller groupings of mankind: for example, the Irish race or the Jewish race. In fact, the National Socialist genocide in the name of "race" is what gave the word a bad name and supported the substitution of "ethnicity."[4] Finally, in the complicated ethnic scene today, are Cuban immigrants or Japanese-Americans races or ethnic groups? I think it is most helpful not to be confused by the heavily charged term "race" and to keep looking at race as one aspect of ethnicity.

The Limits of Ethnicity

Although I use the word "ethnicity" here, I do it more and more hesitantly. In the absence of a better vocabulary, "ethnicity" and "ethnic" shall serve as vehicles which make it easier to talk about conflicts between consent and descent. Often used confusingly, "ethnicity" is still superior to and more inclusive than any other existing term. "Minority" needlessly calls our attention to numbers; "immigration" focuses on the process of traversing space and leads to rather awkwardly forced discussions of people who came as slaves or who were on the American continent before "America." Although "ethnicity" often serves as a code word for "class," it is not identical with "class" and the phenomena discussed under the label "ethnicity" cannot be more easily conceptualized under the label "class." Yet despite these semantic distinctions, the popular associations remain active, even in the word "ethnicity." According to Abner Cohen's introduction to *Urban Ethnicity* (1974), to "many people, the term ethnicity connotes minority status, lower class, or migrancy. This is why sooner or later we shall have to drop it or to find a neutral word for it, though I can see that we shall probably have to live with it for quite a while" (xxi). Ten years after Cohen's assessment, the time has come to reconsider the usefulness of the term. I propose that for the purposes of investigating group formation, inversion, boundary construction and social distancing, myths of origins and fusions, cultural markers and empty symbols, we may be better served, in the long run, by the vocabulary of kinship and cultural codes than by the cultural baggage that the word "ethnicity" contains. My concern has therefore shifted from ethnicity to the cultural construction of the codes of consent and descent, the terms that were outlined more fully in the introduction. Although my examples are drawn from American culture (where weak language loyalties have contributed to the creation of an unusually monolingual polyethnic country), the terminology may prove useful to students of the many other polyethnic nations in the world. Many ethnic movements around the world have been tied to religious symbols; in the United States of America, however, a particular form of Bible interpretation has served as a rationale for the whole country as well as for many ethnic groups. It is therefore useful to review some features of American civil religion.

CHAPTER TWO

Typology and Ethnogenesis

And now the Prisoners sent out, do come
  Padling in their Canooes apace with joyes
Along this blood red Sea, Where joyes do throng,
  And sayling in the Arke of Grace that flies
Drove sweetly by Gailes of the Holy Ghost
Who sweetly briezes all along this Coast.
                    —Edward Taylor, Meditation II, 78

And we Americans are the peculiar, chosen people—the Israel of our time; we bear
the ark of the liberties of the world.
                    —Herman Melville, *White-Jacket* [Cf. 1 Peter 2:9]

In a Jewish Theological Seminary address of 1903, Solomon Schechter located the Americanness of American religion in its pluralism: "it is an especial American feature that no preference is given to any denomination or sect or theological *Richtung*." Schechter then sketched the following context in order to illustrate his assertion:

> The history of the United States does not begin with the Red Indian, and the genesis of its spiritual life is not to be traced back to the vagaries of some peculiar sects. This country is, as everybody knows, a creation of the Bible, particularly the Old Testament, and the Bible is still holding its own, exercising enormous influence as a real spiritual power, in spite of all the destructive tendencies, mostly of foreign make. (*Seminary* 48)

The excerpt is interesting in its combination of nonsectarian pluralism with somewhat exclusionary language, but it documents the widespread assumption that America was Bible-made. How can that be true of a country which is so often identified with the secular spirit of the modern age? And how could these biblical foundations become meaningful to diverse ethnic groups?

Since the seventeenth century biblical images have been applied to the American colonists' new experiences. To be sure, biblical analogies to the drama of seafaring and settling in new worlds were made

in many colonial literatures. In Puritan New England, however, a systematic religious symbolism was applied to transatlantic crossing and
new-world destiny. The religious thinking of seventeenth-century
New Englanders became an important source for the ethnic and cultural definitions of other immigrants. Especially that element of exegesis known as typology has influenced amazingly heterogeneous
ethnic groups in America. As the motto by Edward Taylor shows,
even an Indian canoe could appear in the redemptive context of
American Bible adaptations.[5]

Typology is, according to Ursula Brumm, "a form of prophecy
which sets two successive events into a reciprocal relation of anticipation and fulfillment" (*Thought* 27). Fulfillment generally implies
not just repetition but also a heightening and overshadowing of the
original event. While Paul's Christian typological exegesis was
restricted to an interpretation of Old Testament characters and
events as "types" which foreshadowed the redemptive history of New
Testament "antitypes," Puritan theology related the secular history of
the American colonists to biblical types. Cotton Mather's epithets,
for example, his calling John Winthrop "Nehemias Americanus,"
were thus more than allusions and had typological significance. The
events of early American history were, with the help of typology,
rhetorically transformed and elevated into biblical drama, as New
Englanders interpreted their transatlantic voyage as a new exodus,
their mission as an errand into the wilderness, and their own role as
that of a new chosen people. In this process, even the slur "Puritans,"
the "odious name" (*Oxford English Dictionary*, instance of 1655 listed
under A1) by which they had originally been known, was defiantly
inverted and transformed into an identification they were proud of.
They had become, as Cotton Mather put it, "Good People which had
the Nick-name of *Puritans* put upon them" who transported themselves "into the Desarts of *America*, that they might here peaceably
erect *Congregational Churches*, and therein attend and maintain all the
pure Institutions of the Lord Jesus Christ" (Miller, *Puritans* 499).

The resulting mode of messianic nationalism and consensus construction has recently been made the subject of much inquiry, culminating in the work of Sacvan Bercovitch, who has amply illustrated the extent to which Puritan rhetoric has permeated American
culture through the present. In *The Puritan Origins of the American
Self* (1975) and *The American Jeremiad* (1978), there is much evidence
for the continued importance of the Puritans' vision and of the rhetorical forms in which they expressed it. As Ursula Brumm has
observed, American writing from the seventeenth to the twentieth

century abounds in characters who appear to be not "freshly conceived individuals but based on fixed models, of which the most
important are Adam and Christ" (*Thought* 199). The history of the
American "new man" was intimately interwoven with typology of
this sort. John the Baptist, Exodus, and Christ were constructed as
"types" for America. The sense of peoplehood that emerged among
Puritans and ethnic groups drew on typology; and some cultural
drama in secular America could unfold from different interpretations
of the text of the Bible.

"Go Down Moses": Typology and Chosen Peoplehood

One favorite way in which seventeenth-century New Englanders
connected migration history and sacred mission was, as Ursula
Brumm has shown, through the vitalization of John the Baptist as a
type. A popular point of departure for the development of this type
was Christ's question, concerning John, "What went ye out into the
wilderness to see?" [Matthew 11:7]. This question had an obvious
appeal to emigrants. Francis Higginson, Thomas Shepard, Jonathan
Mitchel, Samuel Danforth, and Cotton Mather all invoked this question in sermons or other writings. Shepard answered that the settlers
came "into this wilderness to see ... more of Jesus Christ"; Danforth
and Mitchel responded with the famous formula of the Puritan
"errand into the wilderness"; and Cotton Mather collected the biographies of five early Puritan ministers (four of whom were actually
baptized "John") under the typological heading *Johannes in Eremo*
(John in the wilderness). They are presented as at least partial fulfillment of the John the Baptist type, having come "to prepare a way
for the Lord in the desert" (Brumm, "What Went You Out into the
Wilderness to See?" 10). The figure of John the Baptist had an advantage over other types: he reminded Puritans that the fulfillment of
one type was also the anticipation of further and higher things to
come. Fulfilling the type of John the Baptist with Puritan John antitypes thus did not close history but prepared the way for Christ's
second coming. This is an illustration of the dynamic, process-ori-
ented way in which typology could become a vehicle for emphasizing
progress and change. It is this dynamism that Frederick Jackson
Turner had in mind when he wrote in "Contributions of the West
to American Democracy" (1903) that "Thomas Jefferson was the John
the Baptist of democracy, not its Moses" (*Frontier* 251). Some work
still remained to be done.

Turner's distinction notwithstanding, one of the most prevalent typological motifs was that of a continued new exodus from Egyptian-old-world bondage to the shores of the American promised land, a motif that could be used with similarly dynamic implications. The image of the new exodus may confer sacral meaning on a secular migration, but also on an always-ongoing process of getting to an ever-elusive Canaan. It was a popular image among English-speaking Protestants. Both Old and New Testament in the Calvinist *Geneva Bible* (1560) depict the escape of the Israelites through the Red Sea, an illustration of Exodus 14, as their frontispiece. In the view of Puritan ministers in New England, God had carried the first settlers "by a mighty hand, and an out-stretched arm, over a greater then the Red Sea" (Carroll 43). Mather described both William Bradford, the leader of the Plymouth Separatists, and John Winthrop of the Massachusetts Bay Company as "new Moses." According to Winthrop's famous "Modell of Christian Charity" (1630), written on board the *Arbella* before his arrival in America, the settlement was the biblical "Citty vpon a Hill" {Matthew 5:14}. Following Revelation, colonists viewed America as a typological "new Canaan," another promised land {Genesis 13:14-15; 17:8}, an association which remained powerful and alive in New England place names as well as in American literature and culture as a whole.

The typological imagination has persisted in American culture. Philip Freneau and Hugh Henry Brackenridge's "Poem, On the Rising Glory of America" (1771) viewed the country typologically: "A Canaan here, / Another Canaan shall excel the old." Timothy Dwight's *Conquest of Canaan* (1785) is another national typological poem which culminates in a praise of America, "by heaven design'd / The last retreat for poor, oppress'd mankind!" The theme of the new world as an asylum, a "refuge for the oppressed" {Psalms 9:9}, is part of a providential view of American history as fulfillment:

> And a new Moses lifts the daring wing,
> Through trackless seas, an unknown flight explores,
> And hails a new Canaan's promis'd shores.
>   (Brumm, *Thought* 93; see Exodus 19:4)

It is hardly an exaggeration to say that the exodus is one of America's central themes. When the choice of an official seal for the United States was discussed in 1776, Franklin suggested the device of "Moses lifting up his wand and dividing the Red Sea while Pharaoh was overwhelmed by its waters, with the motto, 'Rebellion to tyrants is obedience to God'" {Exodus 14:16-17}. Jefferson "proposed the children of Israel in the wilderness 'led by a cloud by day and a pillar of fire at night'" {Exodus 13:21–22} (Stokes 467–68). The exodus design that was recommended for the Great Seal bore considerable resemblance to the frontispiece in the *Geneva Bible* (anon., *History of the Seal* 9–12). The eagle that was finally used for the seal is not just the classical emblem of republics but also the biblical eagle of Exodus {19:4} and Revelation {12:14}, an image of escape and emigration. Jonathan Edwards's disciple David Austin wrote in *The Millennium* (1794): "If any should be disposed to ask ... what has become of the eagle, on whose wings the persecuted woman was borne in to the American wilderness, may it not be answered, that she hath taken her station upon the Civil Seal of the United States" (Bercovitch, *Jeremiad* 124).

In his Thanksgiving sermon *Traits of Resemblance in the People of the United States of America to Ancient Israel* (1799), Abiel Abbot, minister at Haverhill, summarized a widely shared general belief.

> It has been often remarked that the people of the United States come nearer to a parallel with Ancient Israel, than any other nation upon the globe. Hence, "OUR AMERICAN ISRAEL," is a term frequently used; and common consent allows it apt and proper. (6)

Isaac Mitchell's novel, significantly entitled *The Asylum* (1811), again combined the notion of America as a promised land and as a haven for the oppressed of the world: "The new land is the poor man's Canaan; to him it is a land flowing with milk and honey" (Mitchell 1:77; Petter 318){Exodus 33:3; Joshua 5:6}.

The typological hold on the American imagination has affected the literature of writers not just from New England but from diverse regions and ethnic groups as well. When German immigrants came to America from Saxony in 1841, they sang that God had called them to their Canaan: "America ... is a beautiful land that God promised to Abraham" (Roehrich 11).

To many newcomers, America was the promised land that welcomed the immigrants whom Emma Lazarus, in her famous Statue of Liberty poem "The New Colossus" (1883), called the "huddled masses" and the "wretched refuse" (Chapman, *Jewish-American* 308; see Matthew 11:28). Many transatlantic and rural-urban migrations were interpreted typologically as the fulfillment of the second book of Moses.

The association of the Exodus with a deliverance from slavery may explain the widespread use of this theme in Afro-American writing. In some cases the adaptations show the traces of force. In her poem

"To the University of Cambridge, in New England," for example, Phillis Wheatley, who had been captured and enslaved in Senegal and sold to a Boston tailor in 1761, paradoxically described her own enslavement as a typological deliverance from Egypt:

> 'Twas not long since I left my native shore,
> The land of errors and Egyptian gloom;
> Father of mercy! 'twas thy gracious hand
> Brought me in safety from those dark abodes.
> (Renfro, *Wheatley* 46)

Absorbing some universalist and revivalist elements in the American rhetoric surrounding her, however, Wheatley also claimed a full American identity against racial bigotry in "On Being Brought from Africa to America:"

> 'Twas mercy brought me from my Pagan land,
> Taught my benighted soul to understand
> That there's a God, that there's a Saviour too.
> Once I redemption neither sought nor knew.
> Some view our sable race with scornful eye;
> "Their colour is a diabolic dye."
> Remember, Christians, Negroes, black as Cain
> May be refined, and join the angelic train.
> (*Wheatley* 48)

In her acceptance of a rebirth from a pagan past, Wheatley could demand Christian equality in America and rightly denounce prejudice against her "sable race" as un-Christian and Pharisaic. Similarly, Mary Antin, a Russian-Jewish immigrant woman, in her autobiography, *The Promised Land* (1912), took a position of apparent self-effacement only to proclaim proudly her sense of equal entitlement. Antin continued the portraiture of America as a new Canaan from an immigrant's point of view, while leaving no doubt that the metaphor of the promised land was especially suited to Jewish immigrants. Interestingly, both Wheatley and Antin are writers often criticized for having participated in "the cult of gratitude" (Melvin Tumin), characterized by excessive assimilation and submissiveness; yet both claimed the American egalitarian promise defiantly by equating themselves with George Washington (Renfro, *Wheatley* 32; Antin, *Promised* 222-40).

The typological elevation of the migration experience to a new exodus was and continues to be a dominant mode of conceptualizing immigration and ethnicity, as the following titles of some ethnic works suggest: Lewis E. MacBrayne, "The Promised Land" (1902); Sidney Nyburg, *The Chosen People* (1917); W. Forest Cozart, *The Chosen People* (1924); Rudolph Fisher, "The Promised Land" (1927); Martin Wendell Odland, *The New Canaan* (1933); Margaret Marchand, *Pilgrims on the Earth* (1940); Stoyan Christowe, *My American Pilgrimage* (1947); Robert Laxalt, *Sweet Promised Land* (1957); Mario Puzo, *The Fortunate Pilgrim* (1965); and Claude Brown, *Manchild in the Promised Land* (1965).

The adaptations are not always made without irony. In a poem entitled "Otherness," the Chinese-American writer Diana Chang answers the double question "Are you Chinese?" and "Are you American?" with the following lines:

> I
> must
> be
>   Jewish
>
> Leading to an eye-opener:
> *real* Chinese in China,
> not feeling other,
>   not international,
>   not cosmopolitan
>
> are gentiles, no less
>
> no wonder
> I felt the way I did
> in the crowd
>
> my Israel
> not there
>
> not here (Wand 135–36)

Another sophisticated thwarting of Mosaic expectations was undertaken in *Hunger of Memory: The Education of Richard Rodriguez* (1982) when the author describes his image "among certain leaders of America's Ethnic Left": "I am considered a dupe, an ass, the fool—Tom Brown, the brown Uncle Tom, interpreting the writing on the wall to a bunch of cigar-smoking pharaohs" (4). Significantly, Rodriguez goes on to describe a typical hypocrite, a "dainty white lady at the women's club luncheon."

The panethnic rhetoric of the new exodus was pliable and permitted writers to view the providential deliverance as a continual process. For example, the westward movement across the prairie was often seen as a new exodus. In James Fenimore Cooper's *The Prairie*

(1827) and in Ole Rølvaag's *Giants in the Earth* {Genesis 6: 4} (1927), the prairie becomes a new Atlantic Ocean and a typological extension of the Red Sea. The *Book of Mormon* (1830) similarly extended the exodus theme westward. The patterns established by the Puritan settlers found sacred and secular applications to the lore of other peoples in America. In much black literature, the "promised land" was not Phillis Wheatley's America but a truly transcendental realm of liberty, somewhere "over Jordan," as the text of the Spiritual "Deep River" suggests:

> O children, O, don't you want to go to that gospel feast,
> That promised land, that land, where all is peace?
> (Brown, *Negro Caravan* 435)

In some slave narratives that heavenly land of a better life after death was resecularized as "North"; in other stories it could mean Canada or Africa. Following the North Star had a nautical and a messianic connotation {Matthew 2:9–10} in writings which also abounded in descriptions of slaveholders as pharaohs or of the South as Egypt. In *Black Culture and Black Consciousness* (1977), Lawrence Levine, after surveying hundreds of songs, arrives at the conclusion that the "most persistent single image the slave songs contain is that of the chosen people." Levine continues:

> The vast majority of the spirituals identify the singers as "de people
> dat is born of God," "We are the people of God," "we are de people
> of de Lord," "I really do believe I'm a child of God," "I'm a child ob
> God, wid my soul sot free," "I'm born of God, I know I am." (33)

Leslie Pinckney Hill's poem "The Wings of Oppression" (1921) rejects the notion that Negroes are "Ishmaels of an unchosen land" and elevates them instead as a "high-commissioned people, mingled through / With all the bloods of men."

> ... God hath chosen still
> The weak thing, and the foolish, and the base,
> And that which is despised to work His will;
> And humble men are chartered yet to run
> Upon His errands round the groaning sphere.
> (Mays, *Negro's God* 181–82)

It is noteworthy that the adoption of chosen peoplehood and errand comes here—as it did in the case of "Puritans"—by an inversion of a false low image.

It is indicative of the rhetorical power of typological thinking that even America's most ardent black critics resorted to the exodus-promised-land theme, only inverting its use by casting the United States as the new Egypt. In *The Condition, Elevation, Emigration, and Destiny of the Colored People of the United States* (1852), a book full of amazing insights about Afro-Americans as a "nation within a nation" (12–20, 209), Martin Robison Delany, a radical black nationalist who had attended Harvard Medical School, denounced the Liberian colonization plans as an expression of the whites' desire "to get rid of us." In his own plans for a black nation in Central or South America, however, Delany explicitly invoked Exodus (159) and adapted typological rhetoric to his view of the Afro-American situation: "That the continent of America seems to have been designed by Providence as an asylum for all the various nations in the world, is very apparent" (171). Having to face the problem of the aboriginal Americans as owners of the land, he pointed out the relative "consanguinity" of Africans and Indians as opposed to Europeans and used the myth of a lost African tribe in Central America—a remnant of the Carthaginian expedition—in order to justify his colonization scheme, in rhetorical terms not unlike those of the *Book of Mormon*.

When George Harris, toward the end of Harriet Beecher Stowe's *Uncle Tom's Cabin* (1852), outlines his plans for a "new enterprise," the colonization in Africa, his pioneer spirit is expressed in John Winthrop's rhetoric: "As a Christian patriot, as a teacher of Christianity, I go to *my country*,—my chosen, my glorious Africa!" (2:303). George Harris may have been the product of a white Christian's imagination, but his rhetoric reflects that of the colonization movement of a Paul Cuffe. The youngest son of Cuffe Slocum, an African, and Ruth Moses, a Wampanoag Indian, Cuffe was self-taught and became a sea captain and merchant before carrying out his plan of a colonization of Sierra Leone. His journal shows "a Puritan sense of self-scrutiny and introspection" (Harris, *Cuffe* 73). Nathan Huggins ("Afro-Americans" 60) argued that Cuffe impressed upon the emigrants "the need for 'sobriety and steadfastness,' with all faithfulness, so that they might be good examples in all things; 'doing justly, loving mercy, and walking humbly.'" Huggins concluded:

> In all these respects, he echoed John Winthrop's sermon on the {*Arbella*} of a century and a half earlier. One expects Cuffee to claim Sierra Leone to be a "city upon a hill." ... The colony would be the instrument by which Africa would be awakened.
>
> Thus Cuffee was not "going back to Africa" in the sense that he was reclaiming his heritage, nor was he abandoning that which he had come to be. He expected Afro-Americans to go to Africa as they were, products of the New World—new men—and, as such, instru-

ments through which Africa itself would be transformed into a Christian commonwealth. (60)

Typological rhetoric may indicate the Americanization of people who use it. Yet it can, alternately or at the same time, serve to define a new ethnic peoplehood in contradistinction to a general American identity. The rhetoric in support of American group cohesion and consensus can also be used to forge divergent and dissenting ethnic groupings. In *The Souls of Black Folk* (1903), W. E. B. DuBois developed an extended metaphor of the veil that separates Afro-Americans from American culture at large but also gives them a more profound vision and a higher destiny. DuBois imaginatively adapted two biblical images of the veil as a division within the temple [Exodus 26:33] and as the cover that the divinely inspired Moses wore when he came back from Mount Sinai and spoke to the people [Exodus 34:33–35]. Both images are typologically focused in Paul's second letter to the Corinthians [3:13–18], a passage which promises a universal revelation once the Old Testament veil has been sundered in Christ. DuBois cast the Negro as the world's "seventh son, born with a veil, and gifted with second-sight in this American world," for whom emancipation "was the key to a promised land of sweeter beauty than ever stretched before the eyes of the weary Israelites." "Book-learning" soon became "another ideal to guide the unguided, another pillar of fire by night after a clouded day [Exodus 13:21–22]," an ideal which seemed to be "the mountain path to Canaan." Yet, whereas Canaan always remained "dim and far away," the new vision of "self-consciousness, self-realization, self-respect" emerged for the Negro.

> In those sombre forests of his striving his own soul rose before him, and he saw himself—darkly as through a veil; and yet he saw in himself some faint revelation of his power, of his mission. (218)

In Booker T. Washington's autobiography, *Up from Slavery* (1901), chosen peoplehood is similarly invoked, yet this time for Negro industrial education. Hampton Institute is described as a "promised land" (56), and the tasks of building Tuskegee are typologically connected with the preparatory hardships before the emergence from Egyptian bondage:

> I had always sympathized with the "Children of Israel," in their task of "making bricks without straw," but ours was the task of making bricks with no money and no experience. (109) [Exodus 5:7–22]

Later in the twentieth century Marcus Garvey and Elijah Muhammad adapted the chosen-people theme to an Afro-American sense of
mission; Martin Luther King consciously cast himself as a black
Moses when he declaimed, "I've been to the mountain top ... "; and
LeRoi Jones/Amiri Baraka offered himself as a new Noah, ready to
lead his chosen people out of American bondage in his "New Ark"
(the old New Jersey place-name Newark recaptured in the typological
dimensions that were probably intended by its first European settlers). Melvin Tolson planned his volume of poetry *Harlem Gallery*
(1965) as the first of five to follow black history from 1619 to the
present. The projected volumes were to be entitled "Egypt Land,"
"The Red Sea," "The Wilderness," and "The Promised Land." Richard
Wright's story "Bright and Morning Star" (1938) refers both to the
star of Revelation [22:16]—a popular image in American writing
from the times of Increase Mather and Richard Thacher to the
famous ending of Thoreau's *Walden* (Bercovitch, *Puritan* 240 n. 49)—
and to the red star of communism.

If typology served as a literary framework for the articulation of
dissent and reform programs in Afro-American culture, it was also
applied to American business and labor history. In *The Man Nobody
Knows* (1925), Bruce Barton argued that Jesus was "The Founder of
Modern Business." In 1926 Lincoln Steffens published a volume with
the self-explanatory title *Moses in Red*, which contains a very American description of biblical history:

> Moses was a leader; a labor leader; a leader of revolt; and a great
> one. And he was loyal to the people.
> His people, the children of Israel, were the labor of Egypt. They
> were industrious; ... they were highly skilled and very resourceful.
> ... They could, under orders, make bricks and find the straw. (Stef-
> fens 96)

In post-Puritan America, white and black, business and labor, Jew
and Gentile, could follow typological patterns and become biblical
antitypes. The heterogeneous adaptations of typology functioned
most frequently not to lend static sanction to things as they were but
to invite action in order to make things as they should be. Because
it was the promised land, America was promise.

Imitation of Christ

The strongest evidence for the pervasiveness of typology in the
American imagination is provided, as some examples have already

shown, by the countless ways in which Christ was cast as a type. Of course, the imitation of Christ was a duty for Western pilgrims. Thomas à Kempis's book of instruction *Imitatio Christi* appeared in numerous English, German, and French editions which were published in America. Cotton Mather liked the book; in his own autobiography, *Paterna* (1699–1702), he expressed an ardent desire for an imitation of Christ: "I thought, I was arrived unto the highest *Pinnacle* of my *Happiness*, if I might Represent and Exhibit, any *Glory* of my Lord JESUS CHRIST, unto the world. No *Glory*, No, None, Like that of *conformity* to my Lord JESUS CHRIST!" No act could convince Mather of such conformity as successfully as the anonymous libels some "horrid people" threw at Mather's gate: "they drew yᵉ Picture of a Man, hanging on yᵉ *Gallowes*; They wrote *my Name* over it." Mather read this anonymous note by local adversaries as a *"Token For Good"* since it symbolized his own—crucifixion! "Now, Now! my Soul was filled with *unspeakable Joy*! Now I had *Gain'd all my Point*! Now my Resemblance unto my Lord JESUS CHRIST, had a Glorious Addition made unto it" (183).

American writers from the seventeenth to the twentieth century and of the most diverse ethnic backgrounds have continued to develop Christic parallels, sometimes based on what would seem to be minor externals. American protagonists have had more than a "1 in 365" chance to be born on Christmas (like Peder Hansa in Rølvaag's *Giants in the Earth* {1927}) or to die on Good Friday (like Geremio in Di Donato's *Christ in Concrete* {1939}). The titular hero of Charles Brockden Brown's *Wieland* (1798), whose father came to America as a missionary to the Indians after reading the lines "seek and ye shall find" {Luke 11:9}, is transformed into a "Man of Sorrows." When the Virginia slave rebel Nat Turner was asked after his arrest in 1831 whether he found himself mistaken now, he answered: "Was not Christ crucified?" (Foner, *Turner* 45). Harriet Beecher Stowe's Uncle Tom suffers contumely and martyrdom with Christlike dignity. Martin Robison Delany's novel *Blake; or, The Huts* (1859–61) was written in explicit antithesis to Stowe. It was an unusually radical book, both in its creation of a black and beautiful protagonist who is an aristocratic hero, revolutionary superman, and slave conspirator and instigator and in a more or less continuous opposition to American national symbolism. Henry Blake is "black— pure Negro—handsome, manly and intelligent, in size comparing well with his master, but neither so fleshy nor heavy built in person" (16–17). When he sees the American flag on the slave prison in Washington, D.C., he thinks of "stars as the pride of the white man, and stripes as the emblem of power over the blacks" (117).[6] Yet, despite Blake's emphasis on earthly struggle against slavery through a universal slave revolution, his program remains part of *imitatio Christi*: "let us at once drop the religion of our oppressors," he suggests, "and take the Scriptures for our guide and Christ as our example" (197). In American writing, rebels and martyrs are likely to become Christ-like. Thoreau's address to the readers in his "Plea for Captain John Brown" (1860) is characteristic: "You who pretend to care for Christ crucified, consider what you are about to do to him who offered himself to be the saviour of four millions of men" (291). Claude McKay was attracted to radical journalism when he saw the artistic depiction of a lynching as a crucifixion on the cover of the August 1915 issue of *The Masses* (*Passion* 10 and illus. opp. 42). One of the most radical Jewish-American novels, Mike Gold's *Jews without Money* (1930), ends with the call for a new messiah who will raze the world of inequality:

> O, workers' Revolution, you brought hope to me, a lonely suicidal boy. You are the true Messiah. You will destroy the East Side when you come, and build there a garden for the human spirit.
> O revolution, that forced me to think, to struggle and to live.
> O great Beginning!
> THE END. (224)

Gold's revolutionary messianism was not Christian. As David Fine has argued, however, Ezra Brudno's *The Fugitive* (1904) and Edward Steiner's *The Mediator* (1907) are Jewish immigrant novels that specifically embraced Christ as mediator and unifier of Jews and Gentiles in America, where, in Steiner's words, "a new race might be born, which should know nothing of the ancient hate and the ancient wrongs" (285; Fine, *City* 115). American ethnic writing abounds with Christic themes, from the many lynchings rendered as crucifixions to the very titles of Casimir Pijanowski's *Passion Play of Chicago* (1924) and Piri Thomas's *Savior, Savior, Hold My Hand* (1972). William Boelhower called attention to Pascal D'Angelo's interesting autobiography, *Son of Italy* (1924), with its reliance on Christ typology: "A rusty nail pierced my right hand. ... Blood began to come out from both sides" (Boelhower, *Immigrant* 119). As Bonnie Lyons has shown, David Schearl's Christ-like suffering in book 4 of Henry Roth's *Call It Sleep* (1934) is enriched by the image of the chalice and the street voices that talk of Mary and the "T'ree Kings" (Lyons, *Roth* 53). In the third part of James T. Farrell's Studs Lonigan trilogy, significantly entitled *Judgment Day* (1935), the protagonist's death is preceded by his mother's thoughts of "Jesus in Gethsemane, sweating blood for the sins of man, and of Jesus on the cross, wearing a crown of thorns, drinking vinegar and gall, his side pierced with a lance, Jesus crucified ..." (462). Even in Richard Wright's *Native Son* (1940), Bigger Thomas, who explicitly rejects the minister's Jesus, becomes, as Keneth Kinnamon has suggested, a suffering black Christ crucified by white America. "Two men stretched his arms out, as though about to crucify him ..." (Wright 253). Bigger Thomas feels that through his actions the people's "shame was washed away" (Kinnamon 137). Fittingly, his lawyer, Max, pleads for him with the argument that his client resembles the Pilgrim fathers: "In him and men like him is what was in our forefathers when they first came to these strange shores hundreds of years ago" (Wright 362–63). Hisaye Yamamoto, an exciting Japanese-American storyteller whose famous work "The Legend of Miss Sasagawara" (1950) includes a block Christmas party in a Japanese-American detention camp during World War II, described the acceptance of Christ by Mrs. Hosoume in the story "Yoneko's Earthquake" (1951). In a "Baptist church exclusively for Japanese people," the "Christian cousins" sing their version of "Let Us Gather at the River"—in Japanese (Chin, *Aiiieeeee!* 179).

American literature seems Bible-made, indeed. The identification of America with Christ is so strong at times that there are instances in which not only characters accept or resemble Christ but in which the whole country is explicitly equated with Jesus. In an address delivered in New York on April 20, 1915, for example, Woodrow Wilson (still) supported United States neutrality in World War I with a rhetorical flourish, combining an ethnic with a Christic appeal:

> We are the mediating Nation of the world. ... We are compounded of the nations of the world; we mediate their blood, we mediate their traditions, we mediate their sentiments, their tastes, their passions; we are ourselves compounded of those things. (*New Democracy* 1:304)

America may be Christ-like not only in mediation, but also in suffering. Thus Paul Simon's "American Tune" (1973) invokes *Mayflower* and Statue of Liberty only to conclude that you "can't be forever blessed"—all to the tune of "O Haupt voll Blut und Wunden" by Paul Gerhardt (1607–76). Simon's American tune thus merges with one of the most famous Protestant songs of Christ's contumely.

William Faulkner is the most important American writer who apotheosized and transcended the typological tradition. His novels amount to a comprehensive literary counterstatement to America as a promised land and to Christic ethnicity, while remaining firmly

within that tradition, too. *Light in August* (1932) is the most compre-
hensively Christic novel in America and is, at the same time, subversive of the typological assumptions of American culture. Joe Christmas is the Christ figure whose ambiguous racial identity sets different
actions in motion, all of which hinge on the questionable assumption
that he must be black. He is loved and hated, he kills, and he is
lynched for his metaphoric, yet doubtful, ethnic identity. Faulkner
consciously played with all the traditional Christic devices in creating
Joe Christmas, who shares more than his initials with Jesus Christ.
He was found at Christmas, yet Faulkner makes sure to note that he
was not born that day; he is described as thirty-three years of age
when he moves to Jefferson, not when he gets crucified-killed; and
he is arrested, though not lynched, on Good Friday. Faulkner seems
to have realized that the Christic assumptions were so strong in
American culture that his qualifiers were likely to be misread. He
therefore uses the questionable Christic identity to parallel his theme
of doubtful ethnic identity, as the novel becomes an assault on pre-
conceptions.

How Puritanism Shaped American Ethnicity

How was it possible for the sectarian symbol system of a regionally
limited group of early migrants to form the "core," the mainstream,
in a polyethnic culture? Martin Marty, in reviewing the immigration
of Roman Catholics, Jews, and Continental Protestants since 1850,
pointed out that these immigrants "would have found little congenial
in New England village life. But consciously and unconsciously, by
historical study and by osmosis, they share its general outline" ("Spirit's" 172). In a perceptive essay, "Immigration and Puritanism" (1940),
Marcus Lee Hansen noticed how familiar the records of seventeenth-
century Massachusetts sounded to a historian of nineteenth-century
immigration (*Immigrant* 102). Hansen also wrote of "spontaneous
immigrant Puritanism" and the "process of Puritanization" among
immigrant groups (119, 120). Was the process as natural as "osmosis"?
Was it "spontaneous"?

In a rich and resourceful essay, "Religion and Ethnicity in America" (1978), Timothy Smith made a broad attempt to probe the question of ethnic Puritanism. Rather than conceiving of American religion as a static structure that could be imposed upon or absorbed by
newcomers, Smith suggested that the "the acts of uprooting, migration, resettlement, and community-building became for the partici-

pants a theologizing experience" (1181). This view draws on Fredrik Barth's theory, which emphasizes the *emergence*, not the survival, of ethnicity. "The folk theology and religious piety that flourished in immigrant churches from the beginnings of American settlements were not merely traditional but progressive" (1181). This applies, according to Smith, to all immigrants as well as to Afro-Americans, for whom emancipation rather than migration "was the watershed that separated their 'new world' from the old" (1182). Smith concluded his essay with the suggestive remark that, after all, "Moses, Jesus, and Paul were also prophets of process theology" (1185).

Smith's richly documented essay argues persuasively that immigrants whose "conceptions of identity and proper behavior had been wrenched loose from the past" would naturally develop "a deep fascination with the future" (1176).

> From its colonial beginnings, the migration of bonded groups or the formation of such groups in the new land made the biblical imagery of the Exodus seem a metaphor for the American experience, not only for English Puritans and Russian Jews, but for Christian villagers of Catholic, Protestant, and Orthodox persuasions from all parts of Europe. (1176)

> Linking the American future with the Kingdom of God was not, therefore, an exclusively Yankee obsession, nor the Social Gospel a Protestant preserve. Jews of both Reform and Orthodox faith, radical Irish as well as Chicano Catholics, and Mormon converts from Europe ... have also been people of the dream. (1177)

At the center of his argument, Smith keeps emphasizing that migration "was often a theologizing experience—just as it had been when Abraham left the land of his fathers, when the people of the Exodus followed Moses into the wilderness, and when Jeremiah urged the exiles who wept by the rivers of Babylon to make the God of their past the hope of their future" (1175). Timothy Smith offers us much more than "osmosis" or "spontaneity." Instead of naturalizing, he emphasizes the historical experience of migration. The phrasing "theologizing experience" is fortunate and extremely helpful. However, if the experience of migrating alone were the decisive factor, might we not expect that migrants to all countries would have developed typological imagery and jeremiadic exhortations? Yet the United States seems much more strongly affected by such concepts than other new countries, even ones as close by as Canada, Mexico, and Brazil.

For this reason it is justifiable to consider New England typology as a flexible and suggestive way of looking at migration; it was a method that had already taken shape and that could be imposed upon and adapted and altered by later immigrants and by other groups who by adopting a Puritan mode sometimes strengthened their own separateness and group cohesion. Smith deemphasizes the rhetorical dominance of New England in conceptualizing wide-ranging theologizing experiences. "What Marcus Lee Hansen has called 'immigrant Puritanism' owed virtually nothing to colonial New England," Smith says (1176). He is technically right, since Hansen thought of H. L. Mencken's, not Perry Miller's, Puritans: he used "Puritanism" more to describe things like "discipline" than to refer to the New England tradition. In a broader sense, however, Smith underestimates the importance of the Puritan tradition as a culture that defined itself in contrast to an old world, asked questions, set problems, defined the nature of the debate, and used types in ways that made sense to other newcomers and groups who otherwise may have had few things in common with Puritanism. Hans Kohn has thus interpreted the Puritan Revolution as the "first example of modern nationalism" and emphasized that its particular method of community-building on the basis of the biblical idea of a covenanted people was "open," since the community was one "decided not by blood but by faith" (166–68). Once the New-England Puritans had so deeply ingrained the connections between Bible and process toward a prophesied American destiny by consent, later newcomers and other groups could find typology similarly resonant with their own experiences, interests, and hopes—or phrase their divergent interests and aspirations, including their fire-and-brimstone assaults on Puritanism, in the available rhetorical forms. Puritanism had created cultural mechanisms to transmit even discontinuity. The theologizing experience and the need for new images of group emergence thus found a compelling set of codes and images, a *form*, which immigrants and ethnics could fill with their own, varying contents and adapt to their own situations and expectations. Though I am not suggesting the static notion of a New England-controlled monolithic hegemony, I also cannot comfortably accept the notion that "migration experience" is the category that explains it all—even if New England had never existed.

Ethnogenesis: The Naturalization of Group Emergence

I have so far followed Smith's emphasis on migration and have spoken of migrants and newcomers. Yet America is not only a nation of immigrants, and ethnicity does not arise with migrations alone. Under all sorts of diverse circumstances—such as war, conflict, conquest, enslavement, or simply coexistence—what Smith calls "community-building," the growth of a sense of peoplehood among people who previously had other bases of group identification, takes place, bringing about each time, organically speaking, "the birth of a nation." In his book *Ethnicity in the United States* (1974), Andrew Greeley used the term "ethnogenesis" (309) in order to describe the phenomenon of emerging ethnicity, sometimes called "ethnicization" or "ethnification." At the moment of group formation, of the construction of peoplehood, the theologizing that Smith documented so well takes place. It is then that typology and ethnogenesis come together. The very term "ethnogenesis" nicely combines an organic sense (people, birth) with a faint biblical echo (Genesis) and helps to sacralize beginnings.

"Typological ethnogenesis" can clearly be observed in John Winthrop's "A Modell of Christian Charity" (1630), which does typological work and naturalizes a newly formed group by invoking scripture [Ephesians 4:15-16, Romans 12:4-5, and 1 Corinthians 12:12-27]. Winthrop repeatedly addresses the *Arbella* passengers as "the body of Christ" (289). For the purpose of the imaginative construction of the Massachusetts Bay Company as Christ's body, Winthrop can develop an elaborate familistic image of a truly naturalized company (*Gesellschaft* metamorphosed into *Gemeinschaft*), held together by love, not—to reiterate Hans Kohn's point about Puritan "nationalism"—by blood. A whole array of natural images is invoked: "The ligamentes of this body which knitt together are loue" (289); "loue is the fruite of the new birthe" (290); "a reall thing not Imaginarie" (292); or "loue is as absolutely necessary to the being of the body of Christ, as the sinewes and other ligaments of a naturall body are to the being of that body" (292). Perhaps the most interesting moments for our context occur in Winthrop's speech when he actually describes the consent relationship of love as if it were one of descent:

> ... the Lord ... loues his elect because they are like himselfe, he beholds them in his beloued sonne: soe a mother loues her childe, because shee throughly conceiues a resemblance of herselfe in it. Thus it is betweene the members of Christ, each discernes by the worke of the spirit his owne Image and resemblance in another, and therefore cannot but loue him as he loues himselfe. (290)

The relationship of love is equaled with that of "fleshe of my fleshe" (291) and rather wittily given even more importance than "the State of Wedlock" (292). This is one moment of ethnogenesis by typology. Drawing on the New Testament, Winthrop developed a connection between Christian love and ethnicity that was to remain central in American culture.

Although the term "ethnogenesis" is not to be found in the *Oxford English Dictionary* or its supplements, it was used as early as 1861, in Henry Timrod's poem entitled "Ethnogenesis." This poem, written by a grandson of German immigrants to South Carolina, "naturalizes" the emergence of the South as an *ethnos* by constructing a sense of peoplehood with the help of typology. Blessed by the natural elements ("the very sun / Takes part with us; and on our errands run / All breezes of the ocean") and the beauty of the land, the South is born as a new chosen people, about to leave the house of bondage — that is, the Union (*Poems* 92). Timrod's nascent South is thus righteously pitted against "repulsive" and "Pharisaic" northerners who have lost "the pure and Christian faith" and "dare to teach / What Christ and Paul refrained to preach" (i.e., one assumes, the abolition of slavery).

> To doubt the end were want of trust in God,
>> Who, if he has decreed
>> That we must pass a redder sea
> Than that which rang to Miriam's holy glee,
>> Will surely raise at need
>> A Moses with his rod! (*Poems* 94)

Again, the exodus motif sanctions and sacralizes the "birth" of an emerging group, the seceding South. (The use of Miriam is a bit double-edged, however, if one considers not only Exodus 15:20, as Timrod wants us to, but also Numbers 12:1-2.) Ironically, the argument for "a pure and Christian faith" could have come from the sermon of a Puritan divine against whose descendants Timrod's poem is directed. It is interesting to note that the language of ethnogenesis has exerted a centripetal power which may draw outsiders into a sacred group identity; thus the German-Jewish immigrant son Ludwig Lewisohn later identified with the South through Timrod's poetry.

Another example is provided by Lawrence Levine, who states in his study of the sacred music of the slaves that "even outsiders had difficulty resisting the centripetal pull of black religious services and song" (*Black* 29). This was true although many songs were not "totally new creations, but were forged out of many pre-existing bits of old songs mixed together" (29). The mix of individual and collective creativity, these sacred songs engendered ethnogenesis and helped create a different sense of peoplehood even though some of the typological texts (concerning exodus or the promised land) and some of the melodies resembled those sung by other Americans. Long before emancipation (which Timothy Smith considered the ethnicizing watershed in Afro-American history), Afro-American peoplehood could be fashioned out of the extraordinarily diverse Africans and their American descendants with the help of the same typological materials that were used to naturalize national identity. Harriet Beecher Stowe's George Harris was right when he commented:

> In these days, a nation is born in a day. A nation starts now, with all the great problems of republican life and civilization wrought out to its hand;—it has not to discover, but only to apply. (*Uncle* 2:301)

Typology was one of these elements to be applied. Thus typology helps to create ethnicity, and ethnicity feeds on typology.

"One Blood": Acts and Shadows

In *The Invention of Tradition* Eric Hobsbawm reminded us that national paraphernalia such as flags and anthems are of surprisingly recent origin; anthems followed the British example (which can be dated to 1740), whereas flags generally copied the (originally Dutch) tricolor. Yet people who sing very similar anthems or wave flags all of which contain the colors red, white, and blue need not be pursuing the same goals. Similarly, a common typological language is not necessarily an indication for uniformity of thought or feeling. Even if two speakers share the same rhetoric and describe themselves, for example, as "new Moses," they need not be using typology for the same, or even compatible, ends. Their different "promised lands" might be an integrated nation or a separatist ethnic group, a strongly unionized or a laissez-faire business-oriented economy, a unified country or a secessionist region. Their rhetorical codes may support consensus or conflict. What the rhetoric accomplishes, however, is to establish a common language within which dissent can take place. This seems to be of special importance in countries with great diversity in their inhabitants' backgrounds.

An interesting way to illuminate the pervasiveness of biblical phrasing and the flexibility of its uses in American culture is to trace one verse through various texts. The example I have chosen here illustrates how exclusivist scriptural interpretations can be challenged by the invoking of universalist passages, but also how divergently biblical rhetoric may be invoked to support ethnic and national causes which are, after all, secular. Worldly opponents may always, of course, simply cite different sacred passages. In the essay "Slavery and Theology" (1972), Timothy Smith points out that the "favorite text of Black preachers was not the white Christian's John 3:16 at all, but Paul's announcement to the Athenians that God 'made of one blood all nations of men for to dwell on the face of the earth'" (504). Smith cites Benjamin Tanner, Hosea Easton, Austin Steward, and Nathaniel Paul, but the use of Acts 17:26 was even more widespread and diverse in black and white America. Blood imagery—according to David Schneider, belonging to the realm of natural substance—is used in many cultures in order to naturalize kinship or to illustrate ethnogenesis. The proclaiming of the biblical truth of "one blood" in America established a sacred textual basis for the spiritual unity of a secularly divided people.

As early as in 1700 the Puritan Samuel Sewall had invoked the verse in order to support his typological attack on slavery. In *The Selling of Joseph* he argued "that all Men, as they are the Sons of *Adam*, are Coheirs; and have equal Rights unto Liberty, and all other outward Comforts of Life," followed by Psalms 115:16 and Acts 17:26 (Ruchames, *Racial* 47). In 1789 *The Interesting Narrative of the Life of Olaudah Equiano; or, Gustavus Vassa, the African: Written by Himself* invoked Scripture in order to challenge European racial bigotry:

> Let the polished and haughty European recollect that his ancestors were once, like the Africans, uncivilized, and even barbarous .... Let such reflections as these melt the pride of their superiority into sympathy for the wants and miseries of their sable brethren, and compel them to acknowledge that understanding is not confined to feature or color. If, when they look around the world, they feel exultation, let it be tempered with benevolence to others, and gratitude to God, "who hath made of one blood all nations of men for to dwell on all the face of the earth." (Bontemps 18)

In the period after the enactment of the Fugitive Slave Law of 1850, references to Acts 17:26 intensified. In his famous oration "The Meaning of July Fourth for the Negro," delivered in Corinthian Hall, Rochester, on July 5, 1852, Frederick Douglass scolded white Americans for their hypocrisy:

Americans! Your republican politics, not less than your republican religion, are flagrantly inconsistent. ... You invite to your shores fugitives of oppression from abroad, honor them with banquets, greet them with ovations, cheer them, toast them, salute them, protect them, and pour out your money to them like water; but the fugitives from your own land, you advertise, hunt, arrest, shoot, and kill. ... You profess to believe "that, of one blood, God made all nations of men to dwell on the face of all the earth," and hath commanded all men, everywhere, to love one another; yet you notoriously hate, (and glory in your hatred) all men whose skins are not colored like your own. (Foner, *Douglass* 199–200)

Douglass then proceeded to juxtapose the Declaration of Independence with hypocritical American practices. In the same year Martin Robison Delany's *Condition, Elevation, Emigration, and Destiny of the Colored People of the United States* similarly paralleled Bible and Declaration while offering a worldwide exegesis of Acts 17:

We believe in the universal equality of man, and believe in that declaration of God's word, in which it is there positively said, that "God has made of one blood all the nations that dwell on the face of the earth." Now of "the nations that dwell on the face of the earth," that is, all the people—there are one thousand millions of souls, and of this vast number of human beings, two-thirds are colored, from black, tending in complexion to the olive or that of the Chinese, with all the intermediate and admixtures of black and white, with the various "crosses" as they are physiologically, but erroneously termed, to white. (36–37)

In the black writer William Wells Brown's novel *Clotel; or, The President's Daughter* (1853), a sensitive white character gets to invoke Acts. Georgiana Peck, a hypocritical minister's daughter, tries to sway her chosen man, Carlton, by first awakening in him a feeling of Christian love. "Her next aim was," the narrator continues,

to vindicate the Bible from sustaining the monstrous institution of slavery. She said, "God has created of one blood all the nations of men, to dwell on all the face of the earth." To claim, hold and treat a human being as property is felony against God and man. (115)

At the end of Georgiana's two-page address, a regenerate Carlton plays the part of an ideal audience, "a silent tear stealing down the cheek of the newly born child of God" (117). The Afro-American uses of Acts are variations upon the pattern of challenging white exclusivism, of scolding as hypocrites people who make distinctions on the basis of skin color, and of persuading Christian audiences to be reborn in abolitionism.

This is not true of an anonymous anti-evolutionist and of two white antislavery writers of the same period. In an essay entitled "Are the Human Race All of One Blood?" which appeared in volume 6 of the *American Ladies Magazine* in 1833, the anonymous author specifically took Acts 17 as a point of departure for an argument against an evolutionary connection between man and animal. The essay then attempts to explain the presence and future of racial differences in the world, in a fashion that sounds somewhat absurd to twentieth-century readers and must have sounded hypocritical to at least some nineteenth-century readers of Acts. On the one hand, Christianity promises the transcendence of descent:

> True Christianity will make all men brethren, and then the barriers between castes and tribes will be broken down; and it is from hereditary sources that almost all distinctions and peculiarities among the human race originate. (361)

On the other hand, the knowledge of the Christian universalist promise has given whites, and especially Anglo-Americans, distinct advantages, privileges, and even a superiority over other races:

> The efforts to obtain personal liberty, and the influence of the Christian religion have been the chief means of perfecting the faculties of the white man.
>
> Let him then, as far as possible, plant the seeds of freedom and Christianity in the hearts of every people; and then the *brown*, the *red*, the *black*, and the *tawny* man will assimilate with each other, and with the more favored white race, till they learn to *feel* as well as to acknowledge, that "God hath made of one blood all nations of men." (362)

Avowedly in order to teach nonwhites to feel the truth of Acts 17, the *American Ladies Magazine* writer ironically endorses white supremacy in the name of biblical universalism.

In *The Key to Uncle Tom's Cabin* (1853), Harriet Beecher Stowe invokes Acts after telling the story of a slave woman from New England who had felt Christ's comfort "in the distant forest of Africa" (48). "Compare now these experiences with the earnest and beautiful language of Paul" (49). Stowe then quotes Acts 17:26–27 in support of the authenticity of her character Uncle Tom. Stowe's point is that Christ may speak to people *anywhere*: "Is not the veil which divides us from an almighty and most merciful Father much thinner than we, in the pride of our philosophy, are apt to imagine?"

(49). In *Uncle Tom's Cabin*, where much dialogue is drawn from biblical sources, Stowe also alludes to Acts in order to demonstrate the hypocritical character of Marie St. Clare, who gives an unambiguously negative answer to Ophelia's question "Don't you believe that the Lord made them of one blood with us?" (1:251).

Writing in the *Liberator* on May 29, 1863, Wendell Phillips reviewed the historical mission of earlier ages as the bringing of religion and revolution to the world. He continued:

> This generation has another work, which is to say, All races have equal rights. "God hath made of one blood all nations to serve Him on the face of the earth." That is the motto of this generation. (1)

Phillips invoked Acts 17:26 in order to legitimate his own interpretation of America's future. As Gilbert Osofsky (1973) has shown, Phillips derived his vision of a fused and amalgamated American nationality, by "the melting of the negro into the various races that congregate on this continent" in "gradual and harmonizing union, in honorable marriage" (39), from his identification with Puritanism and Revolution: "In my nationality there is but one idea—the harmonious and equal mingling of all races. ... No nation ever became great which was born of one blood" (38–39). This excerpt is an example of the confusing combination in which terms of American ethnic interaction from melting and marriage to generation and national greatness may appear. In nontheological texts, Acts could serve as a basis for abolitionist agitation or for racial supremacy, as well as for special purposes. While subjecting them to the consensus ritual of speaking with the Bible, the quoting of Acts did not make the speakers of a shared rhetoric uniform in spirit.

Comparing these various cultural interpretations with American theological commentaries on Acts 17:26 reveals how much further the political writers went. Of five nineteenth-century book-length commentaries published in the North, only Abiel Abbot Livermore's *Acts* (1857) emphasized that Paul's admonition to Greeks and Jews not to "boast of their descent" meant something special to Americans and that the biblical evidence for the "common origin of the human race furnishes a host of arguments against slavery, oppression, pride, and selfishness" (245). Albert Barnes's *Notes, Explanatory and Practical, on the Acts of the Apostles* (1869) merely alluded to the applicability of the passage to America by mentioning "variety of complexion" (248); and the books by John Owen (1850), Joseph Addison Alexander (1866), and Lyman Abbott (1876) make no reference to contemporary America at all.

The invoking of Acts in secular literature did not go out of fashion with the end of the Civil War, as four final examples may illustrate. Fittingly, the first three come, again, from the realm of black-white relations. In 1896 William Dean Howells responded with an "imaginative prophecy" when he reviewed Paul Laurence Dunbar's poems: "God hath made of one blood all nations of men: perhaps the proof of this saying is to appear in the arts, and our hostilities and prejudices are to vanish in them," Howells wrote with high hopes for ethnic transcendence in literature (Wagenknecht, *Howells* 197; see also Dunbar, *Poems* viii). In the short story "A Matter of Principle," included in the collection *The Wife of His Youth* (1899), Charles W. Chesnutt humorously satirized the race prejudice with which light-skinned Cicero Clayton views Afro-Americans of a darker skin. This folly spoils his daughter's best marriage prospect, yet Mr. Clayton does not learn from his errors. He cannot see the beam in his own eyes, and, though the family Bible is not an object frequently consulted in his house (*Wife* 128), Clayton sticks to an easy line when the future of the colored race is discussed at social meetings: "What the white people of the United States need most, in dealing with this problem, is a higher conception of the brotherhood of man. For of one blood God made all the nations of the earth" (*Wife* 131). Chesnutt's story shows that invoking Acts was perceived as a cliché by black writers at the end of the nineteenth century. This did not keep W. E. B. DuBois from using Acts very prominently at the beginning of *Darkwater* (1920) in order to argue for the universal brotherhood of mankind: "I believe in God, who made of one blood all nations that on earth do dwell. I believe that all men, black and brown and white, are brothers, varying through time and opportunity, in form and gift and feature, but differing in no essential particular, and alike in soul and the possibility of infinite development" (3).

The last example comes from a different area of ethnic interaction in America and illustrates the influence of Howells's phrasing and the continued vitality of the vision of a fused America. Far from attacking hypocrisy, Mary Antin, in *They Who Knock at Our Gates* (1914), felt that Americans were in a unique "position to hasten the climax of the drama of unification." The immigrant Antin saw peoples "merging their interests, their cultures, their bloods," a process that was "approaching completion in our own era." She herself characterized the "process of the removal of barriers" as the major task that still had to be accomplished:

There remain a few ancient prejudices to overcome, a few stumps of ignorance to uproot, before all the nations of the earth shall forget their boundaries, and move about the surface of the earth as congenial guests at a public feast.

This, indeed, will be the proof of the ancient saying, "He hath made of one blood all nations of men, for to dwell on all the face of the earth." It is coming, inevitably it is coming. (138–39)

In this strong concluding example of the dynamic power of typological adaptations, Acts again foreshadows not the America that *is*, but an America that *will be*, because it has been foreshadowed by Acts. Characteristically, prejudices are seen only as a residue of the past, not as the by-products of newly created boundaries; universalism is simply subjugated to progress and becomes the struggle for the future in America and against an old-world past. Mary Antin had a *faible* for condensed Americana as she fused rhetoric of tree stumps, boundaries, ancient prejudice, and inevitable progress into a construction of America as destined fulfillment of Paul's prophecy. This fulfillment was to take place through the melting pot as process and antitype.

CHAPTER THREE

Melting Pots

America is God's Crucible, the great Melting-Pot where all the races of
Europe are melting and re-forming.
                                            —Israel Zangwill, *The Melting-Pot*

But the American nationality is still forming: its processes are mysterious,
and the final form, if there is ever to be a final form, is as yet unknown.
                                        —Nathan Glazer and Daniel Patrick Moynihan,
                                                      Beyond the Melting Pot

Sometimes literary scholars express a yearning for scientific methods
or at least for the clarity and social relevance of sociological thinking.
Yet few examples can illustrate the literary quality of sociological
debates better than the language used in discussions of American
ethnic interaction. Since the beginning of the twentieth century, the
debates have been conducted in the terms of a rarely read, yet universally invoked, play. Whether theorists agreed or disagreed, they
expressed much of their thinking by means of the vague and self-
consciously literary symbolism of a particular playwright. The dram-
atist was Israel Zangwill (1864–1926), an English Jew who in 1905,
two years after marrying the gentile writer Edith Ayrton, had a sud-
den revelation. He told a *New York Times* reporter later: "I shut my
eyes one night; and there before me saw in one vivid flash the whole
play, just as it shall be on the stage" (October 24, 1908). At first he
thought of calling the play-to-be "The Crucible," but he finally settled on the title *The Melting-Pot* for the finished work, which was first
performed in Washington on October 5, 1908, and published in 1909
(Leftwich, *Zangwill* 252). The four-act piece was immensely popular
in the United States, though not in Zangwill's native Britain, and was
greeted with enthusiasm by such diverse figures as Theodore Roosevelt and Jane Addams (Mann, *One* 100–118). More than any social
or political theory, the rhetoric of Zangwill's play shaped American
discourse on immigration and ethnicity, including most notably the
language of self-declared opponents of the melting-pot concept.

66

Just a Four-Act Play

Although Zangwill defined the role of the man of letters as that of a "lay priest" and denounced "art for art's sake" (Mann, *One* 102, 109), he first and foremost presented a story in his drama (illustration 2). The four-act play illustrates the representatively constructed life of a Jewish family in New York. The grandmother, Frau Quixano, remains orthodox and never learns English; the uncle, Mendel, has abandoned orthodoxy and lives in a gentile neighborhood in Staten Island, where he gives music lessons; the young protagonist and composer-genius, David Quixano, falls in love with Vera Revendal, the daughter of an anti-Semitic baron from the very same city, Kishineff, where David's parents had been killed during an anti-Semitic pogrom. The Irish maid, Kathleen, who forms a cultural alliance with Frau Quixano, and the German immigrant musical director, Herr Pappelmeister, round out the ethnic spectrum. Pappelmeister is employed by a native-born philanderer, Quincy Davenport, but quits his job in order to direct David's new world symphony, thus

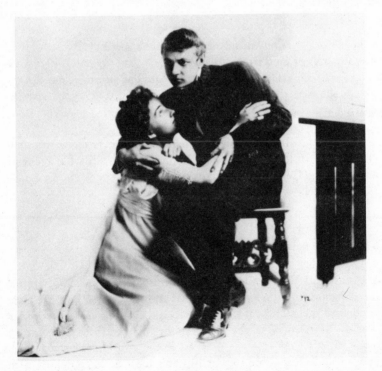

Illustration 2.   Israel Zangwill, *The Melting Pot*, Chrystal Herne and Walker Whiteside star in the 1908 production (Harvard Theatre Collection)

becoming David's artistic "Poppy." The plot consists to a great extent not of action but of the discussion of obstacles to David and Vera's union. Vera's father and stepmother show up from the old world at some point and try to stop the affair; Davenport makes advances to Vera; and Mendel warns his nephew David not to defy the call of the blood.

The magnitude of the gulf that separates David and Vera is made grimly apparent, however, when David learns at the end of act 3 that Vera's father was present at, and responsible for, the pogrom which resulted in the slaughter of David's parents and brother. Yet, with the help of his American symphony and the persistent vision of America as God's melting pot, he overcomes even this obstacle. At the end of the play, after the first performance of the symphony, David and Vera are united on the rooftop of the settlement house. The idealist composer realizes that he must live up to his own ideals and begs Vera: "[C]ling to me till all these ghosts {of Kishineff} are exorcised, cling to me till our love triumphs over death" (197). The lovers kiss, and the play ends with the reaffirmation of David's vision against a glorious sunset.

DAVID
{*Prophetically exalted by the spectacle.*}
It is the fires of God round His Crucible.
{*He drops her hand and points downward.*}
There she lies, the great Melting-Pot—listen! Can't you hear the roaring and the bubbling? There gapes her mouth
{*He points east.*}
—the harbor where a thousand mammoth feeders come from the ends of the world to pour in their human freight. Ah, what a stirring and seething! Celt and Latin, Slav and Teuton, Greek and Syrian,—black and yellow—

VERA
{*Softly, nestling to him.*}
Jew and Gentile—

DAVID
Yes, East and West, and North and South, the palm and the pine, the pole and the equator, the crescent and the cross— how the great Alchemist melts and fuses them with his purging flame! Here shall they all unite to build the Republic of Man and the Kingdom of God. Ah, Vera, what is the glory of Rome and Jerusalem where all nations and races come to worship and look back, compared with the glory of America, where all races and nations come to labour and look forward!

[*He raises his hand in benediction over the shining city.*]
Peace, peace, to all ye unborn millions, fated to fill this giant continent—the God of our *children* give you Peace.
[*An instant's solemn pause. The sunset is swiftly fading, and the vast
panorama is suffused with a more restful twilight, to which the many-
gleaming lights of the town add the tender poetry of the night. Far
back, like a lonely, guiding star, twinkles over the darkening water the
torch of the Statue of Liberty. From below comes up the softened sound
of voices and instruments joining in "My Country, 'tis of Thee." The
curtain falls slowly.*] (198–200)

This carefully constructed (or contrived) national, musical family
drama relied on the heavy assault of cumulative effects. Zangwill
enriched the play with "melting" imagery taken from different
realms. The general background was provided by the metallurgical
and alchemical implications of the crucible. Yet love also melts (101);
souls are melted with carefully orchestrated music (175), ranging
from *Faust* and an "American symphony" to "My Country 'tis of
Thee"; and the seasons change from the wintery February of act 1 to
March (act 2), April (act 3), and the Fourth of July of act 4. Against
this general movement of melting in love, nature, and art, Zangwill
defined a counterimage of "hardness," which is thereby associated
with an icy lack of love and with unoriginal artlessness. On the level
of the characters, hardness is related to the past and the boundaries
of *descent*: under the dispensation of "hardness" people are defined
by the call of the blood (100), as the butcher's daughter (170), or by
looking backward like Lot's wife (176) [Genesis 19:26]. In Equiano's
application of Acts 17, "melt" and "pride" were used as opposites; and
in one of the first American plays, Royall Tyler's *The Contrast* (1787),
acting old-world, looking backward, is similarly perceived as unloving, haughty, hypocritical, and un-American.

"Butcher" Revendal, characteristically described by David as a
"man of stone" (160), looks back to nobility, the Greek church, the
czar, in short, to the hierarchical world of Mother Russia. The unregenerate baroness, Vera's stepmother, is only slightly more flexibly
steeped in an old-world consciousness: she thinks of possessions and
affairs, but she has no understanding of love, loyalty, or spirituality.
Nobody of the new world can be quite as hard as these old-world
types. America softens the ethnic hardness of all characters. On the
side of the "melters," the New World transforms the pogrom orphan
David into an idealistic composer, and the Russian revolutionary
Vera into an American social worker (126); on the other side, the
American equivalent to a Russian butcher is merely a hypocrite—

Quincy Davenport, Jr., whose "squeamishness" on the issue of race is puzzling to the ravingly anti-Semitic Russian baron (117). It is tempting to think of one of those "from ... to" autobiographies, heretically entitled *From Butcher to Hypocrite*. Davenport, an "unemployed millionnaire" who doesn't "take much stock in ... massacres" (117), spends much of his time in Europe. The only white Anglo-Saxon Protestant in Zangwill's play, he has betrayed the vision of his (Pilgrim) fathers as he unpardonably keeps aping the old world. Quincy Davenport is very precisely, almost mathematically, juxtaposed with David Quixano. Their very initials suggest Zangwill's conscious strategy of a "Dav. Qui./Qui. Dav." inversion. (Zangwill worked out his telling names carefully. "Quincy" and "Davenport" evoke the New England ministerial tradition and its debates on universal regeneration; "Quixano" is the name Don Quixote adopts after the conversion at the end of Cervantes's novel.) David will become a pioneering ancestor who fulfills the great promise of Davenport's American heritage, of which Quincy, the heir to an American corn and oil fortune, is merely a weak and ineffectual descendant. Davenport cringes when the Jewish immigrant boy tells him that the American symphony was not written for Davenport and his backward-looking, Europe-fixated Venice imitators, whom David calls "gondola-guzzlers" (90):

> DAVID
>
> Not for you and such as you have I sat here writing and dreaming; not for you who are killing my America!
>
> QUINCY
>
> *Your* America, forsooth, you Jew-immigrant!
>
> DAVID
>
> Yes—Jew-immigrant! But a Jew who knows that your Pilgrim Fathers came straight out of his Old Testament, and that our Jew-immigrants are a greater factor in the glory of this commonwealth than some of you sons of the soil. It is you, freak-fashionables, who are undoing the work of Washington and Lincoln, vulgarising your high heritage, and turning the last and noblest hope of humanity into a caricature.
>
> QUINCY
> {*Rocking with laughter*}
> Ha! Ha! Ha! Ho! Ho! Ho!
>
> {*To* VERA}
> You never told me your Jew-scribbler was a socialist! (91)

According to Zangwill, who is here in good company with much American ethnic sentiment, American ideals are not transmitted by descent but have to be embraced afresh, even if that requires opposing the actual descendants of American founding fathers.

The *Melting-Pot* is thus a drama of an opposition, but also a drama of a development. The past may be anchored in old-world hardness, but the future in America is identified with the melting pot. Three generations of Quixanos are making the transition from past to future. The orthodox and Yiddish-speaking Frau Quixano strikes up an entente with the Irish maid, Kathleen. Mendel, the secularized "second generation" in the Quixano family, reflects, as his name suggests, the mixture of Jewishness and American surrounding. The Quixano house is one of our classic, divided "ethnic rooms," as the stage directions specify:

> Over the street-door is pinned the Stars and Stripes. On the left wall, in the upper corner of which is a music-stand, are bookshelves of large mouldering Hebrew books, and over them is hung a Mizrach, or Hebrew picture, to show it is the East Wall. Other pictures round the room include Wagner, Columbus, Lincoln, and "Jews at the Wailing Place." ... The whole effect is a curious blend of shabbiness, Americanism, Jewishness, and music. ...(1–2)

In his afterword of January 1914 to *The Melting-Pot*, Zangwill emphasized that assimilation is a pervasive and irresistible phenomenon:

> however scrupulously and justifiably America avoids physical intermarriage with the negro, the comic spirit cannot fail to note spiritual miscegenation which, while clothing, commercialising, and Christianising the ex-African, has given "rag-time" and the sex-dances that go with it, first to white America and thence to the whole white world. (207)

Carl Gustav Jung was to make similar observations in his essay "Your Negroid and Indian Behavior" (1930). Zangwill expressed a modern view of ethnic assimilation when he explained that the action of the crucible was not "exclusively physical": "The Jew may be Americanised and the American Judaised without any gamic interaction" (207). This is what happens to Mendel and Frau Quixano and, conversely, to Kathleen and to Herr Pappelmeister. Yet Zangwill's play was very much interested in "gamic interaction" of the exceptional, "heroic souls" who (like Zangwill himself) "dare the adventure of intermarriage" (207). Thus David Quixano's transition to the future comes by a loving union with his absolute "other" (at least by descent definition).

Intermarriage and Immigrant Fidelity

Intermarriage is not an absolute and easily measurable phenomenon, but one dependent upon cultural perception. From a Martian point of view, earthlings are boringly endogamous, because they more or less invariably mate with other earthlings. From the vantage point of 73.9 percent of the first-generation Irish immigrants to Wisconsin who had "out-married" in 1910 or the 46.9 percent of the Filipino men who had taken wives "outside their own group" in 1960, however, intermarriage was a significant American phenomenon (Bernard, *Melting Pot* 66; *HEAEG* 519). A marital union or a love relationship across boundaries that are considered significant, and often in defiance of parental desires and old descent antagonisms, is what constitutes melting-pot love.

The love between David Quixano and Vera Revendal is a case in point. True, they are both white immigrants from the same hometown. Yet, as pogrom orphan and butcher's daughter, they are also poles apart from each other by descent. From David's point of view, his love truly has to overcome the severe wounds of the past and is thus loving proof that any parental past, any descent legacy, can be redeemed by consenting youths. He has fallen in love, not merely with a girl from another ethnic group, but with the daughter of the very man who is responsible for the death of David's parents. In Vera, David loves his true shadow, his absolute other; Vera Revendal (French "rêve") is David's American melting-pot dream precisely because her father is David's old-world nightmare. The first three letters of Vera invert the beginning of her last name, symbolizing her internal conflict between individual identity and parental legacy. David and Vera are constructed as polar opposites who are "made for each other," though this may have seemed contrived to some critics and hair-raising to Vera's father and David's uncle. The Quixano-Revendal alliance is a union of opposites which redeems a specific family history, fuses the old ethnic antagonists "Jew" and "Gentile," and bridges dichotomies of religion and class. True love means, for both, cherishing the absolute antithesis of their own parents. That makes them a chosen couple.

More than just a "pogrom orphan meets butcher's daughter" story, *The Melting-Pot* sacralizes loving consent as the abolition of prejudices of descent. Not merely their specific relationship but also the abstract principle of absolute fidelity to the beloved is idealized to the same degree that loyalties to parents, kin, class, and religion are weakened. This new love is David's "God of our children," who is to replace the biblical God of our fathers {Ezra 7:27}. Loyal love serves as a marker that separates the chosen melters from hard-hearted hypocrites. The immigrant prophet David embraces his new descendant-oriented love religion even though his memories cause him great pain, whereas the *Mayflower* descendant Davenport is ready to sail into adultery, perhaps even bigamy. Quincy is a married man yet makes advances to Vera. The audience is informed that he is not *serious* about her and could never be "true" to "Vera." (This is another parallel with Van Dimple's duplicity in his Chesterfieldian advances toward Maria in *The Contrast*.) Unable to reach his goal—a shallow amorous affair with the profound Vera—Quincy sinks so low as to ask Vera's father and stepmother for assistance in obtaining the "daughter's consent" (114). Yet the baroness's attempt to put in a word for the man "who combines ze manners of Europe viz ze millions of America" (129) is fruitless, as is Baron Revendal's appeal to Vera's loyalty to family, class, and religion:

> BARON
> And you, a Revendal, would mate with an unbaptized dog?
>
> VERA
> Dog! You call my husband a dog!
>
> BARON
> Husband! God in heaven—are you married already?
>
> VERA
> No! But not being unemployed millionnaires like Mr. Davenport, we hold even our troth eternal. (130–31)

Davenport is depraved enough to mock the institution of marriage; but Vera and David, though only engaged, already have a *total* consent relationship. Together, they form a sacred body knit together by "ligaments of love," in marked antithesis to the secular, unloving hypocrite Davenport. More than that, Zangwill clearly suggests a cultural boundary between wealthy old-stock Americans who are unfaithful and poor new-wave immigrants who have a full understanding of the eternal allegiance of love. The last lines by Vera were among the few passages in the play that Zangwill had revised several times. Originally, he had Vera answer: "In the sight of God we are; not being true-born Americans, we hold even our troth eternal." According to the *Baltimore American* of October 13, 1908, Theodore Roosevelt, who was otherwise genuinely enthusiastic about Zangwill's play, and to whom the final version of *The Melting-Pot* was dedicated, successfully implored the author to change this line. The identification of "true-born Americans" with adultery and the idealization of immigrants as *semper fideles* was apparently offensive to Roosevelt. Zangwill gladly obliged by changing the line, first to "not being members of the 400" (richest families), and finally to the version which was quoted first (promptbook ca. 1909, New York Public Library Theatre Collection).

In the world of Zangwill's *Melting-Pot*, descent is secular and temporal, consent is sacred and eternal. It follows logically that the high priests of the cult of consent must be immigrants whose line of descent has been disrupted—like that of the first New England settlers, whose tradition of disruption and love is revitalized by the newcomers. As we shall see in the tales of consent and descent, citizenship by volitional allegiance was modeled upon the consent principle. Immigrants could thus be portrayed as cultural newlyweds, more enthusiastically and loyally in love with the country of their choice than citizens-by-descent. Instead of being a threat to America, as nativists sometimes perceived and portrayed them, Zangwill's immigrants were truly redemptive.

The cultural construction of consent privilege and the deification of the psychological switch from past to future are accompanied in Zangwill's play by the self-conscious creation of the all-immigrant musical symphony and by the new theology of the God of our children who replaces the God of our fathers. Zangwill's phrase "God of our children" was adopted into the humanistic theology of Joseph Blau (Wohlgelernter, *History* 47); however, in Rølvaag's 1931 novel with the programmatically meaningful title *Their Fathers' God* (210), a Reverend Kaldahl is portrayed as an avid critic of the melting pot that prepares a "perfect democracy of barrenness." In Zangwill's play even dates and settings compound the melting and blending symbolism: the Fourth of July is a Sabbath and Plymouth Rock is equated with Ellis Island, a parallel which Mary Antin (*They Who* 54–98), Louis Adamic (*From Many* 291–301), and Salom Rizk (*Syrian Yankee* 317) were to develop further.

The concept of the melting pot that emerged from Zangwill was a centrist one. It provided an imaginative, though immensely pliable, middle ground between ethnic believers in the immutability of descent, radical culture critics, and American opponents of immigration, all of whom it drew into the newly popularized melting imagery, even if they seemed to resent it. Zangwill's rhetoric gave shape to a debate which pulled even the opponents of intermarriage, immigration, and assimilation into the gravitational center of the melting pot. What emerged in these debates were flexible definitions and redefinitions of melting-pot America and attacks from the outside which challenged the term while frequently reaffirming the imagery. Yet, though Zangwill's play popularized the term and made it the key word for discussions of American immigration and minorities, he did not invent the word. A survey of the ancestry of the melting pot is thus in order.

Crèvecoeur, Pocahontas, and Fountain of Youth

To my knowledge, no discussion of the melting pot mentions an occurrence of the term in its ethnic sense prior to the publication of *Letters from an American Farmer* in 1782. Written in English by Michel-Guillaume-Jean de Crèvecoeur—who adopted the name J. Hector St. John upon coming to America in 1759—this early instance of the notion of the melting pot is somewhat incomplete. Crèvecoeur speaks of the process of melting, tells a family story, and is intensely interested in the future of America, but he does not use the word "pot." This may tell us something about the cultural *question* that the notion of the "pot" was intended to answer. Instead of seeing Crèvecoeur merely as the illegitimate father of the complete melting pot of Zangwill, we might ask what the question was he intended to answer, and what the imagery meant that could elsewhere become incorporated into the word "pot," which Crèvecoeur shunned.

Crèvecoeur asked the famous question "What then is the American, this new man?" It is the question concerning the genesis of a new man, or the rebirth, the palingenesis of the old-world migrant that takes place in America. As Russel Nye observed, Crèvecoeur uses the word "new" seventeen times in letter 3, "often in company with such words as *metamorphosis, regeneration,* and *resurrection*" (Nye, *American* 157). The birth of "this new man" is described in the following terms: the cords of an old language and of the "love of a few kindred poor" are cut when the migrant decides to go where he gets "land, bread, protection, and consequence."

> *Ubi panis ibi patria,* is the motto of all emigrants. What then is the American, this new man? He is either an European, or the descendant of an European, hence that strange mixture of blood, which you will find in no other country. I could point out to you a family whose grandfather was an Englishman, whose wife was Dutch, whose son married a French woman, and whose present four sons have now four wives of different nations. *He* is an American, who, leaving behind him all his ancient prejudices and manners, receives new ones from the new mode of life he has embraced, the new government he obeys, and the new rank he holds. He becomes an American by being received in the broad lap of our great *Alma Mater.* Here individuals of all nations are melted into a new race of men, whose

labours and posterity will one day cause great changes in the world. Americans are the western pilgrims, who are carrying along with them that great mass of arts, sciences, vigour, and industry which began long since in the east; they will finish the great circle. (Crèvecoeur 39)

The gender symbolism is striking in this famous passage. The migrant, imagined as *man*, becomes American by "being received" in the "broad lap of our great *Alma Mater*." As Annette Kolodny argued in her study with the telling title *The Lay of the Land* (1975), Crèvecoeur explores "the central metaphor of American pastoral experience, the metaphor of the land as a woman" (54). Crèvecoeur poetically relates the process of becoming American with images of continental sexual procreation and birth. Yet the "broad lap of our great *Alma Mater*" is a very specific phrase for "the land as a woman." What does it mean?

The first volume of the enlarged French edition of 1787, *Lettres d'un cultivateur américain*, carries a frontispiece entitled *Ubi panis, et libertas, ibi Patria*, which illustrates the famous passage from the third letter. This image (illustration 3), designed by C. Bornée and engraved by P. Martini, is quite helpful to any interpreter of Crèvecoeur's text. In the right rear, a sailing ship is anchored in a bay; five men dressed in hats, coats, and pants—presumably immigrants—are arriving in a rowboat; five other immigrant men apparently have landed earlier and are dancing in a circle on the new land (in the very center of the picture). In the foreground are eleven putti-like children without clothes: seven are playing with the fruits of the earth (perhaps corn and potatoes); four are holding on to a plumed goddess who is seated under a tree in the lower left quarter of the engraving; two putti are sucking from the woman's bare breasts; and two are leaning against her shoulders. The woman wears a plumed headband or turban and a skirt made of feathers. Under her bare feet a shield, a bow, and some arrows are resting on the ground. In the background two houses indicate that the land is now inhabited by descendants from Europe.

Howard Rice has interpreted this image as a cumulative allegory of America, within which the putti stand for abundance (*Cultivateur* 96). What is difficult, however, is to account for the immigrants (who apparently *mean* only "immigrants") literally and for the putti figuratively. It may therefore be more plausible to view the frontispiece as a symbolic representation of the *process* of naturalization. Seen this way, the engraving symbolizes the rebirth of immigrants as American infants, sequentially shown in the stages of transatlantic journey, arri-

Illustration 3.

arrival, dance in a mysterious magical circle which leads to the unre-
presented transformation itself, the new birth through a nourishing
Indianized mother figure, and the prosperous settlement in smoke-
stacked houses.

When the Crèvecoeur passage is read against this image, the Indian
princess of the frontispiece illustrates the "broad lap of our great
Alma Mater." In the picture, as in the text, there is not a "pot" but
the lap of an American earth-mother goddess. The cultural affinities
of wombs and pots have been described in great detail by anthropologists and psychologists alike; and even a casual look at the illustrations in Erich Neumann's *Die Grosse Mutter* (1956) provides much
evidence for womb-pots (57 and plate 27a), as well as for transformations (69) and ritual dances (281 and plate 143). An Indian Ceres,
the American mother earth itself was the "pot" in which immigrants
could "melt" in order to be reborn. This places Crèvecoeur and his

engraver in a tradition which ranges from Medea's magic caldron of rejuvenation to the figure of the Statue of Liberty.[7]

Alma Mater may thus be seen as a nonbiblical type to which melting pot was the antitype. Although "alma" was a common epithet of several goddesses, the term "alma mater" occurred very rarely in classical Latin. Neither the *Oxford Latin Dictionary* (1968) nor Lewis and Short's *Latin Dictionary* offers any instances of the term except in Lucretius' *De rerum natura* (55 B.C.). In book 2, Lucretius writes that

> we are all sprung from heavenly seed. All alike have the same father, from whom *all-nourishing mother earth* {my emphasis for this translation of "alma mater"} receives the showering drops of moisture. Thus fertilized, she gives birth to smiling crops and lusty trees, to mankind and all the breeds of beasts. She it is that yields the food on which they all feed their bodies, lead their joyous lives and renew their race. So she has well earned the name of mother. (trans. R. E. Latham, 89)

Lucretius, the Epicurean rationalist, is convinced that "the earth is and always has been an insentient being" and sees the invention of a goddess "Ceres" or "mother earth" ultimately as nothing but a figure of speech, a way of talking about "crops" or "earth."

> If anyone elects to call the sea Neptune and the crops Ceres and would rather take Bacchus' name in vain than denote grape juice by its proper title, we may allow him to refer to the earth as the Mother of Gods, providing that he genuinely refrains from polluting his mind with the foul taint of superstition. (79)

Lucretius' critical relationship to myths was hardly typical of men's attitudes toward mother goddesses. Throughout the centuries they have been appearing in many shapes, one of which was the multi-breasted Artemis of Ephesus—an iconographic precursor of the Roman wolf, who in turn influenced the Crèvecoeur frontispiece. As the goddess of earth and fertility Cybele was the center of many cults in Greece and Rome.

Since Lucretius' time, the term *Alma Mater* was Christianized into an epithet for Mary; thus Herimann von Reichenau or Herrmannus Contractus (1013–54) wrote and composed the well-known antiphon "Alma Redemptoris Mater," which was addressed to Mary (Hansjakob, *Herimann* 79–80). The Humanists applied *alma mater* to universities; and in that sense the term is still in use today. Crèvecoeur participated in the imaginative adaptations of this pliable term when he used it to describe the American land, and his illustrator fleshed out the phrase when he Indianized *Alma Mater* as an American Ceres, in the tradition of allegorizations of the continents. Thus, the image of the Indian princess or queen goes back to allegorical representations of America in sixteenth-century maps. Martin Waldseemüller's world map of 1507 also contained the proposal to name the continent "America" in honor of Amerigo Vespucci.

Allegories of America as an Indian princess have often been combined with Captain John Smith's Pocahontas story. Drawing on the pioneering work by Jay B. Hubbell, Philip Young has described this recurrent figure in the American imagination as "The Mother of Us All: Pocahontas Reconsidered" (1962) without, however, making mention of Crèvecoeur. Young's account of the American Ceres "developed from Pocahontas" is applicable to Crèvecoeur and his illustrator: "We, by descent from her, become a new race, innocent of both European and all human origins—a race from the earth, ... but an earth that is made of her" (408). Young thus sees the melting-pot and rebirth dimensions in the image but also emphasizes that Pocahontas's love makes us feel that "we are chosen, or preferred" and delineates the icon's "imperialistic functions." Pocahontas's consent gives the chosen people of white Americans a new fictional line of noble Indian ancestry.

Modern American writers, including Carl Sandburg, Ernest Hemingway, and William Carlos Williams, have returned with interest to the Pocahontas theme that many earlier poets and playwrights first explored. The theme is often closely allied with melting-pot language, as it weakens static descent-orientation. Vachel Lindsay's little-known poem "Our Mother Pocahontas" gave the fullest expression to Pocahontas as a "transnational" ancestor who can be adopted by consent and who subverts identification by "blood" descent:

> We here renounce our Saxon blood ...
> We here renounce our Teuton pride;
> Our Norse and Slavic boasts have died:
> Italian dreams are swept away,
> And Celtic feuds are lost today. ... (*Poems* 117)

Explaining the flames of the birth of America, Lindsay exclaims:

> gray Europe's rags august
> She tramples in the dust;
> Because we are her fields of corn;
> Because our fires are all reborn
> From her bosom's deathless embers,
> Flaming
> As she remembers

>The springtime
>And Virginia,
>Our Mother, Pocahontas. (116-17)

Trite and corny though these lines may be, they address the same cultural question as the Crèvecoeur frontispiece; in the focus on spring as a season for rebirth, Lindsay has additional affinities with Zangwill's calendar. Another widespread rhetorical feature is Lindsay's assumption that reborn Americans can *choose* their ancestors:

>John Rolfe is not our ancestor
>We rise from out the soul of her
>Held in native wonderland,
>While the sun's rays kissed her hand,
>In the springtime,
>In Virginia,
>Our mother, Pocahontas. (116)

Crèvecoeur's "broad lap of our great *Alma Mater*" and his illustrator's view of the passage were appropriate adaptations of a classical figure to the immigrants' rebirth on the Indianized and female allegory of America. This "rebirth in Pocahontas" furthermore combines elements of the fountain-of-youth motif with the melting pot. Both fountain of youth and melting pot suggest the classical hope for a return to a golden age; alchemists used melting pots and searched for eternal youth; and the visualization of the *process* of transformation also is parallel for American rebirth and European rejuvenation fantasies. In Lucas Cranach's famous painting *Jungbrunnen* (1546) and in Crèvecoeur's text, the transformation is not only a renovation but also a movement from rags to riches. The American rejuvenation in the frontispiece, however, goes even further than many European fountain-of-youth dreams: whereas the ideal age for Cranach's women is the prime age of procreation, Crèvecoeur's illustrator returned the immigrants to the much earlier stage of infancy; instead of being reborn into courtship and amusements with the well-to-do, the American sucklings feed and lean on their Indian Ceres. Sexual polarization, so prominent in Cranach's painting, is absent from the portraiture of the newborn immigrants. What takes place instead is the sexual polarization between men and land, which we also noticed in Crèvecoeur's text. Unlike Cranach's "new women"—who are very much like any other young and rich women who can enjoy life—the melting pot's new men seem to be singled out for a mission more important than enjoyment and procreation: as part of their rebirth they assume a particular, messianic role; in Crèvecoeur's words, "they will finish the great circle."

The Biblical "New Man": The Melting Pot as an Antitype

With a telling allusion to the New Testament, Crèvecoeur described the American as the "new man." It is ironical that precisely in his rhetoric of newness, Crèvecoeur suggests an older, biblical dimension to his myth of America. True to his adopted name St. John, which makes Crèvecoeur a latter-day Johannes in Eremo, he sees Christ as the type of all new men of the future, but especially of reborn Americans. It is no coincidence that the image of Christ occurs in connection with the melting-pot idea. One could thus argue that the melting pot is an antitype for Christ. Not only did Christ represent the new order based on love, or consent, rather than on circumcision as the token of descent, but he also incorporated and merged opposites. Uniting the human with the divine nature in himself, Christ also dissolved the boundaries between man and man. In his commentary upon the New Testament, F. C. Cook (1881) described Christ's work as a peacemaker in the following words:

> The Jewish and the Gentile elements of the human race are fused into one new substance or being, transformed in character ... as well as beginning afresh. ... First [Christ] unites Jew and Gentile, and then he reconciles both, that is, all mankind, to God. (3:553)

As Timothy Smith wrote in his essay on "Religion and Ethnicity," "Jesus's 'good news' was to fulfill God's promise that in Abraham's seed the gentiles would also share the blessings of the covenant" (1183-84). This new universalism would be especially attractive to people who had experienced migrations and culture clashes:

> In a new nation faced from its beginnings with the problems of unity and diversity, the revitalization of religious convictions accentuated the claim of both Judaism and Christianity to universality and renewed the impulse, largely suppressed among Jews since the first century of the Christian era, to recruit all human beings into a common circle of faith and fellowship. (1183)

Christ as the *type* of ethnic fusion and universalism emerges most clearly in diverse passages from Paul's letters. For example:

> For he is our peace, who hath made both one, and hath broken down the middle wall of partition between us; Having abolished in

his flesh the enmity, even the law of commandments contained in ordinances; for to make in himself of twain one new man, so making peace. {Ephesians 2:14-15}

It was this passage that Cook commented on. "Gentiles in the flesh" (and we ought to remember here that "gentile" is the Greek "*ethni-kos*") were "aliens from the commonwealth of Israel, and strangers from the covenants of promise" {Ephesians 2:11-12}. In Christ they are "no more strangers and foreigners, but fellow-citizens with the saints, and of the household of God" {Ephesians 2:19}. The melting-pot parallels are obvious.

Paul also admonished the Colossians to "put off the old man" and to

put on the new man, which is renewed in knowledge after the image of him that created him: Where there is neither Greek nor Jew, circumcision nor uncircumcision, Barbarian, Scythian, bond nor free: but Christ is all, and in all. {Colossians 3:9-11}

Paul's rhetoric, which we encounter again in Zangwill and which can be found in numerous American texts, is that of transcending boundaries in becoming new men as *imitatio Christi*. The visual symbol of the boundary is the "middle wall of partition" from Ephesians 2. According to the detailed explanation of *The Interpreter's Bible* (1953), this is

a reference to the wall which divided the inner court of the temple, open only to Jews, from the outer court to which Gentile visitors were admitted: "the sanctuary" included the inner court, which was therefore open only to those who were sanctified by membership in the holy community. Josephus tells us (*Jewish War* V.5.2) that there were bilingual inscriptions (Greek and Latin) at regular intervals along this wall, warning Gentiles on pain of death not to enter the inner court. One of these inscriptions (in Greek only) was discovered during the excavation on the site of the temple in 1871, and is now in Constantinople. It reads: "No man of another race is to proceed within the partition and enclosing wall about the sanctuary; and anyone arrested there will have himself to blame for the penalty of death which will be imposed as a consequence." The destruction of the temple in A.D. 70 carried with it the destruction of this wall: spiritually, it had already been removed as a barrier to Jewish and Gentile fellowship in religious life by the death of Christ. (10:655)

Seen in this light, Paul's literal "wall of partition" may well be the biblical type of many antitypes in the literature of ethnicity, and an excellent illustration of a boundary in the sense of Fredrik Barth. It is a curious coincidence that the first occurrence of the English word "ethnic" given by the *Oxford English Dictionary* is in a Middle English hagiographical description—of the destruction of the temple: "A part of It fel done & made gret distruccione Of ethnykis" (1375).

Paul's epistle to the Galatians contained the most dramatic formulation of the new creation:

> For ye are all the children of God by faith in Christ Jesus. For as many of you as have been baptized into Christ have put on Christ. There is neither Jew nor Greek, there is neither bond nor free, there is neither male nor female: for ye are all one in Christ Jesus. [Galatians 3:26-28]

The modern annotations to Paul's epistles often sound familiar to any student of the melting pot, as they interpret the prophesied end of discrimination based on race, religion, national origin, or social or sexual difference and envision, with *The Interpreter's Bible*, the "ultimate unity and equality in diversity" (10:519; see also 11:217).

If Paul's Christian must put off the old man and put on the new man, Crèvecoeur's American is he who, "leaving behind him all his ancient prejudices and manners, receives new ones from the new mode of life he has embraced ..." (39). In Crèvecoeur's rhetoric, America's mission is to continue the trans-ethnic demands of Paul's Christianity; and it is in this context that Crèvecoeur uses the image of melting. The rhetorical connections between the trans-ethnic universalism of early Christianity and the American melting pot must have been readily available. New York's Governor DeWitt Clinton, for example, made the same association when he said in 1814 that the

> triumph and general adoption of the english language have been the principal means of melting us down into one people, and of extinguishing those stubborn prejudices and violent animosities which formed a wall of partition between the inhabitants of the same land. (*Discourse* 8)

America was implicitly equated with Christ and was to tear down the ethnic partition walls of mankind: a good reason to think "melting pot."

Israel Zangwill's melting-pot language was heavily and explicitly indebted to the New Testament. In 1916 Zangwill wrote self-critically: "It was vain for Paul to declare that there should be neither Jew nor Greek. Nature will return even if driven out with a pitchfork, still more of driven out with a dogma" (Leftwich 255; see Horace, *Epistles* 1.10.24). But as late as in 1915, Zangwill did believe in Paul's universalism when he wrote in the afterword to *The Melting-Pot*: "There will be neither Jew nor Greek" (209). It was that Pauline maxim which made Zangwill's vision of melting-pot America as the new redeemer and mediator possible. No wonder that in David Quixano's words the voice of America merges with that of Christ {Matthew 11:28}:

> ... when I look at our Statue of Liberty, I just seem to hear the voice of America crying: "Come unto me all ye that labour and are heavy laden and I will give you rest—rest—" (35)

The reference to the Statue of Liberty here recalls the *Alma Mater* tradition, and the conjunction with Matthew 11 throws light on Emma Lazarus's poem "The New Colossus" (Chapman, *Jewish-American* 308.) It is only a small step from religion to ethnicity.

Attempting to describe the state or spiritual ardor achieved after the religious conversion, William James wrote in 1902:

> The stone wall inside of him has fallen, the hardness in his heart has broken down. The rest of us can, I think, imagine this by recalling our state of feeling in those temporary "melting moods" into which either the trials of real life, or the theatre, or a novel sometimes throw us. Especially if we weep! (*Varieties* 267)

The image of the wall is familiar to us from Ephesians 2:14; James uses the word "melting"; and he resorts to an aesthetic analogy—all in the service of accounting for a religious experience! The affinities between religious and ethnic rhetoric can be stunning.

Crèvecoeur and Zangwill are normally looked at in splendid ethnic isolation, so that important religious and cultural contexts for the new man and the melting pot have remained obscure. Yet the melting pot represents an ethnic extension of the religious drama of redemption and rebirth which has also been portrayed in the imagery of melting, and especially in contrast to the stubborn hardness of boundaries. The parallels between American sermons and the rhetoric of ethnicity are compelling.

In 1654, for example, John Cotton made a distinction between "Hypocrites and Saints" in terms which made his sermon a true precursor of the ethnic melting pots of America:

> the Spirit of God ... melteth both, yet hypocrites are melted as iron, which will returne againe to his former hardnes, but his owne people are melted into flesh, which will never returne to his hardnes more, neither can they rest in any measure of softnes unto which they have

attained, but still are carryed toward Jesus Christ: so that one is a temporary faith, and the other persevereth. ... (Miller, *Puritans* 316)

Hardness [see also Ezekiel 36:26 and Mark 3:5] is associated with short-lived hypocrisy; genuine readiness to melt indicates persevering love, the right path to sainthood. And, as in many later ethnic melting pots, the opposition is also one between continuous process—so cherished by Americans—and hardened result.

Samuel Davies (1723–61) preached that baptism is an important ordinance but not "that kind of regeneration which you must be subjects of, if you would enter into the kingdom of God" (*Sermons* 2:496). Though hard to define precisely, rebirth is of central importance: "All external forms of religion, whether Jewish or Christian, are of no avail, without this new creation" (497). He encourages his listeners here and in another sermon to give an honest answer to the question "Have I ever been born again?" (498, 374). Throughout his discussion of regeneration, Davies draws on the same passages from Scriptures that informed Crèvecoeur's "new man."

In 1859 Horace Bushnell consciously made the analogy between Americanization and Christian rebirth when he tried to explain the concept of regeneration to his parishioners:

> Our term *naturalization* signifies essentially the same thing; viz., that the subject is made to be a natural born American, or, in the eye of the law, a native citizen. (*Sermons* 106)

Bushnell adds that their case "is no real exception," but he has established a less than universal regeneration, a "regeneration minus one," so to speak. There is an undeniable theoretical distinction between "citizens" and "aliens" in the kingdom of God, and only "aliens" need regeneration, which Bushnell defines as "the naturalization of a soul in the kingdom of heaven" (106).

In his sermon "The Regeneration" (1873), Ephraim Chamberlain Cummings focused on the misconception of believing in a right of descent when it comes to regeneration. Alluding to John 3:3–4, Cummings exhorts his audience to remember

> that Nicodemus, as a Jew, supposed that the kingdom of God belonged to his people by right of natural descent. They, the children of Abraham, were to see it as a matter of course. It was the very consummation of their national destiny, in whatever way it might be related to the Gentiles. (*Birth* 67)

This narrow and descent-oriented view is wrong, Cummings goes on to say.

If Jesus had said, that the Gentiles must all be born again—meaning that they must be circumcised and keep the law, in a word, be naturalized as Jews—the figure would have been familiar and intelligible ... however, Jesus made no distinction between the Jew and the Gentile. ... In the person of Christ, through the gospel, the kingdom of God knocks at the door of every heart. To Jews and Gentiles, to Greeks and barbarians, to free and bond, to rich and poor, to wise and unwise, this impartial kingdom comes. (67–69)

Not "naturalization as Jews" but rebirth as new men is what Christ demanded, in Cummings's view. There can be no exception: everybody must be reborn, "citizens" and "aliens" alike.

Two positions are sharply at odds with each other and were the source of repeated religious conflicts in America, especially as far as the church membership of children and newcomers was concerned. From the first point of view, a position which Sacvan Bercovitch has termed "genetics of salvation," the still-unregenerate children of church members received grace "through the loyns of godly Parents" (Increase Mather; Bercovitch, *Origins* 94 and *Jeremiad* 62–92). This was, so to speak, redemption by descent, and it formed the theoretical underpinning of the famous Half-Way Covenant of 1662.

From the opposite, evangelical point of view, which we shall call "universal regeneration," nobody was exempt from the requirement of a regeneration experience; those who thought that descent or baptism freed them from the need for a spiritual rebirth were Christians in name only, or hypocrites. The genetics-of-salvation party emphasized descent and the letter of the covenant; the universal-regeneration party stressed consent and the spirit.

If American ministers could resort to the process of naturalization in order to illustrate the theological concept of regeneration, we may reciprocate by looking at the Americanization and melting-pot debates in the redemptive context of the difference between "genetics of salvation" and "universal regeneration." The melting pot may thus be understood as the ethnic variation on a religious theme, its ambiguities more clearly comprehended as part of the conflict between descent and consent. The parallels are so forceful that it is surprising how few attempts have been made to establish that connection in immigration scholarship, though as early as 1928 Robert Park was reminded of William James's *Varieties of Religious Experience* when he read immigrant autobiographies (Park 355) and though Winthrop Hudson included excerpts from Zangwill's play in a section of his *Nationalism and Religion in America* (125–28).

Universal Regeneration

Some newcomers, immigrants, scholars, and radicals have interpreted Americanization in the tradition of universal regeneration. They gave Ephraim Cummings's language a new ethnic content and tended to look at America as an ought, an ideal, reminiscent of the spirit. Emory Bogardus, for example, in his interesting study *Essentials of Americanization* (1922), argues very much in the vein of regeneration sermons:

> The native-born and the foreign-born alike must experience the process of Americanization. In the case of natives, Americanization involves getting acquainted with the best American traditions and current standards, and practicing and trying to improve the quality of these traditions and standards. In the case of the foreign-born, Americanization means giving up one set of well-known and, in part, precious loyalties for another set of loyalties, more or less new and unknown. To renounce one group of loyalties for another group involves a deep-seated and delicate re-adjustment of mental and social attitudes. (16)

The echoes of universal regeneration are also audible in *The Americanization of Edward Bok* (1920), when the successful Dutch immigrant author observes:

> One fundamental trouble with the present desire for Americanization is that the American is anxious to Americanize two classes—if he is a reformer, the foreign-born; if he is an employer, his employees. It never occurs to him that he himself may be in need of Americanization. He seems to take it for granted that because he is American-born, he is an American in spirit and has a right understanding of American ideals. But that, by no means, always follows. There are thousands of American-born who need Americanization just as much as do the foreign-born. (445)

Unregenerate native-born Americans, we might paraphrase Bok, are in danger of becoming hypocrites, Americans in name only. A virtual textbook of universalist-rebirth statements is Robert Spiers Benjamin's collection *I Am an American: By Famous Naturalized Americans* (1941). The actress Luise Rainer said, for example:

> I'm afraid that some native Americans take their democratic citizenship too much for granted. They pay their taxes, obey the laws and vote conscientiously but save their patriotic thoughts for national holidays like Washington's Birthday and the Fourth of July! (9)

And Professor Anton Lang agreed:

Democracy is an experience—like religion—it has to be renewed by every generation—by every citizen. It is growing, not fixed. You can't look at it as something that was won once and for all, a hundred and fifty years ago, and that will always be there when it is needed. To every American it should always be as personal as it is to all new Americans. (18)

Lang is part of a rhetorical tradition that parallels the experience of democracy with that of love.

Perhaps the most famous supporter of the universal regeneration position was not an immigrant but John Dewey, who argued in the frequently cited address "Nationalizing Education," which he delivered in 1916, in the context of the loyalty debates triggered by the war in Europe:

No matter how loudly any one proclaims his Americanism if he assumes that any one racial strain, any one component culture, no matter how early settled it was in our territory, or how effective it has proven in its own land, is to furnish a pattern to which all other strains and cultures are to conform, he is a traitor to an American nationalism. (184–85)

The paradox in this statement is that its own intellectual origins are so clearly traceable to regeneration debates that preceded and, yes, set a pattern for discussions of ethnic pluralism within American boundaries.

Genetics of Salvation

On the other side of the fence are the descent-oriented believers in hereditary election. For them America tends to be a given, an is, reminiscent of the letter. When they approach the subject of Americanization they echo Bushnell's position. Often native-born Americans themselves, they view American identity as something they have safely and easily received by birth and descent, but something that foreign-born workers would have to strive long and hard to achieve. In a frequently quoted letter Barrett Wendell complained on March 31, 1917, that the Russian Jewish immigrant prodigy Mary Antin "has developed an irritating habit of describing herself and her people as Americans, in distinction from such folks as Edith {Wendell's wife} and me, who have been here for three hundred years" (Howe, *Wendell* 282). Wendell clearly thought that Americanness had a greater chance to come by descent; far from "lashing out against the immigrants" (as Gossett had it in *Race* 305), however, he continued:

> whether she has children I don't know. If she has, their children may perhaps come to be American in the sense in which I feel myself so— for better or worse, belonging only here. And that is the kind of miracle which America, for all its faults and its vulgarities, has wrought. (282; see also Solomon, *Ancestors* 172–73)

Wendell's "genetics of salvation" thus included the suggestion of a three-generation residence in this country: the third-generation new-comers are, then, native-born children of native-born parents and have acquired citizenship by birth. This motif will concern us again. We may remember here, however, that Wendell especially liked John Cotton's position against hereditary privileges and note that he discussed Crèvecoeur at some length in his *Literary History* (114).

The genetics-of-salvation perspective could adopt the melting-pot image and reinterpret it by excising the universalism it suggested (just as, conversely, Bogardus and other universal regenerationists sometimes expressed dislike for the *word* melting pot). As Bok had argued, such melting pot proponents usually took the regenerate state of American-born employers for granted and thus limited their efforts to the conversion experience of newcomers. The most famous solution to this problem was offered by the Ford Motor Company English School Melting Pot rituals of 1916, in which the baptismal blessings of the melting pot were conveyed to foreign-born employ-ees who underwent a ritualistic rebirth especially designed for them by their employers (illustration 4). Meant to demonstrate the Amer-ican loyalties of immigrant workers during World War I, the Ford English School graduation exercises put any revivalist meeting to shame. They were described and photographed by various observers; but nowhere have I been able to find a more detailed account of the spectacle than in the company-owned *Ford Times*. In April 1916 an anonymous article under the title "A Motto Wrought into Educa-tion" described the primal scene:

> The feature of the graduation exercises was a unique pageant, for which the big stage of the Light Guard Armory, at Detroit, in which the event was held, had been set. Across the back of the stage was shown the hull and deck of an ocean steamship docked at Ellis Island. In the center of the stage and taking up about half of the entire area was an immense caldron across which was painted the sign "Ford English School Melting Pot." From the deck of the steam-ship the gangway led down into the "Melting Pot." First came the

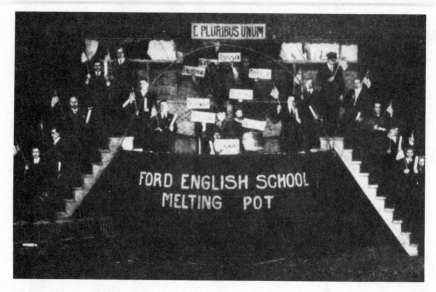

Illustration 4.   (From *Outlook* 44 (1916): 197)

preliminaries of docking the ship and then suddenly a picturesque figure appeared at the top of the gangway. Dressed in a foreign cos- tume and carrying his cherished possessions wrapped in a bundle suspended from a cane, he gazed about with a look of bewilderment and then slowly descended the ladder into the "Melting Pot," hold- ing aloft a sign indicating the country from which he had come.

Another figure followed, and then another — "Syria," "Greece," "Italy," "Austria," "India," read the cards, as the representatives of each of the different countries included in the class filed down the gangway into the "Melting Pot." From it they emerged dressed in American clothes, faces eager with the stimulus of the new oppor- tunities and responsibilities opening out before them. Every man carried a small American flag in his hand.

The graduation exercises were witnessed by an audience of more than 2,000 spectators including representatives of many prominent business concerns. (409)

At the end the graduates received large diplomas. Even more dra- matic than this description was the following account, which was given under the classic heading "The Making of New Americans" in the *Ford Times* of November 1916. The ritual obviously flourished and had been expanded and embellished; this time the celebration took place on the Ford athletic field:

The graduating class filed down from the ship into the melting pot and from this they emerged to take their appointed place in the audience. Any spectator of the stream of 230 graduates who poured from the melting pot at the Ford athletic field saw the pride which shone on the former aliens' faces as they waved little flags on their way down the steps from the huge cauldron, symbolic of the fusing process which makes raw immigrants into loyal Americans.

The "Melting Pot" exercises were dramatic in the extreme: A deckhand came down the gang plank of the ocean liner, represented in canvas facsimile.

"What cargo?" was the hail he received. "About 230 hunkies," he called back. "Send 'em along and we'll see what the melting pot will do for them," said the other and from the ship came a line of immigrants, in the poor garments of their native lands. Into the gaping pot they went. Then six instructors of the Ford school, with long ladles, started stirring. "Stir! Stir!" urged the superintendent of the school. The six bent to greater efforts. From the pot fluttered a flag, held high, then the first of the finished product of the pot appeared, waving his hat. The crowd cheered as he mounted the edge and came down the steps on the side. Many others followed him, gathering in two groups on each side of the cauldron. In contrast to the shabby rags they wore when they were unloaded from the ship, all wore neat suits. They were American in looks. And ask anyone of them what nationality he is, and the reply will come quickly, "American!" "Polish-American?" you might ask. "No, American," would be the answer. For they are taught in the Ford school that the hyphen is a minus sign.

Addresses by prominent speakers and selections by the Ford Motor Band completed a program of enthusiastic interest to the five thousand spectators. (151–52)

The association of the melting-pot image with these anti-universalist spectacles by the Ford Motor Company (which was furthermore compromised by Henry Ford's well-publicized anti-Semitism) is one of the reasons why the very word "melting pot" became offensive to immigrants and to universalist intellectuals (Gossett 371–72) and why the hyphen became a plus sign for ethnic revivalists. For clarity's sake, however, we should point out that this was only *one* interpretation of the melting pot and that the tradition of the "pure" melting pot, from Crèvecoeur to Zangwill, was much closer to universal regeneration than to genetics of salvation. In ethnic terms, genetics of salvation developed into what Milton Gordon discusses as "Anglo-conformity," while universal regeneration was the theological underpinning of the "true" melting pot (*Assimilation* 88–114).

When universalists attacked geneticists—people who make any exemptions from the universal demand for American regeneration on the grounds of descent—they drew on the tradition of Christian attacks on the letter in the name of the spirit and denounced geneticists as "hypocrites," much in the way John Cotton used that biblical term. Abraham Lincoln, for example, wrote to Joshua Speed:

> Our progress in degeneracy appears to me to be pretty rapid. As a nation, we began by declaring that *"all men are created equal."* We now practically read it "all men are created equal, except *negroes.*" When the Know-Nothings get control, it will read "all men are created equal, except negroes, *and foreigners and Catholics.*" When it comes to this I should prefer emigrating to some country where they make no pretense of loving liberty—to Russia, for instance, where despotism can be taken pure, and without the base alloy of hypocracy [*sic*]. (Gordon, *Assimilation* 93–94)

Better an honest reactionary than a hypocritical liberal has remained a valid maxim in American culture. The debate between universalists and geneticists shows that the biblical diatribes against Pharisees and hypocrites were mimicked eagerly by the scribes of America.

American Alchemy and the Melting Pot

A rhetorical element that the melting pot added to debates about consent and descent was the alchemical imagery, to which the "crucible" alluded. In Zangwill's play David marveled how God "the great Alchemist melts and fuses" the diverse human freight (199). A little earlier, David also observed poetically: "In the divine chemistry the very garbage turns to roses" (194). This is reminiscent of alchemical verse and of Emma Lazarus's "New Colossus" with its "wretched refuse." Since immigration historians rarely like to dirty their hands with alchemy, this aspect has not received much attention. Yet New Englanders like John Winthrop, Jr., and Ezra Stiles were actively interested in alchemical experiments. There was much in alchemical processes and imagery that was meaningful to a typological imagination; and there were alchemical illustrations which were iconographical precursors of melting-pot pictures.

Alchemical symbolism made an explicit analogy between Christ and the philosophers' stone, the *Lapis*. "For what reason do philosophers compare the *Lapis* with Christ?" Leonhard Müllner answered this question in his *Bericht von der Generation der Metallen* (1727):

> Therefore, whereas Christ was born of a pure virgin without any sin and without a single man's seed. Thus our *Lapis*, too, gets pregnant

out of pure matter and gives birth to itself without the addition of a single thing. (320–21)

Alchemical illustrations at times literally look like ethnic melting pots. The illuminated initials ascribed to Gerolamo da Cremona (illustration 5) in a manuscript of Raimundus Lullus's *Donum dei* in the National Library in Florence depict the alchemical stage of *nigredo* in the shape of two Mongolian-looking men (Tartarians or Tatars, meant to symbolize Tartarus, the residue of sublimation and distillation) in a boiling caldron. Raimundus Lullus stands by, one hand resting on the brim of the caldron, the other pointing at a dark cloud full of mythical animals that suggest the impurities which have left the matter. One central alchemical image, the Ouroboros, often

Illustration 5.

depicted as a snake biting its own tail, evoked the alchemical yearning for fullness by uniting opposites and, in Crèvecoeur's phrase, finishing the circle. Alchemical imagery has been studied, especially since Carl Gustav Jung's *Psychology and Alchemy* (1944), as an expression of cultural and psychological desires for wholeness achieved through a ritualized process. In some renditions of the Ouroboros, the snake's body is depicted as half-black and half-white; in the alchemical process the stage of *nigredo* is an important encounter of the other; and in the grand vision of the Christic hermaphrodite as the end of the process, even sexual polarization was overcome. It is this yearning for wholeness that has survived in the American melting-pot image of heightened unity out of fused ethnic opposites, an image which emphasizes contrasts and antitheses only to transcend them. Alchemically speaking, Vera was David's shadow, and the play shows the ritual process of unification. On the national level, if American alchemy was successful, America would be the philosophers' stone among nations. This is one reason why melting-pot rhetoric of fused opposites so easily attached itself to the notion of a country's messianic and imperial role and why ethnic fusions work so much better near the Statue of Liberty on the Fourth of July.

Melting Pots before and after Zangwill

Zangwill's image also had nonalchemical precursors in addition to Crèvecoeur. Edward Taylor's poems are rich in rebirth images (49) and include phrasings such as "golden Crucible of Grace" (312) and "Relicks in the Caldron" (219), perhaps influenced by Ezekiel 24:3–6. On November 8, 1702, long before any immigration historians would suspect Americans to be thinking about melting pots, Taylor came very close to using the term in meditation 49 of the second series. The poem, based on John 1:14, develops a parallel between metallurgy and divine grace and begins with the stanza:

> Gold in its Ore, must melted be, to bring
>   It midwift from its mother womb; requires
> To make it shine and a rich market thing,
>   A fining Pot, and Test, and melting fire.
>   So do I, Lord, before thy grace do shine
>   In mee, require, thy fire may mee refine. (169)

Interestingly, Taylor, who here used the words "pot" and "melting" in the same line of a poem, also frequently expressed the infusion of grace or "theanthropy," the union of God and man in Christ, in explicitly musical imagery—to which so many melting-pot writers of the ethnic era also resorted.

Ralph Waldo Emerson's notebook entry of 1845 on the "smelting pot," written in response to the descent-oriented Know-Nothings, reverberates with classical rhetoric and the hope for a national newness out of fusion.

> I hate the narrowness of the Native American party. ... Man is the most composite of all creatures, the wheel-insect, *volvox globator*, is at the beginning. Well, as in the old burning of the Temple at Corinth, by the melting & intermixture of silver & gold & other metals, a new compound more precious than any, called the Corinthian Brass, was formed so in this Continent,—asylum of all nations, the energy of Irish, Germans, Swedes, Poles & (the) Cossacks, & all the European tribes,—of the Africans, & of the Polynesians, will construct a new race, a new religion, a new State, a new literature, which will be as vigorous as the new Europe which came out of the smelting pot of the Dark Ages, or that which earlier emerged from the Pelasgic & Etruscan barbarians. *La Nature aime les croisements*. (*Journals* 9:299–300)

Emerson's smelting pot accompanied the call for an American renaissance and thus drew strength for a new nation's destiny out of its contradictory composition.

An early instance of an ethnic crucible can be found in a strangely typological-nationalistic book written by two authors who were inspired by the European events of 1848. In *The New Rome; or, The United States of the World* (1853), the immigrant Theodore Poesche and the German-American Charles Goepp wrote that

> the American republic is destined to possess the continent of which it bears the name, and to share it, by absorption, with the inhabitants of all the lands of the earth. America is the crucible in which European, Asiatic, and African nationalities and peculiarities are smelted into unity. (47)

Poesche and Goepp give ample room to manifest destiny, the phrase which had come into existence and instant prominence in 1845. In order to support their fervent American nationalism, they develop a curious theory of racial amalgamation based on cohabitation of white males and black females and characteristically combine the notion of a concretely envisioned American melting-pot fusion with that of America's historical mission to bring republicanism and the English language to the four corners of the earth (55–74, 177–79).

In a *Puck* cartoon of June 26, 1889, "The Mortar of Assimilation" (illustration 6), an allegorical America stirs the mixed multitudes with a big ladle; while black and white, Dutch and Jew seem contented, an adherent of the Blaine Irish—denounced as desirous of "rum, roman-ism, and rebellion" (Muzzey 316–25)—refuses to melt. Here the cru-cible was a plea for more American unity addressed to Irish-Ameri-cans, while it also asserted the success of the melting pot apart from that single problem. The rebirth of a new, superior, future-bound America was as central to Emerson and the German 1848ers as it was later to Francis Parkman's public school "crucible" (1890), to Fred-erick Jackson Turner's influential and resonant frontier "crucible" (1893), to Woodrow Wilson's national "melting pot" (1915), and to the host of ethnic melting pots since the Zangwill era (Saveth, *His-torians* 98–149).

Illustration 6.

Zangwill's play was a point of demarcation as it opened the flood-gates for melting-pot rhetoric—a phenomenon which has been carefully documented and interpreted in Philip Gleason's essays. On the one hand, there was a widespread acceptance of the pliable term which could be interpreted, as we have seen, to suit universalist idealists and the Ford Motor Company. In that sense the image lives on in a restaurant in a Pittsburgh airport or on the cover of *Time* magazine. On the other hand, the melting pot has been criticized sharply since the Zangwill era, and on various, contradictory grounds. Yet the images of prophetic meltings, fusions, caldrons, American symphonies, and attacks on "hard" hypocrites infected even Zangwill's opponents. The philosopher Horace Kallen's famous essay "Democracy *versus* the Melting-Pot" (1915) was a specific attack on Zangwill's play, yet it concluded with an image of harmonious musical fusion which was presented as a radical alternative to the melting pot, while it resembles the struggles of Zangwill's protagonist David Quixano to compose an American symphony. Invoking a mystical "multiplicity in a unity, an orchestration of mankind," Kallen embellished the metaphor into an epic simile that serves as a social parable:

> As in an orchestra every type of instrument has its specific *timbre* and *tonality*, founded in its substance and form; as every type has its appropriate theme and melody in the whole symphony, so in society, each ethnic group may be the natural instrument, its temper and culture may be its theme and melody, and the harmony and dissonances and discords of them all make the symphony of civilization. (*Culture* 124–25)

Kallen has, of course, shifted grounds in order to support his federation-of-nationalities theory, which asserts the permanence of ethnic groups, but the rhetorical affinities to Zangwill are striking.

Inspired by Kallen, Randolph Bourne published his attack on the melting pot in "Trans-National America" (1916). As Gleason pointed out, Bourne "referred critically to the melting pot a dozen times, declaring among other things that it had never existed" (Gleason, "Melting Pot" 39). Yet the cosmopolitan dual citizens Bourne envisioned were described in clear melting-pot language: "America has burned most of the baser metal from them." Bourne's essay concluded with a call to the younger intelligentsia of America which could have been exclaimed by David Quixano:

> No mere doubtful triumphs of the past, which redound to the glory of only one of our transnationalities, can satisfy us. [Get thee hence, Davenport!] It must be a future America, on which all can unite, which pulls us irresistibly toward it, as we understand each other more warmly. ... Here is an enterprise of integration into which we

can all pour ourselves, of a spiritual welding which should make us, if the final menace ever came, not weaker, but infinitely strong. (*Radical* 264)

Bourne attacked the melting pot from the left, whereas Henry Pratt Fairchild did it from the right, though he was so much and so admittedly influenced by Zangwill's language that he called his book *The Melting-Pot Mistake* (1926). Gleason observed the curious phenomenon that diverse critics of the most popular image of American ethnic interaction may easily reject the *idea* of the melting pot and then

> go on to deny that it ever had any reality. The conventional wisdom is thus twofold: as an ideal or goal the melting pot is reprehensible, but in the practical order (fortunately, one presumes) it didn't exist, never happened, failed to melt, and is a myth. ("Confusion" 15)

This overdetermination in melting-pot rebuttals has become increasingly popular among intellectuals since the publication of Glazer and Moynihan's *Beyond the Melting Pot.* Whereas perceptive interpreters of American culture such as Robert Park (*Race* 353), D. H. Lawrence (*Studies* 6), and Erik Erikson (*Childhood* 294–95) adopted and freely used the term "melting pot," Richard Basham and David DeGroot noted that in recent years "a virtual academic industry has emerged to counter this metaphor" ("Current" 423).

Michael Novak, for example, one of Gleason's star witnesses, argued that the melting pot "did not exist," though "melting pot ideology ... has dominated the social sciences for three decades." At the same time, Novak used rather elaborate melting-pot rhetoric and stated that "America is a sizzling cauldron for the ethnic American." Novak also claimed that although "we did not have one before ... now national television is our melting pot" (Gleason, "Confusion" 14). Had the melting pot been only half as vicious, unpractical, undesirable, or false as its critics have argued, the image would not continue to be refuted with such ritualistic predictability.

To add to the confusion surrounding the melting pot, there have been rebuttals of Zangwill by religious Jews since the play opened. For example, Rabbi Joel Blau, alluding to the story of Jacob and Esau [Genesis 25:23–34], reminded the Jew of his "oriental soul" that he "claims as his birthright, not to be traded away for the contents of any pot—even though it be the Melting-Pot" (Fairchild, *Mistake* 224); and Rabbi Judah Magnes, an early advocate of America as a "Republic of Nationalities," preached against *The Melting-Pot* and for another symphony, one of "color, of picturesqueness, of character, of distinction," and culminating in the harmony of loyalty (Goren, *Quest* 4).

A recent academic interpreter of the play, Neil Larry Shumsky, has boldly asked us to read the play as if it ended with the third act—with David's recognition who Vera's father is and his despair in his mission! By focusing on that transitory moment of the play, one can make the case that ethnicity persists in Zangwill's play. Shumsky also emphasizes the Judaization of all the non-Jewish characters—as if this were not part of Zangwill's declared program from the cited afterword. The "melting pot" is a *strong*, "centrist" image which has dominated the debates even of its opponents for over seventy years. The meaning of melting pot, best embodied by Crèvecoeur's and Zangwill's *ideal* of universal regeneration, is also usurped in public discourse by ethnicizing and Americanizing interpretations, here represented by Shumsky and Ford. Kallen, Bourne, Novak, and their many followers build up the Ford (mis)interpretation of the melting pot as a straw man and can thus go on to oppose it with their own, varying concepts, yet supported by Zangwill's rhetoric. Blau has a vested interest in opposing radical universalism, and Fairchild, from the other side of the spectrum, can invoke Blau as a witness against the melting pot from the outside.

Other Melting Pots

The very language used to create national unity and a sense of cohesion can also serve to support the ethnogenesis of regional and ethnic groups that could challenge national unity. In 1896 Abraham Cahan described New York's Lower East Side as an all-Jewish melting pot, "a seething human sea fed by streams, streamlets, and rills of immigration flowing from all the Yiddish-speaking centers of Europe." Cahan found the Jewish ghetto inhabited by

> people with all sorts of antecedents, tastes, habits, inclinations, and speaking all sorts of subdialects of the same jargon, thrown pellmell into one social caldron—a human hodgepodge with its component parts changed but not yet fused into one homogeneous whole. (*Yekl* 13–14)

Cahan also gave a characteristic catalog of diverse opposites as ingredients for his Jewish melting-pot ethnogenesis.

In 1925 Alain Locke applied the rhetoric of the "new man" to his own concept of the "New Negro." Locke saw Harlem as the alchemical laboratory for an Afro-American rebirth (the Harlem Renaissance) and described it as "the first concentration in history of so many diverse elements of Negro life" (6). After an extensive cataloging of the intra-ethnic diversity in black Harlem life, Locke concluded with this version of the melting pot: "what began in terms of segregation becomes more and more, as its elements mix and react, the laboratory of a great race-welding" (*Negro* 7).

In a similar way, Edward Spicer (*HEAEG* 82) and Daniel Richter (1983) have described American Indian group formation as "the crucible of Oklahoma" and "the Iroquois melting pot." If other writers thought that ethnic groups were the ideal melting pots, the Irish-American John Gregory envisioned one state as the place of ethnogenesis. Writing in *The Industrial Resources of Wisconsin* in 1855, Gregory (who was rediscovered by the historian Richard Current) saw the population of Wisconsin as "heterogeneous masses collected from every quarter of the globe." Full of characteristic melting-pot hopefulness, Gregory was convinced that

> though these elements may jar for a moment, like different metals in the furnace, yet the amalgamation of the races, by intermarriage, must produce the most perfect race of men that has ever appeared upon earth. (Current 13)

A recent study of Wisconsin, Richard Bernard's *The Melting Pot and the Altar*, develops an argument that suggests that Gregory's hopes were to some extent fulfilled in that state.

One final example may illustrate the possible radical uses of metaphors of regeneration and ethnogenesis. Michael Gold's famous essay "Towards Proletarian Art" (1921) also gives us a belated reason why Davenport thought that David Quixano was a socialist when he talked about *his* melting-pot America. Gold described the process of acquiring a revolutionary identity as ethnogenesis:

> We cling to the old culture, and fight for it against ourselves. But it must die. The old ideals must die. But let us not fear. Let us fling all we are into the cauldron of the Revolution. For out of our death shall arise glories, and out of the final corruption of this old civilization shall spring the new race—the Supermen. (Gold, *Literary* 61)

Like Zangwill, Gold links the melting-pot rebirth to the anticipation of the new man as Superman, though his language also echoes the alchemical hopes for the hermaphrodite and the Ouroboros. In American popular culture, this wish came true with the creation of the most famous Krypto-American immigrant "who fights a never-ending battle, for truth, justice, and the American way." Yet though Superman, in the comic strip created by the immigrants Jerry Siegel and Joe Shuster, could never really marry Lois Lane, the road that generally led to the American melting pot and the fused new men went, as it did for David and Vera, through love and marriage, and, as in *The Melting-Pot*, a parental legacy could easily become an obstacle to that route.

CHAPTER FOUR

Romantic Love, Arranged Marriage, and Indian Melancholy

Say You Red Men You Forgotten Men
Come out from your tepees
Show us Pocahontas For we love her
Bring her from her hiding place Let the sun kiss her eyes
Drape her in a shawl of red wool Tuck her in beside us
—Richard Wright, "Transcontinental"

In the middle decades of the [nineteenth] century, romance was fast losing its negative connotations and emerging as the only acceptable basis for intimacy between women and men. It was no longer associated with wildness and youthful passion; it was made safe. Romance was redefined as the key to domestic harmony rather than as a threat to it. As romantic love became something to celebrate rather than mistrust, "falling in love" would become an increasingly normative part of middle-class courtship.
—Ellen Rothman, Hands and Hearts

Varying the title of a novel by the Austrian-American Charles Sealsfield (né Karl Postl) about American Indians, one may say that the central conflict in Indian-white relations has been that between legitimacy and republicanism. As in Sealsfield's novel Der Legitime und die Republikaner (1833), the legitimate rule of the Indians, based on descent and long residence, was threatened and overthrown by republican immigrants. In the period from the American Revolution to the Civil War, this process was perceived as parallel to that of European bourgeois revolutions against indigenous aristocracies. The American revolutionaries, however, found themselves in a double role as republicans: on the one hand, they overthrew and usurped Indian legitimacy—perceived in European terms as the doomed rule of an aristocratic nobility of chieftains—in the name of European republicanism; on the other hand, they defied the parental authority of the mother country by invoking the spirit of the Indian and by symbolically "acting Indian" in clothing and military strategy. The

102

settlers were metaphoric "Indians" in their attempts to define themselves as "non-British," as "Americans" (a term originally applied exclusively to the Indians); but they were emphatically European when they identified with the destined mission of republicanism against aboriginal legitimacy. Americans could conceive of themselves both as Tammanies following the westward course of empires and as frontiersmen pitted against a savage wilderness.

Indians interpreted the customs and politics of the newcomers in their diverse Indian terms. This may explain, for example, the complicated policy of Powhatan toward the Virginia settlers much better than does melodramatic historiography with its unilateral emphasis on white aggression and greed (Lurie, "Indian" 47n). Cotton Mather's "Life of John Eliot" (1702) may be cited as evidence since it suggests a settler's view of a Narragansett view of the settlers:

> They continue in a Place, till they have burnt up all the *Wood* thereabouts, and then they pluck up Stakes; to follow the *Wood,* which they cannot fetch home unto themselves; hence when they enquire about the *English, Why come they hither!* They have themselves very Learnedly determined the Case, *'Twas because we wanted Firing.*
> (Miller, *Puritans* 505)

Non-Indian Americans (mis)interpreted Indians and were (mis)interpreted by them—a normal fact of acculturation. Yet the much better documented white American side of this process has come under increasing attack in the period since the 1960s, although some scholars in their valiant attempts to denounce past racism and prejudice have inadvertently exhibited their own projections. Thus, the American post-Vietnam ethnohistory of early colonial North America was amusingly described by H. C. Porter as an inversion and a cultural projection. According to recent scholarship on the Indian, the "Last American" (to deserve that name)

> was peaceable, merciful, less violent than the whites ... ; sober, industrious, disciplined, austere ... ; uncomplicated ... ; generous and hospitable ... ; egalitarian ... ; kind to animals. ... Indeed the Indian seems to have had most of the virtues of small-town Middle America, as portrayed in the Andy Hardy films. ([One American historian] adds a Frank Capra touch: Indians were impractical, bohemian, and "quite a bit of fun.") ("Reflections" 245–246)

In their very fervor to tear down the false idols of the past, contemporary critics may help to create another white man's Indian. Modern ethnohistorians also provide us with another example of familiar contrasting ethnic strategies; and the resulting idealization of American Indians has been a pervasive phenomenon in American culture.

American plays from the mid-eighteenth to the mid-nineteenth century idealized Indians with the best intentions. These plays dramatized the conflict between legitimacy and republicanism in several recurring patterns. In many of these "Indian plays," which reached their highest popularity in the decade from 1829 to 1838, the political and national themes were integrated into a family drama. The theatrical spectacles, many of which were extremely popular, combined the traditional comedy motif of a daughter torn between her father's command and the voice of her heart with the serious theme of the end of American Indian legitimacy—the vanishing Indian. The somewhat surprising conjunction of romantic love, arranged marriage, and Indian melancholy in some of these melodramas was also at work in eighteenth- and nineteenth-century American music, painting, sculpture, and folklore.

The Contrast *and "Indian Plays"*

At the beginning of Royall Tyler's play *The Contrast* (1787), right after we have encountered and come to see through the shallow coquettes Charlotte and Letitia, who introduced us to the delicate gossip of Boston society, we see our profound republican heroine, tellingly named Maria, alone and "disconsolate" in the house of her father, Van Rough. Before she says anything, she sings the "Indian death song" known as "Son of Alknomook." Her version concludes with this stanza:

> I go to the land where my father is gone;
> His ghost shall rejoice in the fame of his son:
> Death comes like a friend, he relieves me from pain;
> And thy son, Oh Alknomook! has scorn'd to complain. (10)

The Contrast is not an "Indian play" (the term always refers to dramas *about*, not by, Indians); yet why does Maria Van Rough sing this popular dirge? According to Thomas Tanselle (1979), who tracked down twenty-six early printings of the poem from the years 1783 to 1822, this is "probably the best example of the genre of Indian death songs, depicting the Indian's heroic endurance of adversity and his unyielding spirit in the face of physical defeat" ("Birth" 389–90). But other songs, too, were popular in the period. Why did Maria pick the "Son of Alknomook"?

Fortunately for us, Tyler's play—which Kenneth Silverman has called "the most distinctively American literary work of the eighteenth century" (*Cultural* 559) and which is a perfect example of defining a country by contrast and opposition—also provides a telling context for the song. After the recital, Maria continues with an interpretation of the "Son of Alknomook" and thus preempts speculations by the audience about the implied reader of her text. Maria soliloquizes:

> There is something in this song which ever calls forth my affections. The manly {an allusion to the name of the man of her heart} virtue of courage, that fortitude which steels the heart against the keenest misfortunes, which interweaves the laurel of glory amidst the instruments of torture and death, displays something so noble, so exalted, that in spite of the prejudices of education I cannot but admire it, even in a savage. (10)

For the sentimental reader Maria, the song provides a pure vision of the heroic. Having sung the song and having pronounced the words "noble" and "savage" in a single sentence, Maria now lets her thoughts roam freely as she rambles on about men and women, courage and protection. Her negative foils, Letitia and Charlotte, had revealed their shallow and coquettish selves through a language that included Freudian slips: "I take care never to report anything of my acquaintance, especially if it is to their credit—*discredit* I mean," Charlotte said in scene one (9). The profound woman Maria, however, develops her character through free association prompted by her response to the Indian song. The splitting of female characters into the "sexually predatory and irrational, who appeared in the guise of the 'coquette'" and "the idealized Republican Mother or True Woman" that Ellen Rothman (41) has observed in the first century after Independence is to a certain extent illustrated by *The Contrast*.

As we find out in Maria's monologue, her problem, the root of her depressed state that she describes as "melancholy," lies in the dramatic conflict between her pure love for the heroic Manly and her father's choice of a certain Van Dimple (of patroon descent, he "softened" his name from the original Van Dumpling), ominously a Chesterfield reader of loose morals, as her future spouse. In her stream of consciousness, Maria catches herself dreamily saying:

> Heaven grant that the man with whom I may be connected—may be connected! Whither has my imagination transported me—whither does it now lead me? Am I not indissolubly engaged, "by every obli-

gation of honour which my own consent and my father's approbation can give," to a man who can never share my affections, and
whom a few days hence it will be criminal for me to disapprove—to
disapprove! would to heaven that were all—to despise. For, can the
most frivolous manners, actuated by the most depraved heart, meet,
or merit, anything but contempt from every woman of delicacy and
sentiment? (Tyler 10-11)

Maria cannot easily admit to herself that she loves Manly, but she
knows that she depises her paternally selected prospective bridegroom Van Dimple. Her father cannot comprehend Maria's strange
melancholy: "what good have these books done you? have they not
made you melancholy? as you call it. Pray, what right has a girl of
your age to be in the dumps?"—reminding Maria painfully of Van
Dimple's original name. Putting salt into his daughter's wounded
heart, father Van Rough continues: "haven't you everything your
heart can wish; an't you going to be married to a young man of great
fortune; an't you going to have the quit-rent of twenty miles square?"
(11). As we all know from literature, if not from life, the prospect of
land ownership spells little comfort to a melancholy lover. Though
the metaphors of "courting" and changing one's "state" allude to the
dimension of property, the person who experiences romantic love in
the courtship process does not care to be reminded of the mundane
aspects of the choice of a spouse. Romantic lovers do not consciously
want to think of "property" when the "pursuit of happiness" is at
stake.

In order to dramatize the separation of realms further, *The Contrast*
assigned concern for property to the domain of the father, whereas
the daughter had the prerogative of experiencing love in a pure,
though unfulfilled and sad, form. This is a split which Tyler's play
shared with many of the Indian plays. Interestingly, too, the connection between the father-daughter conflict and the vanishing-Indian
theme recurred and became a mainstay in much American culture of
the nineteenth century.

In Sylvester Judd's novel *Margaret: A Tale of the Real and the Ideal*
(1845), the title heroine, like Tyler's Maria, sings the "Son of Alknomook" when asked to perform something with a "dash of the
heroic." Responding to the comment "you like the Indians, show
them off to their best advantage," she delivers her version of the
"Indian death song." This is a public performance, in sharp contrast
to Maria's solitary recital; but the narrator points out that this is a
song which Margaret "had more than once sung in the loneliness and
grandeur of the hills about them." Her performance is immediately

followed by the men's delirious intonation of a republican song of sorts, "Hoora for the Old Bastille" (262); in *The Contrast* the only other song heard is the equally republican "Yankee Doodle," which is also performed by a man—by Jonathan, an Uncle Sam prototype and Yankee servant (21). The collision between legitimacy and republicanism, symbolized by the different songs, seems frozen into a vignette when the profound heroine sings the Indian death song.

In the first American opera, *The Songs of Tammany*, by Ann Julia Hatton (1794)—which was also connected with the establishment of the republican society of Saint Tammany, out of which Tammany Hall emerged—the title hero and his lover Manana die singing another variant of the "Son of Alknomook," which ends with these lines:

> Together we die for our spirits disdain,
> Ye white children of Europe your rankling chain.
>   (14)

Lewis Deffebach's *Oolaita; or, The Indian Heroine* was an "Indian play" published in Philadelphia in 1821, two years before James Fenimore Cooper's *Leather-Stocking Tales* started to appear. Deffebach presents us with another version of the association between romantic love conflict and Indian theme. The white lovers Stephen and Eumelia have "eloped" (a word omnipresent in this genre) in order to escape a paternally arranged marriage. Together with their humorous Yankee servant, Dominic (who echoes Tyler's famous Jonathan and is another early Uncle Sam prototype), they have ventured into the forest, where they are captured by the Sioux. When asked by Chief Machiwita what brought the paleface "reptiles, spies, marauders, thieves—plunderers of honest toil and labors fruit" into the land of the Sioux, the lovers declare: "[We] have just been married, contrary to the wishes of our families, but in perfect unison with Heaven's decree and our own will" (17). Apparently, they think that Heaven's decrees and their own choices are identical. More surprisingly, they seem to believe that as sentimental defectors from their families they are the kind of people that the Sioux would just *have* to welcome. Yet Machiwita is no sentimentalist. He suspects that they are spies and threatens to give them a "passport" which "leads to the scaffold or the stake" (17). Just at that moment Machiwita's daughter Oolaita "intercedes" (another key word), in best Pocahontas fashion. However, she interposes not for the man of her heart but for the *principle* of romantic love in the shape of the white elopers—who are consequently set free. Yet Oolaita herself is still beset by the same conflict

which she helped to resolve happily for Stephen and Eumelia: Machiwita wants Oolaita to marry the apparently elderly Monoma, but
Oolaita loves young Tullula. She pleads with her father, who is
unwilling to respect her feelings in this matter (though he did set
Stephen and Eumelia free). Machiwita admonishes his daughter,
"Discard Tullula from your thoughts"—thereby transporting her
into a state of melancholy, which Oolaita appropriately describes in
a soliloquy:

> Is fled then every hope? No, no, for there is hope even beyond the
> grave. Sweet peace! thou heavenly goddess of the skies, long have I
> woo'd thee, but alas, in vain. Ungrateful father! hardened, callous
> man, thus to betroth me to a wither'd limb. (Deffebach 19)

Amplifying on the nature of her complaint, Oolaita continues:

> What, wed gray hairs—embrace deformity, declining years, and sec-
> ond childhood? No. I'd rather rend my frame in twain, and strew the
> public highway with my bones—rather perish at the stake—imbibe
> consuming fires, than be an old man's crutch. Nay, ere I'll sacrifice
> my peace of mind, abandon him I love, become Monoma's wife ...
> I'll thwart the mandates of a cruel father, and seek redemption at the
> price of life. ... (19–20)

After kneeling for her solemn vow to follow her heart's voice, Oolaita concludes:

> Tullula is the object of my soul—I love the youth, admire his valour
> and venerate his virtues:—to him I gave my hand, bequeathed my
> heart; and when I violate the sacred pledge may Heaven's just ven-
> geance, crying for revenge, o'ertake the hapless, spotless Oolaita. (20)

Tullula shows his valor and natural Christian virtue in a scene
where he sets free a white would-be assassin hired by Monoma and
echoes Logan's famous speech: "Have you e'er heard that when a
whiteman came, And sued for mercy at a Sioux's cabin, Or ask'd protection, it was e'er denied?" (23). Yet he, too, is thrown into a state of
melancholy when he hears that Monoma is about to marry Oolaita.
Tullula finally manages to convince Chief Machiwita that Monoma
is not only unloving and elderly but also a traitor and a murderer
(43–44); but it is too late. There is no happy ending for Tullula and
Oolaita. In order to escape her fate, Oolaita throws herself from the
"majesty sublime" of a "tremendous precipice" (45) near Lake Pepin
in Minnesota, below the Falls of St. Anthony on the Mississippi
(illustration 7), just as the others enter to bring her the good news.
Tullula stabs himself in grief, and the *Romeo and Juliet* of the Sioux

Illustration 7. Lovers' Leap. Maiden Rock. (From Henry Lewis, *Da sillustrirte Mississippithal*, 1844–45)

has taken its course. The difference in fate for white and red lovers is striking, as is the sense of tableau in the final scene.

The most popular Indian play was undoubtedly John Augustus Stone's *Metamora; or, The Last of the Wampanoags* (1829), the prize-winner in a drama competition instituted by the star actor Edwin Forrest, who specialized in heroic and Indian roles. In *Metamora* the heroine Oceana, the daughter of the fugitive regicide Mordaunt, is faced with the choice of accepting Fitzarnold—probably best described as an English rapist, who blackmails Oceana's father into promising him her hand—or of following her inclination and taking up with Walter and thus endangering her father's safety. "Decide, then, now" Oceana's father, Mordaunt, tells her, "between my honor and my instant death!" (67). Fortunately for her, Oceana does not have to decide, thanks to noble Chief Metamora, who kills Fitzarnold in the presence of the swooning Oceana (86). Though Metamora (like Tullula) is destined to die at the end of the play, he rescues Oceana and resolves her dilemma.

The conflict between parentally arranged marriage and romantic love is connected to the Indian theme in many American plays. What is the culturally felt affinity between pining Maria and Son of Alknomook? Why would Stephen and Eumelia feel that they could safely elope to the Indians? Why does Oceana have such a *strong* relationship with Metamora, who relieves her of the paternally chosen man Fitzarnold (by killing him) and thus permits her to follow her heart and marry Walter—one of the paler figures of the drama? And similarly, in Richard Emmons' play *Tecumseh; or, The Battle of the Thames* (1836), why, if the famous Indian chief is so clearly the hero, does the Englishwoman Lucinda love Edward, an American character who spends most of his time tied to three different trees in the course of the play?

The father-daughter conflict that often results in eloping lovers may be considered merely a melodramatic colonial offshoot of a European comedy motif, but the new American constellation is interesting beyond its literary sources. It is important to discuss a few contexts at this point in order to clarify the connections of romantic love, arranged marriage, and Indian melancholy in the character of Maria and in the other texts.

Romantic Love versus Arranged Marriage

Though poetic illustrations of the state of being in love could easily be assembled from across the ages, romantic love as a socially significant courtship system is of recent origin. Modern romantic love had its origin in the poetry of courtly love of the twelfth century, though that phenomenon was in itself a nostalgic one and probably had its ultimate source in an Arab genre that had come to the Provençal troubadours via Muslim Spain (Boase, *Origin* 123-26). Leonard Benson characterized the features of chivalric love as follows:

> It was supposed to occur outside of marriage, but it did *not* involve sex relations. . . . Unselfish service to a noble lady—a married woman of the ruling class—became the duty of the young knight. . . . The knight had the right to go with his lady to the bedchamber, to help her disrobe, even to put her to bed. Occasionally he could sleep with her, but tenderness alone was allowed, not "carnal knowledge." The knight could have symbolic unity with his beloved by tying her veil to his armor, or perhaps she would wear his blood-stained tunic. (*Family* 113)

At the center of the rites and rituals of courtly love was "the choice of suffering or difficulty in preference to gratification" (Boase 126, 128). It was richly expressed in the medieval troubador songs and *Minne* love lyrics. By the Romantic period, Hugo Beigel wrote, this

> refined concept had filtered down from the castles to the cities. Marriage, to be sure, was still arranged on a family basis with an eye on

business, and the status of the wife was by no means enviable. But the verbiage of courtly love had entered the relation of the sexes. However, it was addressed not to the married woman, but, for the first time, to the marriageable maiden. ("Romantic" 329)

Especially in the time between betrothal and wedding, the man was supposed to "court" the woman. As Niklas Luhmann has carefully documented, the earlier codes of love (before the mid-eighteenth century) had so sharply differentiated love from marriage that the two were considered incompatible (96). In eighteenth-century Anglo-America, strengthened by the codes of fiction established by Samuel Richardson, love increasingly became a cultural prerequisite for bourgeois marriage. As Luhmann wryly puts it: "Love then becomes that strange excitement that one experiences when one notices that one has decided to get married" (159). Luhmann illustrates the dramatic change in literary love codes from the seventeenth to the nineteenth century with the function of a "second declaration," always required by a declaration of love:

> In the seventeenth century this was still the *"déclaration de sa naissance"*; it had to be said or turn out that the lover was a prince or in some other way an equal applicant. In the nineteenth century the declaration of the intention to get married substituted for it. The additional declaration no longer referred to the past, but to the future; and this because the family was no longer continued through generations, but had to be founded anew each time. (*Liebe* 187)

By the yoking of love and marriage, betrothals were removed from the controls of descent (*déclaration de sa naissance*, definition of family by descent) and opened to the forces of consent (romantic love, serious intention to get married, founding of families through marriage).

It became more and more commonplace in the eighteenth century to say that love was needed for marriage. As Beigel illustrates, soon the literature was filled with pleas "for the right of the young people to make their own choice for marriage on the basis of their feelings. No longer was there to be a cleavage between the spirituality of love and the marital sex relation, but the latter was said to be sanctified by the former" (330). Beigel emphasized the parallels between courtly love and adolescence; and he suggested that connection again when he, interestingly for our context, noted that the "romantic love relationship was pervaded by melancholy ... , another trend that is generally encountered in adolescence when the young person, having severed his emotional ties with his protective elders and craving new attachments, finds himself abandoned and . . . inadequate. From the same experience, on the other hand, results the claim to uniqueness and originality" (330).

That romantic love became identified with America may have its reasons in the historical contemporaneity of the movement Beigel, Luhmann, and Rothman described and of American independence; the last excerpt also captures the double focus on adolescence and originality that has been characteristic of many American move-ments. American allegiance, the very concept of citizenship devel-oped in the revolutionary period, was—like love—based on consent, not on descent, which further blended the rhetoric of America with the language of love and the concept of romantic love with Ameri-can identity.

With the Consent of the Governor

Comparatively speaking, Americans enjoyed a great amount of free choice in selecting a spouse in the revolutionary and Jacksonian periods, as was attested by three French interpreters of America. Moreau de St. Méry, not always the most trustworthy observer, who traveled in America from 1793 to 1798, wrote explicitly about Amer-ican women: "They invariably make their own choice of a suitor, and the parents raise no objection because that's the custom of the coun-try" (Moreau 282). Tocqueville related in the second part of *Democ-racy in America* (1840) that in a democracy "the legal part of parental authority vanishes and a species of equality prevails around the domestic hearth" (195). The resulting independence of woman, how-ever, "is irrevocably lost in the bonds of matrimony," Tocqueville continued (201). "As in America paternal discipline is very relaxed and the conjugal tie very strict, a young woman does not contract the latter without considerable circumspection and apprehension. Precocious marriages are rare" (202). Auguste Carlier's *Marriage in the United States* (1867), which took issue with Tocqueville on some accounts (120–51), found that in America "the young girls know that they must depend upon *themselves* to find a husband" (32). Carlier continued:

> When still quite young, ignorant of herself, life not yet a lesson, when circumstances the most frivolous, appearances the most decep-tive, and errors of judgment, may blind reason,—she [the American girl] makes the most important decision of her life. . . . She is . . . nat-urally disposed to receive with the greatest reluctance any opposition

on the part of her parent. ... We can understand, the law not being
more exacting than custom, and therefore not requiring the consent
of the parents to their children's marriage. Consent is in fact nearly
always given. But it would be very curious to inquire and ascertain,
as a trait of manners, how often this consent is not obtained, except
too late, in order to satisfy public opinion. (33–34)

Interestingly, the need for parental consent was not newly questioned in the revolutionary era to accommodate the new sense of
romantic love as a basis for marriage and to reflect the parental parallels with England. It turns out that the Puritans were the important
modernizers in this respect! The secularized concept of marriage as a
civil institution—not a sacrament—induced the earliest New
England migrants to modernize matrimonial law, to relegate it to
local government, and to view the intervention of a minister as out
of place. We saw in the chapter on typology and ethnogenesis how
strongly Winthrop emphasized love in his "Modell of Christian
Charity" (1630) and how he used consent symbolism in order to naturalize the Massachusetts Bay Company. It was in Puritan Massachusetts, too, that marriage law changed, as George Elliott Howard wrote.
Although parental approbation was still formally required, there was
a provision that in case such approval "cannot be had then it shall
be with the consent of the Gover[nor] or some assistant to whom
the persons are knowne whose care it shall be to see the marriage be
fitt before it be allowed by him" (*History* 2:143–44). In a Plymouth
case of 1646, "Richard Taylor complained to the general court ... that
he was prevented from marrying Ruth Wheildon by her father
Gabriel; but when before the court Gabriel yielded and promised no
longer to oppose the marriage" (*History* 2:163). John Winthrop's
grandson Fitz-John wrote in 1707, "[I]t has been the way and custome
of the country for young folkes to choose, and where there is noe
visible exception everybody approves it" (Morgan, *Puritan Family*
85). It is perhaps surprising for us to learn that Puritan parents could
be "prosecuted for 'unreasonably denying any child timely or convenient marriage'" (Howard, *History* 2:166)! It is also clear, however,
that this was only a loophole of modernism in a framework of
assumptions that still strongly stressed "Virgin modesty, which
should make marriage an act rather of 'obedience' than 'choice'" (*History* 2:103).

Yet loopholes may develop into major cultural forces; since the
eighteenth century American culture has increasingly, and more
intensely than many other cultures, emphasized the importance of
romantic love and of the children's free choice (Goode, "Theoretical"

42). Rothman, after surveying substantial private and public documents of the period, concludes:

> By the last quarter of the eighteenth century, middle-class Americans
> enjoyed considerable autonomy when it came to choosing their
> future mates. Legal requirements for parental consent were steadily
> being eroded. (Hands 26)

The pattern that took hold in the early republic still holds, though
occasionally one finds countermovements which attest to the power
of the romantic rule as they express some young people's readiness
to defy the rule by surrendering to a larger power their free will and
their expectation of a marriage based on romantic love. Thus the
Unification Church of Sun Myung Moon in 1981 and 1982 performed mass engagements and marriages in New York's Madison
Square Garden; many of the couples were strangers until, under religious guidance, they exchanged engagement vows. Such exceptions
aside, the belief in romantic love as the basis for marriage is clearly a
cultural norm in America.

Did the first New Englanders pick up the new concepts from the
Indians who were so often portrayed as romantic lovers? American
folklore is especially rich in making the connection between Indians
and love in the countless tales of lovers' leaps. The stories always
involve lovers-against-their-parents'-wishes who find their union
only in death. This motif is "very common all over the United States,
especially in stories told about Indian lovers by whites" (Baughman,
Type 70). The dramatic Oolaita who threw herself from such a precipice near Lake Pepin also appeared in the legend of Oo-la-ita or
Wenona,

> "the pride of the braves of the Dakotas," {who} gave her heart to a
> young Indian, I-ta-tomah (White Eagle), of her own tribe. Her stern
> parents insisted that she marry an old chief. The hopeless lovers
> finally leaped from the limestone bluffs on the east shore of Lake
> Pepin and were dashed to pieces. (Pound, "Nebraska" 309n)

Because the first printed reference to this "Indian legend" given by
folklorists is from 1893, it is possible that the legend is in fact based
on Lewis Deffebach's drama, published some seventy years earlier.
Another representative story, reported by Charles M. Skinner, is
associated with a high cliff on White River, Utah.

> When the Brulés occupied this ground a girl of their tribe was
> bought by an Ogalalla, who paid six horses for her. To the disgust
> of her father she refused to marry the stranger, and that very night

attempted to run away with a friend of her youth who had not three ponies with which to bless himself. They were caught, the young man's career was stopped by an arrow, and the girl was—in short— spanked. Pretending to be converted to the matrimonial views of her parent, she arrayed herself next morning in her best clothes, put flowers into her hair, and gave farewell to her friends. Then, while the Ogalalla waited for her to share in the ceremonies that would make him hers and her his, the girl stole away to the cliff-top and sang her death-song. Her people arrived just as she took the fatal leap. One of them grasped her skirt; but it tore, leaving him with a fragment of it in his hands. And the Ogalalla demanded the return of his horses. (Skinner, *American Myths* 262–63)

Tales of Indian lovers' leaps can fill many volumes of folklore; they have appeared in print at least since William Byrd's *Histories of the Dividing Line* (1728; 232 and 244). Perhaps derived from European legends, these stories were generally of white American origin and merely projected upon the American Indians (Pound, "Nebraska" 308, 313). According to most of the examples included in Edward Westermarck's *History of Human Marriage* (2:279, 284), marriage on the basis of free choice and romantic love was simply not an Indian custom.

What then was the affinity of love and Indian lore? Why did Maria Van Rough sing an Indian death song? She explicitly states her conflict and suffers melancholy. She can express this conflict openly through free association but cannot actively defy her father's wishes. In this disturbed state she turns to the "Son of Alknomook," in order to, as she puts it, "divert {her} melancholy with singing, at {her} leisure hours" (11). The subject she chooses for her diversion, however, was virtually synonymous with "melancholy" in eighteenth- and nineteenth-century America.

Indian Melancholy

Washington Irving wrote in "Traits of Indian Character," included in his *Sketch Book* (1819):

Notwithstanding the obloquy with which the early historians have overshadowed the characters of the unfortunate natives, some bright gleams occasionally break through, which throw a degree of melancholy lustre on their memories. (1009)

"What can be more melancholy than their history?" Justice Joseph Story asked a Salem audience in 1828 about American Indians:

By a law of nature, they seem destined to a slow, but sure extinction. Everywhere, at the approach of the white man, they fade away. We hear the rustling of their footsteps, like that of the withered leaves of autumn, and they are gone for ever. They pass mournfully by us, and they return no more. (Dippie, "Vanishing" 1)

Writing in 1851, Francis Parkman developed the context of this melancholy view of the vanishing Indian more fully:

the Indian is hewn out of rock. You can rarely change the form without destruction of the substance. Races of inferior energy have possessed a power of expansion and assimilation to which he is a stranger; and it is this fixed and rigid quality which has proved his ruin. He will not learn the art of civilization, and he and his forest must perish together. The stern, unchanging features of his mind excite our admiration from their very immutability; and we look with deep interest on the fate of this irreclaimable son of the wilderness, the child who will not be weaned from the breast of his rugged mother. (Rogin, *Fathers* 115)

In 1852 the navy lieutenant George Falconer Emmons observed that "lawless whites" were waging a "war of extermination" on California and Oregon Indians. The Indians "are falling by tens, fifties, and hundreds, before the western rifle," he wrote, only to conclude fatalistically: "It is melancholy to see them melting away so rapidly; but it does not appear to be intended that civilization should prevent it" (Dippie, "Vanishing" 15). In 1853 John William De Forest spoke of the "melancholy character of Pequot history" (xxiv) in the table of contents of his *History of the Indians of Connecticut*.

According to the current *Encyclopaedia Britannica*, "melancholy" is simply a "vague term for desponding grief." For Robert Burton's *Anatomy of Melancholy* (1621), melancholy still was a central concept around which the universe could be organized, though the book also related this brief and common definition: "a kind of dotage without a fever, having for his ordinary companions, fear and sadness, without any apparent occasion" (108). Maria's melancholy is somewhere between Burton's universe and the narrow vagueness of the term in its modern usage. The *Encyclopedia Americana* of 1836, edited by the German-American Francis Lieber, offers the following definition under the heading "mental derangement":

Melancholy (from ... black and ... bile), called also *monomanie* ... a species of mental disorder, consisting in a depression of spirits. Some dark or mournful idea occupies the mind exclusively, so that, by degrees, it becomes unable to judge rightly of existing circumstances, and the faculties are disturbed in their functions. ... If these feelings are allowed to attain a height at which the power of self-control is lost, a settled gloom takes possession of the mind. Consciousness, however, may still continue; the person knows his state. ... A very common cause of melancholy is love. He who loses the great object of his wishes and affections, which has absorbed, we might almost say, the whole activity of his soul, feels more than jealousy at the success of a fortunate rival; existence appears to him a blank and himself the most unhappy of men. (Lieber 8:413)

Research on melancholy is on the ascent again, stimulated by Sigmund Freud's essay "Mourning and Melancholia" (1917). The most significant book in the field is a thorough background study to Albrecht Dürer's engraving *Melencolia I* (1517), *Saturn and Melancholy*, by Raymond Klibansky, Erwin Panofsky, and Fritz Saxl (1964). Among the interesting details which the authors have assembled from the literature on melancholy is the connection between Saturn and melancholy. Saturn was "really to blame for the melancholic's unfortunate character and destiny," which is why a melancholy disposition is sometimes referred to as "Saturnine" (Klibansky 127). Saturn as a planetary power "held the fate of all fathers and old men in his hands" (141). Kronos/Saturn, the deposed father of Zeus, is responsible for melancholy, a mythological aspect which fits nicely with the pains of our theatrical daughters.

Melancholy has an interesting relationship with authority and order, as Wolf Lepenies has shown in his *Melancholie und Gesellschaft* (1969). Lepenies emphasizes Saturn's role as "lord of Utopia" (20) and cites Julian West's melancholy at the beginning of Edward Bellamy's *Looking Backward, 2000–1887* (1888). The questioning of "legitimacy" and the dreaming of power are thus social aspects of the melancholy disposition.

In the rhetoric of the melancholy Indian destiny, the "legitimate" Americans (to go back to Sealsfield's term) were associated with autumn leaves and death, with rocks that are their nature and sepulcher at the same time. In the cult of the vanishing Indian, the children of nature were forever imagined on the brink of the abyss; they were, as Cotton Mather had already put it in "The Life of John Eliot" (1702), the "veriest *Ruines of Mankind*" (Miller, *Puritans* 504). Mather may have used "ruines" as a pejorative term; but by the late eighteenth century ruins had become highly desirable objects for aesthetic contemplation.

The theme of the dying Indian was also connected to republicanism, and it conveyed to American culture a touch of Roman antiquity, as the portraiture of Indian chieftains resembled that of the Latin Stoics. The vogue for Roman drama which preceded and paralleled the Indian cult (Winton, "Theater" 90) was signaled by Joseph Addison's *Cato* (1713), which starts with a motto by Seneca (whose very name must have evoked a synthesis of Rome and American Indians): "I can envisage nothing that Jupiter, if he turned his gaze on earth, would behold there more beautiful than the spectacle of Cato standing stalwart amid the ruins of the state, though the cause to which he had allied himself had been crushed again and again" (Quintana, *Eighteenth* 3). *Cato* was popular in America (Forbes, "Addison's" 210) and may have supported the imperial notion of America as a new Rome as well as the historical return to republicanism. The Seneca motto also supported the promise for a new golden age under Saturn, which Americans had adopted for their enterprise when they chose the Vergilian motto "novus ordo seclorum" (see *Eclogues* 4:4-10) for the obverse of the Great Seal (reproduced on the back of one-dollar bills today). Ferdinand Pettrich's sculpture *The Dying Tecumseh* (1856) equally demonstrates the Roman feeling applied to Indians; this Tecumseh is, as Hugh Honour wrote, "an antique hero in all but costume" (*New Golden* 235).

The spirit of Pettrich's sculpture reflects that of Richard Emmons's play *Tecumseh* (1836), which includes the set speech of the dying Indian:

> [TECUMSEH:] Great Spirit! Thy Red Children's cause avenge! Thick curses light upon the white man's head! Hold not thy thunders back! Blast him with all thy lightnings! May the hawk flap his wing over his steaming carcass! the wolf lap up his—his—blood! (*He sinks; after a desperate effort he revives.*) The Red man's course is run; I die—the last of all my race. (*Dies.*) (35)

The "vanishing Indians" became the subject of songs, poems, plays, paintings, and sculptures, in which they symbolized melancholy reminders of the passage of time—often rhetorically or iconographically connected with waterfalls. This occurred as early as in 1766, the year of Thomas Davies's painting *Niagara Falls from Below* (New-York Historical Society). This picture combines the motif of the Indian on the precipice with Niagara Falls—which was to become a stock element of the genre. Davies's painting also suggests the passage of time (and reminds us of Oolaita) by showing a withering tree stump (see Novak, *Nature* 157-200) on the Indian side of the Falls, and a flourishing tree on the English side. In the same year, Robert Rogers published his unperformed *Ponteach; or, The Savages of Amer-*

ica, so that 1766 can be taken as one historical starting point of the motif which became so popular in the nineteenth century. The pictures and illustrations of Thomas Cole (1830), Vanderlyn (1842/43), and Gustave Doré (1860) suggest the development of the image.[8]

The setting of Niagara Falls reinforced the conjunction of vanishing Indian and marriage based on romantic love. While some legends of Niagara fit into the lovers' leap tradition, the Falls became the most significant destination for honeymooning—a newly invented nineteenth-century tradition of a postmarital journey undertaken by newlyweds alone. The various functions of the wedding tour of visiting relatives or of a joint trip with other relatives and friends changed in the mid-nineteenth century when "the wedding tour developed into an exclusive ritual in which bride and groom alone participated. The demands of exclusive romantic love superseded the need for affirming community ties" (Rothman 175). Niagara Falls became the mecca of loving couples who, in isolation, set out to create new nuclear families. The honeymoon was an additional symbol emphasizing that "the choice of a spouse had to be legitimated autonomously" and gave expression to a dramatic change in social structure (Luhmann 184). Yet, instead of proudly celebrating the innovation, Americans combined the new social forms with supposedly ancient Indian motifs; if lovers eloped or defied parents, they were merely adopting the supposed customs of the original inhabitants of the country. The vanishing Indian provided middle-class lovers with a mythic origin.

Curses and Blessings

The Indian death song may also represent a transformation of a curse into a blessing. Fathers or dying elders may convey curses or blessings upon survivors, descendants, or victors. The "Son of Alknomook" is related to this central element in Indian plays. Like Tecumseh's speech, Alknomook's song defies and curses the white audience. One of the most popular and strongest versions of the dying Indian's curse comes at the end of John Augustus Stone's Metamora (1829; illustration 8):

> My curses on you, white men! May the Great Spirit curse you when he speaks in his war voice from the clouds! Murderers! The last of the Wampanoags' curse be on you! May your graves and the graves of your children be in the path the red man shall trace! And may the wolf and the panther howl o'er your fleshless bones, fit banquet

Illustration 8.   Frederick S. Agate (1807–44), *Metamora—The Last of the Wampanoags.* (From the *Token and Atlantic Souvenir*, Boston, 1842)

for the destroyers! Spirits of the grave, I come! But the curse of Metamora stays with the white man! I die! My wife! My Queen! My Nahmeokee! (92–93)

In the Indian plays, the space allotted to such curses—these secular fire-and-brimstone sermons were played out extensively on nineteenth-century American stages—could sometimes also be taken by the variant of a blessing. The prototypical instant for this substitution is at the end of George Washington Custis's *The Indian Prophecy* (1828), where chief Menawa dies fulfilling his mission to bless Washington, whom he identified despite a masquerade. The author, who was incidentally the son of Washington's stepson John Parke Custis, uses Menawa's blessing—based on a white legend—to convey legitimacy to the ascent of an American empire by casting (his stepgrandfather) Washington as a national father figure. The play, first pro-

duced on July 4, 1827, in Philadelphia, ends with Menawa's last
speech:

> Menawa is old, and soon will be gathered to the Great Council fire
> of his Fathers in the land of the shades; but ere he goes, there is
> something here, which bids him speak in the voice of Prophecy. Lis-
> ten! *The Great Spirit protects that man, and guides his destiny.* He will
> become the Chief of nations, and a people yet unborn, hail him as
> the Founder of a mighty Empire! (*After a pause, his arms outstretched
> to Heaven.*) Fathers! Menawa comes. (*Menawa sinks slowly into the arms
> of his attendants, strain of music, curtain falls.*) (35)

The relationship of the blessed American and an adopted ancestor
figure which is constructed here is an important fixture in American
mythic genealogy. The connection between a dying Indian, cursing
or blessing, and an emergent sense of autonomous American destiny
was made in many other works.

At the end of James Nelson Barker and Raynor Taylor's opera, *The
Indian Princess; or, La Belle Sauvage* (1808), the first theatrical version
of the Pocahontas story, after the treacherous Miami has stabbed
himself and Pocahontas and John Rolfe are united, John Smith
recites the final lines on the promised future of the American empire.
The operatic version (which was recently recorded on New World
Records) bursts out into the finale, "Freedom on the western shores,"
which sounds like a national anthem. (Custis, incidentally, so liked
Barker's script that he lifted some passages from it for his own play
Pocahontas; or, The Settlers of Virginia {1830}.) At this point it may also
be good to repeat that Tyler's play contained only two songs, "Son
of Alknomook" and "Yankee Doodle," and that *Margaret* similarly
contrasted the dying-Indian song with the republican hymn "Hoora
for the Old Bastille." In a parallel juxtaposition, Thomas Crawford's
sculpture *The Dying Indian Chief* (illustration 9), with the classic melancholy pose (1856), was installed in the frieze of the United States
Capitol.

Somewhere between curse and blessing is the most famous Indian
oration, praised and included in *Notes on the State of Virginia* (1785)
by Thomas Jefferson (60–61), reprinted in schoolbooks throughout
the nineteenth century, and, as we saw, alluded to in Indian plays
such as *Oolaita*. It is Logan's speech, which also appeared as the dramatic climax at the very end of Joseph Doddridge's play *Logan: The
Last of the Race of Shikellemus, Chief of the Cayuga Nation* (1823).

> I appeal to any white man to say, if ever he entered Logan's cabin
> hungry, and he gave him not meat: if ever he came cold and naked,
> and he clothed him not {see Matthew 25:35–36}. During the course

Illustration 9. Thomas Crawford (1813?-57), *The Dying Indian Chief* (The New-York Historical Society, New York)

of the last long and bloody war Logan remained idle in his cabin, an advocate for peace [see Romans 12:18]. Such was my love for the whites, that my country-men pointed as they passed, and said, "Logan is the friend of the white men." I had even thought to have lived with you, but for the injuries of one man. Colonel Cresap, the last spring, in cold blood, and unprovoked, murdered all the relations of Logan, not even sparing my women and children. There runs not a drop of my blood in the veins of any living creature. This called on me for revenge. I have sought it. I have killed many: I have fully glutted my vengeance [see Deuteronomy 32:41-42 and Romans 12:19-20]: for my country I rejoice at the beams of peace. But do not harbour a thought that mine is the joy of fear. Logan never felt fear. He will not turn on his heel to save his life. Who is there to mourn for Logan?—Not one. (Doddridge, *Logan* 38)

As Edward Seeber has argued ("Critical" 142), Logan's speech is a medley of New Testament quotes and allusions, giving the Indian chief a Christ-like sacrificial stature. Elements of Logan's speech recur in several other Indian plays. In Nathaniel Deering's *Carabasset* (1830), for example, in a longer scene with many echoes of *Logan*, the titular hero asks: "Who mourns for Carabasset?" (176–78). Stone's *Metamora* also declaims: "If my rarest enemy had crept unarmed into my wigwam and his heart was sore, I would not have driven him from my fire nor forbidden him to lie down upon my mat" (69).

Whether it appears as a curse, a blessing, or a projection of pure Christian conduct, the Indian speech functions as the departing chieftain's last will and testament to his paleface successors and resembles a parent's last wish for his child. Westermarck asked in his *History of Human Marriage*:

> Why are the blessings and curses of parents supposed to possess such an extraordinary power? One reason is no doubt the mystery of old age and the nearness of death. Not parents only, but to some extent old people generally, are held capable of giving due effect to their good and evil wishes, and this capacity is believed to increase when life is drawing to a close. (351)

The dying Indians' speeches and songs cast the Indian chief as a parent figure, an adopted ancestor who could convey curses and blessings and choose successors—which makes these successors chosen people. The image of a melancholy and "Saturnine" Indian promised the return of a golden age to his adoptive descendants. Read as a national allegory, then, the conflict of love, marriage, and Indian melancholy was connected with the search for republican legitimacy in the new world. The oceanic daughters of England received a "legitimate" blessing for their decision to break out of the arranged marriage with old-world aristocracy and rank in order to wed the "natural" republican system of America that they so dearly loved. The romance conflict thus supported the argument for independence, autonomy, and a fresh start in the name of supposedly ancient Indian traditions.

Such rhetorical strategies were popular in the period from the Revolution to the Civil War. The Indian plays, too, give evidence of a national dimension to their concern with parent-child conflicts. In Custis's *Indian Prophecy*, for example, Washington argues:

> As an American, I have all proper respect for the parent which gave us a colonial being here: but really ... we are becoming such well

groomed children, that we shall tire of the trammels of the nursery, and begin to think and act more for ourselves. The parental Government, if wise, will cherish and preserve those ties which are to bind us to allegiance, at a distance of three thousand miles. (17)

In this generational conflict, the Indians take part as well. Despite the common phrase "children of the forest," however, far from appearing as a younger generation (as Rogin suggested in 1974), the melancholy Indians functioned as legitimating ancestors who support the adoptive descendants (especially daughters) in their struggle against the parents and who can even provide alternative parental functions at times. This becomes clear in the famous diatribes in Indian plays.

Apparently, American audiences liked even the "anti-white" curse scenes in the Indian plays—as if they had been blessings! Freud illustrated the antithetical sense of primal words (1910); and the relationship of curses and blessings is the related case of an affinity between antithetical concepts. Inversions of curses into blessings come easily, as easily as transformations of ethnic slurs (such as "Puritans") into sacred names. A famous biblical type for this process appears in Numbers 23:11, when Balak says unto Balaam: "I took thee to curse mine enemies, and, behold, thou hast blessed them altogether." The language of some Indian plays is reminiscent of this biblical chapter, which leads up to Balaam's prophecy of the dominion of Israel in the famous phrase "What hath God wrought!"[Numbers 23:23], the verse Samuel Morse used for the first telegraphic message on May 24, 1844. (Morse also did a well-known painting of Niagara Falls.) Though the Indian plays are full of curses, the structural position of the chieftain as that of a better parent or substitute ancestor may have assured rather than merely intimidated white theatergoers. This is one source for the community-building function of American muckraking. The chieftains can deliver "hymns of revulsion," fire-and-brimstone addresses in which they scold audiences, but they cannot act meanly. Also, if one looks at these rituals from the romantic daughters' point of view, it is only the bad whites, the Goodenoughs and Honnymans, who are justly affected by the Indian curse, while the sentimental ones, capable of romantic love and human empathy, are vindicated in their struggle against fathers and unfeeling suitors.

One indication of this mental transformation of a curse into a blessing is the persistent folk belief which associates Indians with healing waters, blood remedies and cough syrups (Friar and Friar, *Indian* 50–51). A sculpted water fountain in Lebanon, New York, is entitled "The Indian Blessing." Candles which have been for sale in America for many years offer the Indian spirit's "strength, luck and protection." According to Emma Hardinge, nineteenth-century spiritualists found it surprising that in their séances

> the red man, whose highest earthly virtue is revenge, and who, according to the short-sighted policy of human calculations, might reasonably be expected to return in the spirit of an avenger for the intolerable wrongs his race has endured, almost invariably performs, in the modern spiritual movement, the high and blessed function of the beneficent Healer. (*Modern* 481)

The ritualistic invocation of Indian speeches or songs, curses or blessings, becomes most noteworthy where it appears somewhat out of place, as it seems to be in Maria's parlor soliloquy in *The Contrast*. Metamora's speech has a certain logic from the flow of the play; but sometimes Indian speeches are made even against the given plot. The title hero in Robert Rogers' *Ponteach* (1766) delivers a farewell speech, although he is not dying. Alexander Macomb writes in the introduction to his *Pontiac* (1826) that the whole piece is historically "true with the exception of the capture of Pontiac ... and the manner of his death" (6)—a change made just to allow the author to use a death song as the finale (60). In George Washington Custis's *Pocahontas* (1830), Matacoran declaims the standard dying-Indian speech, full of disdain, before simply rushing out and leaving the scene to John Smith, who comments: "Brave, wild, and unconquerable spirit, go whither thou wilt, the esteem of the English goes with thee" (208). Such uses indicate that the Indian curses/blessings had a ritualistic significance which exceeded plot constraints and literary plausibility. They were part of a presumptuous reconstruction of American kinship.

Fixtures

The Indian speech or song was not the only stock element in the dramas which suggests an affinity to ritual. Many of the Indian plays resemble the prefabricated houses that were shipped from Cincinnati to Texas in the 1840s. In many of the plays the focus is not on conflict but on details, not on dramatic development but on tableaux and ingredients. Speaking of *The Contrast*, Thomas Tanselle (*Tyler* 59–77) criticized the playwright's lack of faith in dramatic action. The endings of the Indian plays, too, are a given, though the blessings, curses, or national anthems develop less out of the plots than out of shared beliefs which exist prior to, and independent of, the actual plot lines. Plot development is relegated to very few scenes; melodramatic suffering substitutes for dramatic collision.

Since the stock ingredients of the Indian plays are shared by other artistic representations, we can illustrate the elements of the plays with contemporary art. The Indian chieftain, the last of his nation, is inevitably good and noble; better than any white man in the plays (most notably in *Ponteach*). He is always associated with a rock, cliff, bluff, or precipice, usually near a lake or a waterfall. The stage directions in *Metamora* are representative here: "*Metamora's stronghold: Rocks, bridge and waterfall*" (91). Carabasset is "*discovered reclining on a rock*" (176). The rock on which the Indian chieftain is customarily placed is sometimes specifically identified as a tomb (as in *Metamora*).

At other times the rock is evocative of Mount Sinai, Mount Calvary, or the Sermon on the Mount. In a passage from *Metamora* rendered in Alger's biography of Edwin Forrest (though not included in the final version of the play discovered by Moody), the rock is clearly shaped as the place for an epiphany and for ethnogenesis. Metamora says:

> I have been upon the high mountain-top when the grey mists were beneath my feet [Exodus 24:15], and the Great Spirit passed me by in wrath. He spoke in anger, and the rocks crumbled beneath the flash of his spear. Then I felt proud and smiled. The white man trembles, but Metamora is not afraid. (Alger, *Life* 1:242)

As time passed on, the use of Indian paraphernalia increased. In *Ponteach* the chief is a king, his house a palace, the Indian meeting a senate, and so forth. By the 1820s, with little alteration in the basic plot, we get war whoops, wampum, powwows, wigwams, calumets, tomahawks, moccasins, and all the other generalized ingredients which were still annotated and explained in footnotes in poetry such as Sarah Wentworth Morton's *Ouâbi* (1790) or Thomas Campbell's *Gertrude of Wyoming* (1809).

A frequently recurring plot motif is the frozen moment as the chieftain's tomahawk is raised, often over a white woman. It is at this moment that Indian nobility is most clearly demonstrated because the Indian chieftains of these plays cannot kill their potential victims. Rogers's Ponteach cannot hurt Mrs. Honnyman, the mother of a babe and the wife of a vicious Indian-killer. Deering's Carabasset is implored by Agnes to take her life but to spare her child, whereupon he "drops the tomahawk, turns from her in agony, and motions her away as the curtain falls" (184). The formulaic character of this motif is obvious in Emmons's Tecumseh, who is described as "the most towering chief that ever hatchet raised against the white man" (35). Stone's Metamora confesses to Oceana: "I cannot let the tomahawk descend upon thy head" (77).

This motif brings us back to the relationship of the American Marias and the threatening yet protective Indian benefactors who curse and bless them. Can one say that there is an original configuration of white and Indian relations which, even if it existed only in dreams and folklore, inspired the American imagination? If so, this original tale would be one of red-white fusion, of the newcomers becoming one with the continent, of gaining legitimacy through love and in defiance of the greed for gold and the ruthless politics which were sometimes logically associated with white fathers. Residual evidence of a covered-up love story is omnipresent in American folklore. From Pocahontas to the hundreds of stories—supposedly of Indian origin, but invariably products of the Euro-American imagination—which are associated with America's many lovers' leaps, Indians remain connected with love in the American imagination and, more specifically, with the imagery of chivalric courtly love of the European Middle Ages. Whether as the earth-goddess mother Pocahontas or as youthful lover who interposes on behalf of an endangered founding father; whether as noble warrior who, like a rock, is impervious to the false counsel of greedy Europeans, double-tongued Jesuits, and corrupted tribesmen or as sentimental lover ready to defy two sets of parents—the popular image of the Indian exists in a web of subdued love relationships.[9]

The version of red-white love that is most openly present is the courtly love of Indian chieftains. With the exception of Pocahontas—who is, significantly, another daughter defying her father and who, according to Philip Young, conveys to the European newcomers the sense of being chosen ("Mother" 413)—there is no dream of a red-white marriage. In many of the plays the Indians know that it is better to get wisdom than gold {Proverbs 16:16}. They adhere to a high chivalric ethos of the precapitalist era. Unlike his depraved, greedy, and lustful white male counterpart in most of the plays, the noble Indian chief would never take advantage of the heroine with whom he may occasionally be alone in the forest. (Even in twentieth-century America, Indians are rarely exploited as sexualized images for advertising or pornography—perhaps the only ethnic group in America to escape such collective fantasies.) Characteristic images of Indians from the nineteenth century to this day show a couple in front of a teepee or tent. Following the rituals of courtly love to the letter, the Indian chieftain sometimes exchanges fetishes with his courtly heroine. Metamora receives a scarf as a meaningful bandage from Oceana and gives her a plume in return as a protective talisman. The Indian noblemen live and die for valor and glory—and that is the link they openly establish with the white heroines, who are proponents of love and opponents, sometimes victims, of greed and blunt power. The heroines are in distress and suffer; and the Indians help. The women face a conflict between fathers (who are allied with old-world Chesterfieldian rakes) and lovers, which is resolved or eased by the presence, action, spirit, song, or contemplation of chivalric, noble, melancholy Indians. The chivalric Indians may die, but the heroines live happily ever after. Niklas Luhmann sharply distinguished the old chivalric ethos (to which Metamora adheres) from the newer role of the lover:

> The knights of the Middle Ages had to prove themselves by mastering dangers, by heroic deeds, by realization of the idea of knighthood. In the seventeenth century this proving begins to shift into the role of the lover itself. ... (*Liebe* 90)

The ultimate descendant, the last of his line, blesses romantic love, supports the rebellion against paternally arranged affairs and becomes a patron saint of the new way of doing things in America. Chief Tamenund becomes Saint Tammany. It has a certain cultural logic that M. R. Werner's history of Tammany Hall (1928) has an image supposedly representing "Saint Tammany" as its frontispiece that is actually the well-known engraving by Frederick S. Agate portraying Metamora (illustration 8).

Conclusion

In the first half of the nineteenth century, an American story emerged in which melancholy Indians—always "white man's Indians"—played a crucial part. As European newcomers and postrevolutionary Americans were struggling to legitimate white republicanism, they confronted indigenous Indian legitimacy. In real life this meant conflict, often bloody conflict. In the stories white Americans learned to tell, however, this conflict was transposed into lovers' leap tales and plays about noble chieftains who bless the young ones *against* their physical parents (white parents who are sometimes identified with greed and political ruthlessness in politics). As cursing-blessing elders the Indians conveyed a sense of chosen peoplehood

to the sentimental heroines and heroes as well as to the weeping readers and viewers of these fictions. As melancholy figures they
reminded white Americans of the passage of time and of the march
of empires. As Saturnine characters they seemed to promise the
return of the golden age in the new world while dreaming the power
dream that is so characteristic of melancholy. The noble chieftains
thus conveyed a sense of legitimacy to whites who imagined them:
the idealized imagery of Indians was produced at the height of the
Indian removals. Love melancholy was often connected with this
power dream of the rise of republicanism. In the love plots some
aspects can be distinguished which make sense of this surprising mixture of ethnicity and romanticism.

The heroically noble Indians were portrayed as perfect practitioners of chivalric courtly love. Metamora is the embodiment of the
ideal that was one historical source for the romantic cult of love as
the basis of marriage. The Indians also appeared as champions of the
new *principle* of romantic love without parental consent, supported
white elopers, and actively helped to resolve the white characters'
love melancholy and conflict with elders. As spirits of the lovers'
leaps and of Niagara Falls, they, though they were the only legitimate
and ancient ones, sanctioned the new (and, as we saw, Puritan-
inspired) courtship rituals which culminated in the new American
practice of socially isolated romantic honeymooning. In the world of
nineteenth-century white fantasies, it was as if the Indians had
invented the new love and whites had learned it from them.

Finally, the white-imagined Indians endorsed the right of the
young ones to choose their own spouses on the basis of love, and in
defiance of parents, who were often old-world characters. Indians
were thereby metaphorically portrayed as pseudo-ancestors, yet
nonetheless as advocates of spouses against parents, of consent
against descent, and blessed not only the new principle of marriage
based on love but also young America as the rebellious daughter of
Europe. In Metamora's fire-and-brimstone curses as well as in Menawa's blessing of George Washington, the Indian sacralized the new
form of postrevolutionary citizenship based on the doctrine of consent. "Hymns of revulsion" and "paeans of praise or devotion" may
have similar effects.

Maria Van Rough had compelling cultural reasons to sing the "Son
of Alknomook" in her distress. In the cultural framework of the
period from the War of Independence to the Civil War, the song
virtually sacralized Maria's romantic predicament. She was amply
rewarded for invoking the Son of Alknomook, the melancholy lov-

ers' Indian patron saint. In the course of the play Van Dimple's duplicity, greed, disloyalty, and inability to love are exposed even to Maria's father, and the play ends with the happy union of Maria and Manly—whose Uncle Sam-type servant and "Yankee Doodle" singer, Jonathan, contributes much to the republican cheeriness of Tyler's *Contrast*. As one specific code of consent, the theme of love remained intricately connected with the American ethnic imagination, though the sublime role of the Indian, the idealized natural settings, and the high-serious rhetoric gave way to new modes by the middle of the nineteenth century.

Interlude
From Indian to Urban

The wilderness masters the colonist. It finds him a European in dress, industries, tools, modes of travel, and thought. It takes him from the railroad car and puts him in the birch canoe. It strips off the garments of civilization and arrays him in the hunting shirt and moccasin. It puts him in the log cabin of the Cherokee and Iroquois and runs an Indian palisade around him.

—Frederick Jackson Turner

The American laugh is most impressive. Laughing is a very important expression and one learns a lot about character through careful observation of the way people laugh.

—Carl Gustav Jung

Ethnic Comedy and the Burlesque

The noble Indian became a ridiculous figure in the middle of the nineteenth century. Before we review examples of this development, some reflection on ethnicity and humor is needed. Discussions of ethnic humor are difficult for a variety of reasons. The atmosphere is no longer as piously charged as it was in the 1970s when Michael Novak publicly criticized people who had told anti-Polish jokes. Yet contemporary readers are easily offended when they look at the broad and farcical humor of the mid-nineteenth century. They assume that laughing at mock-Indian plays and Ethiopian sketches is in bad taste, and perhaps even morally bad. Yet the borderline between the funny and the offensive is difficult to draw. It is subject to historical change and personal taste, as well as dependent upon the context in which the joke is made or by whom and to whom it is told. Jokes made at our expense or at the expense of our ancestors are less funny to us than jokes made about others. The outer limit of sympathy stops us from laughing only when we encounter horrifying jokes made at the expense of physical traits of underdogs, of aspects of their fate they cannot possibly control. We are scared at our own capacity to laugh instead of empathizing with others. Laughing at others is a form of boundary construction and can be cruel, not only on an individual level. Humor may help to create serious collective boundaries, too. Anti-Armenian jokes in Turkey or anti-Jewish jokes in Nazi Germany served to support genocidal politics. We are afraid of that collective mechanism and therefore sometimes prefer to be a little pious.

However, in a polyethnic culture humor can also be a very instructive field for observation, as boundaries can be rapidly created and removed, as communities of laughter arise at the expense of some outsiders and then reshape, integrate those outsiders, and pick other targets. If we misjudge our audience, some of the jokes we considered funny in one group may be embarrassing and awkward in another.

Looked at through Fredrik Barth's eyes, jokes fulfill much the same function as slurs and nicknames: they may affirm in-group cohesion (even of newly made in-groups), or they may give us certain symbolic targets on the far side of the boundaries that go up as the jokes are told. In all cases the community of laughter itself is an ethnicizing phenomenon, as we develop a sense of we-ness in laughing with others. As Freud argued in the chapter on jokes as a social process in *Jokes and Their Relation to the Unconscious*, jokes require a social realm in which they are told and shared.

What, then, was the function and target of mid-nineteenth-century ethnic humor? Two burlesques and an "Ethiopian sketch" may help us increase our understanding of ethnicity and humor. These texts were first of all reactions to the serious works of previous years. The cult of the noble Indian—both in its sacralization of love and legitimacy and in its elevation of the vanishing chieftain's curse—had become recognizable as a "cult," a matter of chic among northeastern urban theatergoers. Exaltation lends itself to bathos. Elevation is followed by a fall.

This development was not limited to the stage; as many arts participated in creating and sustaining the high image of the noble Niagara Indian in the first half of the nineteenth century, so many genres after about 1845 took part in letting the exalted stage Indian fall down the cataract from biblical rocks and romantic cliffs into the pit of the ridiculous.

The change is clearly visible in the theater annals of the nineteenth century. When we find mentions that plays like *The Last of the Mohicans* were performed in the second half of the century, we need more information in order to ascertain whether it was a noble-Indian adaptation from Cooper or an "Ethiopian sketch"—as was one text printed in 1870. What is funny about this particular sketch is the ethnic masquerade, in which father Smith outwits his romantic son and West Point cadet, Charles, who refuses to marry Julia Brown, his father's choice, because he believes that he has fallen in love with the Indian maiden Manitoba. As it turns out, Julia has playacted the Indian maiden in order to make doubly sure that Charley will be hers. In the sketch she once again dresses up as Manitoba, Mr. Smith becomes Spotted Tail, and Charles finds out that the woman of his choice is none other than the one his father chose for him in the first place. What makes this play, which was first performed at New York's Theatre Comique in May 1870 (with the author J. C. Stewart, as Smith/chief), most interesting is the fact that all the characters are *black*, a more intricate form of ethnic transvestism, which was so characteristic of the identity shifts in minstrelsy, too. Yet the Indian theme, even in its ethnic vaudeville inversions, remained connected with the problem of the choice of a spouse. If by 1870 the heroic substance of the Indian plays was depleted, this was the result of a theatrical development of iconoclastic writing which started in the 1840s.

An Irish immigrant, John Brougham, was in the avant-garde of the demolition campaign. In his burlesques he took on Edwin Forrest's lofty renditions of *Metamora* and the love conflict of American daughters, the fetishistic exchanges and the audiences' yen for curses, as he combined the familiar plot lines from the Indian-drama tradition with the ethnic mix of urban theatergoers in a dazzling sequence of puns. In Brougham's *Metamora; or, The Last of the Pollywogs* (1847; illustration 10), the chief addresses Oceana with the following words:

> White squaw, approach! Don't tremble, for the
>   storm
> Is past, and Metamora's heart is warm.
> Here, take this tail, plucked from a mongrel rooster.
>
> OCE.
> With pleasure, savage. Tell me, pray, what use, sir?
>
> MET.
> Wear this, and wheresoever be your path,
> 'Twill save the bearer from the red man's wrath. (6)

The chivalric rituals have become at best absurd and fetishistic.

As the following, equally funny passage from his *Po-ca-hon-tas; or, The Gentle Savage* (1855; illustration 11) illustrates, Brougham

Illustration 10.   John Brougham as Metamora (Harvard Theatre Collection)

thought that the whole genre of the serious Indian play and the questions it had asked were quite ridiculous:

SMITH

I visited his majesty's abode,
A portly savage, plump, and pigeon-toed,
Like *Metamora* both in *feet* and *feature*,
I never *met-a-more-a*-musing creature!
Now without fear my love I can avow it,
And *pop* the question boldly?

POCA

My *pop* won't allow it,
I'll *bet* my life!

SMITH

My chance that *betters* still,
For being the *contrary* sex, you will!
In *fact, rare* princess, there's such *rarefaction*
Within my heart, such "*passional attraction*,"
That we must live together spite of fate,

134

Illustration 11. *Po-ca-hon-tas* (Harvard Theatre Collection)

> For all impossibilities that congregate
> Around us, my *free love* despises!
>
> POCA
> Stop! One doubt within my heart arises!
> A great historian before us stands,
> *Bancroft* himself, you know, forbids the *banns!*
>
> SMITH
> *Bancroft* be *banished* from your memory's shelf
> For spite of *fact* I'll marry you myself.
> And happiness you'll have a better *show* for
> With me, than should you wed that *low-bred-loafer!*
> ...
>
> KING
> I've found a husband you must wed tonight!
>
> POCA
> Oh! my prophetic soul, *Bancroft* was right! (18–19)

Brougham's burlesques have the markings of genius. Not only did Brougham mock the fetishism of the chivalric feather, he also let the characters defy the ultimate father, Saturn, Kronos, father time, fate—humorously cast as the American romantic historian George Bancroft! The melancholy contemplation of the fate of the Indians may have reinforced the view that their tragic disappearance was fated and inevitable, that it was beyond the reach of human action. This, incidentally, was a widespread view, shared by such diverse and often perceptive critics as Tocqueville (*Democracy* 1:342) and Georg Lukács (*Historical* 64). Brougham's burlesque plots, however, stressed the possibility of *action*, of making history against Saturnine melancholy. The audience's laughter gives Pocahontas and Smith the power to defy not only King Powhatan but also history: they can finish the story by its own logic, as many readers—including Philip Young ("Mother" 411) and Leslie Fiedler (*Return* 70)—had hoped, and do away with the Dutch-accented surrogate John Rolfe. At the end of his *Metamora*, Brougham, in the same spirit, takes on the cult of the vanishing Indian and the "Son of Alknomook":

MET.
The red man's fading out, and in his place
There comes a bigger, not a better, race.
Just as you've seen the squirming Pollywog
In course of time become a bloated frog. (*Dies*)
    (*Burlesque combat by every body; all fall and die.*)

CHORUS, "*We're all nodding.*"
We're all dying, die, die, dying,
    We're all dying just like a flock of sheep.

SOLO, METAMORA
You're all lying, lie, lie, lying,
    You're all lying; I wouldn't die so cheap.

MET. (*Rises*)
Confound your skins, I will not die to please you. (17–18)

While mocking the pathos of the romantic cult of the vanishing Indian, Brougham concretely resurrected the Indian chief (whom Brougham himself played on stage) and his wife, Tapiokee. While twentieth-century readers may misunderstand Brougham's broad humor, it actually humanized the Indian character by portraying him in a less lofty manner. Brougham's burlesques, far from poking fun at the "Indian character," made audiences laugh at the imaginary Indian they had worshiped earlier.

American audiences loved Brougham's style. *Po-ca-hon-tas*, especially, remained popular into the 1880s as "*the* standard burlesque afterpiece" to many serious plays: "In the almost thirty years of its stage life no theatrical season in any American city was complete without a few performances of 'Pokey'" (Moody, *Dramas* 401). Theater history is full of legends about Brougham, who liked to play the chieftains. He often engaged the music director in comic dialogues, once played the whole thing without the actress who was to star as

Pocahontas, and often included impromptu materials (such as local names and allusions) in his performances.

Brougham's comedy thus has to be interpreted as a satire and parody of a previously popular form. He made fun of the Metamora-language, the pseudo-courtliness, and even the landscape (*Metamora* 9). But Brougham's humor was not only retrospective. It was not an academic exercise in literary parody. He included totally anachronistic elements such as telegraphs (*Metamora* 7) and railroads—as well as the fluctuations of the Erie stock—and made comments on education for women, fashion, Tammany graft, strikes, and the use of tobacco. Brougham was very conscious of the contemporary interests of his audience, and he did not limit their laughter to a now obsolete genre.

Most excitingly, he provides us with a sense of the mixed urban audiences who could laugh alternately at Irish, at German, at Anglo-Italian, at haughty French as well as at Indian and black motifs. It is Brougham's irreverent mix of these polyethnic themes which created an American comic idiom. Brougham makes audiences laugh at the incongruities of his ethnic combinations: Tapiokee sings her lullaby:

> Hush-a-by, baby, on the tree-top;
> I've got no cradle, so thee I must rock;
> If the whites come, upon us they'll fall,
> Then down will go baby, mamma and all. (*Metamora*
> 16)

Brougham's humorous trump card was the pun, which he used without any hesitations, and often to enhance the ethnic incongruities of scenes. Pocahontas discusses Smith's situation in terms of the underground-railway escape from slavery:

> POCA.
>
> Who are you?
> Are you a *fugitive* come here to seek a railway, underground?
>
> SMITH.
>
> Not by a sight!
> Alas! I'm only an unhappy *wight*,
> Without a *shade* of *color* to excuse
> *Canadian Agents* here to chalk my shoes,
> Therefore my passage-money won't be figured,
> For on that head Philanthropy is *niggard!*
>
> (*Po-ca-hon-tas* 17)

Earlier the arriving Smith party appeared as "foreigners, just cast on Castle Garden" (8). The Englishman Smith also doubles as

"Anglo-Italian," and the chorus explains that he came to America for a reason.

> The brilliant game o,
> Man's only aim o,
> To hunt up gold. (10)

King Powhatan, often played by Brougham himself, takes the complementary ethnic role of a pipe-smoking Irishman:

> Let some folks desire,
> To set rivers on fire,
> While some others admire
> To run "wid de machine,"
> I've ambition enough,
> Just to sit here and puff,
> Oh hone! wid a dhudieen! (6-7)

John Rolfe lends himself to a Dutch (i.e., German in mid-nineteenth-century America) caricature, and he performs the yodeling song "With Tyrolean Fixins."

> Like the Tyrolese singers, so gallant and gay,
> I'll sing you a song in the Tyrolese way,
> Fol de dol, de dol lay—it's a very fine day,
> It doesn't much matter—you know what I say. ...
> [Here follows an exhibition of tracheotomous gymnastics, which must be heard to be properly appreciated.]
>
> I wish from mein soul all de rocks round about
> Would to *sausages* turn, and the trees to *sourcrout*.
> The ocean's vast bowl into *lager bier* roll
> And I was an earthquake to swallow the whole.
>
> [More vocal gymnastics]
> And then for mein pipe I'd *Vesuvius* fill full
> Of *kanaster* and through a *pine tree* take a pull
> And after that, p'raps, for fear of mishaps,
> I'd toss down *Niagara Falls* for mein *schnapps*. (23-24)

In burlesque theaters with mixed urban audiences such lines must have created certain communities of laughter and built very flexible and constantly shifting boundaries. For what is interesting about Brougham's polyethnic universe is that the barbs are not directed against only one group—each group gets its turn. The aesthetic ground of the old fixtures of romantic love, arranged marriage, Indian melancholy, and Niagara sublime gave way to a new genre (burlesque) and a new outlook.

The urbanization of noble-Indian materials took place in many art forms of mid-nineteenth-century America. A watercolor of Brough-am's ludicrous performance as Powhatan from the 1850s has some affinities with the cartoon entitled "A Histrionic Savage" from *Harper's Weekly Supplement* of July 29, 1876 (illustration 12), which shows a ranting Forrest-Metamora strutting in front of the footlights and thus satirizes the cult of the Indian curse as a ritual desired as much by modern urban theatergoers as the fire-and-brimstone jeremiads were wanted by churchgoers in former times.

Not even folklore was sacred in the hands of artists who deflated the noble Indian in the second half of the nineteenth century. At a time when folklorists were just beginning to collect and catalog the many serious (though, we ought to remember, generally white-American-made) lovers' leap stories in America, Mark Twain retold the Oolaita story with a devastating new turn. In chapter 59 of *Life on the Mississippi* (1883), Mark Twain returned to the classic scene, connecting the Indian with healing waters and the sublime Maiden's Rock near Lake Pepin on the Mississippi. This is the story he "heard" about that place:

Illustration 12.   (Harvard Theatre Collection)

"Not many years ago this locality was a favorite resort for the Sioux Indians on account of the fine fishing and hunting to be had there, and large numbers of them were always to be found in this locality. Among the families which used to resort here was one belonging to the tribe of Wabasha. We-no-na (firstborn) was the name of a maiden who had plighted her troth to a lover belonging to the same band. But her stern parents had promised her hand to another, a famous warrior, and insisted on her wedding him. The day was fixed by her parents, to her great grief. She appeared to accede to the proposal and accompanied them to the rock, for the purpose of gathering flowers for the feast. On reaching the rock, We-no-na ran to its sum- mit, and, standing on its edge, upbraided her parents who were below, for their cruelty, and then, singing a death-dirge, threw herself from the precipice and dashed them in pieces on the rock below."
"Dashed who in pieces—her parents?"
"Yes."
"Well, it certainly was a tragic business, as you say. And moreover, there is a startling kind of dramatic surprise about it which I was not looking for. It is a distinct improvement upon the threadbare form of Indian legend. There are fifty Lover's Leaps along the Mississippi from whose summit disappointed Indian girls have jumped, but this is the only jump in the lot that turned out in the right and satisfac- tory way. What became of Winona?"
"She was a good deal jarred up and jolted; but she got herself together and disappeared before the coroner reached the fatal spot; and 'tis said she sought and married her true love, and wandered with him to some distant clime, where she lived happy ever after, her gentle spirit mellowed and chastened by the romantic incident which had so early deprived her of the sweet guidance of a mother's love and a father's protecting arm, and thrown her, all unfriended, upon the cold charity of a censorious world." (278)

Mark Twain brilliantly takes us to the edge of our idealized story expectation and then drops us with the heroine on the target of all the lovers' leap stories: on the bad parents who have arranged their daughter's marriage against her will. In his switch from ideal to "low" language, Mark Twain parallels the drop from Maiden's Rock, so that lofty romance and everyday life remain unreconciled through the end of this episode. We know, however, that we shall never trust the language of "romantic incidents" in the same way again. After we have seen John Brougham and read Mark Twain, lovers' leaps cannot possibly be what they used to be.

After the comic use of the sublime theme in cartoons, plays, and stories, the conjunction of romantic love, arranged marriage, and Indian melancholy was weakened. Yet the conflict between consent

and descent that was embodied in it continued even into the mock-
eries of Stewart, Brougham, and Mark Twain. The generational
antagonisms that were expressed even in comic plots, and the Indian-
ization of ancestor figures in the melting-pot-Pocahontas tradition,
continued to be of importance in American culture. In Brougham's
Metamora, Oceana "interposes" and surprisingly pleads for her dad's
life while offering Walter in turn (6). In *Po-ca-hon-tas* the Indian college woman Poo-Tee-Pet argues with Powhatan for her "Anti-marry-
folks-against-their-will Society."

> *King.* Why come you here!—as sorrowful spectators?
> *Poo-tee-pet.* No! on the contrary, we're *very glad*iators!
> For Freedom every heart with ardor glows,
> On Woman's Rights we're *bent*, and *bent* our bows!
> Your daughter dear, must marry whom she may,
> Daughters you know, should *always* have their *way*. (30)

The mix of Indian and immigrant lore, too, had a long afterlife in
the nineteenth and twentieth centuries. Recently, a vaudeville play
from the Yiddish stage of 1895, H. I. Minikes' *Tsvishn indianer*
(Among the Indians), was published by Mark Slobin in English
translation. Perhaps the most profoundly satirical and iconoclastic
cultural statement against fixed views of blacks and Indians can be
found in Mel Brooks's movie *Blazing Saddles* (1974). Brooks's black
railroad workers are sophisticated urbanites who claim not to know
the Stephen Foster song "Camptown Races" or any Negro Spirituals.
When pressed by the white overseers to sing, they present a smoothly
harmonized version of Cole Porter's "I Get a Kick out of You." The
Indian chieftain, played by Brooks himself, is quite unaristocratic,
speaks Yiddish, and releases black captives with the nonchalance of
a Brooklynite. By going back to John Brougham's burlesque mix of
Indian, black, and immigrant lore and to the Indian motifs from the
Yiddish stage, Brooks inverted and exploded some fixtures of perception. In our era of broad ethnic comedy, ranging from Mel Brooks
and Eddie Murphy to Richard Pryor, Madeline Kahn, and Joan Rivers, we may approach the equally broad nineteenth-century ethnic
burlesque without ethnic pieties.

The Tradition of the Mysteries

Carl Gustav Jung once invited his readers to compare "the skyline
of New York or any other great American city with that of a pueblo

like Taos" ("Your Negroid" 199). According to Jung, America Indianizes the children of newcomers since a foreign country somehow "gets under the skin of those born in it" (197). Yet the trails from Indian to urban themes in American culture have not often been traced. In addition to the growth of the urban burlesque, there was another path from Indian to urban in mid-nineteenth-century American culture. One origin of what is sometimes called urban realism was in the imaginary forests of Metamora.

Immigrant writers were generally fascinated by Indian themes— which Europeans sometimes regarded as the true America. In *Jews without Money* (1930) Michael Gold described youth gangs on Manhattan's Lower East Side in Indian terms; when the Jewish narrator is surrounded by Italian boys who are "whooping like Indians" and who call him "Christ-killer," he views the territory of Hester and Mulberry streets as the Wild West and soon yearns for a "Messiah who would look like Buffalo Bill" (134, 136). In Rølvaag's *Giants in the Earth*, the Norwegian settlers often think about the Indians who must have been on their land before; when the brooding Beret Hansa encounters land stakes of Irish settlers, she thinks that the names "Joe Gill" and "O'Hara" must be Indian (119). Abraham Cahan's *Yekl* (1896) depicts the protagonist's wife Gitl as a "squaw" (34).

Immigrants and travelers to America were fascinated by the imaginative possibilities of the ethnic variety of America; at a time when many native-born American authors ritualistically complained about the uniformity and homogeneity of American life that militated against good fiction, European visitors and dreamers adopted and imitated American Indian themes. Among Cooper's German admirers were Karl Postl (Charles Sealsfield), the author of many Indian novels, among them *Der Legitime und die Republikaner* (1833), Friedrich Gerstäcker, and Hans Balduin Möllhausen, whose voluminous novels and travel books earned him the epithet "the German Cooper." In France, Crèvecoeur and Chateaubriand had written up Indian, black, and ethnic scenes well before Cooper; and it was the immensely popular work by one of Cooper's French admirers that somewhat circuitously contributed to the gradual growth of realism in the portraiture of urban ethnicity when it became popular in America.

The book was Eugène Sue's serialized novel *Les Mystères de Paris*, which started to appear in French in 1842. Some 80,000 copies of the English translation were sold in New York within a few months after publication. Ten German translations were in existence by 1844, two of them published in America. Sue's work, which has been made the subject of analyses by diverse critics from Marx and Engels to Umberto Eco, helped to create the image of the city as a "swarming mass of signals, dense, obscure, undecipherable" (Trachtenberg, "Experiments" 265). The book functioned as a tour guide to slummers who were ready for the descent, for the initiation into the underworld—in the age of beginning tourism. Sue openly acknowledged his debt to Cooper; at the beginning of the first edition of his *Mysteries*, he promised his readers nothing but an urban sequel to the *Leather-Stocking Tales*. Instead of Cooper's Indians, Sue said, he was presenting "other barbarians, as far removed from civilization as the savage people so well described by Cooper; only the barbarians of whom we speak live among us, and around us; we can elbow them, if we venture into the dens where they assemble." Sue was referring to the Parisian underworld of crime, poverty, and prostitution; where his French would-be "Apaches" (as they were later called) have "their own customs, women, and language: a mysterious language crowded with wretched imagery and disgusting metaphors of blood" (*Mysteries* 1). Sue took great care in delineating a setting of poverty and misery while agitating for penal reform. His works, which became increasingly concerned with urgent social questions, were immensely popular, because they satisfied the needs both for Indian romance in the forest—the Cooper legacy—and for reformist urban realism. Interestingly, the socialist Daniel De Leon was one of Sue's American translators.

Sue was not merely translated; he was widely copied and adapted to the the mysteries of London, Berlin, Rome, Vienna, and Brussels as well as to many American urban settings. George Lippard's *The Quaker City; or, The Monks of Monk Hall* (1844) transposed the picturesque argot of Sue's Parisians into the ethnic accents of Philadelphians. Translated by Friedrich Gerstäcker in 1846 as *Die Quäkerstadt und ihre Geheimnisse*, Lippard's book enjoyed a German readership on both sides of the Atlantic. Transatlantic crossings were no problem for books of the Sue school. F. Thiele's *The Mysteries of Berlin from the Papers of a Berlin Criminal Officer* appeared in an English translation by C. B. Burckhardt in New York in 1845. Rudolf Lexow published his *Amerikanische Criminal-Mysterien; oder, Das Leben der Verbrecher in New-York* simultaneously in Stuttgart and New York in 1854. An anonymous German-American novel, *Die Geheimnisse von Philadelphia*, came out in 1850. Heinrich Börnstein's *Die Geheimnisse von St. Louis* appeared in 1851. The fad was long-lived in many languages (Edler, *Sue* 49–54). One of the first Italian-American novelists, Bernardino Ciambelli, published such works as *I misteri di Mulberry*

(1893), *I misteri di Bleecker Street* (1899), and *I sotterranei di New York* (1915); a Swedish translation of a book by Burton E. Stevenson, *NewYork-Mysterier*, appeared in 1908. Dion Boucicault tapped the Sue craze for drama; his play *The Poor of New York* (1857), derived from a French drama of the Sue school, was adapted by the author to tenement settings of many different cities, and the title was changed, for example, to *The Streets of Philadelphia*. Harriet Beecher Stowe's *Uncle Tom's Cabin* (1852), with its subtitle *Life among the Lowly*, also follows Sue's strategy of initiating the reader into a hidden world. In the chapter entitled "An Evening in Uncle Tom's Cabin," the narrator openly invites the audience: "Let us enter the dwelling" (1:38). The novel also provides us with panoramic views and a general orientation to the underworld of slavery in America.

Emil Klauprecht's Urban Mysteries

The study of these *Mysteries* provides a true initiation into a popular form which gave expression to urban ethnicity of mid-nineteenth-century America, as a somewhat closer look at a representative example, Emil Klauprecht's *Cincinnati; oder, Geheimnisse des Westens* (1854–55), can demonstrate. It is an immigrant text in an immigrant language and therefore also of special interest in a country where, as DeWitt Clinton said, the English language had torn down the ethnic partition walls between men. Was it weak loyalty to languages other than English that accounted for the power of the myth of America which was conveyed in the English language?

In his "Vorwort" Klauprecht directly attacks the Cooper/Sealsfield school of so-called "Indian" writers who "rarely or never exchanged their blanket in a log cabin or a wigwam for the comfortable rest in an urban hotel." Klauprecht, however, squarely declares himself a *city* writer, and though the American urban grids may cause his painters to despair, they provide a kaleidoscopic vision to the writer who sees his purpose in alerting novelists to this new subject matter.

Sue offered Klauprecht a model for looking at Cincinnati in a way which might engage his readers as slumming tourists to an underworld, as neophytes ready to face secrets unveiled. As in Sue, there is plenty of "romance" in the plots and subplots: a romantic Indian tale of the Pocahontas-like Oneida (despite Klauprecht's attack on Sealsfield and Cooper!); a brief version of Rip Van Winkle (2:110); a story of a white baby and a mulatto baby who were switched; and a worldwide Jesuit conspiracy endangering Cincinnati. Published two years after his fellow Cincinnatian Harriet Beecher Stowe's *Uncle Tom's Cabin*, Klauprecht's novel also includes a New Orleans slave auction and an iced-over-river scene (1:88; 3:127). Appealing to Klauprecht's pervasive and palpable sense of what's new, the contemporary forms of Sue and his successors provided the journalist Klauprecht with a framework for the materials that were at his fingertips at the news desk. Klauprecht used a contemporary form and seemed fascinated by modern subject matter, from prefabricated houses to the telegraph, from the various forms of gaslight to the fastest steamboats and trains. There is a hectic note of sensationalism in the book; and there is much ethnicity.

Some elements in Klauprecht's book separate him from Sue and are connected to the book's peculiarly ethnic position. Published in German, but only in America, it is itself a cultural hybrid, a product of the Cincinnati melting pot that Klauprecht so delights in describing. In the best ethnic tradition, the book is all mixed up. For purists it is, linguistically, as Klauprecht would say, "ein Insult" (1:102)— which makes it an ethnic scholar's delight. The message of his "Jailvogel," "Neuigkeitsitem," "Framehaus," or "fashionable Kleidung," of his careful annotations to such terms as "picanniny," "fisticuffs," or "over the Rhine," or of his "Kettengang" (chaingang), "smartheit," "Businessmann," "Stupidität," "Quadronen," and "Rawinen"—the message of his hodgepodge of expressions seems to be to relax immigrants, to tell them in their own language that this is not Germany anymore, that they are being Americanized, even as they are reading a German-language book which addresses them as immigrants.

To be sure, there are allusions to Jean Paul, Goethe, and Schiller. As one quite funny scene furthermore illustrates, at Cincinnati concerts Beethoven's pearls are thrown before pork aristocrats (they wake up only when the German artist Johanna Steigerwald switches over to play "Yankee Doodle" {3:60–63}). And yet, the book is not very nostalgic for the old world. A *Spaziergang* (stroll) on the Forresthuegel (tellingly named for *Metamora*-actor Edwin Forrest, who won the hill gambling and who was to entertain Cincinnatians at Franconi's Hippodrome, on the site of a former cemetery), enjoying the beautiful panoramic views, having a taste of the good Catawba wine—that is making the best of two worlds (3:169). Loyalty to Germany was last expressed by immigrants who fought in the Schleswig-Holstein conflict against Denmark—but this is contentless structural ethnic loyalty and can be shared by the all-American hero Washington Filson, who also joined the German side while studying in Germany. Germanness here becomes the behavioral abstraction "fighting

Danes" or "fighting for the right cause" and resembles an American involvement in abolition (as espoused by Constanze in the novel {1:77}). Klauprecht's book is not backward looking; it describes ethnic behavior as such—some of the Germans in Cincinnati were acting as if they still lived in the old world, and that was inappropriate and even dangerous in Cincinnati. (It is perhaps functional, then, that the old chestnut of the Roman center of a Jesuit conspiracy is the ultimate old-world evil in a book full of new-world villains.) Unlike the author Klauprecht, who returned to Europe after the Civil War, the German immigrants in his novel do not leave America for good.

What can immigrants learn about ethnicity from Klauprecht? German-Americans are not Irish, not black, not *big business*. They are, in fact, antithetically related to business as artists are to practical men, as the cultured to the moneyed—an antithesis which they share with the Creoles (who, unlike American farmers, decorate their houses not with "Currier's gaudily colored 5 cent lithographs ... but with copper engravings of famous masters" {1:43}). Deep down there is a harmony, perhaps even an identity, between the German and the American ideal, but here and now there are conflicts. These conflicts are brought about by external hostility and boundary-construction-by-slur ("damn the Dutch," or "Sauerkrauts"), but also by inappropriate conduct.

It is for this purpose that Klauprecht creates a German-American immigrant family, the Steigerwalds, who (reminiscent of Cooper's loyalist-revolutionary Wharton family in *The Spy*) experience the tensions of consent and descent in a symbolic fashion. There is Guenther Steigerwald, the patriarch—independent, widowed, towering—who left Schleswig when the cause was lost against Denmark. He has three children: the unhappy weakling, Carl, who is married to the German-hating pork-aristocracy daughter Ellen (née Stevens); the steadfast Wilhelm, who is an artist and highly critical of America and who finally marries the sensitive Constanze Gonzales; and the musical Johanna, who is mysteriously torn between Washington Filson—the clear hero, on whose reputation unjust aspersions have been cast but who is favored by Wilhelm—and John Stevens, Ellen's murderously ruthless but deceptive brother.

It is at first tempting to read Carl as "consent" ("ein perfekter Yankee") and Wilhelm as German "descent," and to see Johanna torn between the two (see 1:26; 2:28, 60–61). To be sure, henpecked Carl shows the false, wide, and fast road to marital assimilation. Yet both his siblings also wed Americans at the end of the novel, which is quite exceptional in the context of American ethnic writing. Johanna and Wilhelm marry Americans, however, who have proved their worthiness and loyalty in the unrelated causes of Denmark, abolition, art, and a critical attitude toward inheritance and hereditary privilege. And even the German patriarch becomes a Jeffersonian yeoman-pioneer at the end of the novel and affirms American ideals by going west.

The muckraking tone, too, is a result of the author's Americanization, and it has an equally Americanizing effect on the audience. Through social criticism newcomers get ethnicized and Americanized at the same time. This is most readily apparent when we ask what Klauprecht's political position was in the novel. There is a context of European literature, but no European-sounding criticism of manifest destiny. There is a lot of muck, but little social program. Condoyannis has noted that Klauprecht did not share Sue's interest in concrete reform plans ("German" 26); but what Klauprecht clearly advocates is "lighting out for the territory," migration instead of pervasive social reform. At the end of the novel the three good couples (the third consists of Isabelle and Alphons Gonzales, Constanze's brother) and the old German paterfamilias and Bertel Thorvaldsen look-alike (an ironic resemblance, given Steigerwald's anti-Danish sentiment) go west, into the redemptive countryside, and leave the Sodom of the porkopolis Cincinnati behind. Filson explicitly rejects his legal title to the land of all of Cincinnati; though he was earlier cast, in a scene on top of Mt. Adams, as the living symbol of the new Cincinnati, he leaves the city gladly and without any hesitation. He now symbolically fulfills the pioneer spirit, his inheritance, by tearing up the letter that contains the legal title and deed (3:164). With this renewed exodus America can start afresh. Since all of this takes place in a novel written in German, we may generalize that you don't have to speak English in order to be a mythic American.

It is not just the Cincinnati suburbs that Klauprecht's heroes and heroines choose; rather, the fertile farmland near Davenport, Iowa, will be the new wilderness in which they will be neighbors and raise cattle (or will help Quincy Davenport's father from The Melting-Pot amass his fortune in corn). As they leave, Klauprecht, like Lot's wife, dares to look back upon Cincinnati, where the mass murderers and businessmen Stevens and Harris are released from jail and are thriving in their various and doubtless nefarious enterprises, while Carl Steigerwald is suffering amid his German-hating family. Cincinnati has become a second old world, presumably even worse than Denmark. The real America, however, lies farther west, in the Bieder-meier pastoral of the little houses on the Iowa prairie.

Klauprecht's concern for Cincinnati's underside, his interest in ethnic types, realistic details, slumming, and muckraking, and his lik-ing for vignettes, clichés, and pathos are not isolated manifestations in nineteenth-century fiction. Klauprecht shares with the later real-ists an eye for precise details and a documentary interest; an urban orientation, focusing on rapid historical changes and modern indus-trial life; a concern with analytical classifications and generalizations; an explicit opposition to embellished form and an incorporation of unpolished journalistic sketches into fiction; and the tone of muckraking.

American "mysteries" in English and immigrant languages provide a fruitful entry into the literature of consent and descent. What emerged in America from Sue's interest in Cooper's Indians was the formal creation of a popular literature which took the path that later realist authors were to follow. This is most apparent in the so-called local-color writers, who were loosely grouped around William Dean Howells and who wrote tales of consent and descent about "their" various regional and ethnic groups. These tales, which further develop the themes of ethnicity and love, sometimes support, and sometimes even expand, current ethnic theorizing.

CHAPTER FIVE

Some Tales of Consent
and Descent

... of course we learned about Love, a very foreign country like maybe
China or Connecticut. It was smooth and slinky, it shone and rustled. It
was petals with Lillian Gish, gay flags with Marion Davies, tiger stripes with
Rudolph Valentino, dog's eyes with Charlie Ray. From what I could see,
and I searched, there was no Love on the block, nor even its fairy-tale end,
Marriage.
— Kate Simon, *Bronx Primitive* (1982)

Mailer finally came to decide that his love for his wife while not at all equal
or congruent to his love for America was damnably parallel.
— Norman Mailer, *The Armies of the Night* (1968)

How do Americans perceive, feel, and conceptualize the harmony or
conflict between ethnic and national loyalties? The correlation of
various excerpts from recent anthropological theories with a few
texts and literary works of different ethnic origins may throw some
light on this question and illustrate how stories support theories and
how theory, too, functions as a form of story-telling. Contemporary
anthropologists have theorized about American kinship and ethnicity; yet late-nineteenth-century writers from Boyesen to Chesnutt
and Cahan provided us with fleshed-out stories long before these
theories were published.

In "Sexuality as Symbolic Form: Performance and Anxiety in
America," David Kemnitzer investigates the cultural construction of
"mediate identities," according to which

one does not exist solely as an individual and as a citizen or a member of a species; the gap between the two is filled by other group
memberships of a particular sort: families, ethnic groups, and so on,
to which one is recruited "by birth" (which is *by blood*: a sharing of
substance, of being between people), and voluntary organizations of

149

which one is a member because of the kind of person one is. . . . (Dolgin, *Symbolic* 301)

This is analogous to David Schneider's distinction between "relationship as natural substance" and "relationship as code for conduct"
(Dolgin 65–66). Schneider's influential work *American Kinship* (1968)
has strongly emphasized the sharp polarization that is made in this
country between "the order of law" and "the order of nature" (29).
As a result, the definition of "relatives" is complicated and varies:

> Relatives by blood are linked by *material* substance; husband and
> wife are linked by *law*. Relatives by blood are related in an entirely
> *objective* way; husband and wife are linked *subjectively*. Blood is a *per-
> manent* tie; marriage can be *terminated*. . . . [B]lood relationships are
> involuntary because a man cannot choose who his blood relatives
> will be. He is born with them and they become his by birth. . . . But
> marriage is not only an institution invented by man; it is an active
> step which a particular person must take. It is a step which is *taken*
> and does not just happen. (Schneider 37–38)

Schneider makes many other differentiations along these lines and
describes the cultural assumptions according to which involuntary
descent relations are associated with blood and material substance,
whereas consent relations are considered as a "matter of volition" and
are symbolized by marital sexual intercourse (38).

Consent and Volitional Allegiance

Schneider's useful distinctions can be pushed even further and
applied to the relationship between American and ethnic identities,
a relationship which is so often expressed in kinship metaphors in
American texts. As James Kettner has shown in *The Development of
American Citizenship, 1608–1870* (1978), the concept of a new American citizenship emerged in the American Revolution and was based
on the "idea of volitional allegiance" (173–209). For instance, Peter
Van Schaack first theorized in the confusing conflicts of loyalties of
1775–76 that

> *every individual* has still a right to choose the State of which he will
> become a member . . . and . . . the subjection of any one to the polit-
> ical power of a State, can arise only from "his own consent." (Kettner
> 189)

According to Kettner this "doctrine of consent" marked the direction in which dominant legal thinking moved. As it was increasingly

assumed that the "Revolution had created a 'state of nature'" (197), it only followed that citizenship "in the new republics was to begin with individual consent" (194). Since republican citizenship was thus based on volitional allegiance, it may symbolically have functioned as a "relationship as code for conduct" in Schneider's sense. American identity alone may take the place of a relationship "in law" (like "husband, wife, step-, -in-law, etc."), leaving ethnicity to fill the place of relationships "in nature" ("the natural child, the illegitimate child, the natural mother, etc.") and "by blood" ("father, mother, brother, sister, uncle, aunt, etc."). In American social symbolism ethnicity may function as a construct evocative of blood, nature, and descent, whereas national identity may be relegated to the order of law, conduct, and consent.

Writers and theorists participate in the delineation of a conflict between contractual and hereditary, self-made and ancestral, definitions of American identity. Against the background of the clash between consent and descent, one leitmotif among ethnicity advocates since Horace Kallen makes sense. The reminder that "you can't change your grandfather," which is central to ethnic rhetoric, present and past, comes as a clear antithesis in Kallen's famous formulation in the essay "Democracy *versus* the Melting Pot" (1916): "Men can change their clothes, their politics, their wives, their religions, their philosophies, to a greater or lesser extent: they cannot change their grandfathers" (122). "Grandfathers" are imagined as "blood"; "wives" are viewed as "law." Kallen elaborated this distinction in *The Structure of Lasting Peace* (1918):

> The citizen of America may become one of England, the Baptist a Methodist, the lawyer a banker, the Elk a Mason, the Republican a Socialist, the capitalist a proletarian. But the son, father, uncle, cousin cannot cease to be these; he cannot reject the relationships these words express, nor alter them. ... Natural groups, like the Irish, the Jews, or any nationality, cannot be destroyed without destroying their members. Artificial groups, like states, churches, professions, castes, can. These are social organizations; natural groups are social organisms. ... (31)

The opposition between the artificial and the organic, between the organization of one's choice and the organism of one's essence, is clear. In America we may *feel* "filiopietism," but we pledge "allegiance" to the country. To say it plainly, American identity is often imagined as volitional consent, as love and marriage, ethnicity as seemingly immutable ancestry and descent.

Wives of Youth: Mothers and Brides

This family symbolism used by Americans to distinguish a "wedded" national from an "innate" ethnic identity is so pervasive as to be both a "logical" aspect of the culture and invisible as a problem to culture critics. The parent-spouse contrast is analogous to the tension between genetics of salvation and universal regeneration; it represents another version of the conflict between parental arrangement and autonomous choice on the basis of romantic love.

John Winthrop's emphasis in his "Modell of Christian Charity" (1630) was, after all, on the ligaments of love which were to knit the members of the Massachusetts Bay Company together into one sacred body. In Cotton Mather's "Life of John Eliot" (1702), a rhetorical drama was constructed between Eliot's native England and his adoptive homeland, New England. Mather calls the Atlantic a "River of *Lethe*" which "may easily cause us to forget many of the things that happened on the other side" (Miller, *Puritans* 497). Appropriately, Mather gives his readers neither the date nor the place of Eliot's "*Nativity*" but informs them instead that Eliot "came to *New-England* in the Month of *November*, A.D. 1631" and argues:

> But whatever *Places* may challenge a share in the Reputation of having enjoy'd the *first Breath* of our *Eliot*, it is *New-England* that with most Right can call him *Hers*; his *best Breath*, and afterwards his *last Breath* was here; and here 'twas, that God bestow'd upon him *Sons and Daughters*. (497)

The disruption of identification by "nativity" goes along with a redefinition by date of arrival in America and by new-world descendants. The sharp contrast embodied by that transformation is mellowed by Mather's emphasis on Eliot's American marriage to an Englishwoman he had left behind, and to his successful family government. "This *Wife of His Youth* {Proverbs 5:18} lived with him until she became to him also the *Staff of his Age*" (497). Mather resolved the drama between past and future in the figure of a virtuous wife who bridges the two and thus helps Eliot to fulfill his typological mission as the American evangelist to the Indians. The drama continued in the writings of later authors, though it was often more sharply polarized than in Mather's "Life of John Eliot."

In a characteristic combination of naturalization and marriage imagery, for example, Frances Wright, an Americanized Englishwoman of the 1820s, declared in a phrasing reminiscent of Mather's:

For what is it to be an American? Is it to have drawn the first breath in Maine, in Pennsylvania, in Florida, or in Missouri? Pshaw! ... Hence with such paltry, pettifogging ... calculations of nativities! *They* are Americans who, having complied with the constitutional regulations of the United States ... wed the principles of America's Declaration to their hearts and render the duties of American citizens practically in their lives. (Mann, *One* 83)

Citizenship by descent ("nativities") is seen as a legalistic calculation, but citizenship by consent ("wed") is consecrated here as an inspiring code for practical conduct.

In *The Divided Heart* Dorothy Burton Skårdal quoted a Danish-American poem of 1895 which "praised America as beloved in immigrant hearts because 'you never demand that we forget or despise our old mother!'" (295). On the other hand, writers like Mary Antin have stressed the chasm between ethnic children and their parents. As Thomas Ferraro has argued, *Hunger of Memory: The Education of Richard Rodriguez* (1982) is a recent example of this tradition; Rodriguez echoes Antin when he testifies that his parents are "no longer my parents, in a cultural sense" (4). In another Danish-American example of the same period, Jacob Riis reflected on his dual identity in his autobiography, *The Making of an American* (1901): "Alas! I am afraid that thirty years in the land of my children's birth have left me as much of a Dane as ever. I no sooner climb the castle hill than I am fighting tooth and nail the hereditary foe of my people whom it was built high to bar" (7). Riis defines Danishness negatively and structurally as opposition to Germans (in a way which complements old Steigerwald's definition of Germanness, in Klauprecht's *Cincinnati* novel, as the defying of Danes). In order to make his situation more vividly imaginable to his American readers, however, Riis continues with a "story":

> Yet, would you have it otherwise? What sort of a husband is the man going to make who begins by pitching his old mother out of the door to make room for his wife? And what sort of a wife would she be to ask or to stand it? (7–8)

Pastor Mac H. Wallace, in an interdenominational Thanksgiving service at Detroit in 1914, invoked the classic expression of an immigrant in order to revitalize the national feeling called for by the occasion. While Wallace, in *A New Emphasis on Some Old American Affirmations*, called "the devotion to the lands of our birth ... beautiful and right," he also felt "moved to inquire if we are really a people here or only a mixed multitude {Exodus 12:38, Nehemia 13:3} of

Europeans abiding on American soil." The pastor of the Brewster Congregational Church was hopeful, however, and answered his Tocquevillean question with the following story:

> One of our Swedish fellow citizens recently was speaking with feel-ings of deep affection for his native country; and concluding he exclaimed, "Sweden is my mother; but America is my bride." He spoke for millions of loyal Americans of foreign descent. Wherever they may have been mothered, America is their bride. If this is not our country, we have no country; it is here that we earn our liveli-hood; it is here that we rear our children; it is here that we are pro-tected in our rights; and it is here that we owe a citizen's duty. If our children ever have a fatherland it will be America; if they ever have patriotic songs of their own to sing they will be "My Country 'tis of Thee" and "Michigan, My Michigan." (New Emphasis, 4)

Wallace's argument outlines the familiar switch from inherited to achieved identity, from being "mothered" to owing a "citizen's duty." The casting of Sweden as a mother makes siblings out of all Swedish-Americans, which is one basic feature of the rhetoric of ethnic broth-erhood. By including the children in his story, Wallace also natural-izes the choice for the "bride" instead of the "mother." With this emphasis on the American-born offspring, the conflict between an old-world and a new-world identity does not appear as one of descent versus consent, but as past ancestry versus future descendants, as par-ents versus children. In Schneider's terms, Wallace allied relations "in nature" and "in law" to outweigh relations "by blood." This strategy was already used in Mather's "Life of John Eliot." It is also precisely what John Quincy Adams appealed to when he informed German immigrants that they must "look forward to their posterity rather than backward to their ancestors" (Rischin, Immigration, 47); and it is at the center of David Quixano's faith in the "God of our children."

Seeking a harmonious relationship between descent and consent, Horace Bridges summarized the reasons that prompted him to leave England and accept citizenship in America:

> America is more generous to me, in regard to all my immediate inter-ests and duties, than was my native land. It is no ingratitude to England that makes me say this. I have always loved her, and I always shall; for, though a man must needs forsake father and mother that he may cleave to his wife [Matthew 19:4-6], it does not follow that he need cease to love his parents or to look back with gratitude to them. (On Becoming 17)

In Bridges's biblical language the family image is rendered as an eter-nal rule, independent of his immigration; he thus tries to harmonize the "interests and duties" of consent with a continued metaphoric definition by descent from his "native land."

"Bluish-American Writing?"

How do kinship theories and metaphoric expressions of experience work in imaginative literature? Can literature help us develop them further? Some tales from the end of the nineteenth century are especially rich for this purpose. Though these stories come from the sphere of influence of William Dean Howells, they are rarely read and never compared with each other. As a result most previous interpretations appeared in separate publications on Scandinavian-American, Jewish-American, and Afro-American writing.

In Hjalmar Hjorth Boyesen's story "A Good-for-Nothing" (1875), the Norwegian-born Ralph Grim, a gentleman, falls in love with the peasant girl Bertha, who tells Ralph that he must do "one manly deed" to prove his independence from the "life of idleness and vanity" which the old-world class structure had provided for him. A student prankster, Ralph propositions six ladies, all of whom accept him as a prospective bridegroom, too; in the ensuing scandal, Ralph emigrates to America, convinced that the new world will provide the opportunity for the manly deed that will prove him worthy of Bertha (a telling name). In America, however, he soon associates with "high-minded and refined women" (*Tales* 163); and when he returns to Norway, intending to marry Bertha, they discover that they have grown too far apart and that "the gulf which separates the New World from the Old ... cannot be bridged" (177). Interestingly, it is Bertha's complexion which signals to Ralph his alienation from the past. While her face reminds him of "those pale, sweet-faced saints of Fra Angelico, ... her forefinger was rough from sewing, and ... the whiteness of her arm ... contrasted strongly with the browned and sun-burned complexion of her hands" (171).

If Boyesen's statement "Howells Americanized me" is typical of American ethnic writers in the late nineteenth century, it is interesting to note that Boyesen often associated the old world with romance and the new world with realism. In "A Good-for-Nothing" Ralph Grim's American inclinations are foreshadowed by the reading of *Robinson Crusoe* (*Tales* 131), whereas *Ivanhoe* represents the more typical old-world fare. Similarly, Mary Antin wrote during her exodus across the Atlantic, "Robinson Crusoe was very real to me" (*Promised* 179); and S. S. McClure specifically mentions that shortly after arriving in America, he first read *Robinson Crusoe* (*Autobiography* 37). Boy-esen's story also parallels Kallen's description of the pioneer as "a col-lective Robinson Crusoe without the literary providence of his author's amenities" (*Culture* 214). Most interestingly, it associates the gulf between old and new world with a man's choice between books (Glasrud, 3, 26), just as Tyler's "contrast" was one between reading Chesterfield or "Son of Alknomook."

A black and a Jewish writer continued the Norwegian-American's rudimentary opposition of "Bertha," a dark-hued reminder of an eth-nic past, with the refined bright women of America. Charles Ches-nutt's "The Wife of His Youth" (1898) and Abraham Cahan's *Yekl: A Tale of the Ghetto* (1896) are parallel attempts at understanding the complicated symbolizations of consent and descent in America. There are such striking similarities between these stories, despite dif-ferences in style, ethos, and literary statement, that one can give a composite plot summary.

In both tales a male protagonist has been transformed from a pre-vious condition of old-world oppression or rural slavery in the American South to a modernized urban existence. The beginnings of the two stories illustrate the newly developed ways of these pro-tagonists. They have changed their names (from Yekl to Jake and from Sam Taylor to Mr. Ryder), and they are trying to succeed on the terms of their new environments. The parties of Chesnutt's "Groveland" Blue Vein Society and Cahan's dance halls on New York's Lower East Side are worlds apart from each other; yet both provide us with an image of an ethnic association as an American-izing agency. The Blue Veins, refined Groveland Afro-Americans, preferably of free birth and such light complexion that the blue veins of their wrists can be seen, explicitly aim to "establish and maintain correct social standards among a people whose social condition pre-sented almost unlimited room for improvement" (Chesnutt, *Wife* 1). Professor Peltner's all-Jewish dancing academy has English as its "offi-cial language," a language "broken and mispronounced in as many different ways as there were Yiddish dialects represented in that insti-tution" (Cahan, *Yekl* 17). Both groupings establish symbolic bound-aries which define the group; and both modernize their members who have to adhere to certain standards and codes of conduct in order to *be* members.

Jake left his old world only three years before the beginning of the story whereas Mr. Ryder has been a free man for twenty-five years; but both protagonists have developed considerably within their dif-ferent modernizing environments; and both find a female within their new reference group who virtually comes to represent America. Mr. Ryder has made the acquaintance of a widow, Mrs. Molly Dixon, who is much younger, lighter skinned, and better educated than Ryder, and who comes from the nation's capital (*Wife* 5). Jake makes friends with Mamie Fein, a woman with a shrewd sense of business and a strong character who has greater fluency in English than Jake has (*Yekl* 19). This apparent upward drift is suddenly questioned as both Jake and Ryder are confronted with emanations of their past. The incarnation of the past is, in both cases, the protagonist's wife. Jake has tried to repress or sentimentalize his memories of marriage; and Ryder appears to have literally forgotten his antebellum bonds. Both marriages were "old-world" arrangements. Ryder's slave marriage has no legally binding quality, since it was not legalized after emancipation. Jake's wedding was—in the familiar pattern from the Indian-drama tradition, which was also the classic old-world Jewish way—perhaps an affair arranged by the parents; in any event, it remains associated with parental obligation, not with romantic love, which is among Jake's new-world discoveries: "Is this what they call love?" Jake asks himself, thinking of Mamie and "the strange, hitherto unexperienced kind of malady, which seemed to be gradually consuming his whole being" (*Yekl* 60). Both tales describe the wife as past and descent from the point of view of the protagonist's Americanized and consentist present.

Mr. Ryder is preparing the engagement ceremony with Mrs. Dixon, leafing through Tennyson's "Dream of Fair Women" and "Guinevere," when he hears the latch of his gate click and sees an apparition more strongly in contrast with the poetry he just read than a raven could be on a bust of Pallas:

> She was a little woman, not five feet tall, and proportioned to her height. Although she stood erect, and looked around her with very bright and restless eyes, she seemed quite old; for her face was crossed and re-crossed with a hundred wrinkles, and around the edges of her bonnet could be seen protruding here and there a tuft of short grey wool. She wore a blue calico gown {see *Yekl* 40} of ancient cut, a little red shawl fastened around her shoulders with an old-fashioned brass-brooch, and a large bonnet profusely ornamented with faded red and yellow artificial flowers. And she was very black,—so black that her toothless gums, revealed when she opened her mouth to speak, were not red, but blue. {Chesnutt thus ironically juxtaposes blue veins with blue gums!} She looked like a bit of the old plantation life, summoned up from the past by the wave of a magician's wand, as the

poet's fancy had called into being the gracious shapes of which Mr. Ryder had just been reading. (*Wife* 9–10)

Liza Jane, this living allegory of Ryder's past, tells him of her twenty-five-year search for her husband, Sam Taylor, with a "shrill and piping voice" and in a broad black rural idiom. Ryder does not immediately reveal his true identity, yet stares at a mirror after she has left.

Jake's past is described in similarly contrastive terms. His wife, Gitl (illustration 13), had become transformed into a fancy in Jake's imagination. Though failing to admit in the dance hall that he is married,

Illustration 13. (From Hutchins Hapgood, *The Spirit of the Ghetto,* 1902)

Jake is fond of remembering his wife at home with "a yearning ten-derness that made him feel like crying. 'I would not exchange her little finger for all the American ladas {ladies},' he soliloqized" (*Yekl* 32). Although he remembers Gitl's "prominent red gums, her little black eyes" (*Yekl* 31), his sentimentalized image is as drastically opposed to the real Gitl as Tennyson's "Guinevere" was to Liza Jane. When Jake goes to meet Gitl at Ellis Island, he goes smartly dressed and is thus younger looking than usual; but his heart sinks at the

> sight of his wife's uncouth and un-American appearance. She was slovenly dressed in a brown jacket and skirt of grotesque cut, and her hair was concealed under a voluminous wig of pitch-black hue. This she had put on just before leaving the steamer, both "in honor of the Sabbath" and by way of sprucing herself up for the great event. Since Yekl had left home she had gained considerably in the measurement of her waist. The wig, however, made her seem stouter and shorter than she would have appeared without it. It also added at least five years to her looks. But she was aware neither of this nor of the fact that in New York even a Jewess of her station and ortho-dox breeding is accustomed to blink at the wickedness of displaying her natural hair, and that none but an elderly matron may wear a wig without being the occasional target for snowballs or stones. She was naturally dark of complexion, and the nine or ten days spent at sea had covered her face with a deep bronze, which combined with her prominent cheek bones, inky little eyes, and, above all, the smooth black wig, to lend her resemblance to a squaw. (*Yekl* 34)

Unlike ethnic revivalists of the 1970s, Chesnutt and Cahan drew no idyllic and easy pictures of past ethnic bonds. Though the literary strategy of presenting spouse figures as absolute "other" is similar to the construction of Zangwill's *Melting-Pot*, these local-color others dif-fer considerably from Vera, the highly desirable "butcher's daughter." These old wives are faithful, stable, and devoted, but they are hardly attractive and youthful spouse images. They seem to be mother (or even grandmother) figures rather than spouses. Both writers' empha-sis on the old wives' gums evokes images of suckling and of very old age. The association of Gitl with a squaw also is evocative of an aged Pocahontas image as the Indianized grandmother of us all in the manner of some popular cartoon squaws of the second half of the nineteenth century—for example, *Harper's* (March 1876: 234) and *The Aldine* (1872: 162). Despite the—partially involuntary—bond, embracing them would seem an artificial, antilibidinal act for the modernized and younger-looking husbands. The central conflict of "The Wife of His Youth" and of *Yekl* is, however, just this question of whether Ryder and Jake will love and cherish their ethnic past or whether they will abandon it. In that respect, the solutions of the two tales seem to differ radically.

Mr. Ryder renounces mobility and upward drift, his position in the Blue Veins, and the attractive Molly Dixon by acknowledging the wife of his youth. He sides with the past against the future, with his moral obligation against his own philosophy. Jake, on the other hand, renounces his much less ancient past (to which he is further-more bound by the presence of a son, Yossele) and plunges into an expectation of freedom, which soon gives way to a sense of unhap-piness, when he gets his divorce from Gitl only to marry Mamie. On Hester Street, love takes the place of arranged marriages, and in America, according to Gitl's neighbor Mrs. Kavarsky, "A father is no father, a wife, no wife—not'ing" (*Yekl* 57). Unlike Mr. Ryder, Jake follows his libidinal drives and his newly found sense of selfhood and turns against duty, tradition, and his old self.

The Ideal and the Real

One possible interpretation of these two old wives' tales is that the black ethos—perhaps because of a stronger and more persistent eth-nic identification from the outside—suggested an affirmation of the party of memory, whereas the Jewish ethos encouraged the party of hope. To be sure, Jake is a divided and other-directed "allrightnik," whereas Mr. Ryder is a gentleman with black consciousness. The cru-cial reason for the different endings, however, is to be located not only in the specific ethnicity of American blacks or Jews but also in the literary mode of the respective tale. Though both Chesnutt and Cahan were explicitly praised by William Dean Howells, they drew their strategies in these stories from the different models of romance and realism (reminding us of Boyesen's hero's choice between *Ivanhoe* and *Robinson Crusoe*). "The Wife of His Youth" takes place in the world of moral and allegorical romance, where human beings are shown in ideal relation. It is a parable that shows the characters' capacity to follow the same biblical precepts that Cotton Mather had invoked to harmonize Eliot's life:

> Let thy fountain be blessed; and rejoice with the wife of thy youth. Let her be as the loving hind and pleasant roe; let her breasts satisfy thee at all times; and be thou ravished always with her love. And why wilt thou, my son, be ravished with a strange woman, and

embrace the bosom of a stranger? {Proverbs 5:18-20} (See Bone, *Down* 98)

In the world of moral ideals, Ryder can be portrayed as living up to that advice. The story also alludes to verses in which God assures the chosen people that "thy Maker is thine husband":

> For the Lord hath called thee as a woman forsaken and grieved in spirit, and a wife of youth, when thou wast refused, saith thy God. For a small moment have I forsaken thee; but with great mercies will I gather thee. In a little wrath, I hid my face from thee for a moment; but with everlasting kindness will I have mercy on thee, saith the Lord thy Redeemer. {Isaiah 54:5-8}

In the light of this parallel, one can say that Ryder plays the part of God and Liza Jane the role of Israel, his covenanted, but temporarily neglected, spouse. "The Wife of His Youth" takes place in an ideal world, indeed. The elements of allegorical romance are reinforced by the references to Tennyson's "Guinevere," which, together with "A Dream of Fair Maidens," also directs us to the conflict of past and present (Buckley, *Tennyson* 55, 190). The story suggests the "what if" world of the *ideal*—in aesthetic and moral terms. It is important that the narrator of the romance story allows us no understanding of the psychological dimensions of Mr. Ryder's decision. Instead, we are given a courtly scene for the denouement. Mr. Ryder, expected to announce his engagement to Mrs. Dixon, presents the assembled Blue Veins with a fable. Making his real dilemma appear like a product of "fancy" (*Wife* 20), he abstracts the story that he tells from his own emotions and secular interests. No wonder, then, that the Blue Veins, led by none other than Mrs. Dixon, should unanimously demand that the hero of Mr. Ryder's fable acknowledge the wife of his youth. In the terms of romance, this is the only "right" answer. It is significant that the story ends with Mr. Ryder's public acknowledgment of Liza Jane (illustration 14) and thus before the Blue Veins (and Mrs. Dixon) or Liza Jane get a chance to respond. Liza Jane, who is South and slavery, black culture and black consciousness, folk and past, mother culture and memory, or, in one word, the world of *descent*, represents everything that the Blue Veins have been trying so hard to eradicate and to build boundaries against. She is defined by contrast and identified by negation. As a living reminder of the upwardly mobile group's contrastive self-definition, she is the most perfect "un-Blue Vein" conceivable. Mr. Ryder's choice may therefore not be "realistically" convincing, but it is the result of a certain aes-

Illustration 14.   Frontispiece to Charles W. Chesnutt, *The Wife of His Youth*, 1899

thetic strategy. Liza Jane could never be realistically accepted as an actual Blue Vein, though she might be idealized one day.

If "The Wife of His Youth" follows the rules of the ideal and of romance, *Yekl* adheres to the logic of the real. What Ryder can do, Jake can only imagine in his dreams of a harmonious synthesis between past and present. In Jake's real world there is no place for a happy ending in a chivalric sense. The maxim is "circumstances alter cases" (*Yekl* 53). (Incidentally, it is a maxim that Chesnutt was not unfamiliar with in other stories, as his tale "The Web of Circum-stance" documents; only in "The Wife of his Youth," Chesnutt chose a different narrative stance.) In Cahan's novel, fresh contact with new environments inevitably and inescapably changes characters, their moral powers, and their allegiances. Although Jake's Gitl is much younger than Ryder's Liza Jane and although they have a son, Jake is so thoroughly alienated from his past that he is unable to love his wife. Even in his struggle to express his love for Mamie, Jake has to contend with the recurrent image of his father's shrouds (*Yekl* 77). The sheets on the rooftop thus symbolize Yekl's father's ghost and demonstrate the force of descent relations; yet they are also literally the "underwear, pillowcases, sheets and what not" (*Yekl* 75) near which the central act of Schneider's consent symbolism often takes place.

On the rooftop Jake exclaims: "Mamie, my treasure, my glory! Say that you are *shatichfied*; my heart will become lighter" (*Yekl* 78); but when he finally approaches city hall to get married to Mamie, he feels like stopping a process which victimizes him. Yet there is no getting off the deterministic cable car of history. Ironically, Gitl has been quite successful at Americanizing herself and at discarding her nar-row old-world religious customs together with her old-fashioned rural apparel. Together with Jake's boarder Bernstein, who—like the story's author—is educated and thus better equipped to synthesize the old and the new, Gitl is about to open a grocery store with the money that Jake had to pay to get the divorce. The source of alien-ation between Jake and Gitl is thus not any absolute distinction between Jake's new-world and Gitl's old-world outlooks but in their separation, which led to different time schedules in Americanization.

The stories by Chesnutt and Cahan illustrate how the tension between consent and descent could be fictionalized by American writers who had a sense of the American as well as the pre-American side of their experience. Their fictional delineations of the territory of consent and descent show striking parallels between black and Jewish writing, parallels which mono-ethnic approaches would surely miss. One could with some justification talk about "bluish" writing in America and thus emphasize the parallels between black and Jew-ish writings in one appropriate word.

The two protagonists are similarly divided selves, whose consent and descent definitions are at odds with each other. Their language is the best indicator of their divided selfhood. Ryder and Jake speak the thin language of renegades, have lost the ability to use the lan-guage of their youth with ease, yet remain distinctly separate from

other speakers of standard English. Cahan shows this beautifully by
introducing the linguistic mix of Yiddish and English; the English of
the dialogue stands for Yiddish; the bastardized language of Jake is
rendered, quite derogatorily, with the inclusion of countless mispronounced words, of Americanisms, and of neologisms from the
hyphen culture ("*oyshgreen*": literally "out-green," "signifying to cease
being green," as Cahan explains in a footnote {*Yekl* 45); or "America
for a country and '*dod'll do*' {that'll do} for a language" [*Yekl* 21}).
Chesnutt, too, masterfully builds up the conflict between Liza Jane's
extensively transcribed folk idiom and the Blue Vein Ryder's thin,
idealized, and somewhat pedantic rhetoric; and the narrator even
states explicitly that Ryder's pronunciation is sometimes faulty when
he recites his memorized English poetry (*Wife* 4).

Whether in the ideal world of Chesnutt's fable or in the real milieu
of Cahan's tale, the ethnic *wives* function as symbols of descent.
Doesn't this sound paradoxical, since marriage would seem to represent the ultimate consent relationship? If we apply Schneider's and
Kemnitzer's theories to Liza Jane, we might conclude that, although
she is a spouse, she symbolizes the involuntary nature of descent relations. But how about Gitl? Jake does break away from her and takes
to city hall Mamie, the woman who appeared to represent consent
and America. Yet at this point a double strategy employed by both
Chesnutt and Cahan becomes apparent. Mamie, like Molly, is, of
course, only partly identical with America. They both also indubit-
ably belong to the ethnic group of the respective protagonist.[10] They
are images of prospective American spouses with maternal-sounding
names and an ethnic ancestry. The dilemma ultimately is not that of
an absolute choice between pure descent and pure consent. No matter how much he acts like an other-directed allrightnik—and, since
"all right" is the ultimate formula of consent in America, we might
here say "consentnik"—Jake remains to some extent socially defined
by his Jewish descent; and even had he opted for Mrs. Dixon, Mr.
Ryder would have remained in the Negro world. However traumatic
the tension between "nature" and "law" may be, the individual's alternative of ethnicity as romance (an idealized acceptance of descent) or
of ethnicity as realism (a truthful account of plausible behavior in
new environments) ultimately appears as an overly dramatized alternative. The splitting of ethnic women into Liza Jane/Molly Dixon
and Gitl/Mamie Fein thus indicates the exaggeration of small differences into vast cultural opposites. The cultural content can be
equated with "loyalty to the past" versus "right of a new beginning."
Ryder-Taylor and Jake-Yekl are and remain hyphenated. However

they may feel about it, they are not given the option of totally losing their past ethnicity. They "cannot change their grandfathers." On the other hand, neither Ryder nor Jake can go back again—except in dreams and fables. However, they *can* change their wives.

As stories imagined in the 1890s, both "The Wife of His Youth" and *Yekl* subtly present the conflicts of a symbolic kinship drama. Ryder and Jake are given the projections of two sets of women: Liza Jane and Molly Dixon, Gitl and Mamie Fein, in order to dramatize their own state of conflict and tension. Seen this way, both tales still show social descent definitions while focusing on the individual's consent choice. Paradoxically, in both stories the ethnic group fosters individualist consent values while an allegorical individual represents the collectivity of descent. In another paradox Liza Jane and Gitl represent "nature" precisely because they symbolize unions not based on "love," whereas Molly and Mamie represent "law" through threatening past legal arrangements.

According to Schneider's kinship theory, we might have expected Ryder's and Yekl's choice to be one between parent and spouse (to make it a pure case of descent versus consent). Yet, interestingly, and quite excitingly, both writers chose two sets of *wives*. When we try to relate these stories to ethnicity theory, we may then learn concretely that casting ethnicity as a relationship "in nature" is in itself a mental construction (not a "natural" phenomenon). The writers' choice is one between a spouse symbolizing mother and descent and another spouse representing love: in other words, the realm of descent is in itself subject to consent, to cultural choice and interpretation, and, in these stories, subject to male polarizations of females.

Chesnutt's and Cahan's fictions create a subtle drama which might in fact inspire future ethnic theory rather than merely serve to illustrate familiar generalities. I know of no better existing theory of the complicated ways in which the relationship of consent and descent has worked in the American imagination. In constructing such a sophisticated opposition, Chesnutt and Cahan retell *the* American story.

Chesnutt and Cahan are not exceptional in the American canon. One can see the conflict between consent and descent reenacted in a great many stories, from *Abie's Irish Rose* to *Freckled Rice* (a 1983 Chinese-American three-generation film set in Boston). In Giuseppe Cautela's *Moon Harvest* (1925), Romualdo is torn between Maria, his static old-world wife and mother figure, and Vincenza DiDedda, the lively new-world incarnate, second-generation Italian-American. As Mary Dearborn has shown, the tension takes the shape of a daughter torn between a father figure and a spouse in much writing by female ethnics (as it also does in some male writings that center on heroines). For example, Anzia Yezierska's *Bread Givers* (1925) is subtitled "A struggle between a father of the Old World and a daughter of the New." Michael DeCapite's *Maria* (1943) shows the disintegration of a family-arranged marriage in America. And, finally, what is Nathaniel Hawthorne's *Scarlet Letter* (1850) but the story of Hester Prynne, a woman who was separated from Chillingworth, the old-world embodiment with whom she had been connected in a marriage that was not based on love and that remained associated with paternal authority? Separated from the old world by the "road" which took her to America, a road she can visualize again from the scaffold, she takes up with Dimmesdale, the living spirit of the new world, love, and a higher law; and their consent relationship had a "consecration of its own" (*Scarlet* 140).

Love and Kinship

In complicating the opposition of descent (imagined as Schneider's "nature") and consent (imagined as "law"), Chesnutt and Cahan were not far off the point that Anthony Wallace made when he reviewed Schneider's *American Kinship* in the *American Anthropologist* (1969). Wallace argued that in American cultural symbolism love-and-marriage was constructed as a more natural form of kinship than Schneider assumed. Marriage is more than an "in-law" relationship and has a more central symbolization than the proper marital coitus, Wallace argued, because it contains the "important archetypal construct of love . . . in the sense of an elemental force of nature, an intense attraction both physical and spiritual that irresistibly draws two people together." Wallace continued:

> Metaphors like "fall in love and get married," and others more explicit, compare this force to other natural forces like magnetism and gravity when no obstacle intervenes; where there is trouble, the comparison is to more violent natural energies like storm and fire. This kind of love is very clearly distinguished from other kinds in American culture, and the distinction is so constantly and conventionally made that one may not hear it even when listening to it. (102)

Since the eighteenth century American culture has in an exceptionally intense way emphasized this naturalized construct of romantic love as the basis for marriage. The lovers' leap dramas, or David and Vera's problems in *The Melting-Pot*, are, in the light of Wallace's observations, experienced less as the conflict of law versus nature than as the clash of two natural forces. Opposing Schneider's focus on marriage as based on volition, legal invention, and actively taken reversible steps and symbolized by the coitus, Wallace emphasizes that in American popular culture the naturalized construct of romantic love

> may happen in inconvenient circumstances, and in that case the force of nature may take precedence—with or without wedlock—over considerations of class, age, race, marital status, and even blood relationship; if too long frustrated, this force of nature turns uncanny and {wreaks} havoc with many lives. ... (102)

One could even go a step further and suppose that one proof of modern American love's "naturalness" is precisely its transcendence of significant secular boundaries or parental desires. There is a certain compulsiveness about the antiparental definition of melting-pot lovers such as David and Vera. It is not all that surprising, then, to see American popular culture involved in a virtually perpetual incantation of love, as the French observer Raoul de Roussy de Sales pointed out in a hilarious piece for the *Atlantic Monthly* (May 1938). Sales also hinted at the parallels between love and the principle of volitional political allegiance and stressed love's symbolic function in distinguishing us from our ancestors:

> The prevailing conception of love, in America, is similar to the idea of democracy. It is fine in theory. It is the grandest system ever evolved by man to differentiate him from his ancestors, the poor brutes who lived in caverns, or from the apes. Love is perfect, in fact, and there is nothing better. But, like democracy, it does not work, and the Americans feel that something should be done about it. President Roosevelt is intent on making democracy work. Everybody is trying to make love work, too. (645)

Sales was fascinated by the cultural obsession with the theme of marriage (and remarriage) "for love" and humorously described Hollywood and the American consumption of an exceptionally "fabulous amount of love songs" as a process of making a construction seem like a natural force. According to Sales's perceptive wit, the American popular mind

> likes to be entertained by the idea (1) that love is the only reason why a man and a woman should get married; (2) that love is always

wholesome, genuine, uplifting, and fresh, like a glass of Grade A
milk; (3) that when, for some reason or other, it fails to keep you
uplifted, wholesome and fresh, the only thing to do is to begin all
over again with another partner. (646)

If love is perceived to be as natural as (mother's?) milk, the clash
between consent as a natural power and descent as an opposing force
is totally lifted into the realm of nature. This cultural process of naturalization, because it balances the colliding elements, is what has
given the conflict such virulence. As Niklas Luhmann also observed,
in the metaphors of "falling in love" or "being made for each other,"
there is a paradoxical tension between free choice and an ineluctably
determined fate (181).

Old Self, New Self: Practical Men
by Visionary Americans

The realms of consent and descent are often envisioned as unified in
the ideal, though separated in the real, world. Consent and descent
may not only be embodied by different characters but also be at odds
with each other in one personality. Many ethnic writers have
sketched the divided interiors of ethnic rooms. But what interior is
more fascinating than the inside of a divided self? By the start of the
twentieth century, ethnic authors were beginning to play with their
audiences' yearning for a literature of initiation and revelation. Two
novels published in 1912 and 1913, James Weldon Johnson's *Autobiography of an Ex-Colored Man* and Abraham Cahan's "Autobiography of an American Jew" (expanded and rewritten for book publication as *The Rise of David Levinsky* in 1917), are strikingly similar in
literary strategy.

Both texts were introduced to their contemporary audiences as
true, and somewhat sensational, confessions as well as, in the tradition of Sue's *Mysteries*, initiations into the mysteries of ethnicity. The
publisher's introduction to the first edition of Johnson's novel states
that though the Negro has been "a sphinx" to the whites, this book
draws aside a (DuBoisian) "veil:" "the reader is given a view of the
inner life of the Negro in America, is initiated into the freemasonry,
as it were, of race" (xii). *McClure's Magazine*, where Cahan's first version of *Levinsky* was serialized in 1913, similarly promises that the
author, who has "probably the most intimate knowledge of Jewish
life of any man in America" is telling the tale of "an actual type: his
story reproduces actual characters, occurrences, and situations taken

from real life." Levinsky's "intense and complicated struggle shows, as no invention could do, the traits of mind and character by which the Jew has made his sensationally rapid progress in the business of America" (April 1913: 92–93).

In the familiar rhetoric of presenting fiction as truth, these introductions promise a symbolic initiation into ethnic riddles. The vehicle of this initiation is, in both novels, an omnipresent first-person narrator, who purports to be telling his own story, confessing his innermost secrets to a larger audience. In fact, there is so much social and historical "revelation" in Cahan's and Johnson's novels that the books can be read as panoramic views of black and Jewish life at the turn of the century. Yet at the center of both books is an initiation into the inner life of one representative man, the narrator.

The picaresque *Autobiography of an Ex-Colored Man* moves rapidly from the nameless narrator's childhood in Georgia and Connecticut to his traumatic realization that he is a Negro. After his mother's death his attempt to go to Atlanta University is thwarted when his inheritance is stolen, and his life takes a new turn. Through the hero's eyes we are shown the worlds of the Pullman porters, the Spanish workers in a Florida cigar factory, and the ragtime bohemia in the "tenderloin" district of New York. After an extended trip to Europe as companion to a rich white benefactor, the narrator-hero returns to America, witnesses a southern lynching, and decides to pass for white. He busies himself with the "interesting and absorbing game" of making money and builds up a fortune by investing in New York City real estate. He marries an unnamed white woman who accepts him even though he confesses to the "drops of African blood" in his veins. After his wife dies, the ex-colored man is left with a son and a daughter, for whom he cherishes high hopes. Yet the novel ends on a gloomy and self-pitying note:

> Sometimes it seems to me that I have never really been a Negro ... ; at other times I feel that I have been a coward, a deserter, and I am possessed by a strange longing for my mother's people.
> Several years ago I attended a great meeting in the interest of Hampton Institute at Carnegie Hall. ... Among the speakers were ... Mark Twain [and] ... Booker T. Washington. ... Even those who oppose them know that these men have the eternal principles of right on their side, and they will be victors even though they should go down in defeat. Beside them I feel small and selfish. I am an ordinarily successful white man who has made a little money. They are men who are making history and a race. I, too, might have taken part in a work so glorious. (*Autobiography* 510–11)

Alluding (as Rabbi Blau did in his rejection of *The Melting-Pot*) to the biblical story of Jacob and Esau, the narrator concludes: "I cannot repress the thought that, after all, I have chosen the lesser part, that I have sold my birthright for a mess of pottage" [Genesis 25:22–34].

Like Johnson's novel, Cahan's *Rise of David Levinsky* covers a wide spectrum of contemporary life. David grows up in Antomir, where he lives with his mother in great poverty. Through hard work, she is able to send her son to a private yeshiva. Pointing to the volumes of the Talmud, she tells David that this is the trade he will learn. But his mother is killed by a group of Russian rowdies, and the Jewish community is in such fear of pogroms that the burial takes place in private in order "not to irritate the Gentiles" (52). David decides to emigrate to America, where he undergoes a rapid transformation. Beginning with the ominous phrase "all right" (91), he learns how to speak English; and soon he is a greenhorn no longer. His locks and ethnic clothes give way to an American haircut and dress. After many ups and downs Levinsky builds up a successful business in the clothing industry by circumventing union regulations and by out-bidding competitors. He never fulfills his often-expressed dream to study at City College, which he calls "my temple." David is also frustrated in his desires for a matrimonial connection. His annual net profits soon exceed $200,000, but he is not a happy man. At the end of the novel, David Levinsky is torn by self-doubt and self-pity and unable to enjoy his wealth or his power:

> Sometimes when I am alone in my beautiful apartments, ... nursing my loneliness, I say to myself:
> "There are cases when success is a tragedy."
> There are moments when I regret my whole career, when my very success seems to be a mistake. ...
> At the height of my business success I feel that if I had my life to live over again I should never think of a business career. ...
> I can never forget the days of my misery. I cannot escape from my old self. My past and my present do not comport well. David, the poor lad swinging over a Talmud volume at the Preacher's Synagogue, seems to have more in common with my inner identity than David Levinsky, the well-known cloak manufacturer. (*Rise* 529–30)

The two novels seem to be another instance for "bluish" literature. Both books depict the externally upward journeys of protagonists (who lose their mothers early in their lives) from poverty to material success, from ethnic marginality to a more "American" identity, and from a small-town background to the urban environment of New York. Inwardly, however, both David Levinsky and the ex-colored

man perceive themselves as victims of circumstance, unhappy cowards, and traitors to kin and authentic, inner descent-self. Their
external rise was really a fall; their very success was their failure.

This ironic point is driven home, in both novels, by a peculiar
narrative technique. The protagonists purport to be narrating their
own stories, using the first-person confessional. Yet throughout their
narratives we feel the intrusion of another, ironic voice, which subverts this basic communicative pattern. Both Johnson and Cahan
shared a common area of experience with their fictional protagonists,
who seem to be moving through stages of their authors' lives in an
inverted fashion. As comparisons between the novels and their
authors' real autobiographies show—Johnson's *Along This Way*
(1933) and *The Education of Abraham Cahan* (1926)—their fictional
narrators were ironically inverted antiselves, shadows, alter ego figures. The protagonists' successful business careers are the ones their
authors did *not* pursue; the educational opportunities missed by the
heroes were the ones their inventors took; and the fictional characters' dreams of what they should have been clearly point in the direction of their creators' real lives.

In Johnson's and Cahan's ironically antithetical construction,
"descent" stands for those facets of self-realization which the retrospective mind of imaginary *practical men* perceives as the lost potential of childhood or as the sacrifice made to consent-America. It is the
visionary, artistic and socially engaged quality somehow associated
with descent which these characters (though not their creators) have
surrendered to selfishness and practical success. When Johnson's hero
speaks of having sold his birthright for a mess of pottage, he virtually
casts himself as Esau, leaving his author, *James* Weldon Johnson, the
vacant place of the chosen *Jacob*, destined to become Israel. After the
disappearance of his money, the narrator simply runs away from
Atlanta University, from which his author, on the other hand, grad-
uated in 1894; and Johnson, unlike the ex-colored man, did speak at
Negro benefits and became an active and nationally known force in
the NAACP. Levinsky's confession is equally obvious in pointing to
the real Abraham Cahan. For example, David reports scornfully that
a collapse of the real-estate market was caused by a "series of rent
strikes inspired and engineered by the Jewish socialists through their
Yiddish daily" (*Rise* 511)—the paper of which Cahan was the well-
known editor! At one point the author lets his character dream: "Had
I then chanced to hear a Socialist speech I might have become an
ardent follower of Karl Marx and my life might have been directed
along lines other than those which brought me to financial power"

(*Rise* 153). When visionaries write fictional autobiographies of invented practical men, it is perhaps not too surprising that these practical men suffer dearly from not having become visionaries. This becomes even more apparent when we ask the novels for the true meaning of the protagonists' betrayed "inner self" and "birthright."

The "ideal" realizations for Johnson's and Cahan's heroes could come about only in a process of *synthesis*, by a fusion of "birthright" and the realm of descent—defined as the legacy of mother, childhood, folk, parish, poverty, education, social vision, and artistic potential—with "mess of pottage"and the world of consent—embodied by manhood, marriage, America, secular world, picaresque roaming, and financial success. In the best tradition of David Quixano's American symphony and the musical imagery that has accompanied discussions of ethnicity, the fusion is seen possible in the process of aesthetic creation, which the novels themselves represent but which their narrators abandoned.

Johnson's suggestion for this creative fusion is incorporated into the ex-colored man's description of an incident at a soiré of artists, musicians, writers, and aristocrats in Berlin at which the narrator most clearly discovers the shape of his artistic mission.

> My millionaire planned, in the midst of the discussion on music, to have me play the "new American music" and astonish everybody present. ... I went to the piano and played the most intricate rag-time piece I knew. Before there was time for anybody to express an opinion on what I had done, a big bespectacled, bushy-headed man rushed over, and, shoving me out of the chair, exclaimed: "Get up! Get up!" He seated himself at the piano, and, taking the theme of my rag-time, played it through first in straight chords; then varied and developed it through every known musical form. I sat amazed. I had been turning classic music into rag-time, a comparatively easy task; and this man had taken rag-time and made it classic. The thought came across me like a flash—It can be done, why can't I do it? From that moment my mind was made up. I clearly saw the way of carrying out the ambition I had formed when a boy. (*Autobiography* 471)

When Carl Van Vechten read this passage, he made the annotation "Rhapsody in Blue foreseen." After this revelatory confrontation with his version of Zangwill's "Poppy," the ex-colored man decides to go to the American South, "to live among the people, and drink in [his] inspiration firsthand." Yet his collection of folk materials remains without consequence. The ex-colored man does not become a George Gershwin or a James Weldon Johnson (who had written many songs for the musical stage of Tin Pan Alley and had toured

Europe with his brother Rosamond and with Bob Cole). He abandons his ideal of collecting black folk art and fusing it with European materials as quickly as it occurs to him; at the end he is left merely with some "fast yellowing manuscripts" which he identifies with the "birthright" that he sold for a mess of pottage (*Autobiography* 511).

David Levinsky has divergent visions of his lost potential. At one point he seriously blames some spilt milk for having prevented him from going to college and putting into reality his conviction that he was "born for a life of intellectual interest." Yet his ideal synthesis prominently includes distinction in the field of music. "I should readily change places," David says self-pityingly at the end of the novel,

> with the Russian Jew who holds the foremost place among American song-writers and whose soulful compositions are sung in almost every English-speaking house in the world. I love music to madness. I yearn for the world of great singers, violinists, pianists. Several of the greatest of them are of my race and country, and I have met them, but all my acquaintance with them has brought me is a sense of being looked down upon as a money-bag striving to play the Maecenas. (*Rise* 529–30)

Yet Levinsky cannot become an Irving Berlin. The gap between an unfulfilling business life and self-realization in music divides David's real life from the dream of his innermost self.

Neither Cahan nor Johnson saw descent statically as a force that American men could return or withdraw to. They knew that consent was here to stay. Their ideal vision was that of a synthesis of specific descent and cosmopolitan consent, a synthesis best expressed in musical metaphors. This harmonization of the descent and consent dimensions within one human being would lead to an existence in which success on American terms was to be realized artistically without compromising self-denials. Locating the tensions between consent and descent within the consciousness of one man—the unreliable narrator and protagonist—Johnson and Cahan cast the opposition in such a way that the figure of the successful musician appears as a possible synthesis.

Nonfictional autobiographies are no less complex than these fictional dreams of a synthesis. In the complicated American landscape of regional, religious, and ethnic affiliations, it could be very difficult to construct the self as autonomous individual *and* as fated group member.

CHAPTER SIX

The Ethics
of Wholesome Provincialism

In a Vision in a Dream,
from the frigid seaport of the proud Xanthrochroid
the good ship Défineznegro
sailed fine, under an unabridged moon,
to reach the archipelago
Nigeridentité.
In the Strait of Octoroon,
off black Scylla,
after the typhoon Phobos, out of the Stereotypus Sea,
had rived her hull and sail to a T,
the Défineznegro sank the rock
and disappeared in the abyss
(Vanitas! vanitatum!)
of white Charybdis.
—Melvin Tolson, *Harlem Gallery* (1965)

An infinite range of individualizing combinations is made possible by the
fact that the individual belongs to a multitude of groups, in which the relationship between competition and socialization varies greatly. . . . [The]
instinctive needs of man prompt him to act in these mutually conflicting
ways: he feels and acts *with* others but also *against* others. . . .
—Georg Simmel, *The Web of Group Affiliations* (1922)

In 1785 a writer who used the pen name "Celadon" (singer) tried to
clarify the meaning of regions in America by making them one with
ethnic groups. The author of the small pamphlet *The Golden Age; or,
Future Glory of North-America Discovered by an Angel to Celadon in Several Entertaining Visions* contemplated the future of America from a
mountain overlooking the whole continent. The narrator was in a
state of rapture when

> the Angel recalled my attention by a gentle touch on my side, and
> pointing his finger a little to the south-west, Celadon, says he, do you

see yonder valley.—. . . That whole region you may call Savagenia: It being designed for the future habitation of your now troublesome Indians.—And that other valley . . . It lies toward the north-west . . . —This you may call Nigrania: It being allotted for the Negroes to dwell there, when the term of their vassalage is come to a period.— And in all those vast spaces westward to the great ocean, there may be seats hereafter for sundry foreign nations.—There may be a French, a Spanish, a Dutch, an Irish, an English, &c. yea, a Jewish State here in process of time.—And all of them united in brotherly affection, will at last form the most potent empire on the face of the earth. (11–12)

The United States did not become Celadon's union of homogeneous ethnic valleys. Although the belief is widespread that there are organic places for each nationality, most American ethnic groups are religiously diverse and spread throughout many regions, while no region has been exclusively populated by only one ethnic group. There are, to be sure, some significant historical exceptions to this, by now well-established pattern. Among the cases that Marcus Lee Hansen discussed in *The Immigrant in American History* (1940) are the German plans for a Teutonic commonwealth in America and the Irish societies' (rejected) petition to Congress in 1818 for an Irish land grant (131–32). In *The Rediscovery of Black Nationalism* (1970), Theodore Draper analyzed the "land question," repeated demands for a black nation in the southern black belt. Mordecai Emanuel Noah embraced a somewhat quirky though sublime plan

to establish a Zion in the New World. In 1825 he proclaimed himself governor and judge over Israel, and persuaded a Christian friend to buy land for a Jewish republic on Grand Island, in the Niagara River in upstate New York. (Schmidt, "Kallen" 12)

Nation-states were only a lovers' leap away. Yet, instead of opting for Celadon's administrative simplicity and organizing America into ethnic arrondissements, Americans have adopted and continue to create complicated and unsystematically overlapping forms of particular regional, ethnic, and religious identities. More than that, these identities are not all, as in Celadon's model, survivals of primordial (or at least, old-world) distinctions; many of them, such as the regional ones, are newly formed in America. The Americans' unsystematic desire to identify with intermediary groups—larger than the family, smaller than the nation—may be based on real or imagined descent, on old or newly adopted religions, on geographic area of origin, socialization, or residence, on external categorization, on voluntary association, or on defiance. In all of these cases, symbolic boundaries are constructed in a perplexing variety of continuously shifting forms. This messy reality challenges us to transcend statically conceived generalizations about regions and ethnic groups in America. Celadon would not make a good real-estate agent in any American city.

What is prominent in ethnic and regional conceptualizations is not the complex model that such an intricate situation would require but a surprisingly resilient pattern that includes the following recurring elements:

1. Dualistic procedures which juxtapose regions and ethnic groups with something elusive one may call the "un-region" and the "un-ethnic group."
2. Dichotomizations of regionalisms and ethnicities into "good" and "bad" forms, usually on the understanding that good and organic group identities are located in the *juste milieu* between two bad ones.
3. Interpretations of regions and ethnic groups that are at once analogous to the nation and to the individual, with the result that even the *scholarly* rhetoric of regionalism and ethnicity reflects the redemptive rhetoric of American civil religion and that the search for "good" group identity permeates American culture.

The Mysteries of Un-Region and Un-Ethnic Group

Studies dedicated to the investigation of American regional and ethnic heterogeneity ironically first set out to construct the homogeneity of their narrower subjects. This is most easily achieved by juxtaposing a slightly purified and improved version of the typically quite messy and mixed region or ethnic group to be studied with the whole country of which it is usually considered a part. It has, for example, become customary to study the South by contrasting it, not with another region (such as the North), but with the whole "rest of the country." Thus John Shelton Reed's study *The Enduring South* (1974) measured the South against the "national norm" on the following grounds: "the relative homogeneity of the non-Southern regions provides a rationale for grouping them as the 'non-South'" (117 n. 23). This dualistic polarization achieves the goal of demonstrating the atypical qualities of the South as region at the expense of creating (contrastively or, as George Devereux would say, "dissociatively") one, homogeneous non-South as un-region, an area ranging from

Bangor to San Diego. Some of the statistical evidence offered for the contrast is striking: for instance, whereas 86 percent of the white Protestants in the South believe that there is a devil, only 52 percent of the white Protestants in the un-South share this belief. We are left with the problem of having to understand a bedeviled region, not as a part of an ensemble of other regions, but in contrast to the mental construct of the "non-region" or "un-region," in which the majority of Americans resides.

What inevitably happens in such polarizing comparisons is the forced homogenization not only of the nonregion not studied but also of the investigated region itself. What many books on the South as region have done implicitly, Reed's *Enduring South* stated explicitly:

> All of the comparisons shown will be between Southern and non-Southern *whites*. While it would be interesting to examine differences between Southern and Northern Negroes, it would be difficult with these data, since so many Northern blacks are Southern-born and since—particularly in the early polls—the black respondents are not representative of the black population. In any event, the group of particular interest here is white Southerners, and white non-Southerners are the appropriate comparison group since we are interested in the effects of being Southern rather than those of being white. (Reed 6)

The dichotomy between region and un-region is more easily sustained in the laboratory setting of relative ethnic homogeneity; and once the category southern comes to stand for white southern it is easier for Reed to describe southernness as a special case of ethnicity.

The same methodology often applies in the study of proper ethnic groups, which are pitted less frequently against other comparable groups than against the antithetical category of Americans. Thus we learn from the introduction to the *Harvard Encyclopedia of American Ethnic Groups* (1980)—which, incidentally, includes an entry on southerners—that there is an "undoubtedly large" number of "plain Americans" who, as "non-ethnic Americans," receive no entry in the book (vii). Yet they are implicitly omnipresent as whites in some entries and as English-speaking, Europeans, Gentiles, or Protestants in others. These abstract people are sometimes described as united in prejudice against the respective ethnic group, at other times as threatening to dilute the ethnic group by intermarrying. The procedure may have the side effect of a flexible community-building in America: in books on American Jewish literature, for example, authors from English, Scotch-Irish, Dutch, Scandinavian, Slavic, and Mediterra-

nean backgrounds as well as black, American Indian, Asian, and His-
panic writers imperceptibly become part of one, single, "gentile" tradition. It seems much harder to conceptualize pervasive polyethnicity
than to construct such neatly contrasted artificial situations.

It is the contrast with people who are *not* considered ethnics which
often shapes the delineation of the various ethnic groups; and both
sides are contrastively homogenized in the process. Thus, the entry
"Russians" invokes the homogeneity of Americans of non-Russian
descent by reminding readers of the periods of "Russophobia in the
United States" (893). At the same time, the essay homogenizes the
immigrants from Russia by saying this about their religion:

> Religion plays a central role in the life of Russian-American immi-
> grants, whether they be adherents of the Eastern Orthodox Church,
> Old Believers, or sectarians like the Molokans. (*HEAEG* 888)

What is interesting about this statement on religious diversity is that
the numerically significant Russian Jews are not even mentioned as
a religious grouping among immigrants from Russia. However, they
are never absolutely excluded from the category "Russians" either
and receive some passing comments as socialists under "Politics." Yet
the entry on Russians ends with another statement which separates
Jewish from Russian ethnicity:

> Finally, recent immigrants from the Soviet Union cannot fit easily
> into existing Russian-American secular or religious organizations.
> The vast majority of the newcomers are Jewish, while the others have
> little in common with the religious beliefs and political ideologies of
> the older immigrants. (*HEAEG* 894)

Paradoxically, some regional and ethnic studies set out with the
contention that generalizations about "America" often exclude
southerners or Russian immigrants; yet in their own generalizations
about the South or Russians, these studies may exclude blacks and
Jews.

These examples illustrate the dualistic tendencies in studies of
regions and ethnic groups. Such a procedure serves to give the particular a more distinctive character. On the one hand the group or
region is individualized. It is not contrasted with another individualized form of particularism but juxtaposed with the undifferentiated
national norm of the "un-region" and the "un-ethnic group." On the
other hand the group or region in question is made more distinctive
by homogenization. This yields a non-black South and non-Jewish
immigrants from Russia as more clear-cut subjects for study than the
actual diversity to be found in a biracial South and among gentile-
Jewish Russians. In this fashion, scholars participate in the creation

of the ethnicizing process which always defines the ethnic content of x dissociatively and contrastively as being not a y. (In the same vein, an Italian-American speaker can evoke a homogeneous nation of non-lasagna eaters.) The yearning for a vision of America as a structured society composed of neatly defined "ethnic regions" is a pervasive theme in American conceptualizations of "pluralistic diversity." The dualistic lens will do for one valley at a time what Celadon's angel could display in a grand total vision.

So far I have described the dualistic methodology merely as a pragmatic device that contributes to create and legitimate its own subject. Yet this same procedure also frequently serves to make moral distinctions, which are often accompanied by semantic ones. Thus we are accustomed to separating "sectionalism" (bad) from "regionalism" (good), and "ethnocentrism" (bad) from "ethnicity" (good). This moral polarization is sometimes made overtly and sometimes covertly, but it pervades the literature of regionalism and ethnicity to a surprising degree. More than that, it seems to follow the systematic arrangement of vices and virtues established in Aristotle's *Ethics*.

Josiah Royce and the Ethics of Wholesome Provincialism

A classic formulation of regionalism and ethnicity was made by the Harvard philosophy professor Josiah Royce in 1908. Unlike Frederick Jackson Turner, Royce did not adopt John Wesley Powell's terms "regions" and "regionalism" (Jensen, *Regionalism* 84). Instead, he discussed the phenomenon under the term "provincialism," which he used despite its pejorative implications in everyday speech. In his influential work Royce argued for provincialism as a positive value, as a moral and aesthetic *ideal* to be realized in America, and as a form of identification which may lead to a harmonious and organic relationship with other group identities.

Royce left no doubt about his positive evaluation of "provincialism" when he wrote that

> the time has come to emphasize, with a new meaning and intensity, the positive value, the absolute necessity for our welfare, of a wholesome provincialism, as a saving power to which the world in the near future will need more and more to appeal. (Royce 62)

Royce's provincialism is conceived as an agency of redemption. But from what is it to save us? To answer this question, we must proceed to what at first seems merely to be the other side of the dualistic coin. Royce mentions several interrelated evils: uprootedness caused by immigration and mobility; homogeneity of thought spawned by modernization; and the resulting "mob-spirit" through which a "nation composed of many millions of people may fall rapidly under the hypnotic influence of a few leaders, of a few fatal phrases" (95). The nation as such is helpless and can do little for the "salvation of the individual from the overwhelming forces of consolidation. ... The nation by itself, apart from the influence of the province, is in danger of becoming an incomprehensible monster. ..." So it is up to the province to "save the individual" (98).

How can the province do it? By functioning in an essentially paradoxical way. First, provincialism must avoid backsliding into "the ancient narrowness" (98)—which we might customarily associate with the very word "provincialism," as distinct from Royce's "wholesome provincialism," that is. Second, in opposition to "ancient narrowness" and "false sectionalism which disunites," Royce's wholesome provincialism must transcend the province into the direction of broad humanity:

> Just because the true issues of human life are brought to a finish not in time but in eternity, it is necessary that in our temporal existence what is most worthy should appear to us as an ideal, as an Ought, rather than as something that is already in our hands. ... Hence the ideal in the bush, so to speak, is always worth infinitely more to him [the moral agent working under human limitations] than the food or the plaything of time that happens to be just now in his hands. (Royce 101)

Analogously, "the better aspect of our provincial consciousness is always its longing for the improvement of the community" (102).

Provincialism is equated by Royce with an aesthetic ideal, with Friedrich Schiller's world of dreams and poetry. Paraphrasing Royce in the language of today's bumper stickers, we might say that "provincialism is beautiful." Yet the ideals in the bush have to be possessed, according to Royce's admonition, in a unique fashion. "The way to win independence is by learning freely from abroad, but by then insisting upon our own interpretation of the common good" (103). We should wander, but return to the province. This is the way for provincialism to function, "like monogamy," as "an essential basis of true civilization" (67). The marriage analogy—reminiscent of a long line of such rhetorical figures, starting with John Winthrop's ligaments of love—illustrates that Royce, who was, incidentally, a Californian, was not thinking of a long-standing, traditional provincialism based on descent: that would have come too close to "ancient narrowness." He was thinking of a willed, an acquired, a consent-based provincialism as an organic ideal. His wholesome provincialism applied to *chosen* more than to inherited provinces.

Will "wholesome provincialism" present a threat to national cohesion? On the contrary:

> As our country grows in social organization, there will be, in absolute measure, more and not less provincialism amongst our people. To be sure, as I hope, there will also be, in absolute measure, more and not less patriotism, closer and not looser national ties, less and not more mutual sectional misunderstanding. But the two tendencies, the tendency toward national unity and that toward local independence of spirit, must henceforth grow together. (Royce 66)

It deserves emphasis that Royce pervasively resorted to the province as a metaphor of the individual and to the individual as a metaphor of the province. For Royce "it is with provinces as with individuals" (103). As we shall see, Ludwig Lewisohn's attempts at finding his individual province illustrate the same analogy.

Royce made it quite clear that he conceived of "provincialism" as an ideal, opposed to mob spirit on the one hand and to ancient narrowness on the other. This location of a virtue between two evils representing excess (too much provincialism = narrowness) and deficiency (too little provincialism = mob spirit) is reminiscent of Aristotle's *Ethics*. Royce's "Higher Provincialism" (his capitals), characterized by organic, redemptive, and individual metaphors, is the golden mean, the *juste milieu*; and it is thus revealing to put Royce's argument into an Aristotelian table (*Ethics* 104), which we may call "The Ethics of Wholesome Provincialism." This table gives us a mental landscape, a "map" of regionalism and ethnicity; and its principles have been operative in much American writing and thinking. Horace Kallen, who coined the term "cultural pluralism" in 1924, was one of Royce's Harvard students, and W. E. B. DuBois was another; Randolph Bourne, whose concept of "trans-nationalism" was inspired by Kallen, studied Royce in his classes at Columbia; and Ludwig Lewisohn read and admired Royce. Yet the Roycean conceptualization is pervasive in American culture, and although Frederick Jackson Turner, too, explicitly acknowledged the importance of Royce's work on provincialism (*Frontier* 157–58), Royce's significance extends far beyond direct lines of influence.

Kallen, Bourne, and DuBois

Horace Kallen received a variety of impulses from his teachers William James, George Santayana, and Barrett Wendell; yet, in his think-

ing on groups, he was also clearly a Roycean. Kallen's essay "Democracy *versus* the Melting Pot" (1915) has been of concern to us before.
However, an earlier, even more Roycean formulation can be found
in Horace Kallen's paper of 1906 entitled "The Ethics of Zionism," to
which Sarah Schmidt called attention in her dissertation, "Horace
Kallen and the Americanization of Zionism" (1973). In his essay,
which Kallen delivered on the Fourth of July weekend at the Federation of American Zionists convention in the Catskills and published a month later in the *Maccabean*, he rejected some "traditional"
Zionist positions, among them the view of Zionism as the fulfillment
of an age-old religious instinct. This attack on a definition of Jewish-
ness as ancient narrowness was balanced by Kallen's opposite dislike
of assimilationism: "We have to crush out the ... chameleon ... and
spiritual mongrel; we have to assert the Israelite" ("Ethics" 71). Kallen's "Israelite" is neither quite the old religious Jew (reminiscent of
Kallen's own "God-fearing proud father") nor the totally deracinated
convert who, like young Kallen at Harvard, might think of the Old
Testament merely as a "narrow, bigoted" book (Schmidt, "Kallen"
38). Kallen's ideal Zionist is the born-again adherent of what Kallen
elsewhere calls "the Jewish idea" and which he modeled on the
"American idea" of one of his mentors; for it was, as Kallen later
remembered, at Harvard College, "where a Yankee, named Barrett
Wendell, re-Judaized me" (Schmidt 36). Like Royce's provincialism,
Kallen's Zionism is an ideal in the bush, a goal, an ought: "our duty
is," Kallen says, "to Judaize the Jew" ("Ethics" 71). This is grounded
in Kallen's pluralistic faith that "each man in the human family" has
"the right to live and to give his life ideal expression." Again, the
group is imagined as an individual, as Kallen also envisioned "the
realization of the race-self." In 1972 Kallen remembered his "Ethics
of Zionism:"

> In that paper I automatically applied what I had learned in my
> courses. ... most auditors either couldn't make out what I was driving
> at or were opposed anyhow. (Schmidt 46–47)

Kallen continued to develop his Roycean conception of culture as
a harmonious federation of different provincialisms. By 1910, when
he published the essay "Judaism, Hebraism, Zionism," Kallen had
already found the musical image to express the integrative qualities
of his group ideal:

> Culture thus constitutes a harmony, of which peoples and nations
> are the producing instruments, to which each contributes its unique
> tone, in which the whole human past is present as ... a background
> from which the present comes to light. (Schmidt 78)

Although he still focused on the "Hebraic note" here, his later work gave full expression to the American symphony as an equivalent of Royce's Schiller. Yet, as Waldo Frank pointed out, Kallen's thought "proceeds on a strangely unmusical idea of the symphonic form: it presumes that a lot of instruments playing their own perpetual tune will somehow make a music together if they leave each other alone and smile during their pauses" (Frank, *Re-Discovery* 260n). Despite Kallen's modern definition of Zionism as a new group affiliation that structurally resembled Americanism, Kallen, of all the Royceans discussed here, was most given to considering descent-based identifications eternal and static; he believed in what David Hollinger described as "durable ethnic units" ("Ethnic Diversity" 142). By the time Kallen wrote *The Structure of Lasting Peace* (1918), he had completely naturalized ethnicity as an immutable category:

> So an Irishman is always an Irishman, a Jew always a Jew. Irishman or Jew is born, citizen, lawyer, or church-member is made. Irishman and Jew are facts in nature; citizen and church-member are artefacts in civilization. (31)

Kallen made a particularly sharp distinction between natural descent affiliations and artificial consent relations which affected his Roycean construction of ethnic harmony.

Randolph Bourne's "Trans-National America" (1916) is an invocation of the cosmopolitan ideal in quasi-aesthetic and organic terms which also echo Royce's "Higher Provincialism." America may be pitted against the old nationalism of Europe and Anglo-Saxonism, on the one hand, and threatened by the leveling power of the melting pot, on the other; yet there is still hope for the emergence of a truly transnational America, a country which would retain the "savor" of ethnic diversity and thus develop great moral and creative force. Bourne, too, was worried about the power of Americanization (as homogenization) and mass culture ("the cheap newspaper ... , the popular song, the ubiquitous automobile, our vapid moving pictures, our popular novels") upon the "flotsam and jetsam of American life" (*Radical* 255). Depressed by the "vacuous faces of the crowds in the city street," Bourne was especially imaginative in providing us with synonyms for the Roycean "deficiency" of homogeneity. In his "postmodern" America (of 1916!), Bourne saw "a tasteless, colorless fluid of uniformity," "insipidity," "flabbiness," "leering cheapness and falseness of taste and spiritual outlook," in short, "cultural wreckage" (254, 255). "Our cities are filled with these half-breeds who retain their foreign names but have lost their foreign savor" (254). He was equally indignant about the excess: wartime outbursts of "narrow 'Americanism' or forced chauvinism" (260), the "wave of reactionary enthusiasm to play the orthodox nationalistic game" (256), "that fiercely heightened pride" and "scarcely veiled belligerency" (257).

Yet between the excess and the deficiency lies the ideal middle ground of hope and redemption, which Bourne called "trans-nation-alism." Only when perceived as a "federation of cultures" (Kallen's term, which Bourne adopts, 256)—based on region (Bourne cites the South and New England) and on ethnicity—will America fulfill its ideal spirit (264). In the closely related essay "The Jew and Trans-National America" (1916), Bourne said that the so-called hyphenate (far from signaling a "minus sign") "has actually been our salvation" (Bourne, War 125), considered modern Zionism a model for Ameri-can transnationalism, and specifically termed the Jewish aspiration "wholesome" (War 131). In "Trans-National America" Bourne envi-sioned a "trans-national" federal culture of hyphenate dual citizens that could, in the tradition of "wholesome provincialism," "unite and not divide" (Radical 260) and help to save the world from suicide (259), which he rather realistically feared might result from the fierce nationalisms unleashed by World War I.

Bourne's perception is sharp, and occasionally his insights are astounding. He undermined arrogant nativism based on putative descent with the famous phrasing "We are all foreign-born or the descendants of foreign-born, and if distinctions are to be made between us they should rightly be on some other grounds than indig-enousness" (Radical 249). Although he often associates modern America with the pop culture of deficient provincialism, he occasion-ally has a very clear sense of the *modernity* of his own ideal hyphen-ates, whom he wants to be more than mere descendants (the Anglo-Saxons' flaw, 252): "Assimilation ... instead of washing out the mem-ories of Europe, made them more intensely real. Just as these clusters {of immigrants} became more and more objectively American, did they become more and more German or Scandinavian or Bohemian or Polish" (248). As if he were a part of the "ethnicization" and "eth-nogenesis" arguments of present-day theorists, Bourne, in "The Jew and Trans-National America," cites Zionism as the purest pattern of his transnationalism (War 128) and emphasizes that the immigrants' indiscriminate clinging to the past may be a case of arrested development:

> They fondly imagine that they are keeping the faith. But in merely not changing, these expatriated groups have not really kept the faith.

The faith is a certain way of facing the world, of accepting experience. It is a spirit and not any particular forms. A genuine transnationalism would be modern, reflecting not only the peculiar gifts
and temperament of the people, but reflecting it in its contemporary
form. America runs a very real danger of becoming not the modern
cosmopolitan grouping that we desire, but a queer conglomeration
of the prejudices of past generations, miraculously preserved here,
after they have mercifully perished at home. (*War* 131)

Bourne made the distinction between false antiquarian ethnicity
and truly modern and dynamic, cosmopolitan transnationalism
along the lines of the New Testament opposition of "letter" and
"spirit" [e.g., 2 Corinthians 3:6]. For Bourne, spiritual ethnicization
was "good" modernization. These are impressive insights in an essay
that was published in the same year in which Madison Grant's nativist *The Passing of a Great Race* appeared in print.

Yet there are shortcomings, too, in Bourne's thinking, flaws which
he shares with Kallen. Despite his understanding of the modern,
dynamic, and "spiritual" nature of ethnicity, Bourne as a matter of
course opposed the melting pot. He still wanted to "fix" his dual citizens and identify them with typical, characteristic traits (illiterate
Slavs, French clarity, etc.) which are more statically conceived and
descent based than Bourne would desire them to be. It is the image
of the orchestra and the instruments that seems to provide the mental map for his faith that "harmonious" diversity can be achieved
only if the ethnic parts are identifiable and in themselves homogeneous. Once a trombone, always a trombone!

Nowhere is this more apparent than in Bourne's venomous disdain for the (un-savor-y) marginal man who defies his static descent
identity, which alone seems to ensure the categorical variety of the
whole enterprise:

It is not the Jew who sticks proudly to the faith of his fathers and
boasts of that venerable culture of his who is dangerous to America,
but the Jew who has lost the Jewish fire and become a mere elemen-
tary, grasping animal. (*Radical* 254)

The understanding that keeping the faith doesn't work was forgotten, as Bourne surrendered to a strikingly paradoxical argument for
homogeneity and ethnic purity in the service of cosmopolitan diversity. This ideal diversity is achieved schematically and statically and
requires homogeneous components. In order to construct a dynamic
pluralistic transnationalism based on consent, Bourne needed mon-
istic little nationalities based on statically conceived descent. Without

recognizing it clearly, Bourne needed and constructed boundaries and ostracized types that challenged these walls of partition.

This is the dilemma of many pluralistic models of America's regional and ethnic provinces. Persons who do not fit into Celadon's valleys (blacks in the southern valley, Jews in the Russian valley, or Americanized ethnics who leave their ethnic valleys) are ignored, rationalized out of the valley, or scorned as they threaten the homogeneous units on which the scheme of diversity is based. The theme song of American regional and ethnic studies might well be "How monochrome was my valley. . . ."

Although Bourne and Kallen make no mention at all of Afro-Americans in their transnational federal republics and orchestras, Josiah Royce had a Negro student in his Harvard classes on argumentative composition, English C and D, who undertook an earlier, parallel attempt at charting black attitudes between the excess of revolt and the deficiency of hypocrisy. The student was W. E. B. DuBois; and the tenth chapter of his famous *The Souls of Black Folk* (1903) contains this passage:

> ... the Negro faces no enviable dilemma. Conscious of his impotence, and pessimistic; he often becomes bitter and vindictive; and his religion, instead of a worship, is a complaint and a curse, a wail rather than a hope, a sneer rather than a faith. On the other hand, another type of mind, shrewder and keener and more tortuous too, sees in the very strength of the anti-Negro movement its patent weaknesses, and with Jesuitic casuistry is deterred by no ethical considerations in the endeavor to turn this weakness to the black man's strength. Thus we have two great and hardly reconcilable streams of thought and ethical strivings; the danger of the one lies in anarchy, that of the other in hypocrisy. The one type of Negro stands almost ready to curse God and die, and the other is too often found a traitor to right and a coward before force; the one is wedded to ideals remote, whimsical, perhaps impossible of realization; the other forgets that life is more than meat and the body more than raiment. But, after all, is not this simply the writhing of the age translated into black,—the triumph of the Lie which, to-day, with its false culture, faces the hideousness of the anarchist assassin? (346–47)

DuBois emphasized that between "the two extreme types of ethical attitude ... wavers the mass of the millions of Negroes, North and South." He ended the chapter by presenting these ten million Negroes as waiting for "a new religious ideal," an "Awakening" which would lead them out of the "Valley of the Shadow of death" [Psalms

23:4} "where all that makes life worth living—Liberty, Justice, and Right—is marked 'For White People Only'" (348, 349).

In the related, though less well known essay, "On the Conservation of Races" (1897), DuBois, like Royce, delighted in the fact that "human beings differ widely" (Bracey, *Black* 251). He described the physical variations of mankind only to conclude that the deeper differences were "spiritual, psychical" (254). A "race" for DuBois was "a vast family of human beings, generally of common blood and language, always of common history, traditions and impulses, who are both voluntarily and involuntarily striving together for the accomplishment of certain more or less vividly conceived ideals of life" (252–53). DuBois's proposal, then, was, like Royce's, a plea for the conservation of these "ideals," which might encourage cooperation rather than friction. If, according to DuBois,

> there is substantial agreement in laws, language and religion; if there is a satisfactory adjustment of economic life, then there is no reason why, in the same country and on the same street, two or three great national ideals might not thrive and develop, that men of different races might not strive together for their race ideals as well, perhaps even better, than in isolation. (257)

The shared areas of the American ideal can be realized more fully by diverse provincialisms in harmonious cooperation: "We are Americans, not only by birth and by citizenship, but by our political ideals, our language, our religion" (258). Though DuBois also articulated the limits of the American identity, he was confident that the Negro would fulfill his "distinct mission as a race" (257) on this shared common ground.

> We believe in the duty of the Americans of Negro descent, as a body, to maintain their race identity until this mission of the Negro people is accomplished, and the ideal of human brotherhood has become a practical possibility. (261)

Paradoxically, would the conserving of Negro provincialism not make it easier to achieve the cosmopolitan and universalist ideal in America? This is particularly appropriate since the American Negro (like Royce's Californian) is understood by DuBois as a new formation:

> We are the first fruits of this new nation, the harbinger of that black to-morrow which is yet destined to soften the whiteness of the Teutonic to-day. We are that people whose subtle sense of song has given America its only American music, its only American fairy tales, its

only touch of pathos and humor amid its mad money-getting plu-
tocracy. As such, it is our duty to conserve our physical powers, our
intellectual endowments, our spiritual ideals. ... (258)

The aesthetic idealization of the province is here juxtaposed with an
incomplete nation dedicated to the madness of acquisition. As is so
often true in images of ethnicity, ethnics are idealist visionaries, un-
ethnics are practical men. Again, the vision of a redeemed pluralistic
future needs "conserved" redemptive ingredients.

The various applications of Royce's ethics of wholesome provincialism, including the distaste for the colorless fluid of homogenized
and acquisitive America and the distinction between good, excessive,
and deficient parochialism, are reflected in the conceptualizations of
regionalism which became prominent in the 1930s and the post-
World War II period.

The classic definition of regionalism appeared in Howard Odum
and Harry Estill Moore's *American Regionalism: A Cultural-Historical
Approach to National Integration* (1938), the very subtitle of which suggested the programmatic organic unity of the region as an integrative
(and corrective) element of the nation. Odum's regionalism, like
Royce's provincialism, was located between an excess and a deficiency: for Odum's (as for Frederick Jackson Turner's) regionalism,
the negative poles were divisive sectionalism and total national uniformity. Discussing the "essential quality of sectionalism" (the excess),
Odum wrote that

> inherent in it is the idea of separatism and isolation; of separate units
> with separate interests. It must be clear that, since the very definition
> of regionalism implies a unifying function, it must be different from
> sectionalism as everywhere defined by the historians. Here the dis-
> tinctions are clear between the divisive power of self-seeking *sections*
> and the integrating power of co-ordinate regions fabricated into a
> united whole. (39)

Odum's concept is, in Royce's sense, one of "wholesome" regionalism.
Whether or not the whole was "fabricated" and constructed, Odum
wrote: "Regionalism is organic, basic to the evolution of all culture.
Sectionalism is mechanical and is basic to specialized and temporary
ends" (43). This opposition is characteristic of the writings of many
later theorists who have made distinctions between natural, organic,
and timeless regionalism and mechanical, schismatic, and temporal
sectionalism. So much for the Aristotelian excess; but Odum also
dealt with the problem of deficiency, as his regions protected organic
variety against the "uniformities of machinery and techniques."

Odum furthermore saw regionalism as an important part of structuring the whole, of supplying an order to what might otherwise be unmanageable and out of balance.

> In American society there must be a strong national character and organization before the nation can be made strong through the strength and integration of its diverse regions so that regionalism may supplant the older separatism and isolationism of sectional development. (Jensen, *Regionalism* 403)

The semantic distinction between integrative region and separatist section is unmistakable. On several occasions Odum emphasized that part and whole were not to be perceived as alternative or conflicting concepts. Thinking of appropriate conjunctions to describe the relationship of regionalism and universalism, Odum declared that "it is not regionalism *or*, but regionalism *and*" (Jensen 401), an antithesis which remained important in Roycean America.

In a famous essay, "The Historian's Use of Nationalism," David Potter summarized the Roycean position when he wrote:

> Historians frequently write about national loyalty as if it were exclusive, and inconsistent with other loyalties, which are described as "competing" or "divided" and which are viewed as detracting from the primary loyalty to the nation. Yet it is self-evident that national loyalty flourishes not by challenging and overpowering all other loyalties, but by subsuming them all in a mutually supportive relation to one another. The strength of the whole is not enhanced by destroying the parts, but is made up of the sum of the parts. (Potter, *History* 75)

Potter humorously echoed Odum's "and"/"or" definition when he summarized: "A well-known phrase runs, 'for God, for Country, and for Yale'—not 'for God, or for Country, or for Yale." It does seem self-evident, yet it is based on a presumed harmony. What would we do if Yale seceded and the country started to open fire on New Haven? Perhaps we might then see studies contrasting deconstructionist Yale with the national norm of un-Yale—are there more or fewer believers in the devil in New Haven? The Roycean model leaves us with a moral geography which endows us with the capacity to overcome the excess and the deficiency so that we can practice "wholesome" regionalism. By making the part an organic and harmonious ingredient of the whole, one obviates conflict.

I would now like to broaden the Aristotelian table that was first applied only to Royce and incorporate into it some of the key terms surrounding the literature on regionalism and ethnicity. The model has a considerable range of possible applications. The underlying theme of many studies in regionalism and ethnicity is the search for a viable middle course of virtuous loyalties as an integrative force— expressive again, of the yearning for structure that is neither hier-archy nor mobocracy and an individualized concept of group life that is neither rigidly polarized nor colorlessly monotonous. We may do well to remember that Royce substituted, at some point in his essay, the hope of entertaining wholesome and transcendent provin-cialism in America for Schiller's fear that ideals might live only in poetry and in dreams. Royce's concept of the province is thus the result of an aesthetic ideal "in the bush" made manifest in the hands of Americans.

Many American intellectuals and ethnic writers have explicitly or implicitly adhered to variants of an "Aristotelian Table for the Ethics of Wholesome Provincialism" and defined a good ethnic attitude as a "new," an acquired, or an achieved identity, located between the ancient narrowness of a hierarchical old-world orientation (embod-ied by the nationalist spirit of World War I) and the dangers of

Aristotelian Table for the Ethics of Wholesome Provincialism

SPHERE OF ACTION OR FEELING	EXCESS	MEAN	DEFICIENCY
ETHNIC GROUP	ethnocentrism	proper ethnicity	deracination
REGION	sectionalism	regionalism	mobility
COUNTRY OF . . .	divisiveness	diversity	homogeneity
SOCIAL ORDER	hierarchy	structure	mobocracy
CLASS	aristocrat	middle class	plebeian
CONCERN	status	vision	money
INTENSITY	fanaticism	consciousness	indifference
REACTION	prejudice	celebration	ignorance
MIGRATION METAPHOR	old world	third generation	second generation
AESTHETIC METAPHOR	rigid, harsh	beautiful, harmonious	colorless, bland, monotonous
REALM METAPHOR	ancient, schismatic	natural, organic, individual	modern, artificial, mass-produced
WHERE TO FIND IT?	other countries	true America	un-South, melting-pot America
CONJUNCTION	either . . . or	and	neither . . . nor
KAFKA MOTTO	sentence one	sentence three	sentence two
MY TERMS	descent only	consent/descent	consent only

homogenization by total assimilation (symbolized by American popular culture); or, in our terms, between an identity based exclusively
on divisive descent and one primarily founded on bland universalist
consent. To invoke yet one further example, the English-born immigrant Horace Bridges in his meditations *On Becoming an American*
(1919) hoped for a nationalism that would be an internationalism at
the same time. "Only by taking such a view of its mission in the
world," Bridges continued, "can a free people escape both the Scylla
of aggressive jingoism and the Charybdis of a denationalized cosmopolitanism" (170). The American odyssey continues. . . .

The Problem of Cultural Dominance

As in the case of the diffusion of typological thinking in the varied
examples of regional and ethnic provincialisms, it has been striking
to observe how easily an American concept of idealized diversity
traveled across ethnic and regional lines. Ironically, one could say
that the theoretical basis on which American diversification takes
place is universally shared. And yet, there are enormous gradations
in intensity and meaning in these provincialisms, distinctions which
are connected with the question of power. In the examples we have
looked at, there is a difference between Royce, on the one hand, and
DuBois and Bourne, on the other, which deserves further attention.
Whereas Royce investigates his provincialism as such, without too
much regard for external pressures for or against the expression of
group cohesion, DuBois structures his Aristotelian table against the
pressure emanating from the excesses of white ethnocentrism, while
Bourne polemicizes against the Americanization campaign during
World War I. It may therefore be appropriate to take into consideration how dominance and power affect the ethics of wholesome
provincialism.

The virtuous spot on the spectrum between vices changes once we
admit the categories of class, stratification, and cultural dominance.
The Aristotelian excess seems more defiantly hopeless, the deficiency
more cowardly when we look at groups which lack dominance and
are more often than not defined from the outside. The self-definition
by consent is denied only to that part of a group's population which
tends to deny the importance of descent: since they are externally
defined by powerful descent myths, their adoption of the culture's
dominant individual consent definitions can at best be defined as
"passing" and "assimilationism." Afro-American narrators, most com-

prehensively embodied by Ralph Ellison's *Invisible Man* (1952), have illustrated how external definitions by racial categories persistently interfere with individual definitions from the inside. This is also the cultural tension of Melvin Tolson's "Défineznegro," steering a hazardous course through the narrowing opening between a Scylla and Charybdis. For the Aristotelian middle ground shrinks dramatically as we go down on the social ladder, so that an underdog group's very Roycean ideal of wholesome provincialism may look either like dangerously narrow group pride or like self-hating and unreal conformism to dominant writers, observers, and critics—and sometimes even to underdogs themselves.

What is healthily "provincial" in a position of cultural dominance is considered both vulgar and narrow when it appears lower on the scale. The dominant category often wants to portray itself as universal, yet at the same time it excludes dominated, or simply *defined*, groups from practicing that very universalism and categorizes them by descent only. To take another example, in *The Mark of Oppression* (1951), Abram Kardiner and Lionel Ovesey left very little room for a "wholesome" race consciousness for American blacks between the Scylla of (self-hating) assimilationism and the Charybdis of (aggressively antiwhite) nationalism. In *The Omni-Americans* (1970) Albert Murray mocks such narrowing strategies as "social science fiction"; among other examples, Murray points out that one study "actually indicts Negroes {as deviant} for having a low suicide rate" (*Omni-Americans* 67). For culturally besieged and externally defined groups, the Roycean middle ground, the spot of ideal wholesome provincialism, may thus simply be squeezed out of existence by dominant groups. In American ethnic symbolism some groups may fluctuate: white southerners, for example, function both as an (often negatively) defined group in the American context and at the same time as a defining group in relation to southern blacks and other groups (such as Appalachians).

If we add the dimension of power to our chart, we have to indicate a V-shaped overlay to describe the narrowing of the healthy ideal. What would be called healthy group consciousness at the top (sometimes semantically excluded from the very term "ethnicity") may get defined externally as angry ethnocentrism or bland escapist Americanism for groups at the bottom. New York folk wisdom has it that when a patient comes early to therapy he's anxious, when he is late he's hostile, and when he arrives on time he's compulsive. Once he accepts the therapist's definition as dominant (as a universal concern, not as a hostile idiosyncrasy), a patient can do nothing right. "How does it feel to be a problem?" is the hidden question DuBois said he so often sensed (*Souls* 213). (In this context it is interesting to reflect upon the array of metaphors from the realm of mental health that were applied to the "problem" of black "social pathology," especially since *The Mark of Oppression* appeared.) Once a problem, always a problem!

Cultural dominance is expressed in the power of definition, the power of constructing boundaries, and—this is certainly a theme of regional and ethnic writing—people wrongly or carelessly defined may even externally accept but then internally invert a false definition or a confining slur out of defiance. This is perhaps why so many names, including that of the "odious" Puritans, originated in frozen curses, why some southerners delight in viewing themselves as "unreconstructed rebels," or why terms such as "funky" or "jazz" changed from frankly derogatory into subtly subversive and finally positive and descriptive terms. As Ulf Hannerz argued in 1976, this tendency for people to make such defiant reinterpretations is a source of cultural vitality ("Some Comments" 435). But this almost inevitably means standing the dominant ethics on its head and refusing to accept its universal goodness by challenging the boundaries on which it is constructed. This is one theoretical context in which the frequent appearances of tricksters in ethnic writing make sense: the trickster, after all, is "the enemy of boundaries" (Radin, *Trickster* 185).

The Aristotelian table, schematic though it may be, can help to illuminate the tone of idealism that is so pervasive in regional and ethnic studies and, at the same time, clarify the notion of provincialism as an agency of a hoped-for redemption. Yet we also saw how dominance affected the Roycean model, so that at some point the power-contaminated ethics had to be inverted in order to permit the oppressed group's realization of the ethical ideal.

What seems to have happened with the Roycean provinces, Bourne's ethnic groups, DuBois's races, and Odum's regions is that they have been endowed with the ability to carry forth the banner of hope to let America be America again—as Langston Hughes put it (Brown, *Caravan* 370). If the codes of American exceptionalism identified the sacred rhetoric of religious redemption with the secular place of America, then the concepts of American regionalism identify that same language of typological ethnogenesis with the region, while ethnic thinking applies it to the ethnic group. That may be the deeper meaning of the persistent yearning for a unified structure of the country, a structure that would be virtuous, aesthetic, harmoniously conflict-free, and redemptive at the same time. America seems to be filled not just with Celadon's valleys but also with harmoniously coexisting and overlapping ethnic groups on errands into the wilderness, and regions on the hill—here to save us from the surrounding evils. This may be one reason for the aestheticization of regional and ethnic life, the pervasiveness of moralism in ethnic and regional studies, and the individualization of region and ethnic group. But how can individuality be constructed as a representation and metaphor of group identity?

I would like to break the spell of virtue, salvation, and harmonious structure and turn to the individual as a version of Royce's province. Provincialism is conceived as a way to realize true individuality, and the individual provides discussions of regionalism and ethnicity with pervasive metaphors. In analogy to Sacvan Bercovitch's term "auto-American-biography" (*Puritan* 179), one might speak of "auto-regional-biography" or "the American self as region and ethnic group." A surprisingly Roycean illustration of this process is given in Louis Adamic's discussion of ethnic name changing in *What's Your Name* (1942). Adamic describes his own name as the organic ideal, located between the original "Adamič" (which a narrow-minded ethnic spokesman named Valjavec asked him to retain) and the unorganic Anglicization "Adams" (which Chapman, an ardent Americanizer, urged him to adopt). He argues that "Adamič became Adamic *organically*" and that he "yielded to no pressure" (22). The applicability of the ethics of wholesome provincialism is self-evident as the individual steers a middle course between old-world haughtiness and self-annihilating assimilation.

Ludwig Lewisohn's autobiography, *Up Stream: An American Chronicle* (1922), is a more complicated example for the identity choices of a nonsouthern southerner and non-Jewish Jew who, however, shared Bourne's and Royce's yearning for a province of his own. Yet, in the symphony of American pluralism, which instrument was Lewisohn to play? In relating an individual autobiography to regional and ethnic identity, one is strongly tempted to repeat the methodology of wholesome provincialism and to juxtapose the regional and ethnic "norm" with the "isolato experience" of a writer who is unusually hard to identify. I might then end up with the individual writer (here Lewisohn) as the true embodiment of America against all attempts to strip him of his particular "savor" by subjecting him to homogenizing ethnic and regional categories or looking at him with some ancient narrowness. I am not trying to do that. Instead, I would like to emphasize that the concept of individual identity—natural though it seems to be—is as much the result of cultural construction as are the notions of regional and ethnic-group identities.

The "Real" Ludwig Lewisohn: American Identities of a German Jewish Immigrant to the South

Ludwig Lewisohn's problematic use of the first person singular notwithstanding, he wanted to follow Royce's advice that wanderers should return to their own province after learning freely from abroad: But to which province was Lewisohn to return? In his autobiography Lewisohn presents himself as a man with a dazzling variety of identity choices. He attributes some of his character traits to his German background, others to his tenuous Jewishness, and still others to his southern upbringing or to his voracious reading. Far from soberly describing the confluence of these different elements in the narrator of the book, he is strongly evaluative and curiously Roycean in accounting for the process during which he absorbed, "unconsciously, of course, a very large set of moral and social conventions that are basic to the life of the average American" (Up Stream 51). On the one hand he sees the religious practices of his orthodox relatives as an indication of the "ancient narrowness" which had to be overcome. On the other hand the immersion in southern Christian values provides an illustration of being hypnotized by a few fatal phrases. Finally, when his "true individuality" emerges, it appears with the same gesture of defiance which earlier prompted Royce to use the very term "provincialism."

Descended from assimilated Prussian Jews ("they were Germans first and Jews afterwards" {17}), Ludwig Lewisohn was born in Berlin on May 30, 1882. After attending school in Berlin for a few years, the nine-year-old Lewisohn went to America—where his father Jacques decided to emigrate after being financially ruined because of an unwise business deal. The family first moved in with Minna's (the mother's) youngest brother, Siegfried Eloesser, who lived in St. Matthews, a small village in South Carolina, which Lewisohn dubs "St. Marks" in Up Stream (Chyet, "Ludwig" 296-322). At the point of migration Lewisohn, an only child, was already affected by a number of forces on his identity. Berlin is associated with his "earliest glimpses of beauty," and Pariser Platz—which was then, ironically, the site of the American embassy in Berlin—left an indelible imprint as a significant mental region, since Lewisohn remembers that it

spread out with an airiness, a fine and noble amplitude of shape and
proportion, a grace and majesty at once that I despair of rendering
into words. I have seen nothing like it since. (12)

The child feels more at home with the German Christmas celebration than with that of the Jewish New Year and the Day of Atone-
ment; yet while Germany remains associated with festiveness and
beauty, he speaks of Jewish melancholy as "the badge of all our tribe"
(17). Lewisohn's relatives in South Carolina function in the sense of
Royce's ancient narrowness: "My aunt," Lewisohn writes without
much sympathy, "was a Jewess of the Eastern tradition, narrow-
minded, given over to the clattering ritual of pots and pans—'meaty'
and 'milky'—and very ignorant" (41).

The southern landscape appears to have had a more formative
force, though this force is understood by an "I" who exists prior to
regional category here:

> In spring the dogwood showed its white blossoms there; in the mild
> Southern autumn a child could lie on the deep layers of brownish
> pine-needles and play with the aromatic cones and gaze up at the
> brilliant blue of the sky. The summer stirred me deeply. I had been
> used to the cool, chaste, frugal summers of the North. Here the heat
> smote; the vegetation sprang into rank and hot luxuriance—noi-
> some weeds with white ooze in their stems and bell-like pink flowers
> invaded the paths and streets. I felt a strange throbbing, followed by
> sickish languor and a dumb terror at the frequent, fierce thunder-
> storms. Both my intelligence and my instincts ripened with morbid
> rapidity and I attribute many abnormalities of temper and taste that
> are mine to that sudden transplantation into a semi-tropical world.
> (39)

This excerpt, taken from a chapter ambitiously entitled "The American Scene" (as Lewisohn writes in the same book, "I didn't, I must
say in justice to myself, imitate Henry James at all" {133}), shows the
power Lewisohn ascribed to the place of socialization; at the same
time it invests the narrator with the superior power to attribute character traits to regional influences, while the language is evocative of
Henry Timrod's "Cotton Boll."

In St. Matthews, that little southern village, Lewisohn also becomes
aware of the diverse ethnic backgrounds of its inhabitants. His attention is first attracted by the Negroes; he notes that on Saturdays many
hundreds of them "came in from the sparsely settled country; they
rode in on horses or mules or oxen or drove rough carts and primitive wagons, and were themselves generally clad in garments of which

the original homespun had disappeared in a mass of gaudy patches"
(38). This sounds like the dichotomy of homespun provincialism versus vulgar standardization. Lewisohn's ethnoreligious profile of the
villagers is detailed:

> The people of the village, storekeepers, a few retired farmers, three
> physicians, three or four lawyers, came of various stocks—English,
> Scotch-Irish, German, even French and Dutch. But they were all
> descended from early nineteenth century settlers and had become
> thorough Americans. Everybody belonged to either the Baptist or
> the Methodist church. The Methodists were, upon the whole, more
> refined, had better manners than the Baptists and were less illiterate.
> Among the villagers there was a moderate amount of hard drinking
> and a good deal of sexual irregularity, especially with Mulatto
> women. I have since wondered that there was not more. The life was
> sterile and monotonous enough. (42)

The contrast developed is, again, between ethnic variety—for Lewisohn even in the shape of sexual irregularity—and monotony.

How did Lewisohn's parents fit into this setting? His account is
reminiscent of Bourne's strictures against marginal men in his vision
of cosmopolitan ethnic group life—only that Lewisohn's own father
played the role of Bourne's assimilated Jew! Lewisohn emphasizes
that the Christian villagers were quite liberal toward the Jews in the
village:

> Only one Jew and that was my father, was looked upon with some
> suspicion by the severer among his Gentile neighbors. The reason
> was curious and significant; he did not perform the external rites of
> the Jewish faith and, upon entering a fraternal life insurance order,
> he smiled and hesitated when asked to affirm categorically his belief
> in a personal God. (43)

Though at first solitary in school, Lewisohn learns English fast and
becomes a Methodist. "In the phraseology of our Protestant sects, I
accepted Jesus as my personal Savior and cultivated, with vivid faith,
the habit of prayer in which I persisted for many years" (51). He
writes about his whole family: "We saw a good deal of my uncle and
his family and their friends. But culturally we really felt closer to the
better sort of Americans in the community, and so there began in
those early days that alienation from my own race which has been
the source to me of some good but of more evil" (44). It is surprising
that Lewisohn uses the terms "alienation" and "my own race" here,
though so far he has fairly consistently portrayed himself as alien
among Jews.

While his parents did "not so rapidly adapt themselves to the folk-ways of the surprising land in which they found themselves" (52), Lewisohn's own Americanization is more complete. Discussing the process in retrospect, Lewisohn develops a telling distinction between his Americanized self then, at the time of the experience, and his "real" self now, at the time of writing. Though he often uses distancing devices in talking about his childhood and youth, Lewisohn here openly discusses the distance for the first time. He emphasizes that his "American" values came by absorption:

> There can be no question of reflection or conviction on the part of the child. But at the age of ten my emotional assimilation into the social group of which I was a physical member was complete. I would not have touched any alcoholic drink; I would have shrunk in horror from a divorced person; I would have felt a sense of moral discomfort in the presence of an avowed sceptic. I believed in the Blood of the Lamb. ... (51)

The transformation was, however, according to the narrator of 1922 an inorganic and artificial one; when the voice of the narrator intervenes, he establishes his new and "real" self as that of a skeptic and an opponent of Prohibition who views his own, past immersion into southernness as a typical case of shallow second-generation deficiency:

> I find it hard not to let an ironic note slip into these phrases. But they mark the sober facts. If ever the child of immigrants embraced the faith of the folk among whom it came—I was that child. Insensibly almost I withdrew myself from my cousins and from the other Jewish children in the village. (51)

A rather complicated life line is thus simplified with the help of a Roycean value system; instead of coming to terms with the complexity of the assimilated and secularized German-Jewish background exposed to southern methodism, Lewisohn suggests a somewhat melodramatic antagonism between a "real," organic self and an unreal, adopted identity which the narrator can easily denounce. The real and authentic self, moreover, seems to have become the true identity precisely because it followed (and therefore also must have preceded?) the phase of southern immersion. The "true" Lewisohn is thus born out of the oppositional denunciation of a false "un-Lewisohn."

And yet, Lewisohn's transformations are also seen as inevitable: the old world was left behind; the South, and not Berlin, exerted its geographic influence on the formative mind; there was no peer group for the boy to associate with except the one that he did become a part of, since his parents failed to cultivate a wholesome provincialism of their own. Lewisohn is particularly astute in accounting for his parents' failure to become part of an ethnic or religious group in America. After they moved to Charleston ("Queenshaven" in *Up Stream*), his parents experienced more social distancing from the city's inhabitants. Lewisohn asks:

> Why, then, did not my parents join either one of two other groups — a German-American or a Jewish one? Their instinct in this matter was a fine although a quite tragically mistaken one. They conceived the country in which they had made their home as obviously one of English speech and culture. Hence, without a shadow of disloyalty to their German training, they desired to be at one with such of their English-speaking countrymen as shared their tastes in art and literature and — *mutatis mutandis* — their outlook on life. They saw no reason for associating with North German peasants turned grocers (although they had the kindliest feeling toward these sturdy and excellent people), nor with rather ignorant, semi-orthodox Jews from Posen. They had not done so in Berlin. Why should they in America where, as my father used to observe, in those earliest years, a democratic spirit must prevail, and where neither poverty nor a humble employment could keep an educated man from the society of his intellectual equals. That was, according to him, the precise virtue of America, the fundamental spiritual implication of American life! The result of my parents' acceptance of this principle was utter friendlessness. (58–59)

In other words, according to the judgment of their son, the immigrants Jacques and Minna Lewisohn overlooked the importance of ethnicity and overestimated the rhetoric of individualism. They did not know that in America it is commendable for newcomers to consent to belong to an ethnic group of their choice. Thus they did not fit into "a city of very rigid social groups" (57). Lewisohn writes — as if he wanted to illustrate Fredrik Barth's thesis that it is the boundary and not the cultural content that defines ethnic groups — that immediately upon the family's move to Charleston "there came to us in some impalpable way a sense of something we had never felt in St. Marks: invisible barriers seemed to arise about us, a silence seemed to fall where we were, an iron isolation to be established" (57).

Young Lewisohn appears to have been able to break down at least some of these walls of partition; and his own group integration in his high school years, which he discusses in a part of *Up Stream* entitled — in classic ethnic fashion — "The Making of an American," seems to have been more successful than that of his parents. To be sure, he experiences the ultimate humiliation of hostile categorization by peers in an episode that is reminiscent of much ethnic literature from the "Christ-killer" passage in Michael Gold's *Jews without Money* (1930) and the phrase "Oh, you're a nigger too" hurled at the narrator of James Weldon Johnson's *Autobiography of an Ex-Colored Man* (1912) to the titular insult of the narrator's grandfather in John Fante's "Odyssey of a Wop" (1940). Lewisohn writes that during his first school year in Charleston, he was "taunted with being a foreigner and a Jew" (65). Lewisohn's antagonist and tormentor was a much stronger schoolboy who excelled in such rituals of insult; he is described by Lewisohn, not totally dispassionately, as "a tallish fellow with huge mouth always distorted by idiotic laughter, hateful, off-standing ears and small, greenish eyes" (65). Lewisohn reports that he heroically fought this ogre of a classmate and "had no trouble after that" (66). It would be tempting to compare such descriptions of youthful ethnic antagonists and interpret them as the writers' delayed revenge.

Later, when the adolescent Lewisohn is beset by a growing "consciousness of sex," he feels the need to denounce this new awareness as something vulgar and disconcerting, a reaction which the libertine narrator now retrospectively ascribes to an "Anglo-American" character trait:

> And my Americanization was complete. . . . I attended a Methodist church. . . . Naturally I soon fell into a wretched conviction of sin and tried to double the zeal of my religious exercises. Yet all my inner life was like a clear pool that had been muddied and defiled. . . . Relentlessly my mind drifted off into imaginings that filled me with terror, but that seem to me now, as I recall them, not only harmless, but rather poetical. I was the more convinced of the wickedness of my thoughts by the absurd exaltation of woman which is so characteristic a note of Southern life. (73–74)

The writer's new self can see the poetry of the tormented soul of his adolescent and Americanized old self: then even the conventional belief that "woman is a being without passion" had "entered the very texture" of his life. The very act of writing about this topic is seen as proof of his conversion and as a dramatic departure from the old stage of delusion brought about by his Americanization in its southern form:

> Nothing could have persuaded me that I would ever have thoughts as "ungentlemanly" as those I have just set down. A gentleman

believed that the South was in the right in the War between the States, that Christianity was the true religion ... that the Democratic party was the only means, under Providence, of saving the White Race from obliteration by the Nigger, that good women are sexless— "sweet and pure" was the formula—and that in a harlot's house you must keep on your hat. (74)

Lewisohn apparently at one point or another believed in and acted upon all of those tenets, including the last one (though he "wanted hard to take {his} hat off"). Yet the conversion formula of the first-person-singular narrative permits him to cast his sins as not really "his own" but as "theirs," under whose spell he once was. He describes the youth's militant Americanism as artificial and external, acquired at the expense of his truer self:

> It is clear then that, at the age of fifteen, I was an American, a South-erner and a Christian. ... It was at this time that, in my thoughts and emotions, I came upon a distinct and involuntary hostility to every-thing either Jewish or German. (77)

As Stanley Chyet has shown, Lewisohn's mental southernization was intense. Most notably, Lewisohn read and identified with white southern literature and thought of the Confederacy as his own ver-sion of Celadon's valley. No matter how much the Lewisohn of 1922 wanted to play this phase down as the inauthentic one, the Lewisohn of 1902–1904 was a true local patriot of Charleston who had made the southern cause his own. In a series of articles for the *Charleston News-and-Courier*, entitled "Books We Have Made," Lewisohn's pub-lic voice emerged as that of a southern apologist. Lewisohn identified strongly with southern antagonism to New England ("Nor hanging witches, nor abjuring plays") and even with white southern prejudice against blacks; the valley had to be homogeneous. Explaining the low literary output of Carolina since the Civil War, Lewisohn wrote in the *News-and-Courier* of September 20, 1903: "For over a decade the State lay prostrate under the intolerable tyranny of a barbarous and inferior race" (Chyet, "Ludwig" 321). As Chyet has also documented, in Lewisohn's introduction to an edition of Crèvecoeur's *Letters from an American Farmer* (which the author coedited with his Columbia University professor William Peterfield Trent), Lewisohn considers the Frenchman's critical remarks on slavery "untrustworthy" since, as a "humanitarian of the Age of the Revolution, a member of the Soci-ety of Friends, or, at least closely connected with it," Crèvecoeur was "incapable of approaching the slavery problem dispassionately" (Chyet, "Crèvecoeur" 134). With such comments Lewisohn, who otherwise liked Crèvecoeur's ability to capture the "aroma of life," could fend off the horrifying account of the Charleston slave who was left to die in a cage at the end of Crèvecoeur's ninth letter. More to Lewisohn's southern taste were the poems by Henry Timrod, quite appropriately the author of "Ethnogenesis" (1861); Lewisohn considered him "the most perfect lyricist of the ante-bellum Republic," who "produced no work that is technically crude" and who deserves "a high recognition."

As many ethnic births seem to take place in sacralized defiance against otherness, so the "true" Lewisohn is (re)born when he begins his exodus from the bondage of the earlier and false "not-me." In the narrator's attempt to criticize his Americanization as self-denying conformity experienced by his inner self, he resorts to the ethics of wholesome provincialism, though it is, ironically, the South—a province—which provides Lewisohn with the primary false slogans of an unorganic group identity. The writer's approach to his past is thus characterized by a critique of his Americanization from an American point of view. His "real" or "inner" self emerges out of defiance against the inauthentic (nearly "brainwashed") southern Christian self—in which, however, he clearly and confidently believed during much of his adolescence and early manhood. As he puts it in the conversion formula so familiar from immigrant autobiographies, "my present self is so far removed from that old, boyish self in Queenshaven with its deep faith and ardor" (92). In the College of Charleston, Lewisohn decides to major in English and go on to graduate school at Columbia University in New York. Now, as he recognizes the "uncriticalness of Southern culture" (95), Lewisohn wants to be a poet—of all unsouthern professions! He characterizes himself in retrospect as a "Pan-Angle of the purest type" (87):

> I was passionately Anglo-American in all my sympathies, I wanted above all things to be a poet in the English tongue, and my name and physiognomy were characteristically Jewish. I had ill-cut, provincial clothes and just money enough to get through one semester. Such was my inner and outer equipment for pursuing in a metropolitan graduate school the course which was to lead to a college appointment to teach English. (103)

The Anglo-Saxon/Jewish conflict is enriched by Lewisohn's encounter with modern German poetry, where he finds

> the haunting echoes of my inner life, the deep things, the true things of which I had been ashamed and which I had tried to transmute into the correct sentiments of my Anglo-American environment. . . .

They spoke my thoughts, they felt my conflicts; they dared to be themselves—these modern men and women who were impassioned and troubled like myself, who had not snared the universe in barren {formulae}, but who were seekers and strivers! ... They made me free; they set me on the road of trying to be not what was thought correct without reference to reality, but what I was naturally meant to be. They taught me, not directly, but by the luminous implications of their works, the complete spiritual unveracity in which I had been living and in which most of my Anglo-American friends seemed to be living. (114)

As in Royce's analogy with Schiller's realm of poetry, and resonant with Lewisohn's idealization of a Berlin square as the place of aesthetics, and his southernization as a Timrod reader—group identity, true organic selfhood, and "what I was naturally meant to be" become intertwined with an aesthetic ideal. For Lewisohn "nature" revealed itself in modern German poetry, pitted against the "unveracity" of his actual life. As Jules Chametzky has suggested, at times ethnoregional group identity "ain't what you do, or what you are but an image created by what you read" ("Styron's" 435–36). Lewisohn became immersed in German literature in 1903 as a result of his friendship with George Sylvester Viereck. The fact that the Lewisohn of 1922 still describes having found his "natural" self in *German* poetry seems to be at least in part affected by the author's defiant dissent against the pervasive anti-German spirit during World War I.

According to the account in *Up Stream*, the idealistic search for elective affinities, for poetic Kunta Kintes of Lewisohn's roots, the consent (or dissent) construction of his "natural" descent line, comes to a halt when he encounters first the possibility and then the reality of anti-Semitism in university English departments. The episode is based on a letter in which Professor Carpenter of Columbia told Lewisohn not to expect an appointment in English at any university because of his Jewish background. Now the narrator is closer to the protagonist in indignation and confusion when he bitterly complains that American "guardianship of the native tongue is far fiercer than it is in an, after all, racially homogeneous state like Germany" (124). He now has to grapple with the problem of an external definition based on descent myths that is not matched by his consent or an inner sense of belonging to that group: "I could take no refuge in the spirit and traditions of my own people. I knew little of them. My psychical life was Aryan through and through" (125). Again, there is a sense of individual identity prior to group membership for an "I" who has the power to attribute character traits to groups:

> Slowly, in the course of the years, I have discovered traits in me which I sometimes call Jewish. But that interpretation is open to grave doubt. I can, in reality, find no difference between my own inner life and thought and impulse and that of my very close friends whether American or German.

In the face of such complications, who can blame Lewisohn for one of the ways in which he tried to resolve his dilemma: "In my confusion of mind I didn't revise my dissertation and left the university without my doctor's degree" (127). His working for "Singleton, Leaf and Company" (i.e., Doubleday, Page, and Co.), the publishing firm which had rejected *Sister Carrie* but printed "a most slanderous and ignorant piece of anti-Semitic propaganda" (129), did not help either.

An author in search of his organic ethnic province, Lewisohn was overwhelmed by the complicated options he faced. Except when *he* was the object of such typecasting, he was not opposed to external ascription of ethnic character traits and strongly believed in regional and ethnic group identities, as his remarks throughout *Up Stream* indicate. We already noted Jewish melancholy and southern gentility; Lewisohn also speaks of "child-like" Negroes, "interesting and vital" Mexicans, and a New England Brahmin student who lost his indigenous coldness and stiffness only after absorbing "the sunny comradeship and spiritual freedom" of the University of Bonn (38, 90, 109). For an instant Lewisohn was attracted to the tramps at Union Square: "I understood the temptation of stepping out of the ranks and drifting off into the land of unconsidered men ..." (130).

Yet Lewisohn resisted that temptation and concentrated, in the last chapters, on finding his identity by responding to the most important negative categorization to which he had been subjected. Having confessed earlier that he could never wholeheartedly "root" (an interesting word) for his school and college teams (75), he now seemed to take it upon himself to root for all those potential aspects of his identity which were antithetical to his immediate environments. He refused to change his name in order to increase his chances of getting published (133). He became a stubborn, European-oriented professor of German literature in the Midwest, in a very pronounced antithesis to students and administrators who had no trouble rooting for their home teams and who never permitted themselves "to see the rival team, the competing institution, or the other party" (158).

During World War I the anti-German sentiment at "Central City" (i.e., Ohio State) University provoked Lewisohn to identify himself antithetically and defiantly:

> The middle-aged professors with homely and withered wives and strong moral opinions shouted and flared up and wreaked themselves on William II—and Kant and Nietzsche and Wagner. . . . When they saw me their eyes glowed strangely or turned fiercely cold. I would not join the lynching-party. I had a weakness for the lynchee. . . . I was regarded as good, loyal Southerners—guardians of Christianity, morality, democracy—regard a "nigger-lover." The parallel is exact. (205)

Lewisohn, who had shown little interest in black civil rights and who in his own loyal southern period had expressed some rather problematic ideas about race, here adopts the convenient strategy of an "un-Southern," transethnic, and defiant bohemian who scorns the mainstream on a whole slate of contradictory grounds: he navigates his own position in self-contradictory antithesis as he opposes middle age and withered wives in the name of youthful vitality, speaks against America in the name of its ethnic victims, and counters war propaganda in the name of German culture. This hodgepodge of heterogeneous identity formations is held together by antithesis. The act of defiance is directed against external categorization and, at the same time, against his own old self. In this antithetical structure, not in the cultural content of his opinions, Lewisohn remained constant through the years. For all the variety of identity options he accepted in the course of his life, he always defined himself as an opponent, a rebel, a renegade.

At the end of *Up Stream*, Lewisohn—now "in all fundamental sense ... an American" (219)—sketched vignettes (similar ones appeared in his *Cities and Men* [1927]) of some cultural victims of Americanization and came to a conclusion which is, again, evocative of Royce:

> If you drain a man of spiritual and intellectual content, if you cut him off from the cultural continuity that is native to him and then fling him into a world where his choice lies between an impossible religiosity and Prohibition on the one hand, and the naked vulgarity of the streets and of the baseball diamond on the other, you have robbed him of the foundation on which character can be built. (239)

Wholesome character had to be developed somewhere between the excess of Prohibition and the deficiency of popular sports. Lewisohn saw the problem, both in the psychological and in the social sphere, in the terms of the ethics of wholesome provincialism (though he used the term "provincialism" in its pejorative sense). Describing the cultural situation at the beginning of World War I in *Expression in America*, Lewisohn constructed the familiar Roycean threat of two opposite evils:

> We had the just terror of those who saw the danger of a rickety poly-glot polity, like the Austrian, and we had the equally just terror of those who feared a blank British provincialism in which all but Smith and Jones would be helots by anterior decree. (369)

Lewisohn saw the redemptive synthesis in the emergence and sup-port of an ethnic-minority literature of critical protest which invited the sons and daughters of the Puritans to join in and "destroy and transform Puritanism" (370).

The complications of his own sets of conflicting identities notwith-standing, Lewisohn the American wanted men to have their adopted wholesome provincialism, even if there was no province readily avail-able to claim them. He arrived at the point which the villagers of St. Matthews had maintained all along when they were suspicious of Lewisohn's father for not being Jewish enough. He arrived at this point in the precise terms of Josiah Royce, "perhaps the most pow-erful writer of the period," as he called him in *Expression in America* (297). The unreligious Jew, the southern Christian of German birth, the secret tramp and open bohemian, the Pan-Angle and inner Aryan, the American poet on a perennial quest for his inner, organic, authentic self—all these Lewisohns become "un-Lewisohns" and give way to a structural acceptance of a new, mediate identity achieved by defiance. If English departments from Virginia to Min-nesota were prejudiced enough not to hire Lewisohn because he was Jewish, then he *had to be* Jewish! The external definition of an ethnic identity may thus help to create an internal one. Years after the pub-lication of *Up Stream*, Lewisohn identified himself as a "Zionist" in the *Who's Who*—but this was, like Kallen's "Hebraic idea," a Jewish-ness based not on the "narrowness" of tradition but on wholesome provincialism. It was a case not of organic identity by descent and unbroken tradition but of constructed, symbolic ethnicity, built on consent, modernity, and defiance.

Lewisohn's untypical situation may yet be—as the author claimed in the epilogue to *Up Stream*—representatively American. Embrac-ing a regional or group identity in voluntary defiance (as in Faulk-ner's "I don't hate it, I don't hate it!") allows Americans to steer a Roycean middle course between ancient narrowness and vulgar

monotony. By creating new, not traditionally anchored, group identities and by authenticating them, they may represent individuality
and American identity at the same time. Organically belonging to an
ethnic group of their choice, these Adamics who are neither Adam-
ičes nor Adamses can now proceed to fight ancient narrowness and
mob spirit, and do it all in the name of their province and of America. Celadon and his angel would have been very puzzled indeed. ...
Lewisohn's career and shifting self-identification demonstrate the
validity of examining the dynamic nature of the Aristotelian categories that constitute individualized modern provincialism. In the
system of "Wholesome Provincialism" provinces are a moral escape
into space for ethnic discourse. But escape also occurs in the dimension of time. This is where "generations," which can serve to naturalize time and to allow for a plausible construction of mythical
descent lines, come into the picture.

CHAPTER SEVEN

First Generation, Second Generation, Third Generation ... : The Cultural Construction of Descent

I desire that the mantle of the New England prophets should rest on the shoulders of our own children.

—Mary Antin

Washington does not represent the past to which one belongs by birth, but the past to which one tries to belong by effort.

—Margaret Mead

The term "generation" often appears as an answer to all sorts of questions. Why wasn't a certain ethnic language maintained in the United States? Because of the second generation. Why is there an ethnic revival in a given group at some point? Because the third generation has arrived. What is often overlooked in such uses of the term "generation" is that it is less an exact answer than an escape hatch and a metaphor. To be precise, it is what Donald Schön called a "problem-setting, generative metaphor," which frames our perception of reality while largely remaining invisible.

Generations are perceived to be so obviously natural that they have become rather inconspicuous. Quentin Anderson has described "the psychic need manifested by a particular generation" as what "a good many historians of culture now posit without being explicit about it" (*Imperial* 232). Students of American culture feel that invoking "generations" may help explain a great variety of other phenomena, such as historical change, social conflict, progress or declension, immigrant adaptation, certain aesthetic movements, as well as the scholars' own interests; yet more often than not, the concept of the "generation" itself remains unexplained and unquestioned. When David Quixano says in *The Melting-Pot*, "Each gener-

208

ation must live and die for its own dream" (157), he is vague, yet he can count on widespread approval.

Omnipresent and invisible at the same time, the word "generation" may not even appear in the indexes of studies which use it as an explanatory category. It is easier to find generational analyses of the history of American Studies than to encounter American Studies debates about the concept of the generation.[11] Robert Spiller started his preface to the *Literary History of the United States* (1947) with the pronouncement: "Each generation should produce at least one literary history of the United States, for each generation must define the past in its own terms" (vii). Reviewing the history of his field of specialization, Jay Mechling wrote in 1977: "American Studies is now fully into its third generation of practitioners" (Wise, *Paradigm* 327). In 1981 Houston Baker wrote a historical account of Black Studies under the title "Generational Shifts and the Recent Criticism of Afro-American Literature." One is reminded of Marvin Rintala's suspicion that "generational differences are being used as *deus ex machina* in much the same way that differences in national character are sometimes invoked when there seems to be no other explanation" of some phenomenon (Sills 6:94).

Are not generations as natural as days? Who would be pedantic enough to consult the index of Lewis Mumford's *The Golden Day* (1926) for a definition of "day"? Can we not simply invoke the Bible, as did Hemingway's Lost Generation, and conclude: "One generation passeth away, and another generation cometh: but the earth abideth forever. The sun also ariseth and the sun goeth down, and hasteth to his place where he arose" {Ecclesiastes 1:4–5}. Generations constantly do pass away, and new ones are constantly emerging, but at intervals which, unlike days, cannot easily be determined. "It is not easy to say when one generation ends and another begins," David Riesman writes wryly, "for people are not produced in batches, as are pancakes, but are born continuously" (*Abundance* 309).

Thomas Jefferson developed a theory of generations which Daniel Boorstin has described as ensuring "the sovereignty of the present generation." Many of the colonists perceived their relationship to England in generational terms; in turn, Jefferson theorized that generations were as separate from each other as America was from England. "We may consider each generation as a distinct nation," Jefferson wrote, "with a right to bind themselves, but none to bind the succeeding generation, more than the inhabitants of another country" (Boorstin, *Lost* 205). Jefferson thus needed boundaries for his generation-nations; and he meticulously calculated that the natural life span of a political generation measured eighteen years and eight months. Consequently, he felt that no government should have the right to take up loans which could not be paid back within nineteen years. Other attempts to determine the length of generations have yielded figures ranging from fifteen to thirty-three years. F. Scott Fitzgerald, for example, writes in the posthumously published piece "My Generation" (1968): "... by a generation I mean that reaction against the fathers which seems to occur about three times in a century" (Cowley, *Second* 233).

Though it defies measurability, the generation is first and foremost a mental concept which has been experienced as well as used to interpret experience throughout American history. Generations are no less real because their duration cannot be precisely determined. As Edwin Burrows and Michael Wallace conclude in a detailed study of generational imagery in the American Revolution, "once a symbol has come into existence it becomes a social datum with a life and coercive authority of its own" ("Revolution" 272). "Generations" are such a social datum, part of American folklore as well as of what James Willkie has termed "elitelore" (Zelman 111). Generational metaphors have served to support (and have sometimes even shaped) interpretations of the conflicts which have emerged from the clash between descent and consent in American culture. Seen this way, the construct of "generations" has been useful both as an instrument of cultural criticism and as a rhetorical device that is used to create a sense of cohesive kinship among the diverse inhabitants of this country.[12]

By far the most probing theoretical essay on the general subject is Karl Mannheim's "The Problem of Generations" (1928). Mannheim first criticizes the positivist interpretations by Hume, Comte, and others who focus on determining the duration, the precise life span, of generations in the belief that here is "the framework of human destiny in comprehensible, even measurable form" ("Problem" 276). For Mannheim these positivistic attempts—to which we might add Jefferson's—suffer from a "unilinear conception of progress" (281). Mannheim then shows the limits of the romantic-historical interpretation of generations (by Dilthey, Pindar, and others) as an expression of felt experience which sometimes "degenerates into a kind of arithmetical mysticism," a sense of "interior time which can only be grasped by intuitive understanding" (282). This "romantic tendency ... obscured the fact that between the natural and physical and the mental spheres there is a level of existence at which social forces operate" (284).

Instead of the positivist and romantic-historical interpretations, Mannheim suggests focusing on generation units and their inherent potentials in the context of social and historical forces by examining the "social location" of presumptive members of a generation. "Only when contemporaries definitely are in a position to participate as an integrated group in certain common experiences can we rightly speak of community of location of a generation" ("Problem" 298). Contemporaries living in countries remote from each other, for example, may not share such a community of location. Social and historical forces alone transform a group of contemporaries from a "generation as potentiality" into a "generation as actuality" "where a concrete bond is created" among them (303). (Similarly, one could fruitfully speak about ethnicity as potentiality and actuality.) Imagining a society in which "one generation lived on forever and none followed to replace it" (292), Mannheim describes our world by contrast as one "developed by individuals who come into contact anew with the accumulated heritage" (293). Mannheim calls this phenomenon "fresh contact" and makes an aside which sheds some light on the prominence of generational rhetoric in America:

> The phenomenon of "fresh contact" is ... of great significance in many social contexts; the problem of generations is only one among those upon which it has a bearing. Fresh contacts play an important part in the life of the individual when he is forced by events to leave his own social group and enter a new one—when, for example, an adolescent leaves home, or a peasant the countryside for the town, or when an emigrant changes his home, or a social climber his social status or class. ("Problem" 293)

Many motifs of American culture stem from the stresses of adolescence and ethnogenesis (the individual and the collective "coming of age" after separating from a parent/country), of urbanization, of immigration, and of social mobility. In the United States what Mannheim terms "fresh contact" is experienced in a persistent and cumulative fashion. Many stories told in this country are stories of several "fresh contact" themes combined. Generational rhetoric may be one appropriate expression and vehicle of this experience. In America, more than in Europe, generational imagery—in both its positivist and its romantic-historical versions—has provided a mental map for newcomers and their descendants, one that may have been more suited than historical or social analysis. This is true from the time of the first fresh-contact experience of the Puritans to twentieth-century interpretations of immigration.

First, Second, Third . . . : Gradual Degeneracy?

The model of successive generations—mostly limited to three in American discourse—provides a specific lens through which the general problem can be more sharply focused. The familiar sequence of "first," "second," and "third" generations has become a commonplace orientation device in the historiography of Puritan New England as well as of nineteenth- and twentieth-century immigration to the United States. I have not been able to find a more precisely detailed description of generational succession than the one given by John Higginson (1616–1708) in his "Attestation" (1697) to Cotton Mather's *Magnalia Christi Americana* (1702). Minister Higginson appropriately takes Ecclesiastes as his point of departure, connecting it with a phrasing from Isaiah 58:12 and, later in the "Attestation," with the passage from Genesis 17:7–9 which formed the basis of Puritan covenant theology; yet Higginson's numerical scheme is more New-English than biblical. He writes:

> Now, *One Generation passeth away, and another cometh.* The *First Generation* of our Fathers, that began this Plantation of *New-England,* most of them in their *middle Age,* and many of them in their *declining Years,* who, *after they had served the Will of God,* in laying the *Foundation* (as we hope) of *many Generations,* and given an *Example* of true *Reformed Religion* in the *Faith* and *Order* of the Gospel, according to the best Light from the *Words* of God, they are now *gathered unto their Fathers.* There hath been *another Generation* succeeding the *First,* either of such as come over with their Parents very Young, or were born in the Country, and these have had the managing of the Publick Affairs for many Years, but are apparently *passing away,* as their *Fathers* before them. There is also a *Third Generation,* who are grown up, and begin to stand thick upon the Stage of *Action,* at this Day, and these were all born in the Country, and may call *New-England* their *Native Land.* Now, in respect of what the Lord hath done for these generations, succeeding one another, we have aboundant cause of Thanksgiving to the Lord our God, who hath so Increased and Blessed this People, that from a *Day of small things,* he has brought us to be, what we now are. (Higginson 64)

Higginson's definitions clarify the point from which the generational enumeration starts (founding fathers who had to be of middle age or older at the time of migration), elucidate the complicated composition of the second generation (brought over by their parents when very young, or born here), and point to the distinctive feature of the third (all born in this country, and of parents who were born or at least raised in America). John Higginson had come with his father from England to Massachusetts at age thirteen, which makes him, by his own account, a member of the second generation. Yet despite his soberly neutral definitions, Higginson is not without fears about that position; when he looks at it from the "dark side," he exclaims: "may we, the *Children* of such *Fathers*, lament our *Gradual Degeneracy* from that *Life* and *Power of Godliness* that was in them, and the many *Provoking Evils* that are amongst us; which have moved God severely to witness against us" (65). It is this fear of a *"Gradual Degeneracy"* embodied especially by the second generation that has become a cliché in the history of migrations to America, from Perry Miller's account of the "declension" that resulted in the Half-Way Covenant to the immigration historiography of Marcus Lee Hansen.

Generalizations about "the" immigrant family and generational successions that characterize its change are ubiquitous. Americans seem to be eager to fit their own, often more complicated historical location and line of ancestry into the Procrustean bed of three generations. It seems to be misleadingly easy, for example, to find authentications of "the" second generation in autobiographies and essays, since in many cases the authors experienced their "social location" in terms of a generational scheme—which seems to exist prior, and give cohesion, to their lives. "If ever the child of immigrants embraced the faith of the folk among whom it came," we heard Lewisohn confess in *Up Stream: An American Chronicle* (1922), "I was that child" (51). Similarly, Joseph Freeman writes in *An American Testament: A Narrative of Rebels and Romantics* (1936): "My friends and I were the second generation of immigrants—the 'educated' people who spoke English and read books. Our fathers were tailors, grocers, storekeepers, salesmen, brokers on the pettiest scale" (28). However, the writers evaluate their past experiences retrospectively in the generational scheme, often, as we saw in the case of Lewisohn, with the suggestion that they have reformed their erroneous second-generation ways in a rebirth as third generation. Three recent interviews quoted in Andrew Rolle's *The Italian Americans: Troubled Roots* (1980) may be considered classic expressions of the felt generational location at the moment it is experienced:

> *First Generation:* I don't know to express myself. A sixteen year old kid ... I didn't have no trade, I didn't have no money, only a little education. ... I can't express you how I was feeling, scared ... no money, a few dollars I think I had ... I don't know where to go ... go to America, what is America ... where is America? ... You know

where I was sleeping? I had no bed. There was a pile of rope ... I was sleeping inside the rope.

Second Generation: I'm a second generation Italian. My name is Jodi Desmond, but I was born Josephina Dessimone and oh how I hated that. For the first fourteen years of my life I was Josephina Dessimone and rebelling every moment.

I was ashamed of my parents, they spoke with a broken accent and I am ashamed of being ashamed now, but I wasn't then. I just ignored them.

Third Generation: Just being part of an ethnic group is really great because you belong to something, and you can't always belong to something if you're just plain old American.

Being a melting pot doesn't mean all the cultures have to combine and lose our identity. It means that all cultures can come together ... maintain our identity, but still proud we're American. (183–84)

These excerpts from interviewees, which would be worth a linguistic analysis, illustrate the broad acceptance of the code, the cultural construct of the generational succession by people, not just by writers of autobiographies and fiction. Such examples can be found across all ethnic groups, from the Afro-American Chester Himes's *The Third Generation* (1954) to the specialized Japanese-American vocabulary of Issei, Nisei, and Sansei for the three generations.

The Third Generation as Redemption: Hansen's "Law" Revisited

The best-known modern formulation of generational succession among immigrants was developed by Marcus Lee Hansen in a 1938 address to the Augustana Historical Society, an association devoted to the study of Swedish immigrants to the United States. The speech was reprinted, in an abridged form, under the title "The Third Generation in America," in *Commentary* in November 1952, with an introduction by Oscar Handlin. Handlin suggested that, judging by his "own experience," there were "uncanny similarities between patterns in the adjustment of other groups of settlers and those ... thought to be peculiar to the newcomers of the Jewish group" (493). The one characteristic which is perceived to transcend ethnicity and even history is the second generation's proclivity to what Higginson described as gradual degeneracy and what Hansen views as downright treason. According to Hansen the typical member of the second generation wanted to forget everything: the foreign language that left an unmistakable trace in his English speech, the religion that continually recalled childhood struggles, the family customs that should have been the happiest of all memories. He wanted to be away from all physical reminders of early days, in an environment so different, so American, that all associates naturally assumed that he was as American as they. ("Third" 494)

Hansen exculpates the first generation, whose efforts were taken up with material cares; "but nothing," he thunders, "can absolve the traitors of the second generation who deliberately threw away what had been preserved in the home." It should be emphasized that Hansen did not invent this assessment of the second generation, which has traditionally received a bad press in America. Repudiating Zangwill's *Melting-Pot* in 1916, the Norwegian-American immigrant writer Waldemar Ager argued that the

legions of prostitutes in this country are not drawn from the ranks of the poor newcomer girls, notwithstanding the fact that in certain quarters poverty is inaccurately cited as the major cause of prostitution. These women are most frequently recruited from the immigrants' daughters, who grow up with the feeling that they are something better and greater than their "old-country-ish" and hardworking parents. They have often not learned any mother tongue. (Ager, *Cultural* 82)

Randolph Bourne, in "The Jew and Trans-National America" (1916), saw the "large masses of our foreign-born of the second generation" as the perfect illustration for "that cultural pointlessness and vacuity which our critics of American life are never weary of deploring" (*War* 124–25). According to Julius Drachsler's study *Democracy and Assimilation* (1920), "the fatal disease gnawing at the vitals of the immigrant community is the 'diluted' second generation" (79). Traitors, prostitutes, vacuous dilutees: the second generation has not been portrayed very flatteringly. For Hansen, however, there was hope:

All has not been lost. After the second generation comes the third, and with the third appears a new force and a new opportunity which, if recognized in time, can not only do a good job of salvaging, but probably can accomplish more than either the first or the second could ever have achieved. ("Third" 495)

The hope for redemption comes from the "principle of third-generation interest" that Hansen, a disciple of Frederick Jackson Turner's, develops in the following resonant phrase: "what the son wishes to forget the grandson wishes to remember" (495). Hansen's statement has become so widely accepted that it is now commonly referred to not merely as a thesis (like Turner's frontier thesis) but as "Hansen's law." This was first proposed by Will Herberg in his widely read study *Protestant-Catholic-Jew: An Essay in American Religious Sociology* (1955), which was dedicated to "the Third Generation upon whose 'return' so much of the future of religion in America depends." Hansen strongly polarized second-generation traitors and third-generation redeemers on the basis of very little evidence. For Hansen, the historians of Swedish immigration who were gathered in Augustana in 1938 were a case in point, and so was *Gone with the Wind* (1936), written by a "granddaughter of the confederacy" (495).

Hansen's one-issue theory has not remained without critics, influential though it continues to be. Nahirny and Fishman have subtly argued that the first generation's attachment was to a specific place in the old world, an attachment the second generation could not possibly share. "While estranged from their parental heritage, the sons, nevertheless, remained more conscious of their ethnic identity than were their immigrant fathers" (Nahirny, "Immigrant" 322). The third generation could form only a generalized attachment to the ethnic group in the abstract that lacks a specific localism. This movement from concrete to abstract attachments is well exposed in Rolle's three generations of Italians. Nahirny and Fishman thus moved the debate outside of the pervasive moralism. As Hansen offered no evidence beyond that of intellectuals (Swedish-American historians, a southern writer), Herbert Gans has suggested that "Hansen's Law applies only to academics and intellectuals," an argument that he weaves into a broader fabric. For Gans, the so-called ethnic revival of the 1970s becomes a revival limited to intellectuals. In the foreword to Neil Sandberg's *Ethnicity, Acculturation and Assimilation* (1974), Gans points out that this study of Polish-American immigrants to California "does not provide any evidence that the rest of the third generation is more interested in its ethnic origins than the first or second" (xiii). Looking at second-generation Jewish immigrants from a different perspective, Deborah Dash Moore finds that they "synthesized American and Jewish values into a pattern of acculturation that was not simply a prelude to assimilation." According to Moore's "Defining American Jewish Ethnicity" (1981), the second generation was no obstacle to their successors' ethnicity: "Third-generation Jews continued to elaborate the same associational ties and patterns of behavior that form the framework of community adjusting Jewish ethnicity to the American context" (390, 391). Recent immigration research seems to suggest that perhaps the masses of the second generation did not act "second generation" and that the "third generation" did not act "third."

Can Hansen's "law," then, as Gans proposes, be amended to apply only to the group that is of special interest to us—the writers, aca-demics, and intellectuals? Though Hansen specifically offers the "broad generalization" that "the second generation is not interested in and does not write any history" (495), there are good reasons to doubt even such a limited applicability of Hansen's hypothesis. Han-sen explicitly pointed out to his own audience of Swedish immigrant historians: "Among the leaders of this society are men of the first generation and of the second generation but they are the proverbial exception, or it may be better to say they are third generation in spirit" (497). This is an astounding statement, especially in an essay that supposedly established a "law."

Even more puzzling is the noteworthy fact that Oscar Handlin who helped to popularize Hansen's famous diatribe against second-gen-eration traitors was, as the jacket flap of The Uprooted (1951) reads, "himself a part of the epic he was writing about, the son of one of those 35 million immigrants who had come to this country in search of freedom and opportunity." And yet, Handlin suggested that his own experience validated Hansen's observations. How could one of America's foremost immigrant historians, who was himself of the sec-ond generation, accept the "broad generalizations" and implications of Hansen's law? Handlin was certainly interested in history and unwilling to "forget" his generational location. In the introductory materials to his reader, revealingly entitled Children of the Uprooted (1966)—a collection of writings by second-generation Americans from 1845 to 1965—Handlin makes the interesting assertion that, at least for writers born between 1890 and 1920, second-generation sta-tus was more significant than actual ethnic background. Though they were a less cohesive group than writers born earlier, they were very aware of their second-generation location. They were a generation as actuality; and that generation's members, Handlin writes, were the

> children of parents of the most diverse antecedents—English, Ger-mans, and Scandinavians, as before, but also French-Canadians, Armenians, Chinese, Italians, Dutch, and eastern European Jews. Yet in important respects the writers who were the products of so many different heritages had more in common with one another than had their predecessors. (Children 224)

Many second-generation writers included in Handlin's reader were consciously and actively interested in ethnicity and quite unwilling to forget the past, among them Josiah Royce, Finley Peter Dunne, Carl Sandburg, Arthur Meier Schlesinger, and—perhaps especially surprisingly—Marcus Lee Hansen, too. Hansen was born at Neenah, Wisconsin, in 1892; his father had emigrated from Denmark, his mother from Norway; both had come to the United States in 1871. There is some mystery surrounding Hansen's language loyalties and skills: in a recent essay Moses Rischin reports some Scandinavian colleagues' suspicions that Hansen had to rely on others in researching the Scandinavian documents he used in his works. Rischin also mentions in passing that in 1929, in a letter to his mentor Frederick Jackson Turner, Hansen paid homage to his America with what Rischin calls "the characteristic ardor of a second-generation American" ("Hansen" 329). What ever happened to Hansen's "law"? If it wasn't applicable to the masses of the second generation, it certainly doesn't describe the second-generation intellectuals any better. It does not even apply to the historian who phrased it.

Higginson had at least openly characterized himself as a second-generation New Englander and had juxtaposed his worries on the dark side about a gradual degeneracy with some hope on the lighter side that "the *Glory of God* which was with our *Fathers*, is not wholly departed from us their *Children*" ("Attestation" 65). Yet what could it mean for Hansen as a second-generation immigrant historian to vilify the second generation in terms which were hardly commensurate with his own location? And why would Oscar Handlin, another second-generation immigrant historian, give credence to Hansen's condemnation of that generation as a group of unhistorical and forgetful traitors to their heritage? These are puzzling questions. Perhaps fictional second-generation stories by other second-generation storytellers will give us clues.

In the aesthetic creation of a contemporary second-generation artist, we learn about a young American professor of surgery who—after having lived a thoroughly assimilated life for many years—decides literally to "return" to the old world of his long-forgotten, previously denied roots and to fulfill his grandfather's (or great-grandfather's) mission. "We all know what he did," the young surgeon who has changed the pronunciation of his name to "Fron-kon-steen" remarks wearily when a student asks him about his Transylvanian ancestor whose memory is much of an embarrassment to "Young Frankenstein" (brilliantly played by Gene Wilder in Mel Brooks's 1974 movie of that title). Fortunately for the plot of the movie as well as for our speculations, Young Frankenstein—whose parents are never mentioned in the film—symbolically plays both second and third generation in the sense of Hansen's "law." At first he is the second-generation new-world doctor who "would rather be remembered for [his] own small contributions to science and not because of [his] accidental relationship to a famous cuckoo" (at which point he is washing his hands in the lecture room). Then he is reborn as the loyal grandson (or is it great-grandson?) who "returns" to fulfill his ancestor's work. When he says, "My grandfather's work was doo-doo," he is acting second generation; yet when he finds the old baron's account ("HOW I DID IT"), follows the secret family recipe, screams, "It can work!" and even accepts the original, more familiar pronunciation of his family name, he irrevocably becomes third generation in spirit. "Destiny, destiny, no escaping destiny," he yells in a crucial nightmare which started with his refusal to accept his ancestral identity: "I am not a Frankenstein." At the end of the dream, he says, "You win," to a portrait of Gene Wilder representing Old Frankenstein—and soon he sets out, in the old family tradition, to work on the creation of the "new man."

Though *Young Frankenstein* is not the kind of story customarily consulted by immigration historians, it complements and elucidates Hansen's essay nicely. In American culture it is apparently possible for one man to be both second and third generation. He may be numerically second generation, though third generation "in spirit" (as Hansen attested to members of the Swedish immigrant society); or, like Young Frankenstein, he may be third generation by descent (or fourth—the movie never resolves that) but act second generation—until a life crisis brings out his true third-generation character formation and destiny.

Generational switches of this nature are not unusual in American culture. Dorothy Burton Skårdal writes (with an explanation) that she has "considered Anna Olsson and Dorthea Dahl, both of whom came to the United States at the age of two, second-generation authors, whereas Simon Johnson, who was eight when he arrived, has been regarded as first generation" (*Divided* 52). In *Power and the Pulpit in Puritan New England* (1975), a study which persuasively emphasizes that Puritan fears of a declension of the second generation were largely unfounded and unjustified, Emory Elliott defines "first" and "second generation." (His is one of the rare books which attempt to define the generational concept and which list "generation" in the index.) Then he adds the following intriguing statement:

To some degree, however, my terms "first" and "second" generations become metaphors, as in the case of the Winthrop family with the

second-generation founder and patriarch, John Jr. ... , considered a
member of the first generation. (ix)

Metaphorically speaking, then, two first generations succeeded
each other in the Winthrop family. This is a striking departure from
traditional notions of filiation and descent, and in contrast, too, to
other interpretations of the Winthrop family, which cast John
Winthrop, Jr., as a representative second-generation New Englander
(Dunn, *Puritans* 59). Yet Elliott's procedure is justifiable, since generational numbering is always a metaphoric enterprise and generational identity a matter of potentiality. Elliott's book argues forcefully that the older interpretations of the real existence of a declining
second generation in Puritan New England were based on rhetoric,
not on historical facts. Contrary to common seventeenth-century
accusations against "the Bastard Sons," the second generation was
"actually quite religious and needed only a little encouragement to
be brought into the churches." Elliott concludes:

> The discrepancy between the facts and the rhetoric, between the
> reality and the ideals, that has puzzled historians was created by the
> fathers of New England themselves in their attempt to construct an
> imaginative vision of the way their society had been and to impose
> that vision upon the reality they rejected. Cotton Mather's *Magnalia
> Christi Americana* is a third-generation man's supreme effort to make
> this vision supplant the reality; the illusion is so convincing that
> only recently have we seen that his history is really an epic, a work
> of imaginative expression and power. (*Power* 61–62)

If the "fathers" and the third generation created this image of the
declining second generation, the example of John Higginson suggests
that the second generation, too, was ready to accept the notion of
"gradual degeneracy" as at least partially true. The twentieth-century
parallels of Hansen and Handlin furthermore illustrate that the vision
of second-generation immigrant traitors was propagated by the second generation itself, allowing, however, for the possibility of "proverbial exceptions," attitudinal switches, and conversions.

From Cotton Mather's epic to Oscar Handlin's, Americans have
never lost interest in the concept of generations in order to account
for doctrinal changes in religion (Half-Way Covenant), for independence from the mother country, for a form of republican government which would not burden future generations, for the process of
immigrant adjustment, and for many generational renaissances and
literary revival movements. The reason for this popularity of generational rhetoric is to be found not in its explicatory precision but in

its delineation of a moral map. Hansen developed not a "law" of historical progression but a moral choice between a wholesome third and a deficient second generation. Any reader of Hansen's essay would rather strive to be third generation than to be classified as second generation. Hansen's "law" has the markings of a moral antithesis, of a melodramatic choice between good and bad. Mel Brooks, too, showed that numbered generations may stand for moral alternatives rather than for a precise way to determine a human being's historical location. Even a member of the name-changing second generation can take advantage of the opportunity to become third generation in spirit. It is this moral exhortation that is at the root of much agitation against the second generation.

The melodrama of numbered generations obscures the tension in human desire between the wish to escape ancestors and the yearning to fulfill them. As Hawthorne put it in his sketch "Main-Street" (1849), "Let us thank God for having given us such ancestors; and let each successive generation thank Him, not less fervently, for being one step further from them in the march of ages" (*Tales* 540). The cultural construction of the "bad" second generation is a reminder that origins can never be preserved unless they are depleted to meaninglessness. Klaus Heinrich argues similarly in an essay on the function of genealogy in myth:

> To derive from an origin means on the one hand to come from the origin, to carry on the power of origins. On the other hand it means to separate oneself from this origin, to have escaped from origins. (*Vernunft* 14–15)

One way of dealing with this doubleness is to split it into opposed attitudes which can be labeled by a generational number (second = bad; third = good). Another way is to exaggerate our constant, continuous, and inevitable escape from origins into the fear of the coming generation's degeneration.

Generations Lost to the Pied Piper: Community-building Jeremiads

Puritan New England allowed members of the second generation into the Half-Way Covenant, yet exhorted them with a continual barrage of anti-second-generation propaganda which was meant to ensure the rising progress of the city upon a hill. On the surface, the metaphor of degeneracy or declension of the second generation was

an expression of the concern and even despair among New Englanders that they were "losing their children." This, too, is a persistent
theme in American culture, a kind of Pied Piper of Hamlin motif,
reenacted from the time of William Bradford to that of Margaret
Mead. In his *History of Plymouth Plantation* (1651), Bradford writes
that in Holland the future Pilgrim fathers "saw their posterities would
be in danger to degenerate and be corrupted" (46). In *The Lost Generation: A Portrait of American Youth Today* (1936), Maxine Davis has
practically given up on the next generation after which her book is
entitled: "It will remain ... a decadent, vitiated generation, a cancer
in the vitals of our people, rearing its children in its own dun and
dreary twilight" (Susman, *Culture* 245). Yet, on the other hand, for
Davis these "boys and girls are our responsibility. If we do not assume
it, some self-appointed piper may take it from us, and lead our youth
God knows where" (245). Addressing secondary-school and college
teachers in 1940, Margaret Mead described the pied piper as a fascist
organizer at the beginning of World War II:

> At a time when we need the enthusiasm and devotion of every
> young adult, we have let conditions develop which promote just the
> opposite. The typical American sulks and when he sulks he provides
> good material for the fascist organizer, who at least offers him a place
> in a group in which there is some hope of doing something.
> ("Conflicts" 42)

The pattern is familiar from countless similar expressions of fear that
the next generation will become one of little fascists, brain-washed
communists, hypnotized rock fans, Moonies, zombies, androids, *them.*
The mental landscape of such fears is beautifully developed in countless science fiction movies about body snatchers. The people who are
portrayed as hypnotized in such fashion are also at home in Royce's
category of deficiency as flavorless mob. (Characteristically, they also
usually lack the ability to love.)

On a deeper level, however, the metaphor of a declining second
generation—precisely, perhaps, because it was such a prominent
focus for the migrants' fears—strenghtened the sense of common
peoplehood and destiny: by scolding different people as a degenerate
second generation one may in fact be molding a family. A people of
diverse ancestries thus develops a familistic sense of belonging, complete with (adopted) founding fathers and a sense of mission for
future generations from which the (perhaps invented) attitude of the
second generation can be seen swerving. This leads to a rhetorical
fire-and-brimstone barrage against the upcoming second generation.

The jeremiadic solution of the generational metaphor may thus function as a community-building symbol. This is one reason why generational rhetoric, even rhetoric that seemingly expresses sheer
despair at the degeneracy of the coming generation, powerfully
cements heterogeneous newcomers into a pseudo-family. It is a code
which, like that of romantic love, functions to naturalize consent
relations. If love emphasizes the new foundation of nuclear families
in each generation, generational counting—even if enacted dispar-
agingly—gives these atomized units a semblance of cohesion. Many
individuals or nuclear families (often mixed ones) can become "second-generation Italian-Americans" as they are challenged to rally
against certain dangers (such as defamation or dilution). This is
equally true in generational interpretations of, for example, the
American Studies movement, or Black Studies, which have the powerful side effect of creating the sense of togetherness in a discipline,
of a familistic community of scholars united in an enterprise, an effect
that could never be reached with a soberly chronological account.

The concern with creating community (Susman, "Thirties" 179-
210) that underlies generational thinking has strong intellectual
roots in the period from the Depression through the early 1950s. It
was then, within a very short span of time, that Marcus Lee Hansen
formulated his "law" (1938), Odum and Moore published their *American Regionalism* (1938), Raoul de Roussy de Sales mused about the
parallels of love and democracy (1938), Perry Miller published the
first volume of *The New England Mind* (1939), and the second-generation historian Arthur M. Schlesinger edited Hansen's essays under
the title *The Immigrant in American History* (1940), a volume which
connects Puritan and immigrant historiography. Schlesinger also
published his famous Crèvecoeurian national-character essay "The
American—A New Man" [1942-43] in the *American Historical
Review*. W. Lloyd Warner coined the term "ethnicity" in 1941. Hansen's and Miller's conceptualizations became dominant in the 1950s,
when Handlin, too, wrote about jeremiads ("Prophets" 49-51) and
Miller described Bradford in terms of *The Uprooted* (*Errand* 4). Significant challenges to all these conceptualizations were published in
the 1970s. In any other context I would probably have argued that
this must be a generational phenomenon.

Intermarriage and "Half-Breeds"

The second generation, seen from the point of view of both a first
and a third generation, and even by members of its own ranks, takes

the cultural space in America that is equivalent to deficiency in the ethics of wholesome provincialism. The code phrase "second generation" also evokes the animosities that "melting pot" and "intermarriage" sometimes receive as threats to "ethnic purity" and human identity over more than one lifetime.

One fear that emanates from the tirades against lost generations is the fear of "loss of substance" that the theme of "intermarriage" can evoke. Zangwill's *Melting-Pot*, the discussions of which sometimes focus on denouncing intermarriage, raised one such fear when the baroness suggested to the Gentile Revendal that "a hook-nosed brat to call you grandpa" (137) might be the result of his daughter's intermarriage with David Quixano. The fear that lurks behind the aggressive response to the famous question "But would you like your daughter to marry one?" is the fear of "losing" the children to a further progeny that bears only little resemblance to the addressee of the question.

The dream of the ethnic purist is the eternal likeness of all after-generations to his or her own image; on a global scale it is the eternal perpetuation of the boundaries between races or stocks or groups that have been classified and organized hierarchically to the advantage of the purist. This static dream of ethnic cloning is constantly challenged by second generations and intermarriages. Unable to recognize themselves in their necessarily mixed progeny, purists have preferred to develop elaborate fictions of an "inky curse" (Aaron 170) upon their descendants. The purists' own unwillingness to accept the mixed after-generations as theirs is seen as the "loss" of the children, and the projection of this self-constructed loss upon the descendants of mixed marriages is the cultural belief—widespread in nineteenth- and early-twentieth-century America—that "mixed bloods," "mulattoes," and "half-breeds" were sterile. Even Horace Kallen fell victim to this line of thinking, though he contemplated the fate of Jewish-Gentile alliances when he wrote in 1906:

> It is the Jew that dominates in the child of a mixed marriage, and after a few generations, if sterility does not supervene, as it usually does, what is not Jewish dies out or is transmuted. ("Ethics" 69)

Mixed marriages of all sorts, and especially marital unions between whites and Indians or whites and Afro-Americans, often appeared dangerous in American literature, the offspring of such unions doomed. The mulatto and half-breed themes were inevitably tragic or horrifying. Edgar Allan Poe's half-Indian Dirk Peters, in the *Narrative of Arthur Gordon Pym* (1838), is as awesome as Nathaniel Hawthorne's Septimius Felton, descended from an Indian wizard and a Puritan witch, is morbid. On a lighter note, in John Huston's film *The Unforgiven* (1960), Burt Lancaster has to contain the Indians who claimed his half-sister, the half-breed Audrey Hepburn, as theirs; when he plays classical music on a grand piano which he carried into the wilderness, he silences the Indian war whoops and finally wins his sister back from one set of her descent claims.

The mulatto story most central to a nervous national self-consciousness was Callender's apocryphal account of Jefferson's reputed slave mistress and children. William Wells Brown, the first Afro-American novelist, used the story of the children Jefferson supposedly fathered with the slave woman Sally Hemings (whom Brown calls "Currer") as the plot of his abolitionist novel *Clotel; or, The President's Daughter* (1853). Brown's Clotel is a national symbol of the injustice slavery perpetrates upon womanhood; she dies as a Christ-like martyr with arms outstretched and eyes lifted up to heaven, pursued by slave catchers onto a bridge across the Potomac, "within plain sight of the President's house and the capital of the Union" (217). She dies for the national sin of slavery, but also for the president's sin of the flesh or, more precisely, for his failure to acknowledge his own offspring. Only one of her daughters survives the novel, significantly by going to England. In 1859 the Irish-American Dion Boucicault published *The Octoroon*, the most influential "tragic mulatto" melodrama, which includes a camera with a self-developing liquid as a crime detector. Revealingly, a British version of Boucicault's play allowed a happy ending for the title heroine Zoe (whose name means "life") and a marital union between her and her white lover and first cousin, George Peyton; but the American version ended sadly with Zoe's suicide (Hogan, *Boucicault* 74-75). The cause for the mulattoes' tragic roles may be found in the sin of "miscegenation" or in social prejudice, but the life expectancy of mulatto characters in American literature is low.

In the 1920s Sherwood Anderson and William Faulkner debated the question whether mulattoes—like mules, from which they are etymologically derived—were sterile by nature (Blotner 1:498-99). Their conversations, facetious though they may have been, were not aberrations by literary types, but influenced by popular thinking since the mid-nineteenth century as well as by sociologists like Ulysses Weatherly, who published his thoughts in the *American Journal of Sociology* (1910). As Joel Williamson wrote in *New People*, only E. Franklin Frazier's publication "Children in Black and Mulatto Families" (1933) finally discredited this widely shared assumption (Wil-

liamson 123). In a striking difference from Latin American belief systems, the North American cultural maxim to prevent racial mixing
was that culturally unacceptable consent relations were considered
punished by a natural lack of descendants, an ideological exaggeration of the general fear of losing a generation. In the cultural fear of
boundary-dissolving characters between categories, an American paradox manifested itself. The products of consent relations across dramatic boundaries were, well into the twentieth century, considered
to be exclusively and negatively shaped by one aspect of their
descent. In the United States, the country of consent, mulattoes were
not to be viewed as architects of their own fates. In the American
imagination, mixed bloods were the culmination of the fear of losing
generations.

Revolutionary Genealogy and Fear of Frankensteins

In many instances the American Revolution was, as Edwin Burrows
and Michael Wallace have amply demonstrated, experienced as the
American children's coming of age. As one colonist wrote in 1775:

> Some suppose there is a superintending power in the British Parlia-
> ment over the Colonies, resulting from the nature of colonization
> and their relation to the parent State. ... But how can parental
> authority be applied to support or illustrate such a principle? A par-
> ent has a natural right to govern his children during their minority
> and continuance in his family, but has no such authority over them
> as they arrive at full age. (Burrows, "Revolution" 212)

The classic American text for generational and familistic images of
revolutionary America is Thomas Paine's Common Sense (1776),
which plays the theme of parents and children in many variations.
In Paine's rhetoric, America, as England's child, has come of age and
can change its diet from milk to meat. The parent, however, has
become a pharaoh and a monster, who is ready, like Saturn, to
devour his offspring, and therefore is undeserving of the very name
parent. In his interesting essay "Burke's American Tragedy" (1983),
Gerald Chapman cites many examples from Cobbett's Parliamentary
History of England (1806–1820) which document that the English side
accepted the complementary parental metaphor. For example, Dow-
deswell: "the ridiculous doctrine that parents are apt to instil into
their children, of 'you shall do it—you shall do it,' is oftentimes the
means of enforcing the same disposition in the child, of 'I won't.'"

Or *Burgoyne*: "Sir, I look upon America to be our child, which I think we have already spoiled by too much indulgence."

The American revolutionary imagery of coming of age, being emancipated from a parent country, ready for "fresh contact," was also anchored, as Sacvan Bercovitch has argued, in a larger typological framework of fulfilling the *New England* fathers. This "revolutionary genealogy," Bercovitch writes, "helped to project the movement from colony to republic forward to the transition from Jeffersonian fathers to Jacksonian sons, and later to celebrate the Civil War as a confirmation of the revolution begun in New England over two hundred years before" (*Jeremiad* 123n). Revolutionaries were, then, defying a "parent" (Britain) in the name of adopted "ancestors" (American beginnings), which is, of course, a widespread revolutionary strategy. In other words, American rebels defined themselves as third rather than second generation. Vladimir Nahirny and Joshua Fishman (1965) have noted the phenomenon that

> the uneasy and, at times, derogatory attitude of the sons toward the heritage of their close ancestors—their own fathers and mothers— made them prone to fall back upon the heritage of remote ancestors—from Pericles to Marx, from Columbus to Kosciusko. . . . [The] more determined they were to be weaned from those aspects of ethnicity which had been transmitted to them by their natural fathers, the more inclined they were to embrace the intangible values attributed to the distant past of their adopted fathers. ("Immigrant" 321)

"Revolutionary genealogy" is, in our terms, not really a descent relationship but more an act of consent. Adopted ancestors are elective affinities who may help revolutionaries overcome their physical parents; instead of continuously acting merely as rebellious children, they may play the part of pious heirs.

However, revolutionaries had to worry—not unlike seventeenth-century founders and immigrants throughout American history— about their own succeeding generations. How could a new sense of family cohesion, community, and continuity be created after the experience of a rupture? Echoes of the revolutionary rhetoric of generations have reverberated in American culture, from the transcendentalist yearnings for an American aesthetic to more recent conceptualizations of the American identity. Writing in 1846, Margaret Fuller gave expression to what had become a commonplace in American literary theory: "there is often," Fuller says, "between child and parent, a reaction from excessive influence having been exerted, and such a one we have experienced, in behalf of our country against

England." Fuller finds that what is appropriate for an insular culture does not necessarily "suit a mixed race, continually enriched with new blood from other stocks the most unlike that of our first descent." An "American genius ... rooted in strength as the rocks on which the Puritan fathers landed," will not emerge, Fuller feels, in a jeremiadic vein, "till the fusion of races among us is more complete" (Fuller 231). There is danger of something resembling second-generation swerving in the premature "birth" of the national spirit, which may then "end in abortions like the monster of Frankenstein, things with forms and the instincts of forms, but soulless and therefore revolting" (232). In America, Frankenstein's (literally "brainwashed") monster is not only the image of the old world turned pharaoh but also "the dark side" of Young America's mission, the embodiment of the fear of second-generation degeneracy. (This is reminiscent of Royce's vision of the nation as a "monster"—if it weren't for the provinces.) It is also noteworthy that Fuller invokes "Puritan fathers" against a British "parent" and sees the moment of national flourishing in the establishment of an ethnically fused community which would fulfill the ancestors precisely by not being exclusively descended from them. This is another version of melting-pot destiny, not just for Fuller's time but for all future generations. If only all Americans could give up the monstrosity of the second generation and be wholesomely third generation!

We Are All Third Generation: A Cultural Grandfather Complex?

In chapter 3 of *And Keep Your Powder Dry* (1942)—which opens with an echo of Crèvecoeur's famous question in the third of his *Letters from an American Farmer*—the anthropologist Margaret Mead develops a three-generation model which resembles that of Marcus Lee Hansen; only instead of making it apply just to immigrants, Mead sees in it the representative American character formation. She also adds a surprise ending to the progression from first generation of strong immigrant founders to second generation of culturally thin Americanizers, when she concludes with this paradoxical formulation:

> In our behavior, however many generations we may actually boast of in this country, however real our lack of ties in the old world may be, we are all third generation, our European ancestry tucked away

and half forgotten, the recent steps in our wanderings over America immortalized and over-emphasized. (*Keep* 31)

This is a phrasing which makes the metaphoric and moral use of "generation" exceptionally conspicuous. Mead explains that this cultural formation accounts for the obsolescence of American fathers (perceived as second generation) and tells us an American (all-male) family saga:

> Father is to be outdistanced and outmoded, but not because he is a strong representative of another culture, well entrenched, not because he is a weak and ineffectual attempt to imitate the new culture; he did very well in his way, but he is out of date. ...
> Therefore it is not necessary to fight him, to knock him out of the race. It is much easier and quicker to pass him. (52–53)

According to Mead, this is not only the individual immigrant pattern but also the collective kinship drama of American history and throws a new light on the obsession with founding fathers:

> Washington does not represent the past to which one belongs by birth, but the past to which one tries to belong by effort. ... Washington is not that to which Americans passionately cling but that to which they want to belong, and fear, in the bottom of their hearts, that they cannot and do not.
> This odd blending of the future and the past, in which another man's great-grandfather becomes the symbol of one's grandson's future, is an essential part of American culture. (49–50)

Invoking the danger of "backsliding" in the process of achieving an American identity, Mead concludes:

> Only if one slackens, loses one's interest in the race toward success, does one slip back. Otherwise, it is onward and upward, *towards* the world of Washington and Lincoln; a world in which we don't fully belong, but which we feel, if we work at it, we sometime may achieve. (53)

Mead's observation answers Perry Miller's question why Americans are so anxious about achieving an identity (*Nature's* 3). In American mythology, ancestors may be adopted by consent. Mead has also pushed the metaphor of the third generation to the point at which it applies to Americans in general as well as to newcomers. No method of generational counting can validate her verdict that "we are all third generation"—even if Americans were all descended from the same few boatloads of imaginary immigrants who were all the same age when they arrived in America at the same time. Only as a metaphor, as an *ideal*, can all Americans be third generation. Or, to put it differently, if we count from our parents, we are all second generation; if we count from real or putative grandparents or ancestors, we are third; yet our own parents turn into the problematic second generation. What does it mean to have that choice of self-definition?

The psychological interpretation of the American national character as "third generation" sheds much light on the function of generations as metaphors. If we are all third generation (at least as an ideal), we may have parents who, for all practical purposes, are more ethnic than we are; but we can transcend them by invoking real or imaginary grandparents or founding fathers. The achieving of an identity in the world of Lincoln and Washington thus proceeds along the same lines as the invoking of a focal figure of national or ethnic authenticity. Hansen's third generation is, at the same time, more American and more ethnic than its predecessors. In fact, not being like their immediate predecessors—the parents—is what helps to authenticate third-generation members, who yet avoid oedipal confrontations by aggrandizing their own position as rooted in meaningful origins. We may thus create an independent self in the name of America or a modern identity in the name of ethnicity. Typologically speaking, a self-declared third generation represents the antitype, the redemptive fulfillment of types, of original ancestors (real or adopted). This is similar to the claims of lovers' leap couples that they fulfilled an Indian legacy. The range of applications of this third-generation code is wide.

Religiously orthodox parents may be perceived by their children as swerving from the "Jewish idea" of, for example, newly invented Zionism (Schmidt, "Kallen" 38–39). Children may transcend their parents' supposed narrowness in the name of the very ethnicity the parents embody more authentically than their offspring. Or they may cast themselves as visionaries, grounded in America's first principles, and assign the guilt of acquisitiveness only to their parents. Continuing the argument in Mead's tone, one might say that Americans can confront parental authority with the phrase "I am not swerving, Dad (or Mom). I am fulfilling Grandpa (or Grandma)!" Thus, Americans can continuously perceive themselves as capable of fulfilling the third-generation ideal while avoiding second-generation pitfalls.

In America the young ones surpass the old ones in the name of even older ones. This is a cultural process which resembles, on the family level, the "grandfather complex" as described by Ernest Jones and Karl Abraham in 1913. According to these psychoanalytic theorists, many children have the wish to be the parents of their own parents—and the identification with the grandparents permits this fantasy to be acted out symbolically. The wish is nourished, according to Jones, by an exaggeration of the desire to be one's own father; and its realization would permit the child to act out its hostilities toward its own parents. The wish also forms one of the bases of the notion of reincarnation.

In the introduction to her autobiography, *The Promised Land* (1912), Mary Antin expressly described the feeling of becoming her own parents' progenitrix as she started to build a "world of her own" by reading books: "did I not begin to make my father and mother, as truly as they had ever made me? Did I not become the parent and they the children, in those relations of teacher and learner? And so I can say that there has been more than one birth of myself ..." (xii). This casts a new light on the meaning of rebirth in the American melting pot. Even pornographic yearning for otherness and transcendence has occasionally satisfied the wish for generational inversions; for example, Ingrid Bengis writes in *Combat in the Erogenous Zone* (1972), in a scene the context of which I need not here elaborate: "I was simultaneously Rona's mother and her child, her lover and her guardian" (143).

In 1915, two years after Jones and Abraham argued the grandfather complex, Horace Kallen made the following interesting comment: "Men change their clothes, their politics, their wives, their religions, their philosophies, to a greater or lesser extent: they cannot change their grandfathers." When I cited these lines earlier I focused on the clash of relationships "in nature" and those "in law" which is expressed in this excerpt. Yet significantly, Kallen juxtaposes "wives" not with "fathers" (or "mothers") but with "grandfathers." When we recall the stories "The Wife of His Youth" and *Yekl* in this connection, we remember that the mother figure characters have certain grandmotherly qualities and are likened to "squaws" (the ultimate in American female adoptive ancestors). More fuel for our cultural grandparent complex is provided by Michael Novak, who writes in his best-selling jeremiad *The Rise of the Unmeltable Ethnics* (1972):

> My grandparents, I am sure, never guessed what it would cost them and their children to become "Americanized." ... My parents decided never to teach us Slovak. They hoped that thereby we would gain a generation in the process of becoming full Americans. ... *Pirohi* ... more or less died with my grandmother, who used to work all day making huge, steaming pots of potato dumplings and prune

dumplings for her grandchildren. No other food shall ever taste so sweet. . . .

What has happened to my people since they came to this land nearly a century ago? Where are they now, that long-awaited fully Americanized third generation? Are we living the dream our grandparents dreamed when on creaking decks they stood silent, afraid, hopeful at the sight of the Statue of Liberty? Will we ever find that secret relief, that door, that hidden entrance? Did our grandparents choose for us, and our posterity, what they should have chosen? (xxxiii–xxxv)

This excerpt is characteristic in its organization of biographical data through the grid of a generational scheme. Novak's and Kallen's association of grandparents with "changing" and "choosing" may point to a semantic inversion process according to which members of the third generation may in fact be choosing and changing their own ancestors, shaping them in their own image, while maintaining that the elders chose for them. By choosing to fulfill a grandfather (even a largely invented one) we become, in fact, a "chosen generation." American culture is rich in such uses of a grandparent. It may be well to remember that in *Young Frankenstein* the descendant Gene Wilder accepts as his destiny an ancestral image also portraying Gene Wilder. In a *People* magazine article in 1980, Oscar Handlin criticized Alex Haley's *Roots* (1976) for having created his significant ancestor Kunta Kinte in the image of a twentieth-century civil rights activist—which is to say, in Haley's own image. Both Hawthorne and Faulkner demonstrated much concern for their powerfully imagined ancestors, whom they sometimes created as "types" for their own parts as "antitypes." *The Americanization of Edward Bok* (1920) starts with "An Introduction of Two Persons," a tale of an island-cultivating founding father (a kindred spirit to Faulkner's Thomas Sutpen) who is set up as the significant ancestor of all his children's children, including, presumably, the narrator. Inspired by his grandparents, Edward Bok also built the Bok Tower Gardens at Lake Wales in Florida. John Fante's classic ethnic story "The Odyssey of a Wop" (1940) is about the narrator's grandfather. Karl Shapiro's poem "My Grandmother" (1941), which is appropriately included in some anthologies of ethnic literature, closes with these telling lines:

> I pity her life of deaths, the agony of her own,
> But most that history moved her through
> Stranger lands and many houses,
> Taking her exile for granted, confusing
> The tongues and tasks of her children's children.
> (Simon, *Ethnic* 326)

American literature is full of imaginative portrayals of the character Margaret Mead called "the epic grandfather" (*Keep* 49).

The anthropologist David Schneider's observations on some American idiosyncrasies in the establishing of genealogies nicely parallel the imaginative writers' texts. Schneider describes the shape of a typical American family tree as that of a Christmas tree with the capital *A* Ancestor on top, "like the star," and the respective informant, or "Ego," as the trunk. The trees may be "pyramids of greater or lesser range, but they include far fewer kinsmen than the definition of a relative as anyone related by blood or marriage would lead one to expect" (*Kinship* 67–68). In-laws and other relatives of spouses are among the most frequently omitted kinsmen. This selectiveness, which may be a result of the mental splitting of descent and consent relations, aligns kinship more easily along a line which leads from the significant Ancestor to Ego. As the title of Nancy Wilson Ross's novel (based on a motto by Ralph Hodgson) suggests, the American Ego may identify as *I, My Ancestor* (1950); there is also the once popular song "I Am My Own Grandpa."

Without taking notice of Jones or Abraham, but with a specific indebtedness to Margaret Mead, Erik Erikson also emphasizes the importance of the "myth of the grandfather" in his "Reflections on the American Identity" (1950). Erikson notes "the overwhelming importance of the grandfather" in American psychoanalytic patients. He adds:

> He may have been a blacksmith of the old world or a railroad builder of the new, an as yet proud Jew or an unreconstructed Southerner. What these grandfathers have in common is the fact that they were the last representatives of a more homogeneous world, masterly and cruel with good conscience, disciplined and pious without loss of self-esteem. ... Their mastery persists in their grandsons as a stubborn, an angry sense of superiority. Overtly inhibited, they yet can accept others only on terms of prearranged privilege. (*Childhood* 314–15n)

This suggestive note sheds some light on the phenomenon of angry, unmeltable ethnics who constantly invoke their unchangeable grandfathers. It illuminates some of the static assumptions surrounding "founding fathers"; they are connected here, very intriguingly, with some rhetorical affinities to an autumnal American Indian ancestry in the manner of "The Last of the Wampanoags." Finally, Erikson, whose book is dedicated to "OUR *children's children*," returns us to the pied piper motif of the Puritan founders' worries about their descendants: the development from railroad builder to psychoanalytic patient with an angry sense of superiority fits neatly with the "dark side" of Higginson's account.

Generational rhetoric confers, as we saw earlier, a sense of kinship and community upon the descendants of heterogeneous ancestors. The metaphoric interpretation of all Americans as members of numbered generations subjugates powerful and potentially divisive myths of descent to the democratic rhetoric of consent. Generational language has served founding fathers and revolutionaries as a community-building device, whereas it helps contemporary Americans wrap a cloak of ancestral and communal legitimacy around their individuality. At the same time it perpetuates one cultural moment, freezes the historical process into ahistorical conceptions and into metaphors of timeless identity as sameness. It is when Americans speak of generations, numbered or unnumbered, that they easily leave history and enter "the myth of America." Apparently talking about lineage, they are actually inventing not only a sense of communal descendants—the coming generation so much worried about—but also a metaphoric ancestry in order to authenticate their own identity. Even supposedly pure descent definitions are far from natural, being largely based on a consent construction.

Generational rhetoric may function as an American lingua franca in trans-ethnic discourse and contribute to its own perpetuation in America. While ethnics often claim to be making specific insiders' points about their culture that were not accessible to the outside, they may be making these points in familiar American family patterns. David Schneider has given an amusing account of the trans-ethnic interchangeability of some of his findings in *American Kinship*:

> During the fieldwork in Chicago, informants often insisted that their particular ethnic groups had distinctive or typical family characteristics which were unlike anything else in America. ... For the Italians the matter was quite simple; it is not possible to fully understand the Italian family in America until one has understood the Italian mother. For the Irish the matter was equally clear; it is not really possible to understand the Irish family until one has understood the special place of the Irish mother. For the Jews the matter was beyond dispute; it is impossible to fully comprehend the complexities and special qualities of Jewish family life without understanding the Jewish mother. (15)

Generations function very much as Schneider's mothers did. As readers browse with the intention to find out about the other, they get the American generational constructions—in different-looking, sometimes downright exotic, yet ultimately interchangeable ethnic guises. This may be one reason why ethnic family sagas like *Roots* could become so widely popular despite an ostensible antimajority message. While Alex Haley set out to trace all of his family roots on three continents, his novel quite dramatically selects people who count as "Ancestors." Tellingly, his parents are insignificant compared with the grandparents; and, most important, Tom Lea—who raped Kizzy—is, as Leslie Fiedler perceptively emphasized in *The Inadvertent Epic* (1979),

> a male ancestor, two generations closer to … Haley than the African Kunta Kinte; yet we are not permitted in this [rape] scene to think of "roots," since Massa Lea is White and therefore does not mythically count as an ancestor, only as a source of "pollution. …" (82)

This principle of selectively adopted descent relations may look "antiwhite" here, but, more important, it reaffirms the American pattern of mythological ancestry construction Margaret Mead discussed in the opposite case of the "daughters of the American Revolution." George S. Schuyler recognized the absurd potential in such constructions when he dedicated his novel *Black No More* (1931) to "all Caucasians in the great republic who can trace their ancestry back ten generations and confidently assert that there are no Black leaves, twigs, limbs or branches on their family trees." The consent construction of generations unites Americans across ethnic divisions, and, as Oscar Handlin recognized in *Children of the Uprooted*, generational location may in some cases be more salient than ethnicity, which would be yet another interesting point of departure for a study of the Beat Generation.

Many questions and paradoxes remain. It seems ironical, for example, that the generative metaphor of the three generations actually obscured the generative process. There is little sense of a dialectical family development in American generational rhetoric. There is no dominant family model of a man, a woman, and a child, as in an early version of Hegel's dialectic. American family symbolism seems more drawn to the quasi-typological sequence of grandparent (foundation, type), parent (declension), and grandchild-Ego (fulfillment, antitype). Few studies of generations are devoted to the mixed origins of Americans in the sense of Crèvecoeur's description of a family "whose grandfather was an Englishman, whose wife was Dutch, whose son marries a French woman, and whose present four sons have now four wives of different nations." Instead, writers help to create versions of a mono-ethnic, single-sex ancestry, often with only *one* grandparent (or an even further removed capital A Ancestor) as type, one parent as declension, and the Ego as heightened fulfillment. This is also true in some recent feminist attempts to construct a supposed countertradition of "generations of women" which yet affirm the same old construction in a different gender, so that we now get a "foremother" as the epic, capital A Ancestor. The more popular conceptualizations of American generations show little awareness that relations of law—or, consent—are usually necessary to produce relations of nature—descent. Judging by this widespread and purist mythology, Americans might as well have been cloned (or sewn together by third-generation Transylvanian surgeons). Students of American literature and culture will have to pay more attention to the problem of numbered and unnumbered generations. I might add that if the next generation fails to do it, then undoubtedly our children's children will. . . .

The themes of consent and descent in America—typology, melting pot, love, provincialism, and generations—are surprisingly interconnected and intertwined. Yet these thematic aspects of consent and descent have been expressed in particular forms. It is important to conclude with at least some consideration of the formal side of ethnic culture in America.

CHAPTER EIGHT

Ethnicity and Literary Form

There are some families and some of them are being living and some of them have been dead then and some of them are remembering that some are dead then and that time has been passing very quickly all the time any one has been a dead one.

—Gertrude Stein

The settlers of New England were at the same time ardent sectarians and daring innovators.

—Alexis de Tocqueville

It is customary to ascribe the origins of America's most characteristic art forms—jazz, musicals, and movies—to the influences of ethnic diversity. Yet only a few attempts have been made to investigate the relationship of American ethnicity to cultural media and literary forms. Readers are most curious about the *content* of ethnic writing and often look for the survival of cultural baggage. Influenced by older approaches to ethnic survivals, they search for supposedly "authentic" literature and are less concerned with formal aspects, let alone syncretisms and stylistic innovations.

Ethnic Encyclopedias, American Odysseys

Ethnicity has been a factor in the choice of many interesting formal patterns. The tension between consent and descent sometimes expresses itself as uneasiness about the incongruity of putting new-world content into old-world forms, or minority writing in majority forms. The belief is widespread that a new national or ethnic consciousness has to be rendered in appropriate forms; and works which express American themes in English forms or ethnic themes in mainstream forms are often criticized for doing so. Since there is no ontological connection between a country and a form, however, such critiques are often based on the political impulse of the moment. On

237

the individual level, it seems to be the particular writer's encounters with art during early socialization that shape his or her later understanding of what were the natural and organic forms of the respective nation or ethnic group. Moreover, since it is hard to define precisely and persuasively what constitutes an adequate national or ethnic form, the point of departure is frequently in the form of a polemic against an opponent. This is one aspect of ethnicity where the legacy of folk romanticism, with its belief in the organic connection of national/ethnic groups and cultural forms, is most stubbornly persistent.

Yet, despite professions to the contrary, there is very little that is natural in the relationship of ethnicity and forms or symbols. Those that seem most ancient, meaningful, and indigenous may be of relatively recent fabrication and may have been adopted simply for reasons of contrast. For example, the defining of what is an American form can be accomplished by a defying of something that is perceived as its antithesis, as un-American. The word "un-American" made its debut in 1818 (*Oxford English Dictionary*) in protest against the import of Italian marble. Analogously, English Popian couplets could be viewed as un-American. As we saw earlier, however, Sir Walter Scott could be regarded as un-American, while *Robinson Crusoe* seemed, in the eyes of immigrants, quite compatible with the United States. National and ethnic parallels are strong here: in 1788, to use another field, Nicholas Pike, the author of a mathematical textbook, hoped for the emergence of "American arithmetic"; in 1969 Nathan Hare predicted the rise of "Black math." Where American writers were criticized for using "English" forms, the Afro-American writer Claude McKay's work in the sonnet form, for example, in "If We Must Die" (1919), has sometimes been read as a contradiction of his themes of black pride and self-defense.

If there is one genre that is exempted from such debates, it is the epic, which is generally associated with ethnogenesis, the emergence of a people, and can therefore seemingly be appropriated transnationally by all peoples. The image of an American "Odyssey" is almost as widespread as that of a new-world exodus, as it appears in the very titles of countless fiction and nonfiction books; for example, in the Italian-American John Fante's "Odyssey of a Wop" (1940), in the Scotch-Swedish Frederick Philip Grove's *A Search for America: The Odyssey of an Immigrant* (1928), in the historian Nathan Huggins's *Black Odyssey: The Afro-American Ordeal in Slavery* (1977), in Julius Haber's *The Odyssey of an American Zionist: Fifty Years of Zionist History* (1956), or in the story of a Puerto Rican who came to New York in

the 1930s, entitled "The Odyssey of a Jíbaro" (1974). If Homer influenced American book titles, it was the *Aeneid* that shaped the *form*
of American epics. In itself the product of the continuation of a tradition, the *Aeneid* lent itself to a sanctioning of the further transporting west of empires. Among the earliest colonial writings in
America is Gaspar Pérez de Villagra's ambitious and consciously Vergilian epic, *Historia de la Nueva Mexico* (1610); and Cotton Mather's
famous introduction to the *Magnalia Christi Americana* (1702) begins
with the Vergilian formula: "I write the *Wonders* of the CHRISTIAN
RELIGION, flying from the Depravations of *Europe*, to the American
Strand" (Miller, *Puritans* 163). Epic epithets, such as "Nehemias
Americanus" or "the American evangelist," and catalogs, such as the
listings of different people in melting pots, are further epic elements
which recur quite frequently.

The polyethnic character of America has sometimes stimulated the
creation of exuberantly multilingual forms, in which ethnic contrad-
ictions could be absorbed as into a sponge, or organized in an encyclopedic and panoramic fashion. The panoramic approaches to
whole cities or ethnic groups were particularly popular among Sue's
American disciples. Encyclopedic collections of American ethnic-
group life are an appropriately open-ended, popular nonfiction
genre, in which one group is discussed after the other. The tradition
ranges from numerous efforts of this sort in the period of Edward
Steiner's *On the Trail of the Immigrant* (1906) through Louis Adamic's
never-realized project of an encyclopedia of the "nation of nations"
to the recently published *Harvard Encyclopedia of American Ethnic
Groups* (1980). In his insightful study *Immigrant Autobiography in the
United States* (1982), William Boelhower calls attention to Pascal
D'Angelo's "encyclopedic approach to culture" in *Son of Italy* (1924),
where the narrator masters the challenge of finding words that his
listeners would not know:

> I began, "Troglodyte," "sebaceous," "wen," "helot," "indeciduity,"
> "muringe," "bantling," "ubiquity," "clinthrophobia," "nadir," ... And
> with a pencil against the office façade I wrote seven words so that
> everyone might see their eternal defeat, "abettor," "caballine," "phle-
> botomy," "coeval," "[octoroon}," "risible," "anorexia," "arable," then
> to complete, I added, "asininity." (147; Boelhower 124)

A manuscript by "the Pennsylvania Pilgrim" and founder of Germantown, Francis Daniel Pastorius, entitled *Bee-Hive or Bee-Stock*
(1697; first printed in 1897), is a conglomerate of proverbs and folk
wisdom, personal observations and messages for the second genera-

tion, and has been called by Marion Dexter Learned "the *Magna Charta* of German culture in colonial America and a veritable *speculum scientiarum* of the seventeenth century"—the first American encyclopedia. Pastorius, who describes modern English as "a Mingle-mangle of Latin, Dutch & French," uses seven languages in his own book, but mostly German, English, and Latin. The focus and central image of the book is the "bee-hive" in its literal, metaphoric, and cultural implications (Learned, *Pastorius* 241–54). The comprehensiveness of Pastorius's method makes his work a minor precursor of Melville's encyclopedic view of whales ("cetology") in *Moby-Dick* (1851). Pastorius's learned and multilingual facility is reminiscent of Nathaniel Ward's Rabelaisian *Simple Cobbler of Aggawam* (1647) and much of Cotton Mather's work. The culmination of this rhetorical strain was reached in Walt Whitman's poetry. Whitman's all-absorbing, panethnic, and future-oriented poetic consciousness has often been considered peculiarly American.

> Ages, precedents, have long been accumulating undirected materials,
> America brings builders, and brings its own styles.
> The immortal poets of Asia and Europe have done their work and pass'd to other spheres,
> A work remains, the work of surpassing all they have done.
> . . . .
> These States are the amplest poem,
> Here is not merely a nation but a teeming Nation of nations,
> Here the doings of men correspond with the broadcast doings of the day and night,
> Here is what moves in magnificent masses careless of particulars,
> Here are the roughs, beards, friendliness, combativeness, the soul loves,
> Here the flowing trains, here the crowds, equality, diversity, the soul loves. (Ifkovic, *Letter* 370–71)

Older concepts of ethnicity alert the antiquarian in us when we think of ethnic literature. How does this Hungarian-American poem relate to an old-world prototype? How does that Afro-American writer draw on African folklore? How Portuguese is Dos Passos?—these are the questions often triggered when we think about American literature and ethnicity. Less frequently studied are the innovative aspects of ethnic writing, the invention of ethnic traditions, the syncretism and modernism that characterize so many of the forms of ethnic culture in America. For instance, we are accustomed to think of the development of American literature as "growth," as a process of increasing formal complexity from travelogues and letters (starting with John Smith's *True Relation* {1608}, which is the first "America letter"), sermons, essays, and biographies to the increasingly successful mastery of poetry, prose fiction, and drama. Analogously, we may see the historical unfolding of ethnic writing as a process of growth; and again, the beginning is with immigrant and migrant letters (collected, for example, by Everett Emerson for British emigrants, Alan Conway for the Welsh, Karl Larsen for Danes, Abraham Cahan for Jews, Thomas and Znaniecki for Poles, and by the *Journal of Negro History* for black migrants). The literature then "grows" from nonfictional to fictional forms (e.g., from *A Bintel Brief* to *Miss Lonelyhearts*; or from an autobiography to an autobiographic novel); from folk and popular forms to high forms (e.g., from Uncle Remus tales to Charles Chesnutt's *The Conjure Woman*; from Indian folklore to N. Scott Momaday's *House Made of Dawn*, Hyemeyohsts Storm's *Seven Arrows*, or Leslie Silko's *Ceremony*; or from Mexican-American popular culture to Luis Valdez's dramatic Actos and Richard Rodriguez's *Education*); from lower to higher degrees of complexity (e.g., from Dion Boucicault to Eugene O'Neill, from Abraham Cahan to Saul Bellow, or from James Weldon Johnson to Ralph Ellison); and from "parochial" marginality to "universal" significance in the literary mainstream (and the American mainstream now includes more and more writers with identifiable "ethnic" backgrounds). Characteristically, the transition from provincialism (of the unwholesome kind) to modernity is often marked by a collective rebirth experience of a tradition, which literary historians (and sometimes the cultural participants) customarily term "renaissance" (American and Harlem) and renascence (southern) or describe with the ominous epithet "new" (as in "American drama," "Negro" or "ethnicity"). In some instances, these "growth" models yield a plausible picture of literary developments against the background of an opposition between parochial ethnicity and modern movements in art and literature. This was, as we saw in the first chapter, the gist of much sociological theory through the 1960s as well. In theories of the past, modernization simply meant emancipation from ethnicity. This view also nicely supported a general belief in human progress, taking place in ethnic units; and to this day, this belief affects the very definition of what constitutes ethnic literature.

What Is Ethnic Writing?

Writers of national fame or of striking formal accomplishments or of international fame are often categorically excluded from the realm of ethnic writing. This is illustrated by the cases of Nathanael West, Eugene O'Neill, or Vladimir Nabokov and suggests the limited scope of what we define—sometimes quite tautologically—as ethnic literature.

Carl Sandburg is an interesting example of a popular ethnic who may be excluded from ethnic definitions because of his very popularity. The Illinois-born son of Swedish immigrants married Lillian Steichen, the daughter of Luxembourgers and, because of this intermarriage, made it into Richard Bernard's recent study *The Melting Pot and the Altar* (1980). As a person who was second generation by descent and melting pot by consent, and as an author of many poems on ethnic themes (including, as we saw, redemptive Hungarians), Sandburg would seem to be the perfect author for ethnic critics. Yet so eminent and magisterial a scholar of Scandinavian-American writing as Dorothy Burton Skårdal does not consider Sandburg part of her field. In her study *The Divided Heart* (1974), Skårdal calls him the "greatest of the completely assimilated authors of Scandinavian background," who "has become a symbol of the American Middle West." She then makes Sandburg a virtual test case:

> Such authors help define the limits of immigrant literature because—in spite of their parentage—they fall so indisputably outside it. By no stretch of definition can they be considered anything but wholly American. (47–48)

This is as if a discussion of nineteenth-century American literature started with a brief statement to the effect that the works of Cooper, Poe, Melville, Harriet Beecher Stowe, and Mark Twain fell outside the scope of the survey since by no stretch of definition could they be considered anything but world literature—despite the accident of their authors' American birth. If an author's descent is what matters (and not, say, subject matter of a non-Scandinavian author who wrote about Swedes in America), then there is no good reason for excluding a Sandburg. If descent does not matter, then why use it as a category at all? Skårdal further formulated what sounds like a "law" of immigrant writing:

> authors in English who betray no trace of their foreign origin should probably be classified as American writers, regardless of their parentage. Nelson Algren is no more an immigrant author than James T. Farrell. (51)

Skårdal's fine line of distinction *appears* to be between the immigrant writer "with insight arising from his special heritage" and the author who has "no more perception than if he was not of Scandinavian origin" (which is to say that much insight comes by descent). What is really juxtaposed here is the famous, nationally known and modern writer and the unknown, modestly parochial immigrant author. "Insight" is the code word for *minor* insider, otherwise Farrell or Algren could not conceivably be excluded. Ethnic writing is equated with parochialism, and ethnic writers who were not parochial are simply classified not as ethnic but as "wholly American." According to such definitions ethnic writing is interesting if it is "authentic" in a rather narrow sense, and whatever Sandburg or Farrell are, they are not, in this sense, authentic. The forms of American ethnic literature surely deserve to be treated more seriously than if they were humble and involuntary by-products of "genuine" ethnic themes or unmediated results of a minor author's parentage. While tautologically narrowing definitions are of little persuasive power, a broader and more inclusive definition of ethnic literature is helpful: works written by, about, or for persons who perceived themselves, or were perceived by others, as members of ethnic groups, including even nationally and internationally popular writings by "major" authors and formally intricate and modernist texts. Even ethnic writers who seem to be "traditional" may have been brazen inventors of these traditions. In any event, much thinking has been done about the affinities of ethnicity and modernity; and there is no reason why readers of ethnic literature should not benefit from these efforts in their own interpretations.

In his interesting essay "The Intellectual Pre-eminence of Jews in Western Europe" (1919), Thorstein Veblen argued that it is exposure to culture contact and to doubleness that encourages "pioneering" and "*Unbefangenheit*, release from the dead hand of conventional finality." It is only when the Jew, Veblen's exemplary case,

> falls into the alien lines of gentile inquiry and becomes a naturalised, though hyphenate, citizen in the gentile republic of learning, that he comes into his own as a creative leader in the world's intellectual enterprise. It is by loss of allegiance, or at best by force of a divided allegiance to the people of his origin, that he finds himself in the vanguard of modern inquiry. (*Veblen* 475, 474)

The hyphen, again far from being considered a minus sign, is seen as a token of avant-garde modernism. It is only a small step from Veblen's special case to the general situation of cultural doubleness in America, a step that Robert Park took when he interpreted the situation of all "marginal men" who have migrated to American cities, "these vast melting pots of races and cultures," as characterized by emancipation, enlightenment, and modern liberation from conventionality (*Race*, 345–56; see also Gordon, *Nature* 269–95). This is not only true for renegades, exceptional and intrepid souls. In modern polyethnic societies most men and women can play the part of Veblen's exceptional Jews in relation to others; and this applies to artists as well as to other ethnics, and even to those active in ethnic and ethnocentric movements.

In an amazing number of instances, ethnic artists have embraced innovation and modernity in form. We ought to remember that though many ethnic writers used realistic techniques, realism was nineteenth-century modernism. As has become increasingly clear from scholarship in the past twenty years, ethnicity and modernity are not opposites. This is true in life, in cultural media, as well as in literature. We quite instinctively tend to equate America with modernity and ethnicity with tradition, without much regard for the astounding evidence which contradicts that assumption. It is not emancipation from ethnicity that spells modernism; Veblen appropriately added at least the "force of a divided allegiance." Recent ethnic theorists, inspired particularly by Fredrik Barth's *Ethnic Groups and Boundaries* (1969), have emphasized the emergence, even the invention, of ethnic markers, which were later sometimes passed off as "traditional." The black "natural" hairdo ("Afro") and the clenched fist symbol of the Jewish Defense League are, in this sense, very "modern" markers. In his seminal contribution to the reader *On the Making of Americans* (1979), Herbert Gans calls attention to the invention of the Jewish bas mitzvah (the initiation ceremony for thirteen-year-old girls) in America and to the newly emphasized importance of Chanukah. "Americans," Gans concludes, "increasingly perceive themselves as undergoing cultural homogenization, and whether or not this perception is justified, they are constantly looking for new ways to establish their differences from each other" (205, 215). Drawing on LeRoi Jones/Amiri Baraka's *Blues People* (1963), Ulf Hannerz argues similarly, in an essay included in Frances Henry's *Ethnicity in the Americas* (1976), that

> black music has been undergoing a continuous revitalization as a reaction to the equally continuous assimilation of its forms into mainstream music. ... [Thus] the desire to maintain ethnic boundaries despite cultural diffusion may be a source of cultural vitality in a multiethnic society. (Hannerz 435)

Not only the assault on ethnic boundaries but also ethnic boundary construction itself may generate innovation and modernization.

As Americans of different backgrounds share larger and larger areas of an overlapping culture, they keep insisting on symbolic distinctions (often not those of "ancient origin" but freshly invented ones), the process known as "ethnicization." Instead of looking at various ethnic traditions as merely growing from very parochial beginnings to modernist assimilation, we may also see ethnic identification itself as a modern phenomenon. It is in this context that Franz Kafka's sketch "The Trees"—which serves as the motto of this book—can be read as a profound illustration of this new understanding. "We are all uprooted" is the first proposition (shared by the older universalist historians and sociologists); "no, we are all firmly wedded to the ground" is the counterproposition, equally false (and advanced by the spokesmen for the "new ethnicity"). No, we are only apparently rooted, but seem to be acting as if these constructed connections were natural ones. One may say that ethnicity is continuously created anew and that assimilation and modernization take place in ethnic and even ethnocentric forms. The Marcus Garvey movement, for example, which appears in the "growth" model as the link in a chain from Martin Robison Delany's nineteenth-century black nationalism to Elijah Muhammad's Nation of Islam in the twentieth, has now been studied as a "trendy" ethnocentric movement which actually modernized its members. Judith Stein thus placed Garvey's focus on the Black Star Line into the context of other attempts at establishing shipping lines as ethnic or national symbols at the end of World War I. She found that Garvey's Black Star Line was in good ethnocentric company with an Irish-American Green Star Line and a Cuban Star Line. These ships were modern markers. Or, to return to *Blues People* (1963), the avant-garde art of bebop was not the result of cultural diffusion from the mainstream and of the emancipation from ethnic solidarity; instead, it functioned as a reaction against white swing and as an "anti-assimilationist" symbolic marker which, in the words of LeRoi Jones/Amiri Baraka, dragged black music "outside the mainstream of American culture again" (181).

The old antithesis between ethnicity and modernism was often flawed by a one-dimensional view of the power of cultural diffusion, of assimilation as homogenization. In an essay on modern communication included in *Race and Culture*, Robert Park observes that "the oil cans of the Standard Oil Company and the Singer sewing-machine ... are now possibly the most widely dispersed of all our modern cultural artifacts" (46). Yet precisely these widely diffused cultural artifacts have not only engendered homogenization but also prompted "ethnic," that is to say, in this context, boundary-constructing responses. Apart from inspiring Perry Miller to contemplate the meaning of America, as he writes in the introduction to *Errand into the Wilderness* (1956), the oil drums also led to the invention of the Trinidadian steel bands which have become, as Abner Cohen (1980) has brilliantly argued, a central ethnic symbol for West Indians in London. The worldwide marketing of the Singer sewing machine has not only promulgated western dress codes but also, as Peter Marzio vividly illustrates in *A Nation of Nations* (1976), facilitated the "making of intricately ornamented folk costumes" in different countries (530–37). A postcard currently for sale at the Museum of the American Indian in New York City shows a Seminole Indian woman sewing a folk dress in front of a tent—on a Singer sewing machine. Perhaps ethnic scholars ought to develop as much joy in syncretism as they have found in purity and authenticity in the past.

Mass-market paperbacks and television docudramas may not only homogenize a national and international audience but also—as the examples of *Roots* and *Holocaust* show—help to rally ethnic groups around certain symbols. Ethnocentric novels may be composed on word processors these days. Ethnicization and modernization often go hand in hand. Any close reader of immigrant and ethnic writing who is not looking exclusively for the loss of traditional culture must notice the persistent concern with the new and the modern. I have been impressed again and again with how much interest immigrants displayed, for example, in the development of modern media of communication. The Irish-born Henry O'Rielly (né O'Reilly), an urban journalist in the boom years of Rochester, was instrumental in developing the brand-new telegraph line known then as "O'Rielly's Lightning Line" and in finding investors for the new medium in the 1840s and 1850s. The Danish-born muckraker Jacob Riis describes in his autobiography, *The Making of an American* (1901), how he used and adapted the most recently developed flashlight in order to photograph how the other half lives (268–73) in support of social reform plans. The Irish-born Samuel Sidney McClure, according to his account in *My Autobiography* (1914)—ghostwritten by Willa Cather—sat down one evening in his East Orange, New Jersey, home and invented the newspaper syndicate: "I saw it all, in all its ramifications, as completely as I ever did afterward, and I don't think I ever added anything to my first conception" (164). The first American writer whose story S. S. McClure sold to many newspapers at $5 to $20 each was the Norwegian-American Hjalmar Hjorth Boyesen, who received $250 for it (168).

If modern ethnicization is a form of symbolic boundary-construct-ing which increases cultural vitality, and if ethnic writers have dis-played much interest in modern forms of communication, then the literary forms of ethnic writing can hardly be expected to be exclu-sively traditional. Indeed, the affinities to new forms as adequate expressions of rebirth experiences are strong. There are good reasons why many ethnic artists do not fit into the older developmental schemes from ethnic to modern. One of America's most recent immi-grants, or, as they are for some reason called when they come from Russia, émigrés, Slava Tsukerman directed the supermodernist punk science fiction film *Liquid Sky* (1983). While it includes an unusual melting-pot scene and shows some concern for the characters' national and ethnic backgrounds, it is formally so radical (with Yuri Neyman's high-tech camera style, heat photography, and neon cold-ness) and so convincingly embraces a new-wave sensibility (which makes *Easy Rider* seem cute, old-fashioned, warmhearted, and upbeat by comparison) that it probably won't be discussed much as a "mod-ernist immigrant movie," which is precisely what it is. Tsukerman also characterized himself in the American tradition of immigrant rebirths when he said: "People who see *Liquid Sky* expect me to be a younger person. I think that's because I had to start life as a new person when I was 33. Maybe I just started my life after I left Moscow. In this life, I'm much younger" (*Boston Globe* January 31, 1984). Did Tsukerman listen to Bob Dylan's "I Was So Much Older Then" in the Soviet Union?

Ethnic Modernism and Double Audience

One problem with artists between cultures is where they ought to be fit in the developmental line of progress: in the old world from which they may come (or which may have emerged after their ancestors arrived in America), in America, or in a specific line of ethnic descent. Writers may adhere to old-world languages and yet be more modern than their Americanized and American counterparts. Ethnic writers, alerted to cultural clashes, may feel the need for new forms earlier or more intensely than mainstream authors. Furthermore, the rhetoric of ethnicity as conflict between consent and descent has mil-itated in favor of consent and the "new" and thus supported drives toward formal innovation.

Because of their close connections to other cultures or to interna-tional reading matter, American ethnic writers sometimes participated in literary innovations of other national literatures before such innovations became more widespread in America. At the beginning of the twentieth century, for example, the Scandinavian, German, and Yiddish stages were more "modern" than the average American theater. Hutchins Hapgood devoted a large section of his study of the "Jewish quarter" of New York, *The Spirit of the Ghetto* (1902), to the Yiddish stage, and especially to the serious drama by Jacob Gordin (136–49). In his volume of sketches from ethnic low life, *Types from City Streets* (1910), Hapgood advised writers: "You can take not only your plots from the lives of these people, but you can also derive the vigor and vitality, the figurative quality, of your style, from the slang and racy expression of your lowly friends" (22). While this may have just been a late echo to Sue's pseudo-Indian argot of Paris lowlifes, in 1915 Hapgood did support the Provincetown group which helped to create the new American drama and which gave prominent exposure to the modernist plays of an Irish-American, Eugene O'Neill. This example illustrates that acculturation and modernization work in more complicated ways than by literary diffusion from more modern American mainstream to more traditional ethnic group, in the course of which ethnic literature supposedly "matures" and immigrant writers become "wholly American."

Similarly, marginal and less assimilated writers may be more in tune with international avant-gardist literary movements than their wholly American or fully Americanized colleagues. Ethnic poets who used languages other than English were sometimes more willing to work with the new forms of Whitman and the French symbolists than immigrant or native American poets who wrote in Whitman's native tongue. The rebellious and aggressive Yiddish poets who, in 1907, formed *Die Yunge* (the young ones) and published their path-breaking anthology *Yugend* (youth) by "self press," shared a common ground with the modernist rebels in Europe and America, despite the language barrier. At a time when Jewish-American writing in English showed few traces of modernist influences—Henry Roth's *Call It Sleep* marked the full breakthrough of high modernism only in 1934—*Die Yunge* and *Insichisten* (introspectivists) created a Yiddish avant-gardism in America, well expressed in Aaron Glantz-Leyeles's manifesto *Labyrinth* (1918): "Create new rhythms, as an expression of new moods. ... Permit absolute freedom of thematic selection. ... Present images ... create clear and definite poetic concentration—the quintessence of poetry" (Madison, *Yiddish* 307). There are parallels to this case in the literature by Chinese-Americans, Puerto Ricans, as well as most other groups that have produced writers in old-world tongues. One recent collection of ethnic poetry which emphasizes the avant-garde is David Kherdian's *Settling America: The Ethnic Expressions of 14 Contemporary Poets* (1974).

Yet, whether they write in other languages or in English, ethnic writers have an acute sense of doubleness. "Double consciousness," that Emersonian term used in W. E. B. DuBois's well-known formula of "an American, a Negro," exerted its particular pressure—sometimes an intensely stimulating one—upon ethnic writers as cultural producers. Johan G. R. Banér's *Barr* (1926) unabashedly makes an asset out of ethnic dualism and considers it superior to any measly single national identity: "You are ONE, but—I am TWO!" (Skårdal 295). This attitude implies a degree of imperviousness to traditional sex roles; the human being with a double identity in literature is related to Christ and Superman rather than to average mortals; and he is both yin and yang in himself. Hyphenate writers may think of themselves as far advanced over single-consciousness competitors. Double-consciousness characters may be attracted to mirrors, reflecting windows, or smooth-surfaced ponds. This is a central motif in *Liquid Sky*, where the new-wave fashion model Margaret (played by Anne Carlisle) represents only the most recent cutting edge in androgynous narcissism, a latter-day fulfillment of the alchemists' vision of the hermaphrodite. An earlier narcissist is Abraham Cahan's David Levinsky, who feels attracted by his own new image— without sidelocks and in American clothes—an image he sees reflected in mirrors and shop windows. Confronted for the first time in his life with the ultimate slur "Nigger, nigger, never die, Black face and shiny eye," the narrator-hero of James Weldon Johnson's *Autobiography of an Ex-Colored Man* (1912) rushes to the mirror and discovers his own beauty in black-white ambiguity: "I noticed the ivory whiteness of my skin, the beauty of my mouth, the size and liquid darkness of my eyes, and how the long, black lashes that fringed and shaded them produced an effect that was strangely fascinating even to me" (401).

Johnson in 1928 also described the "dilemma of the Negro author" as the "problem of the double audience" ("Dilemma" 477). Ethnic writers in general confront an actual or imagined double audience, composed of "insiders" and of readers, listeners, or spectators who are not familiar with the writer's ethnic group. Here the opportunity presents itself for the writer to play a variety of roles. He or she may, like Harriet Beecher Stowe or James Weldon Johnson, take the general readers by the hand and initiate them into the mysteries of low life and ethnicity or, like Emil Klauprecht, address the immigrant readers and tell them about America. Yet their audience may well be ethnic *and* American. Imperceptibly and sometimes involuntarily, writers begin to function as translators of ethnicity to ignorant, and sometimes hostile, outsiders and, at the same time, as mediators between "America" and greenhorns. Footnotes, lengthy asides, explanations which at times seem superfluous or even offensive to some readers, bibliographies, and glossaries become the signposts of this situation. Mary Antin's *The Promised Land* (1911) ends with a seven-page multilingual glossary which includes, according to Mary Dearborn, several words that are never used in the book. O. E. Rølvaag's *Giants in the Earth* (1927) explains Beret Hansa's growing obsession with tampered landmarks with the following footnote:

> In the light of Norwegian peasant psychology, Beret's fear is easily understandable; for a more heinous crime than meddling with other people's landmarks could hardly be imagined. In fact, the crime was so dark that a special punishment after death was meted out to it. The visionary literature of the Middle Ages gives many examples. (120–21)

Sometimes, especially when stories appear in different languages or media, the authors change plot lines to suit what they think of as the respective audience. In Boucicault's *Octoroon* (1859) an English audience was assumed to be ready for an ending different from the one the American audiences saw. If the Hollywood studios are indicative of a larger pattern, the transformation of stories which were originally aimed at smaller markets into national and even international popular culture requires significant changes in plot lines, among them the well-known convention of the happy ending. It might be interesting to compare the formal changes of literature written for an ethnic group and rewritten for an "American" audience. Abraham Cahan, for example, rewrote his Yiddish story "Mottke Arbel" (1891–92) in English under the title "A Providential Match" (1895). In both versions the hero is an Americanized immigrant who, ironically, changed his name to "Friedman." He is thus in a long tradition of ethnic puns on "freed man," from Frederick Douglass's *Narrative* (1845) to Bernard Malamud's "The Lady of the Lake" (1953). In both versions of Cahan's story, this Friedman is duped in his expectations of marriage with the daughter of his former employer in Russia. In the English story, however, Cahan adds, as Jules Chametzky has shown in *From the Ghetto* (1977), a distinctive formal element of much immigrant literature: "the superior narrator explaining to a reader, whose values he presumably shares, some inside information about the Jewish immigrant culture in America" (49).

What is important about this strategy is the word "presumably." In order to mediate properly, the writer has to act, put on the ethnic costume here, sound an American voice there. Writer, narrator, or character may begin to resemble a "chameleon," a crucial term in ethnic discourse. Horace Kallen used the word to chide assimilated Jews in "The Ethics of Zionism"; James Weldon Johnson contemplated using it as the title of the book that became *The Autobiography of an Ex-Colored Man* (1912), and Woody Allen metaphorically is a chameleon in *Zelig* (1983). Even language is, after all, not an absolute indicator telling us who will read a story. So the doubleness gets more complicated, and writers often play around with expectations of double or multiple audiences.

Writing in dialect is one formal strategy by which ethnic writers can play with double audiences—in popular national humor columns, for example. Reaching their high point in Finley Peter Dunne's *Mr. Dooley Says* (1910) and Langston Hughes's *The Best of Simple* (1961), these humorous figures beautifully illustrate the ploy. Serialized in periodicals such as *McClure's Magazine* and the *New York Post* and collected in books by major publishing houses, these monologues and dialogues consciously take the *appearance* of ingroup conversations and pretend a little that the national audience does not exist or is merely permitted to eavesdrop—which gives the writers much leeway in avoiding pieties. Abraham Cahan's *Yekl: A Tale of the New York Ghetto* (1896), published in English, makes the readers believe that the characters speak Yiddish by using an influential strategy, described in the following footnote: "English words {such as *feller, preticly,* and *greenhornsh*} incorporated into the Yiddish of the characters of this narrative are given in italics" (3). There are storytellers who, like Charles W. Chesnutt's John in *The Conjure Woman* (1899), are ethnic versions of the unreliable narrator: John speaks with an authoritative and self-righteous white American voice and at times obviously misinterprets Uncle Julius and Afro-American character and tradition. Elements frequently used to orient readers in strange worlds are sometimes humorously turned against the reader's expectations. Carl Van Vechten's *Nigger Heaven* (1926) ends with a "Glossary of Negro Words and Phrases," which contains the entries "*boody:* see hootchie-pap" and "*hootchie-pap:* see boody." Vladimir Nabokov's *Pale Fire* (1962), written in the form of a paranoid line-by-line commentary upon a poem, has a ten-page index which does nothing but add circularity to an already maddening array of untrustworthy information by a Zemblan-American: for example, "All brown-bearded, apple-cheeked, blue-eyed Zemblans look alike, and I who have not shaved for a year, resemble my disguised king" (55). Ishmael Reed somewhat ironically appends a 104-item bibliography, including Freud, Olmsted's *Cotton Kingdom*, and Zora Neale Hurston, to his postmodern novel *Mumbo Jumbo* (1972).

Double consciousness, far from stifling American ethnic authors, alerts them to possibilities of playfulness in establishing their voice. Raising and thwarting initiation expectations, feeding the gullibility of readers and then pulling the rug from under their feet, or ironically undercutting the image of a presumably stable relationship between in-group and out-group are among the weapons in the rich arsenal of ethnic writers. This is delightfully illustrated by the ethnic transvestism of many fake ethnic writers, from the times of Henry Harland, who published "Jewish" novels under the pen name Sidney Luska, to the recent case of Daniel James, who wrote "Chicano" stories under the assumed name Danny Santiago and fooled critics for a while. In America's multigroup landscape, one individual could also alternately play the secret-cult member of an ethnic in-group ritual, the duped outsider who goes slumming somewhere else, and the general American who shares a syncretistic culture. Faulkner, for example, delighted in playacting the professional existential southerner, who needed bourbon for his painful imaginary World War I wound, at the expense of gullible outsiders like Sherwood Anderson; yet he asked Carl Van Vechten for a tour of Harlem nightclubs, where he, somewhat awkwardly, requested to hear the "St. Louis Blues." These switches from insider to outsider are also interesting because they suggest the complicated variety with which cultural boundaries are continually constructed in this country against "squares," "Anglos," "honkies," or other modern "hypocrites" or "philistines." Jack Kerouac once claimed "that all this 'Beat' guts ... goes back to my ancestors who were Bretons," only to add: "Breton, Wiking, Irishman, Indian, madboy, it doesn't make any difference, there is no doubt about the Beat Generation, at least the core of it, being a swinging group of new American men intent on joy" (*Road* 359; see Austern). In the sense of Georg Simmel's famous essay of 1908, *all* American writers can be in the role of "The Stranger" at times.

The intensely ironic relationship of ethnic authors to in-group and out-group audiences, from both of whom they must have felt alienated at times, could also lend itself to a pioneeringly transcending leap ahead in literary form. On an international scale, perhaps even James Joyce's venture into modernism was related to his com-

plex sense of Irish ethnicity; and Franz Kafka's own minority literature was written by a German-speaking Jew in Czechoslovakia, in a
situation of not just double but multiple group consciousness. American writers, too, could go further than just playing with doubleness:
they could push themselves into linguistic innovation as an assault
on conventions, patterns, and habits which also formed one basis of
group hostilities. Some writers would even attempt to deny the ade-
quacy of *any* existing language for their vision, while others developed an alliance between modernist forms and ethnic subject matter.

Among the many interesting ethnic modernists between the world
wars were Jean Toomer and José García Villa. Toomer, a light-
skinned Afro-American whose family had been living on both sides
of the color line for generations, viewed racial as well as other "Lin-
naean" categories with great detachment and ironical distance. In his
collection of aphorisms, *Essentials* (1931), he opposed ethnicity and
other divisive categories while advocating a Whitmanesque sense of
panethnic and pansexual cosmic wholeness, a return to the alchemical dreams of the Ouroboros and the hermaphrodite:

> I am of no particular race. I am of the human race, a man at large in
> the human world, preparing a new race.
>
> I am of no specific region. I am of earth.
>
> I am of no particular class. I am of the human class, preparing a new
> class.
>
> I am neither male nor female nor in-between. I am of sex, with male
> differentiations.
>
> I am of no special field. I am of the field of being. (XXIV)

In his open-verse poem "Blue Meridian" (1936), Toomer sounded a
similar theme and saw the coming synthesis of "the seven regions of
America." Toomer's *Cane* (1923), a book that significantly defies
genre categorization, is an experimental search for reality beyond
labels and for mankind above race and nationality. The section entitled "Bona and Paul" opposes imaginative vision to the ethnic blind-
ness of a priori assumptions. Interestingly, as Robert Bone has argued,
"Toomer's central metaphor ... is drawn from St. Paul's first epistle
to the Corinthians: 'For now we see through a glass darkly; but then
face to face: now I know in part; but then shall I know even as I am
known'" (*Down* 227). Challenging the "split spirit" of the past,
Toomer expressed a complex vision of the new America of the
future. He wanted his readers to understand the essential unity
beyond phenomenal diversity, including that created by ethnic
categories.

José García Villa's poetry similarly attempted to create its own formal rules and its own area of freedom and true vision. In *Have Come,
Am Here* (1942), García Villa—who was born in the Philippines—
proudly used "a new method of rhyming, a method which has never
been used in the history of English poetry, nor in any poetry," the
principle of "*reversed* consonance" (151). For example:

> Nobody yet knows who I am,
> Nor myself may;
> Nor yet what I deal,
> Nor yet where I lead. (18)

The new principle connects "I am" and "may," "deal" and "lead," and
the poem asks a common question for identity in a new way.

Ethnic literature abounds in musical imagery, so that the notion
of a multi-ethnic harmony, a polyphonic symphony, has become a
cliché since David Quixano's compositions in Zangwill's *Melting-Pot*
and Horace Kallen's problematic definition of American civilization
as an orchestration of mankind. On his quest for the new, away from
the commonplace, Villa found an adequate formal prototype for ethnic poetry in modern painting. In his most famous poems, ethnic
mediator that he was, Villa "translated" Seurat's pointillism into
punctuation, which blurs the sequence of lines and forces the reader
to take a total view from a certain distance (Casper, *New Writing* 109).
Villa ended the poem "Christ, Oppositor, / Christ, Foeman" with
these lines:

> After,pure,eyes,have,peeled,
>
> Off,skin,who,can,gaze,unburned? Who,
> Can,stand,unbowed? Well,be,perceived,
> And,well,perceive. Receive,be,received. (Casper 275)

Villa's comma poems may be an "extreme and absurd extravagance"
even in the context of avant-gardism, as Renato Poggioli has argued
(*Theory* 134), but they indicate a radical *formal* response to the ethnic
writer's need for a new poetic language. At the same time, Villa and
Toomer show affinities with Christic imagery of fusion and revelation that we have encountered in formally less radical writers.

Washingtonian and Mosaic Modernism

Since the appearance of artists' subcultures, ethnic writers could often
be found in the sometimes nationally visible bohemias of the avant-

garde. One could write a substantial history of ethnic American modernism in the first half of the twentieth century, from the serious realist immigrant stages to Ralph Ellison's *Invisible Man* (1952). Yet if ethnicity and modernity go well together, there are also important modernist writers who challenge all the clichés of ethnic discourse, if not ethnicity itself, just as Ellison poked fun at national symbolism in the "Liberty Paints" chapter of his novel. Grace Paley's "The Immigrant Story" (1975) appears to be intensely detached from the subject that the title promises. Paley separates a long conversation about the difficulty of remembering accurately from a consciously trite and clichéd ethnic memoir:

> My mother and father came from a small town in Poland. They had three sons. My father decided to go to America, to 1. stay out of the army, 2. stay out of jail, 3. save his children from everyday wars and pogroms. (*Enormous* 180)

The reasons are the familiar history book clichés, and despite all the reflections on remembering the concrete, we get a formula, "The Immigrant Story" at its most abstract.

Gertrude Stein's *The Making of Americans* (1925) is a consciously constructed counterpiece to the realistic and semiautobiographical novels one might expect from its title. In the book, the rhetoric of new world and ethnicity is churningly regurgitated and spewed out as a comment on its literary prototype. Yet, despite this formal antithesis, *The Making of Americans* remains part of its tradition. We noted earlier that ethnic writers such as Phillis Wheatley and Mary Antin sometimes defined their identity through a connection with George Washington. What could illustrate her new consciousness better than Antin's awareness that she was "nobly related": "Undoubtedly I was a Fellow Citizen, and George Washington was another" (*Promised* 224). Susannah Rowson, the author of the first American best-seller, *Charlotte* (1791), considered American authors more fortunate than Homer, who had only "barbarous chieftains" to write about, while they had "matchless Washington" (Nye, *Cultural* 245). The relationship to Washington is crucial to Cooper's *Spy*. In *Moby-Dick* Melville refers to Queequeg as "George Washington cannibalistically developed" (49). In his autobiography, *Up from Slavery* (1901), Booker T. Washington, an ardent advocate of cleanliness and the gospel of the toothbrush, describes how he adopted his last name and proudly proclaims: "[T]here are not many men in our country who have had the privilege of naming themselves in the way that I have" (47). In much American literature George Washington appears as a spouse and a name giver, an adopted ancestor (by consent) who is superior to a blood relative since he symbolizes Americanness by achievement. Gertrude Stein's *The Making of Americans* persistently alludes to, and works within, such Washington rhetoric and, at the same time, linguistically responds to the epithet "dirty," which is so often hurled against minorities. Stein writes of the immigrant boy George who "was not named after his grandfather" (a phrasing that evokes Margaret Mead's discussion of American ancestry). At age fourteen George Dehning was "strong in sport and washing. He was not foreign in his washing. Oh, no, he was really an american" (14). Stein continues in her unique style, which has been called cubist:

> It's a great question this question of washing. One never can find any one who can be satisfied with anybody else's washing. I knew a man once who never as far as any one could see ever did any washing, and yet he described another with contempt, why he is a dirty hog sir, he never does any washing. The French tell me it's the Italians who never do any washing, the French and the Italians both find the Spanish a little short in their washing, the English find all the world lax in this business of washing, and the East finds all the West a pig, which never is clean with just the little cold water washing. And so it goes. (14–15)

In Stein's writing, as in Toomer's or Henry Roth's, the "new style" is related to ethnicity. In the mode of ethnic modernism, ethnicity remains palpable while the writing transcends it, too. "Yes, George Dehning was not at all foreign in his washing but for him, too, the old world was not altogether lost behind him" (16).

In *The Autobiography of Emanuel Carnevali* (1967), an Italian-American modernist, the narrator attempts, as Boelhower has shown, to "draw the mythic dimension out of commonplace reality, as the new Whitman, the American poet who could absorb all things into himself" (Boelhower, *Immigrant* 168). Donning the mask of Jesus Christ, "this great blond poet," Carnevali delivers a new, modernist sermon on the mount (168, 169):

> I began to live in a glorious mist. My work on earth was different. . . . Maybe I would save the whole bloody world. . . . Save it from what? . . . Save the world from being too difficult to understand, too hard to die in and too hard to live in . . . have you ever, like a young and marvelous God, given life lavishly away with both open hands? (99; Boelhower 168)

If ethnic identification is to a good extent a matter of consent, of constructing modern and symbolic boundaries, then trans-ethnic art movements have to set out, melting-pot fashion, to tear down Barth's boundaries and biblical walls of partition. Ironically, as Carnevali's example illustrates, this may lead to the creation of a new (trans-)ethnogenesis, which remains firmly in the typological tradition. By questioning, sometimes even denying, the power of ethnicity, writers may be helping to create it anew. Some American modernists who set out to tear down ethnic categories and were associated with trans-ethnic art movements developed a pseudo-ethnic identity as bohemians. Andrew Greeley once suggested that intellectuals form an ethnic group (*New York Times Magazine* July 12, 1970), and Waldo Frank saw artists, in the familiar terms of ethnicity and typology, as a new "chosen people." Modernists might denounce "Puritanism" (by which they often meant moralism and nativist arrogance rather than the belief system of seventeenth-century New England), but they defined even their defiantly embraced "transnationalism" in the same typological tradition of American ethnicity that was first fully developed by the Puritans. Van Wyck Brooks, for example, described the (trans)"nationalism of the poets, novelists, and thinkers" as "a golden world in which one finds neither Roman, Jew, Barbarian nor Greek, for the prejudices of the brazen world are left behind there" (*Writer* 97–98). Describing the harmonious cooperation of Nordic, black, Jew, and Italian at Max Eastman's *Liberator* office, Joseph Freeman similarly observes in *An American Testament* (1936):

> Traditional racial barriers were transcended not only in the common work of the publication and in personal friendship, but even in the more intimate relations of love and marriage. I felt that on a small scale the *Liberator* group represented that ideal society which we all wanted, that society in which no racial barriers could possibly exist. (246)

Universal republics in a new golden age are, not surprisingly for students of melting-pot language, described as worlds without boundaries. In his essay "Transnationalism," Van Wyck Brooks cites Frank Lloyd Wright's "open plan" in architecture as an appropriate example of what we might call "melting-pot art forms" since it "abolishes all the partitions that have divided room from room" in the same way the "human laboratory" of America "abolishes the barriers between man and man in the interest of a wide sociality and all-human freedom. Wright has translated Walt Whitman into architecture" (Brooks, *Writer* 106). The passage is rich, as it evokes temple segregation, melting-pot ideal, art as translation, and Whitman.

Whitman was, indeed, often viewed as the formal prototype, the adoptive ancestor, of ethnic modernists; he was the Moses of the new chosen people, the (transnational) bohemians. By following their adopted epic grandfather and capital A Ancestor Moses Whitman, the self-chosen descendants could witness the birth of their own (trans)nation. In Waldo Frank's suggestive phrasing,

> this man was born among us: ... he never left our lands. He talked with God, standing upon America as Moses upon Sinai. He talked with God, speaking our tongue. America therefore is holy land to us. Not because Whitman stood upon it, but because we have faith that there is meaning in the fact that Whitman stood upon it. Because we cannot be so weak as to doubt that in this juncture of his spirit and our land is revelation. (*Our America* 204)

Frank may have written these lines with the intention of expressing an artistic opposition to bourgeois and puritanical America, yet one could not invent a paragraph more congruous with the typological underpinnings of American exceptionalism. Literary forms are not organically connected with ethnic groups; ethnicity and modernism form a false set of opposites; and the very desire to transcend ethnicity may lead writers back into the most familiar territory of ethnogenesis and typology.

Conclusion

No candidate can expect unanimous support from any given community.
All candidates must get their votes from the open market, and none of the
candidates have inherited any votes, nor can anyone bequeath any votes.
—Jesse Jackson announces he will run
for the presidency, October 30, 1983

I'd like to be the Moses who leads the schools out of the wilderness.
—Albert Shanker, president of
American Federation of Teachers, November 13, 1983

The tradition that this book has reported lives on. The intricate ways
persist in which a sense of kinship has been created by such elements
as boundary-constructing antithesis, biblically derived constructions
of chosen peoplehood, mixed rhetoric of melting pots, naturalization
of love as a ligament, curses and blessings by adoptive ancestors, symbolic tensions of parent and spouse figures, regionalist ethics, and
generational thinking. The language of consent and descent has been
flexibly adapted to the most diverse kinds of ends and has amazingly
helped to create a sense of Americanness among the heterogeneous
inhabitants of this country. As I have emphasized throughout, however, all of these elements have also been available and were used for
the creation of seriously divergent models of peoplehood; the same
ligament constructions that spelled consensus among Americans
could also be adapted to formulate secessionist and separatist peoplehoods. At times, the very glue could become dynamite.

The ways in which stories have helped create the rites and rituals
which can impart to the diverse populace of the United States a
shared sense of destiny are impressive. However, some final points of
criticism are also in order, if only to place the domestic debates about
consent and descent into some international contexts. To be sure,
American culture has tended to deemphasize hereditary privilege to
a greater extent than that of many other countries has. However, the
American Ladies Magazine's use of Acts 17 showed that even the

invoking of universalism could serve exclusivist ends. Tearing down the partition walls of mankind with a loud flourish could take place in conjunction with the quiet and sometimes less clearly observed construction of new boundaries. In the name of the new golden age in America, some provinces may have been kept in the brass age. Freedom from the fetters of descent was achieved while other forms of descent were literally thought of as deserving fetters.

These paradoxical processes are not stumps of inherited prejudice, colonial remnants that will slowly wither away as republicanism triumphs. As David Smiley said in a lecture on southern history, "when I was a kid in Mississippi, my town was so backward, it didn't even have segregation yet." Enough ethnic distinctions have *emerged* in the United States to put the theory of old-world survivals to rest.

The popular contrasts with the ethnically homogeneous and hierarchically structured old worlds are also often melodramatically overdrawn. It is not as if the American ethos was all Manly's and the rest of the world's all Van Dimple's. This oppositional strategy is often based on freezing the old world at a static point, which is, in some cases, the point of migration (Mead, *Keep* 40), and on exempting the new world from the secular realms of hierarchy, class, history, and conflict.

Somebody's claim to universalism may easily become somebody else's restriction to particularism, as long as an ideal is identified not with total human striving but with a place on the map or a secular interest. The rhetoric of American exceptionalism, while coming out of utopian hopes for the universal republic of man and for the return of the golden age, may easily subvert its own idealistic origins and speak only for one of the world's superpowers' nationalism—even when it is called transnationalism. By imagining America as the Christ-like mediator among nations one makes it artificially separate from all other secular nations. A century after Whitman, it is useful to think of America as a polyethnic nation among polyethnic nations instead of *the* nation of nations. After all, polyethnic countries are the rule and not the exception in the world today, so that if diversity is the touchstone for divinely chosen peoplehood, then there must be many nations among the elect.

America is not all alone with its cultural codes, either. "I am a 16-year-old Indian girl and my parents are very strict. I'm not allowed to have boyfriends or go to parties. What I dread is that when I'm older I'm expected to have an arranged marriage. Marriage to Indian people is nothing to do with love. It revolts me! I'm going to marry for love. But how can I get out of my parents' clutches? If my parents knew how I was thinking they'd kill me." Does this sound familiar? This letter to the editor appeared on December 11, 1983, in the British magazine *Woman*; and the writer's odious parents came from India! Many of the patterns we have looked at as characteristically American may be more and more widely shared in the world today. Romantic love was, after all, an Arab invention that inspired chivalry in twelfth-century Europe. Even though the myth of America has traveled to many places since 1776, America's is not the only road to modernism; and some ancient prejudices survive even in a country studded with skyscrapers (where the thirteenth floors are often mysteriously missing), while some new ones constantly emerge there, as elsewhere in the world. Modernization continues to take the form of ethnicization in many places around the globe.

It is important in a book of this nature to conclude with the clear statement that America was not Bible-made and that, the old seminary address notwithstanding, it did begin—and has always continued—with the many diverse nations known as American Indians, with slaves and their descendants, and with annexed territories. God did not prosper this undertaking any more than any others. The motto "annuit coeptis" from the Great Seal of the United States, reproduced on the back of every dollar bill, is a revealing adaptation of the Vergilian plea for divine approval, "audacibus adnue coeptis" (*Georgics* 1:40). American revolutionaries simply presumed that the nod had already been given to their undertaking (Escherig 105). In the very terms of the American belief system, the equating of redemption with being American is contrary to the need for *universal* regeneration. In other words, to think of America as the model of redemption is thus hypocritical by America's own revivalist standards.

If Paul had to address the Americans today, he might add "where there is neither American nor un-American" to his list of opposites in order to break down yet another partition wall of mankind. Once America thinks of itself as the only place of grace and once true human universalism is narrowly compacted into the American Dream, it becomes an obstacle to its own self-declared transcendent ends. It may be appropriate to end this book (with an apology to all Martians and to E.T.) by continuing in Josiah Royce's unforgettable idiom: the American Dream may be in our hands, but it is the human dream in the bush that matters.

Notes

[1]There are, of course, many noteworthy exceptions to the pattern I am describing, and I would like to mention at least a few of them. The sociologist Herbert Gans, for example, presented an unusually detailed and subtle interpretation, "Love Story: A Romance of Upward Mobility," in *The Popular Arts*, ed. William H. Hammel (New York: Harcourt Brace, © 1972), 431–35; the historian Nathan Huggins showed exceptional literary sensitivity in his *Harlem Renaissance* (New York: Oxford University Press, © 1971); the literary critic William Boelhower published a theoretically exciting study, *Immigrant Autobiography in the United States* (Verona: Essedue Edizioni, 1982); more recently, Boelhower published a superb and broadly conceived study of American literature, *Through a Glass Darkly: Ethnic Semiosis in American Literature* (Venice: Edizioni Helvetia, © 1984); and the literary historian Simone Vauthier has presented a number of psychologically and anthropologically sophisticated readings of plantation and mulatto fictions, which ought to be collected in book form and made more widely accessible. Of great value to literary, sociological, and historical orientations are the following pioneers: Carter Davidson, "The Immigrant Strain in Contemporaray American Literature," *English Journal* 25 (December 1936): 862–68; Howard Mumford Jones, "American Literature and the Melting Pot," *Ideas in America* (Cambridge, 1944), 185–204; David F. Bowers, ed., *Foreign Influences in American Life* (Princeton, 1944); Carl Wittke, "Melting-Pot Literature," *College English* 7 (January 1946): 189–97; Van Wyck Brooks, "Transnationalism," *Writer*, 86–108; Henry Pochmann, "The Mingling of Tongues," *Literary History of the United States*, ed. Robert E. Spiller, rev. ed. (New York, 1953), 676–93; Malcolm Cowley, "Where Writers Come From," *Literary*, 152–61; Daniel Aaron, "The Hyphenate Writer and American Letters," *Smith Alumnae Quarterly* (July 1964): 213–17; and Jules Chametzky, "Our Decentralized Literature: A Consideration of Regional, Ethnic, and Sexual Factors," *Jahrbuch für Amerikastudien* 17 (1972): 56–72. The following books document the intensified interest in American literary ethnicity in the past decade: Maxine Seller, *To Seek America: A History of Ethnic Group Life in the United States*, [Englewood, N. J.]: J. S. Ozer, © 1977; Ronald T. Takaki, *Iron Cages: Race and Culture in Nineteenth-Century America* (New York: Knopf, 1979); Marcus Klein, *Foreigners: The Making of American Literature, 1900–1940* (Chicago: University of Chicago Press, 1981); and Kristin Herzog, *Women, Ethnics, and Exotics: Images of Power in Mid-Nineteenth-Century American Fiction* (Knoxville: University of Tennessee Press, 1983).

[2]Carla Cappetti, "Quest for American Sociology: Richard Wright and the Chicago School," forthcoming in *MELUS*. See also Park's dream to become a novelist reported in Fred Matthews, *Quest for an American Sociology: Robert E. Park and the Chicago School* (Montreal and London: McGill-Queen's University Press, 1977), 108.

[3]See Hobsbawm and Ranger, eds., *Invention of Tradition*, with its devastating implications for American ethnic studies, esp. 1–14, 263–307.

[4]See Oscar Handlin, "What Happened to Race?" *Race and Nationality in American Life* (Garden City, N.Y.: Doubleday, 1957), 150-64; and Egal Feldman's letter to *Commentary*, January 1975, 8.

[5]Frederick Jackson Turner echoed this motif when he wrote: "The wilderness masters the colonist. ... It takes him from the railroad car and puts him in the birch canoe" (*Frontier* 4).

[6]An expression of symbolic ethnicity, this example further explains why national symbols were wholly absent in the Hotel Dumas.

[7]For discussions of this iconography see E. McClung Fleming, "Symbols of the United States: From Indian Queen to Uncle Sam," in *Frontiers of American Culture*, ed. Ray B. Browne et al. (Lafayette, Ind.: Purdue University Studies, 1968), 1-24; and Rayna Green, "The Pocahontas Perplex: The Image of Indian Women in American Culture," *Massachusetts Review* 16 (1975): 698-714. In her anti-melting-pot essay "The Modest Immigrant," Agnes Repplier writes that Americans "believe in the miracle of the melting-pot, which, like Medea's magic cauldron, will turn the old and decrepit races of Europe into a young and vigorous people, new-born in soul and body" (*Counter-Currents* {Boston and New York: Houghton Mifflin, 1916}, 202).

[8]Elizabeth McKinsey has argued that Indians appeared on paintings of the Falls long after they lived in its vicinity; see her *Niagara Falls: Icon of the American Sublime* (Cambridge, Eng., and New York: Cambridge University Press, 1985).

[9]The wish of so many white Americans to become Indian—as Crèvecoeur wrote at the end of his *Letters*—was directed toward such fantasy constructions of love, melancholy, and republicanism.

[10]This aspect makes Chesnutt's and Cahan's stories different from Klauprecht's triple intermarriage plot in his Cincinnati novel.

[11]In the 1914 essay "The West and American Ideals," Frederick Jackson Turner described his historical interest in the westward movement in the following terms: "We are the first generation of Americans who can look back upon that era as a historic movement now coming to its end. Other generations have been so much a part of it that they could hardly comprehend its significance" (*Frontier* 293).

[12]In recent years the concept of the generation has been subjected to some scrutiny and used with increased subtlety. Since the publication of S{hmuel} N{oah} Eisenstadt's classic *From Generation to Generation: Age Groups and Social Structure* (Glencoe, Ill.: Free Press, 1956), several good essayists have offered conceptual insight. Among them, Norman Ryder suggested the significance of the cohort in "The Cohort as a Concept in the Study of Social Change," *American Sociological Review* 30 (December 1965): 843-61; Alan Spitzer made the case for the historical importance of the collective experiences of coevals in "The Historical Problem of Generations," *American Historical Review* 78 (December 1973): 1353-85; and, most important, Vladimir Nahirny and Joshua Fishman convincingly interpreted the meaning of numbered generations in "American Immigrant Groups: Ethnic Identification and the Problem of Generations," *Sociological Review*, ns 13 (1965): 311-26. An exceptionally nuanced and detailed discussion of the concept of a "literary generation" is sustained in Cowley's *A Second Flowering*. George Forgie offered a methodologically sophisticated interpretation of Lincoln's generation as a "post-heroic" second generation in *Patricide in the House Divided: A Psychological Interpretation of Lincoln and His Age* (New York: Norton, 1979). Robert Wohl in *The Generation of 1914* (Cambridge: Harvard University Press, 1979) described that generation with great terminological clarity and developed a generational concept drawing on Karl Mannheim.

Bibliography

Aaron, Daniel. "The 'Inky Curse': Miscegenation in the White American Literary Imagination." *Social Science Information* 22 (1983): 169–90.

Abbot, Abiel. *Traits of Resemblance in the People of the United States of America to Ancient Israel. In a Sermon, Delivered at Haverhill, on the Twenty-Eighth of November, 1799, the Day of Anniversary Thanksgiving.*

Abbott, Lyman. *The Acts of the Apostles.* New York, Chicago, and New Orleans: Barnes, 1876.

Abraham, Karl. "Einige Bemerkungen über die Rolle der Grosseltern in der Psychologie der Neurosen." *Internationale Zeitschrift für ärztliche Psychoanalyse* 1 (1913): 224–27. English abstracts of Abraham and Ernest Jones appeared in *Psychoanalytic Review* 1 (July 1914): 337–42.

Abramson, Harold J. *Ethnic Diversity in Catholic America.* New York, London, etc.: John Wiley, 1973.

Adamic, Louis. *From Many Lands.* New York: Harper, 1940.

Adamic, Louis. *What's Your Name?* New York: Harper, 1942.

Ager, Waldemar. *Cultural Pluralism vs. Assimilation.* Ed. Odd S. Lovell. Northfield, Minn.: Norwegian-American Historical Association, © 1977.

Alexander, Joseph Addison. *The Acts of the Apostles Explained.* 2 vols. New York: Scribner, 1866.

Alger, William Rounseville. *Life of Edwin Forrest, the American Tragedian.* 2 vols. Philadelphia: Lippincott, 1877.

Anderson, Quentin. *The Imperial Self: An Essay in American Literary and Cultural History.* New York: Knopf, 1971.

———. "Practical and Visionary Americans." *American Scholar* 45 (Summer 1976): 405–18.

Anon. "Are the Human Race All of One Blood?" *American Ladies Magazine* 6 (1833): 359–62.

Anon. *Die Emigranten: Deutsch-Amerikanisches Lebensbild in fünf Akten.* St. Louis: Aug. Wiebusch & Son, 1882.

Anon. *History of the Seal of the United States.* Washington, D.C.: Department of State, 1909.

Anon. "The Making of New Americans." *Ford Times* November 1916: 151–52.

Anon. "A Motto Wrought into Education." *Ford Times* April 1916: 406–9.

Antin, Mary. *The Promised Land.* Boston and New York: Houghton Mifflin, 1912.

———. *They Who Knock at Our Gates: A Complete Gospel of Immigration.* Boston and New York: Houghton Mifflin, 1914.

Aristotle. *The Ethics of Aristotle: The Nicomachean Ethics.* Trans. J. A. K. Thompson. 1953. Harmondsworth: Penguin, 1977.

Austern, Nathan. "Ethnicity and Popular Culture in the Beat Generation." Forthcoming in *MELUS*.

Baker, Houston A. "Generational Shifts and the Recent Criticism of Afro-American Literature." *Black American Literature Forum* 15.1 (Spring 1981): 3–21.

Barker, J[ames] N[elson]. *The Indian Princess; or, La Belle Sauvage: An Operatic Melo-Drame*. Philadelphia: Palmer, 1808.

Barnes, Albert. *Notes, Explanatory and Practical, on the Acts of the Apostles*. New York: Harper & Bros., 1869.

Barth, Fredrik. *Ethnic Groups and Boundaries: The Social Organization of Culture Difference*. Boston: Little, Brown, © 1969.

Basham, Richard, and David DeGroot. "Current Approaches to Urban and Complex Societies." *American Anthropologist* 79 (1977): 414–40.

Baughman, Ernst W. *Type and Motif-Index of the Folktales of England and North America*. Indiana University Folklore Series, vol. 20. The Hague: Mouton, 1966.

Beigel, Hugo G. "Romantic Love." *American Sociological Review* 16 (1951): 326–34.

Bell, Michael Davitt. *Hawthorne and the Historical Romance of New England*. Princeton: Princeton University Press, 1971.

Bengis, Ingrid. *Combat in the Erogenous Zone*. New York: Knopf, 1972.

Benjamin, Robert Spiers, ed. *I Am an American: By Famous Naturalized Americans*. Introd. Archibald MacLeish. 1941. Freeport, N.Y.: Books for Library Series, 1970.

Benson, Leonard. *The Family Bond: Marriage, Love and Sex in America*. New York: Random House, 1971.

Bercovitch, Sacvan. *The American Jeremiad*. Madison: University of Wisconsin Press, 1978.

———. *The Puritan Origins of the American Self*. New Haven and London: Yale University Press, 1975.

Bernard, Richard M. *The Melting Pot and the Altar: Marital Assimilation in Early Twentieth-Century Wisconsin*. Minneapolis: University of Minnesota Press, 1980.

Bigsby, C. W. E. *The Black American Writer*. Vol. 1, *Fiction*. Baltimore: Penguin, 1969.

Blotner, Joseph. *Faulkner: A Bibliography*. 2 vols. New York: Random House, © 1974.

Boase, Roger. *The Origin and Meaning of Courtly Love: A Critical Study of European Scholarship*. Manchester:Manchester University Press, 1977.

Boelhower, William. *Immigrant Autobiography in the United States: Four Versions of the American Self*. Verona: Essedue Edizione, 1982.

Bogardus, Emory S. *Essentials of Americanization*. 3rd ed. Los Angeles: University of Southern California Press, 1923.

Bok, Edward. *The Americanization of Edward Bok: The Autobiography of a Dutch Boy Fifty Years After*. 1920. 50th ed., New York: Scribner, 1930.

Bone, Robert A. *Down Home: A History of Afro-American Short Fiction from Its Beginnings to the End of the Harlem Renaissance*. New York: Putnam's, 1975.

Bontemps, Arna, ed. *Great Slave Narratives*. Boston: Beacon Press, 1969.

Boorstin, Daniel J. *The Lost World of Thomas Jefferson*. Boston: Beacon Press, 1960.

Bourne, Randolph S. *The Radical Will: Randolph Bourne—Selected Writings, 1911–1918*. Ed. Olaf Hansen. New York: Urizen, 1977).

———. *War and the Intellectuals: Collected Essays, 1915–1919*. Ed. Carl Resek. New York: Harper, 1964.

Boyesen, Hjalmar Hjorth. *Tales from Two Hemispheres*. New York: Scribner, 1881.

Bracey, John H., Jr., August Meier, and Elliott Rudwick, eds. *Black Nationalism in America*. Indianapolis and New York: Bobbs-Merrill, 1970.

Bradford, William. *History of Plymouth Plantation*. 1651. Ed. William T. Davis. Original Narratives of Early American History Series. New York: Barnes & Noble, 1971.

Bridges, Horace J. *On Becoming an American: Some Meditations of a Newly Naturalized Immigrant*. Boston: Marshall Jones, 1919.

Brooks, Van Wyck. *The Writer in America*. New York: Dutton, 1953.

Brougham, John. *Metamora; or, The Last of the Pollywogs: A Burlesque, in Two Acts*. New York: French, {1847}.

————. *Po-ca-hon-tas; or, The Gentle Savage. In Two Acts*. New York: Samuel French,{1855}.

Brown, Sterling A., Arthur P. Davis, and Ulysses Lee, eds. *The Negro Caravan*. 1941. New York: Arno Press and New York Times, 1970.

Brown, William Wells. *Clotel; or, The President's Daughter*. 1853. New York: Arno Press and New York Times, 1969.

Brumm, Ursula. *American Thought and Religious Typology*. New Brunswick, N.J.: Rutgers University Press, 1970.

————. "'What Went You Out into the Wilderness to See?' Nonconformity and Wilderness in Cotton Mather's *Magnalia Christi Americana*." *Prospects* 6 (1981): 1–17.

Buckley, Jerome Hamilton. *Tennyson: The Growth of a Poet*. Cambridge: Harvard University Press, 1960.

Burrows, Edwin G., and Michael Wallace. "The American Revolution: The Ideology and Psychology of National Liberation." *Perspectives in American History* 6 (1972): 165–306.

{Burton, Robert.} "Democritus Junior." *Anatomy of Melancholy*. 1621. London: Tegg, 1845.

Bushnell, Horace. *Sermons for the New Life*. 4th ed. New York: Scribner, 1859.

Byrd, William. *Histories of the Dividing Line betwixt Virginia and North Carolina*. Ed. William K. Boyd. Raleigh, N.C.: North Carolina Historical Commission, 1929.

Cahan, Abraham. "The Autobiography of an American Jew: The Rise of David Levinsky." *McClure's Magazine* April 1913: 92–106; May 1913: 73–85; June 1913: 131–52; July 1913: 116–28.

————. *The Education of Abraham Cahan*. 1926. Trans. from the Yiddish autobiography *Bleter fun mein Leben*, vols. 1 and 2, by Leon Stein, Abraham P. Conan, and Lynn Davison. Philadelphia: Jewish Publication Society of America, 1969.

————. *The Rise of David Levinsky*. 1917. New York: Harper, 1966.

————. *Yekl and the Imported Bridegroom and Other Stories of the New York Ghetto*. New York: Dover Press, 1970.

Carlier, Auguste. *Marriage in the United States*. Trans. B. Joy Jeffries. Boston: De Vries, Iberra, 1867.

Carroll, Peter N. *Puritanism and the Wilderness: The Intellectual Significance of the New England Frontier, 1629–1700*. New York: Columbia University Press, 1969.

Casper, Leonard, ed. *New Writing from the Philippines: A Critique and Anthology*. Syracuse: Syracuse University Press, 1966.

"Celadon." *The Golden Age; or, Future Glory of North America Discovered by an Angel to Celadon in Several Entertaining Visions*. N.p.: 1785.

Chametzky, Jules. *From the Ghetto: The Fiction of Abraham Cahan*. Amherst: University of Massachusetts Press, 1977.

─────."Styron's *Sophie's Choice*, Jews and Other Marginals, and the Mainstream." *Prospects* 9 (1984): 433–41.

Chapman, Abraham, ed. *Jewish-American Literature: An Anthology of Fiction, Poetry, Autobiography, and Criticism.* New York: Mentor NAL, 1974.

Chapman, Gerald. "Burke's American Tragedy." MS 1983. Shorter version to be published in *Harvard English Studies.*

Chesnutt, Charles W. *The Wife of His Youth and Other Stories of the Color Line.* 1899. Ann Arbor: University of Michigan Press, 1969.

Chin, Frank, et al., eds. *Aiiieeeee! An Anthology of Asian-American Writers.* Washington, D.C.: Howard University Press, 1974.

Chyet, Stanley F. "Lewisohn and Crèvecoeur." *Chicago Jewish Forum* 22.2 (Winter 1963–64): 130–36.

─────. "Ludwig Lewisohn in Charleston (1892–1903)." *American Jewish Historical Quarterly* 54 (1964–65): 296–322.

Clinton, DeWitt. *An Introductory Discourse Delivered before the Literary and Philosophical Society of New-York on the 4th of May, 1814.* New York: Longworth, 1815.

Cohen, Abner. "Drama and Politics in the Development of a London Carnival." *Man* ns 15 (1980): 65–87.

─────, ed. *Urban Ethnicity.* London: Tavistock Publications, 1974.

Condoyannis, George E. "German American Prose Fiction from 1850 to 1914." Diss., Columbia University, 1953.

Cook, F. C. *The Holy Bible According to the Authorized Version (A.D. 1611) with an Explanation and Critical Commentary . . . New Testament.* Vol. 3. London: John Murray, 1881.

Cowley, Malcolm. *The Literary Situation.* New York: Viking Press, © 1954.

─────. *A Second Flowering: Works and Days of the Lost Generation.* New York: Viking Press, 1973.

Crèvecoeur, J. Hector St. John de. *Letters from an American Farmer.* 1782. New York: Dutton, 1957.

─────. *Lettres d'un cultivateur américain.* Paris: Cuchet Libraire, 1787.

Cummings, Ephraim Chamberlain. *Birth and Baptism: Discourses on First Principles.* Portland: B. Thurston, 1873.

Current, Richard N. "The 'New Ethnicity' and American History." Paper read at American Historical Society meeting in Detroit, 1981.

[Custis, George Washington.] *The Indian Prophecy: A National Drama in Two Acts.* Georgetown, D.C.: James Thomas, 1828.

Custis, George Washington. *Pocahontas; or, The Settlers of Virginia: A National Drama in Three Acts."* In *Representative American Plays, 1767–1923,* ed. Arthur Hobson Quinn. 3rd ed. New York: Century, 1925. 183–208.

Davies, Samuel. *Sermons.* Vol. 2. Philadelphia: Presbyterian Board of Publication, 1864.

Dearborn, Mary. "Pocahontas Revisited: Gender and Ethnicity in American Culture from the Civil War to the Present." Diss., Columbia University, 1983.

Deering, Nathaniel. *Carabasset: A Tragedy.* In Leola Bowie Chaplin, *The Life and Works of Nathaniel Deering (1791–1881).* Orono, Maine: University Press, 1934. 155–91.

Deffebach, Lewis. *Oolaita; or, The Indian Heroine. A Melo Drama in Three Acts.* Philadelphia, printed for the author, 1821.

De Forest, John William. *History of the Indians of Connecticut from the Earliest Known Period to 1850*. Hartford: Hammersley, 1853.

Delany, Martin R. *Blake; or, The Huts of America*. 1859–61. Introd. Floyd Miller. Boston: Beacon Press, 1970.

————. *The Condition, Elevation, Emigration, and Destiny of the Colored People of the United States*. 1852. New York: Arno Press and New York Times, 1969.

Devereux, George, and Edwin M. Loeb. "Antagonistic Acculturation." *American Sociological Review* 7 (1943): 133–47.

Devereux, George. "Ethnic Identity: Its Logical Foundations and Its Dysfunctions." In *Ethnic Identity: Cultural Continuities and Change*, ed. George de Vos and Lola Romanucci-Ross. Palo Alto: Mayfield, 1975. 42–70.

Dewey, John. "Nationalizing Education." In National Education Association of the United States, *Addresses and Proceedings of the Fifty-Fourth Annual Meeting ...* 54 (1916): 183–89.

Di Donato, Pietro. *Christ in Concrete*. 1939. Indianapolis and New York: Bobbs-Merrill, n.d.

Di Pietro, Robert J. "Language, Culture and the Specialist in Ethnic Literature." *MELUS* 4.1 (Spring 1977): 2–4.

Dippie, Brian William. "The Vanishing American: Popular Attitudes and American Indian Policy in the Nineteenth Century." Diss., University of Texas, Austin, 1970.

Doddridge, Joseph. *Logan: The Last of the Race of Shikellemus, Chief of the Cayuga Nation*. 1823. Cincinnati: Dodge, 1868.

Dolgin, Janet L., David S. Kemnitzer, and David M. Schneider, eds. *Symbolic Anthropology: A Reader in the Study of Symbols and Meanings*. New York: Columbia University Press, 1977.

Drachsler, Julius. *Democracy and Assimilation: The Blending of Immigrant Heritages in America*. New York: Macmillan, 1920.

Draper, Theodore. *The Rediscovery of Black Nationalism*. New York: Viking Press, 1970.

DuBois, W. E. B. *Darkwater: Voices from Within the Veil*. New York: Harcourt, Brace & Howe, 1920.

————. *The Souls of Black Folk*. 1903. In *Three Negro Classics*, introd. John Hope Franklin. New York: Avon, 1965.

Dunbar, Paul Laurence. *Complete Poems*. New York: Dodd, Mead, n.d.

Dunn, Richard S. *Puritans and Yankees: The Winthrop Dynasty of New England, 1630–1717*. Princeton: Princeton University Press, 1962.

Easton, H[osea]. *A Treatise on the Intellectual Character and Civil and Political Condition of the Colored People of the United States*. Boston: Isaac Knapp, 1837.

Edler, Erich. *Eugène Sue und die deutsche Mysterienliteratur*. Diss., Berlin, 1932.

Elliott, Emory. *Power and the Pulpit in Puritan New England*. Princeton: Princeton University Press, © 1975.

Ellison, Ralph. *Shadow and Act*. 1964. New York: Signet, 1966.

Emerson, Ralph Waldo. *The Journals and Miscellaneous Notebooks of Ralph Waldo Emerson*. Ed. Ralph H. Orth and Alfred R. Ferguson. Vol. 9. Cambridge: Harvard University Press, 1971.

Emmons, Dr. [Richard]. *Tecumseh; or, The Battle of the Thames: A National Drama in Five Acts*. Philadelphia, 1836.

Erikson, Erik H. *Childhood and Society*. 2nd rev. ed. New York: Norton, 1963.

Escherig, Manfred. "Die Geburt des göttlichen Amerikaners." *Sprache im technischen Zeitalter* 54 (1976): 80–126.

Fabre, Michel. *The Unfinished Quest of Richard Wright.* Trans. Isabel Barzun. New York: Morrow, 1973.

Fairchild, Henry Pratt. *The Melting-Pot Mistake.* Boston: Little, Brown, 1926.

Farrell, James T. *Studs Lonigan: A Trilogy.* New York: Modern Library, © 1938.

Ferraro, Thomas. "Ethnic Passages." Diss., Yale University, in progress.

Fiedler, Leslie A. *The Inadvertent Epic: From "Uncle Tom's Cabin" to "Roots."* New York: Simon and Schuster, 1979.

————. *Love and Death in the American Novel.* Rev. ed. 1966. New York: Stein and Day, 1975.

————. *The Return of the Vanishing American.* 1968. London: Paladin, 1972.

Fine, David M. *The City, the Immigrant, and American Fiction, 1880–1920.* Metuchen, N.J., and London: Scarecrow Press, 1971.

Fishman, J[oshua] A. "Language and Ethnicity." In *Language, Ethnicity and Intergroup Relations,* ed. Howard Giles. London, New York, and San Francisco: Academic Press, 1977. 15–57.

Fishman, Joshua A. *See also* Nahirny, Vladimir C.

Foner, Eric, ed. *Nat Turner.* Englewood Cliffs, N.J.: Prentice-Hall, 1971.

Foner, Philip S. *The Life and Writings of Fredrick Douglass.* Vol. 2, *Pre-Civil War Decade, 1850–1860.* New York: International Publishers, 1950.

Forbes, Margaret M. "Addison's Cato and George Washington." *Classical Journal* 55 (February 1960): 210–12.

Forrester, Frank {i.e., William Herbert}. *The Fair Puritan: An Historical Romance of the Days of Witchcraft.* Boston, 1844–45.

Francis, E. K. "The Nature of the Ethnic Group." *American Journal of Sociology* 52 (March 1947): 393–400.

Frank, Waldo. *Our America.* New York: Boni and Liveright, 1919.

————. *The Re-Discovery of America: An Introduction to a Philosophy of American Life.* New York and London: Scribner, 1929.

Frazier, E. Franklin. "Children in Black and Mulatto Families." *American Journal of Sociology* 39 (July 1933): 12–29.

Fredrickson, George M. *The Black Image in the White Mind: The Debate on Afro-American Character and Destiny, 1817–1914.* New York: Harper, 1972.

Freeman, Joseph. *An American Testament: A Narrative of Rebels and Romantics.* New York: Farrar, Rinehart, 1936.

Freud, Sigmund. *Jokes and Their Relation to the Unconscious.* 1905. In *The Standard Edition of the Complete Psychological Works,* trans. and ed. James Strachey and Anna Freud. Vol. 8. London: Hogarth Press, 1960.

————. "The Antithetical Sense of Primal Words." 1910. In *Collected Papers,* ed. Ernest Jones, trans. Joan Riviere. Vol. 4. New York: Basic Books, 1959. 184–91.

————. "Mourning and Melancholia." 1917. In *Collected Papers,* ed. Ernest Jones, trans. Joan Riviere. Vol. 4. New York: Basic Books, 1959. 152–70.

————. *Totem and Taboo: Some Points of Agreement between the Mental Lives of Savages and Neurotics.* 1913. Trans. James Strachey. New York: Norton, 1950.

Friar, Ralph E., and Natasha A. Friar. *The Only Good Indian . . . : The Hollywood Gospel.* New York: Drama Book Specialists, 1972.

Fuller, Margaret. *Margaret Fuller: American Romantic: A Selection from Her Writings and Correspondence.* Ed. Perry Miller. Ithaca: Cornell University Press, 1970.

Gans, Herbert J. "Ethnicity, Acculturation and Assimilation." Foreword to Neil Sandberg, *Ethnic Identity and Assimilation,* New York: Praeger, 1974. vii–xiii.

Gans, Herbert J., et al., eds. *On the Making of Americans: Essays in Honor of David Riesman.* Philadelphia: University of Pennsylvania Press, 1979.

Glasrud, Clarence A. *Hjalmar Hjorth Boyesen.* Northfield, Minn.: Norwegian-American Historical Association, 1963. Authors series, vol. 1.

Glazer, Nathan, and Daniel Patrick Moynihan. *Beyond the Melting Pot: The Negroes, Puerto Ricans, Jews, Italians, and Irish of New York City.* Cambridge: MIT Press, 1963.

————, eds. *Ethnicity: Theory and Experience.* Cambridge: Harvard University Press, 1975.

Gleason, Philip. "The Melting Pot: Symbol of Fusion or Confusion." *American Quarterly* 16 (1964): 20–46.

————. "Confusion Compounded: The Melting Pot in the 1960s and 1970s." *Ethnicity* 6.1 (March 1979): 10–20.

Gold, Michael. *Jews without Money.* 1930. New York: Avon, 1965.

————. *A Literary Anthology.* Ed. Michael Folsom. New York: International Publishers, 1972.

Goode, William J. "The Theoretical Importance of Love." *American Sociological Review* 24 (1959): 38–47.

Gordon, Milton M. *Assimilation in American Life: The Role of Race, Religion, and National Origins.* New York: Oxford University Press, 1964.

————. *Human Nature, Class, and Ethnicity.* New York: Oxford University Press, 1978.

Goren, Arthur A. *New York Jews and the Quest for Community: The Kehillah Experiment, 1908–1922.* New York and London: Columbia University Press, 1970.

Gossett, Thomas F. *Race: The History of an Idea in America.* New York: Schocken, 1965.

Greeley, Andrew M. *Ethnicity in the United States: A Preliminary Reconnaissance.* New York, London, etc.: John Wiley, 1974.

————. "Intellectuals as an 'Ethnic Group.'" *New York Times Magazine* July 12, 1970: 22–34.

Haley, Alex. *Roots: The Saga of an American Family.* 1976. New York: Dell, 1977.

Handlin, Oscar, ed. *Children of the Uprooted.* New York: George Braziller, 1966.

————. "The Prophets of Gloom." *Atlantic Monthly* April 1950: 49–51.

————. *The Uprooted: The Epic Story of the Great Migrations That Made the American People.* Boston: Little, Brown, 1951.

Hannerz, Ulf. "Some Comments on the Anthropology of Ethnicity in the United States." In *Ethnicity in the Americas,* ed. Frances Henry. The Hague and Paris: Mouton, 1976.

Hansen, Marcus Lee. *The Atlantic Migration, 1607–1860.* 1940. Ed. with a foreword by Arthur M. Schlesinger. Introd. Oscar Handlin. New York: Harper, 1961.

————. *The Immigrant in American History.* 1940. Ed. with an introd. by Arthur M. Schlesinger. New York, Evanston, and London: Harper, 1964.

————. "The Third Generation in America." [Originally entitled "The Problem of the Third Generation Immigrant." 1938.} *Commentary* 14 (November 1952): 492–500.

Hansjakob, Heinrich. *Herimann der Lahme von der Reichenau: Sein Leben und seine Wissenschaft.* Mainz: Kirchheim, 1875.

Hapgood, Hutchins. *The Spirit of the Ghetto: Studies of the Jewish Quarter of New York.* 1902. New York: Schocken, 1966.

———. *Types from City Streets.* New York and London: Funk and Wagnalls, 1910.

Hardinge, Emma. *Modern American Spiritualism: A Twenty Years' Record of the Communion between Earth and the World of the Spirits.* 1869. Introd. E. J. Dingwall. New Hyde Park, N.Y.: University Books, 1970.

Harris, Sheldon H. *Paul Cuffe: Black America and the African Return.* New York: Simon and Schuster, 1972.

Hatton, Ann Julia. *The Songs of Tammany; or, The Indian Chief: A Serious Opera.* [New York:] John Harrison and Faulkner, [1794].

Hawthorne, Nathaniel. *Selected Tales and Sketches.* Introd. Hyatt H. Waggoner. 3rd ed. New York: Holt, Rinehart and Winston, 1970.

———. *The Scarlet Letter.* 1850. Ed. Sculley Bradley, Richmond Croom Beatty, and E. Hudson Long. New York: Norton, 1962.

HEAEG. See Thernstrom, Stephan.

Heinrich, Klaus. *Vernunft und Mythos: Ausgewählte Texte.* Frankfurt: Fischer Alternative, 1983.

Heller, Agnes. "Can Cultures Be Compared?" *Dialectical Anthropology* 8 (April 1984): 269–74.

Herberg, Will. *Protestant-Catholic-Jew: An Essay in American Religious Sociology.* 1955. Rev. ed. Garden City, N.Y.: Doubleday Anchor, 1960.

Higginson, John. "An Attestation to This Church-History of NEW-ENGLAND." In Cotton Mather, *Magnalia Christi Americana. Books I and II,* ed. Kenneth B. Murdock. Cambridge, Mass., and London: Harvard University Press, 1977. 63–73.

Higham, John. *Send These to Me: Jews and Other Immigrants in Urban America.* New York: Atheneum, 1975.

Hoagland, Edward. "The Job Is to Pour Out Your Heart." *New York Times Book Review* October 4, 1981: 3, 36–37.

Hobsbawm, Eric, and Terence Ranger, eds. *The Invention of Tradition.* Cambridge, New York, etc.: Cambridge University Press, 1983.

Hogan, Robert. *Dion Boucicault.* New York: Twayne, 1969.

Hollinger, David A. "Ethnic Diversity, Cosmopolitanism and the Emergence of the American Liberal Intelligentsia." *American Quarterly* 27 (May 1975): 133–51.

Honour, Hugh. *The New Golden Land: European Images of America from the Discoveries to the Present Time.* New York: Pantheon, © 1975.

Horace. *The Epistles and Art of Poetry of Horace.* Ed. Philip Francis. London, 1778.

Howard, George Elliott. *A History of Matrimonial Institutions Chiefly in England and the United States.* 1904. Vol. 2. New York: Humanities Press, 1964.

Howe, Irving. "The Limits of Ethnicity." *New Republic* June 25, 1977: 17–19.

Howe, M. A. DeWolfe. *Barrett Wendell and His Letters.* Boston: Atlantic Monthly Press, 1924.

Hubbell, Jay B. "The Smith-Pocahontas Story in Literature." *Virginia Magazine* 65 (July 1957): 275–300.

Hudson, Winthrop S., ed. *Nationalism and Religion in America: Concepts of American Identity and Mission.* New York: Harper, 1970.

Huggins, Nathan I. "Afro-Americans: National Character and Community." *Center Magazine* July/August 1974: 51–66.

Hughes, Everett Cherrington, and Helen MacGill Hughes. *Where Peoples Meet: Racial and Ethnic Frontiers*. Glencoe, Ill.: Free Press, 1952.

Hutchinson, Thomas. *The History of the Colony and Province of Massachusetts Bay*. Ed. Lawrence Shaw Mayo. Cambridge: Harvard University Press, 1936.

Ifkovic, Edward, ed. *American Letter: Immigrant and Ethnic Writing*. Englewood Cliffs, N.J.: Prentice-Hall, © 1975.

Interpreter's Bible, The. New York and Nashville: Abingdon-Cokesbury. Vol. 10, 1953; vol. 11, 1955.

Irving, Washington. *History, Tales and Sketches*. New York: Library of America, 1983.

Irwin, John T. *Doubling and Incest/Repetition and Revenge: A Speculative Reading of Faulkner*. Baltimore and London: Johns Hopkins University Press, 1975.

James, William. *The Varieties of Religious Experience*. 1902. Harmondsworth: Penguin, 1982.

Jefferson, Thomas. *Notes on the State of Virginia*. 1785. New York: Harper, 1964.

Jensen, Merrill. *Regionalism in America*. Madison: University of Wisconsin Press, 1952.

Johnson, James Weldon. *Along This Way: The Autobiography of James Weldon Johnson*. 1933. New York: Viking, 1968.

———. *The Autobiography of an Ex-Colored Man*. 1912. In *Three Negro Classics*, introd. John Hope Franklin. New York: Avon, 1965. The publisher's "Preface to the Original Edition of 1912" reprinted in *The Autobiography of an Ex-Coloured Man*, ed. Arna Bontemps. New York: Hill and Wang, 1960. xi–xii.

———. "The Dilemma of the Negro Author." *American Mercury* December 1928: 477–81.

Jones, Ernest. "Die Bedeutung des Grossvaters für das Schicksal des Einzelnen." *Internationale Zeitschrift für Psychoanalyse* 1 (1913): 219–23. Reference to English abstract under Abraham, Karl.

Jones, LeRoi. *Blues People: Negro Music in White America*. New York: Morrow, 1967.

———. *Home: Social Essays*. New York: Morrow, 1966.

Judd, Sylvester. *Margaret: A Tale of the Real and the Ideal, Blight and Bloom*. Boston: Jordan and Wiley, 1845.

Jung, C[arl] G[ustav]. *Psychology and Alchemy*. 1944. Trans. R. F. C. Hull. In *Collected Works*, vol. 12. 2nd ed. Princeton: Princeton University Press, 1968.

———."Your Negroid and Indian Behavior." *Forum* 83.4 (April 1930): 193–99.

Kafka, Franz. "The Trees." 1913. In *The Penal Colony: Stories and Short Pieces*, trans. Willa and Edwin Muir. New York: Schocken, 1948.

Kallen, Horace M. *Culture and Democracy in the United States: Studies in the Group Psychology of the American Peoples*. New York: Boni and Liveright, 1924.

———."The Ethics of Zionism." *Maccabean* 11.2 (August 1906): 61–71.

———. *The Structure of Lasting Peace: An Inquiry into the Motives of Peace*. Boston: Marshall Jones, 1918.

Kardiner, Abram, and Lionel Ovesey. *The Mark of Oppression: Explorations in the Personality of the American Negro*. 1951. Cleveland and New York: Meridian Books, 1964.

Kennedy, John F. *A Nation of Immigrants*. New York: Harper, 1964.

Kerouac, Jack. *On the Road: Text and Criticism*. Ed. Scott Donaldson. New York: Penguin, © 1979.

Kettner, James. *The Development of American Citizenship, 1608–1870*. Chapel Hill: University of North Carolina Press, 1978.

Kinnamon, Keneth. *The Emergence of Richard Wright: A Study in Literature and Society*. Urbana: University of Illinois Press, 1972.

Klauprecht, Emil. *Cincinnati; oder, Geheimnisse des Westens*. Cincinnati: C. F. Schmidt, 1854–55.

Klibansky, Raymond, Erwin Panofsky, and Fritz Saxl. *Saturn and Melancholy: Studies in the History of Natural Philosophy, Religion and Art*. Cambridge, Eng.: Thomas Nelson, 1964.

Kohn, Hans. *The Idea of Nationalism*. New York: Macmillan, 1945.

Kolodny, Annette. *The Lay of the Land: Metaphor as Experience and History in American Life and Letters*. Chapel Hill: University of North Carolina Press, © 1975.

Kroes, Rob, ed. *The American Identity: Fusion and Fragmentation*. European Contributions to American Studies 3. Amsterdam: Amerika-Instituut, 1980.

Lasch, Christopher. "Mass Culture Reconsidered." *Democracy* October 1981: 7–22.

Lawrence, D. H. *Studies in Classic American Literature*. 1923. New York: Viking Press, 1964.

Learned, Marion Dexter. *The Life of Francis Daniel Pastorius, the Founder of Germantown*. Philadelphia: Campbell, 1908.

Leftwich, Joseph. *Israel Zangwill*. New York: Thomas Yoseloff, 1957.

Lepenies, Wolfgang. *Melancholie und Gesellschaft*. Frankfurt: Suhrkamp, 1969.

Levine, Lawrence W. *Black Culture and Black Consciousness: Afro-American Folk Thought from Slavery to Freedom*. New York: Oxford University Press, 1977.

Lewisohn, Ludwig. *Expression in America*. New York: Harper, 1932.

———. *Cities and Men*. New York and London: Harper, 1927.

———. *Up Stream: An American Chronicle*. New York: Boni and Liveright, 1922.

Lieber, Francis, ed. *Encyclopedia Americana*. Vol. 8. Philadelphia: Desilver, Thomas, 1836.

Lindsay, Vachel. *Selected Poems*. Ed. Mark Harris. New York: Macmillan, 1963.

Lippard, George. *The Monks of Monk Hall* [i.e., *The Quaker City*. 1844.] Ed. with an introd. by Leslie Fiedler. New York: Odyssey, 1970.

Livermore, Abiel Abbot. *The Acts of the Apostles: With a Commentary*. Boston and Cambridge: James Munroe; London: Sampson Low, 1857.

Locke, Alain, ed. *The New Negro*. 1925. New York: Atheneum, 1969.

Lucretius. *On the Nature of the Universe*. Trans. R. E. Latham. Harmondsworth: Penguin, 1977.

Luhmann, Niklas. *Liebe als Passion: Zur Codierung von Intimität*. Frankfurt: Suhrkamp Wissenschaft, 1982.

Lukács, Georg. *The Historical Novel*. Trans. Hannah and Stanley Mitchell. Boston: Beacon Press, 1962.

Lurie, Nancy Oestreich. "Indian Cultural Adjustment to European Civilization." In *Seventeenth-Century America: Essays in Colonial History*, ed. James Morton Smith. Chapel Hill: University of North Carolina Press, 1959. 33–60.

Lyons, Bonnie. *Henry Roth: The Man and His Work*. New York: Cooper Square Publishers, 1976.

McClure, S[amuel] S[idney], [and Willa Cather]. *My Autobiography*. 1914. Introd. Louis Filler. New York: Ungar, 1963.

[Macomb, Alexander.] *Pontiac; or, The Siege of Detroit: A Drama*. Boston: Colman, 1835.

McKay, Claude. *The Passion of Claude McKay: Selected Prose and Poetry, 1912–1948.* Ed. Wayne Cooper. New York: Schocken, 1973.

Madison, Charles A. *Yiddish Literature: Its Scope and Major Works.* 1968. New York: Schocken, 1971.

Mailer, Norman. *The Armies of the Night: History as a Novel: The Novel as History.* New York: Signet, 1968.

Malcolm X. *The Autobiography of Malcolm X,* with the assistance of Alex Haley. New York: Grove Press, © 1965.

Mangione, Jerre. *Mount Allegro: A Memoir of Italian American Life.* 1942. Ed. with an introd. by Herbert J. Gans. New York: Columbia University Press, 1981.

Mann, Arthur. *The One and the Many: Reflections on the American Identity.* Chicago and London: University of Chicago Press, 1979.

Mannheim, Karl. "The Problem of Generations." 1928. In *Essays on the Sociology of Knowledge,* ed. Paul Kecskemeti. New York: Oxford University Press, 1952. 276–322.

Marty, Martin E. "The Spirit's Holy Errand: The Search for a Spiritual Style in Secular America." In *Religion in America,* ed. Robert W. Bellah and William McLoughlin. Boston: Houghton Mifflin, 1968. 167–83.

Marzio, Peter C., ed. *A Nation of Nations: The People Who Came to America as Seen through Objects and Documents Exhibited at the Smithsonian Institution.* New York: Harper, 1976.

Mather, Cotton. *Magnalia Christi Americana; or, The Ecclesiastical History of New-England, from its First Planting in the Year 1620, unto the Year of Our Lord 1698: In seven books.* 2 vols. Hartford: Silas Andrews and Sons, 1853.

———. *Paterna: The Autobiography of Cotton Mather.* 1699–1702. Ed. Ronald A. Bosco. Delmar, N.Y.: Scholars' Facsimiles and Reprints, 1976.

Matthews, F{red} H. "The Revolt against Americanism: Cultural Pluralism and Cultural Relativism as an Ideology of Liberation." *Canadian Review of American Studies* 1.1 (Spring 1970): 4–31.

Mayer, J{acob} P. *Prophet of the Mass Age: A Study of Alexis de Tocqueville.* Trans. M. M. Bozman and C. Hahn. London: J. M. Dent, 1939.

Mays, Benjamin E. *The Negro's God as Reflected in His Literature.* 1938. New York: Atheneum, 1973.

Mead, Margaret. *And Keep Your Powder Dry: An Anthropologist Looks at America.* 1942. Expanded ed. New York: Morrow, 1965.

———. "Conflicts of Cultures in America." *Proceedings of the 54th Annual Convention of the Middle States Association of Colleges and Secondary Schools . . . 1940.* Philadelphia: Middle States Association, 1940. 30–44.

Melville, Herman. *Mardi and a Voyage Thither.* 1849. 2 vols. London, Bombay, Sidney: Constable, 1922.

———. *Moby-Dick; or, The Whale.* 1851. Ed. Luther S. Mansfield and Howard P. Vincent. New York: Hendricks House, 1962.

———. *White-Jacket or The World in a Man-of-War.* 1850. Boston: L. C. Page, 1950.

Miller, Perry. *Errand into the Wilderness.* Cambridge: Harvard University Press, 1956.

———. *Nature's Nation.* Cambridge: Harvard University Press, 1967.

———. *The New England Mind: From Colony to Province.* Cambridge: Harvard University Press, 1953.

Miller, Perry, and Thomas H. Johnson. *The Puritans: A Sourcebook of Their Writings.* 1938. Rev. ed. New York: Harper, 1963.

Minikes, H. I. *Among the Indians; or, The Country Peddler.* Ed. and trans. Mark Slobin. *Drama Review* 24.3 (September 1980): 17–26.

Mitchell, Isaac. *The Asylum; or, Alonzo and Melissa: An American Tale, Founded on Fact.* Poughkeepsie: Joseph Nelson, 1811.

Moody, Richard, ed. *Dramas from the American Theatre, 1762–1909.* Cleveland and New York: World, 1966.

Moore, Deborah Dash. "Defining American Jewish Ethnicity." *Prospects* 6 (1981): 387–409.

"Moreau de St. Méry's American Journey." Trans. and ed. Kenneth and Anna M. Roberts. In *Literature of the Early Republic,* ed. Edwin H. Cady. 2nd ed. New York: Holt, Rinehart and Winston, 1969. 272–84.

Morgan, Edmund S. *The Puritan Family: Religion and Domestic Relations in Seventeenth Century New England.* 1944. New York: Harper, 1966.

Müllner, Leonhard. "Bericht von der Generation der Metallen." In *Jo. Franc. Buddei Historisch = und politische Untersuchung der Alchemie und was davon zu halten sey?* Nürnberg, 1727.

Murdock, George P. "Ethnocentrism." In *Encyclopedia of the Social Sciences,* ed. Edwin A. Seligman and Alvin Johnson. Vol. 5, New York: Macmillan, 1931. 613–14.

Murphy, Geraldine Anne. "The Ideology of American Romance Theory." Diss., Columbia University, 1985.

Murray, Albert. *The Omni-Americans: New Perspectives on Black Experience and American Culture.* New York: Avon, 1970.

Muzzey, David Saville. *James G. Blaine. A Political Idol of Other Days.* New York: Dodd, Mead, 1934.

Myrdal, Gunnar. "The Case against Romantic Ethnicity." *Center Magazine* July/August 1974: 26–30.

Nabokov, Vladimir. *Pale Fire.* 1962. New York: Berkley Medallion, n.d.

Nahirny, Vladimir C., and Joshua A. Fishman. "American Immigrant Groups: Ethnic Identification and the Problem of Generations." *Sociological Review* ns 13 (1965): 311–26.

Neumann, Erich. *Die grosse Mutter: Der Archetyp des grossen Weiblichen.* Zürich: Rhein-verlag, 1956.

Newman, Katharine D., ed. *The American Equation: Literature in a Multiethnic Culture.* Boston: Allyn and Bacon, 1971.

Novak, Barbara. *Nature and Culture: American Landscape and Painting, 1825–1875.* New York: Oxford University Press, © 1980.

Novak, Michael. *The Rise of the Unmeltable Ethnics: Politics and Culture in the Seventies.* 1972. New York: Macmillan, 1975.

Nye, Russel B{laine}. *American Literary History: 1607–1830.* New York: Knopf, 1970.

————. *The Cultural Life of the New Nation, 1776–1830.* 1960. New York: Harper, 1963.

Odum, Howard, and Harry Estill Moore. *American Regionalism: A Cultural-Historical Approach to National Integration.* New York: H. Holt, 1938.

Osofsky, Gilbert. "Wendell Phillips and the Quest for a New American Identity." *Canadian Review of Studies in Nationalism* 1.1 (Fall 1973): 15–46.

Owen, John J. *The Acts of the Apostles.* New York: Leavitt, 1850.

Paine, Thomas. *Common Sense.* 1776. Ed. Isaac Kramnick. New York and Harmond-sworth: Penguin, 1983.

Paley, Grace. *Enormous Changes at the Last Minute.* New York: Dell, 1975.

Park, Robert Ezra. *Race and Culture: Essays in the Sociology of Contemporary Man.* New York: Free Press of Glencoe, 1964.

Parsons, Talcott, and Kenneth B. Clark, eds. *The Negro American.* Boston: Beacon Press, 1967.

Patterson, G. James. "A Critique of 'The New Ethnicity.'" *American Anthropologist* 81 (1979): 103–5.

Patterson, Orlando. *Ethnic Chauvinism: The Reactionary Impulse.* New York: Stein and Day, 1977.

————. *Slavery and Social Death: A Comparative Study.* Cambridge, Mass., and London: Harvard University Press, 1982.

Petter, Henri. *The Early American Novel.* {n.p.}: Ohio State University Press, © 1971.

Phillips, Wendell. "Speech of Wendell Phillips, Esq.: At the Anniversary of the American Anti-Slavery Society, in the Cooper Institute, New York." *Liberator* May 29, 1863: 1.

Poesche, Theodore, and Charles Goepp. *The New Rome; or, The United States of the World.* New York: G. P. Putnam, 1853.

Poggioli, Renato. *The Theory of the Avant-Garde.* New York: Harper, 1971.

Poirier, Richard. *A World Elsewhere: The Place of Style in American Literature.* New York: Oxford University Press, 1966.

Porter, H. C. "Reflections on the Ethnohistory of Early Colonial North America." *Journal of American Studies* 16 (August 1982): 243–54.

Potter, David M. *History and American Society: Essays.* Ed. Don E. Fehrenbacher. New York: Oxford University Press, 1973.

Pound, Louise. "Nebraska Legends of Lovers' Leaps." *Western Folklore* 8 (October 1949): 304–13.

Powell, John W. "Physiographic Regions of the United States." In National Geographic Society, *The Physiography of the United States.* New York, 1896.

Quintana, Ricardo, ed. *Eighteenth-Century Plays.* New York: Modern Library, 1952.

Radin, Paul. *The Trickster: A Study in American Indian Mythology.* With commentaries by C. G. Jung and Karl Kerényi. London: Routledge and Kegan Paul, 1956.

Reed, Ishmael. *Mumbo Jumbo.* 1972. New York: Bantam, 1973.

Reed, John Shelton. *The Enduring South: Subcultural Persistence in Mass Society.* Chapel Hill: University of North Carolina Press, 1974.

Renfro, G. Herbert. *Life and Works of Phillis Wheatley.* 1916. Miami: Mnemosyne, 1969.

Rice, Howard. *Le Cultivateur américain: Étude sur l'oeuvre de Saint John de Crèvecoeur.* Paris: Librairie Ancienne Honoré Champion, 1933.

Richter, Daniel K. "The Iroquois Melting Pot: Seventeenth-Century War Captives of the Five Nations." Paper presented to the Shelby Cullom Davis Center Conference on War and Society in Early America, March 11–12, 1983.

Riesman, David. *Abundance for What? and Other Essays.* Garden City, N.Y.: Doubleday, 1964.

————. "Some Observations on Intellectual Freedom." *American Scholar* 23 (Winter 1953–54): 9–25.

Riis, Jacob. *The Making of an American.* 1901. New York: Macmillan, 1904.

Rischin, Moses, ed. *Immigration and the American Tradition.* Indianapolis: Bobbs-Merrill, 1976.

————. "Marcus Lee Hansen: America's First Transethnic Historian." In *Uprooted Americans: Essays to Honor Oscar Handlin*, ed. Richard L. Bushman et al. Boston: Little, Brown, 1979. 319–47.

Rizk, Salom. *Syrian Yankee*. Garden City, N.Y.: Doubleday, Doran, 1943.

Rodriguez, Richard. *Hunger of Memory: The Education of Richard Rodriguez*. 1982. Toronto, New York, etc.: Bantam, 1983.

Roehrich, Lutz. "Auswandererlieder." Mimeogr. handout for lecture on October 8, 1983, University of Cincinnati.

Rølvaag, O[le] E. *Giants in the Earth*. 1927. Trans. Lincoln Colcord and O. E. Rølvaag. New York: Harper, 1966.

————. *Their Fathers' God*. 1931. Trans. Trygve M. Ager. Lincoln and London: University of Nebraska Press, 1983.

Rogers, Robert. *Ponteach; or, The Savages of America: A Tragedy*. London, 1766.

Rogin, Michael Paul. *Fathers and Children: Andrew Jackson and the Subjugation of the American Indian*. New York: Vintage, 1975.

Rolle, Andrew F. *The Italian Americans: Troubled Roots*. New York and London: Free Press, 1980.

Roth, Henry. *Call It Sleep*. New York: Robert O. Ballou, 1934.

Rothman, Ellen K. *Hands and Hearts: A History of Courtship in America*. New York: Basic Books, 1984.

Royce, Josiah. *Race Questions, Provincialism, and Other American Problems*. 1908. Freeport: Books for Library Press, 1967.

Ruchames, Louis, ed. *Racial Thought in America*. Vol. 1, *From the Puritans to Abraham Lincoln: A Documentary History*. New York: Grosset and Dunlap, 1970.

Sales, Raoul de Roussy de. "Love in America." *Atlantic Monthly* May 1938: 645–51.

Saveth, Edward N. *American Historians and European Immigrants, 1875–1925*. 1948. New York: Russell and Russell, 1965.

Schechter, Solomon. *Seminary Addresses and Other Papers*. Ed. Louis Finkelstein. Cincinnati: Ark, 1915.

Schmidt, Sarah L. "Horace Kallen and the Americanization of Zionism." Diss., University of Maryland, 1973.

Schneider, David M. *American Kinship: A Cultural Account*. 1968. 2nd ed. Chicago and London: University of Chicago Press, 1980.

Schön, Donald. "Generative Metaphor: A Perspective on Problem-Setting in Social Policy." In *Metaphor and Thought*, ed. Andrew Ortony. Cambridge, Eng.: Cambridge University Press, 1979. 254–83.

Schoolcraft, Henry R. *The American Indians: Their History, Condition and Prospects, from Original Notes and Manuscripts*. Buffalo: Derby, 1851.

Sealsfield, Charles [i.e., Karl Postl]. *Der Legitime und die Republikaner: Eine Geschichte aus dem letzten amerikanisch-englischen Kriege*. Zürich: Orell, Füssli, 1833.

Seeber, Edward D. "Critical Views on Logan's Speech." *Journal of American Folklore* 60 (April-June 1947): 130–46.

Shumsky, Neil Larry. "Zangwill's *The Melting Pot*: Ethnic Tensions on Stage." *American Quarterly* 27 (1975): 29–41.

Sills, David L., ed. *International Encyclopedia of the Social Sciences*. New York: Macmillan and Free Press, 1968.

Silverman, Kenneth. *A Cultural History of the American Revolution*. New York: Thomas Y. Crowell, 1976.

Simmel, Georg. *Conflict and The Web of Group Affiliations*, ed. Everett C. Hughes. New York: Macmillan and Free Press, 1964.

Simmen, Edward, ed. *Pain and Promise: The Chicano Today*. New York and Scarborough, Ont.: Mentor, 1972.

Simon, Kate. *Bronx Primitive: Portraits in a Childhood*. 1982. New York: Harper, 1983.

Simon, Myron, ed. *Ethnic Writers in America*. New York: Harcourt, Brace, 1972.

Simon, Paul. "American Tune." On *There Goes Rhymin' Simon*. CBS 69035, © 1973.

Skårdal, Dorothy Burton. *The Divided Heart: Scandinavian Immigrant Experience through Literary Sources*. Lincoln: University of Nebraska Press, 1974.

Skinner, Charles M. *American Myths and Legends*. Vol. 2. Philadelphia and London: Lippincott, 1903.

Smith, M. G. "Ethnicity and Ethnic Groups in America: The View from Harvard." *Ethnic and Racial Studies* 5 (1982): 1–22.

Smith, Timothy L. "Religion and Ethnicity in America." *American Historical Review* 83 (December 1978): 1155–85.

———. "Slavery and Theology: The Emergence of Black Christian Consciousness in Nineteenth-Century America." *Church History* 41 (December 1972): 497–512.

Solomon, Barbara Miller. *Ancestors and Immigrants: A Changing New England Tradition*. 1956. Chicago and London: University of Chicago Press, 1972.

Spiller, Robert E., et al. *Literary History of the United States*. 4th ed. New York: Macmillan, 1975.

Steffens, Lincoln. "Moses in Red." In *The World of Lincoln Steffens*, ed. Ella Winter and Herbert Shapiro. New York: Hill and Wang, 1962.

Stein, Gertrude. *The Making of Americans: The Hersland Family*. 1934. Introd. Bernard Fay. New York: Harcourt, Brace and World, 1962.

Stein, Judith. *The World of Marcus Garvey: Race and Class in Mordern Society*. Baton Rouge: Louisiana State University Press, 1985.

Stewart, J. C. *The Last of the Mohicans: An Ethiopian Sketch*. New York: DeWitt, 1870.

Stokes, Anson Phelps. *Church and State in the United States*. Introd. Ralph Henry Gabriel. Vol. 1. New York: Harper and Brothers, 1950.

Stone, John Augustus. *Metamora; or, The Last of the Wampanoags*. 1829. In *Six Early American Plays, 1798–1890*, ed. William Coyle and Harvey Damaser. Columbus, Ohio: Charles Merrill, 1968. 47–95.

Stowe, Harriet Beecher. *The Key to Uncle Tom's Cabin*. 1853. New York: Arno Press and New York Times, 1969.

———. *Uncle Tom's Cabin; or, Life among the Lowly*. 1852. Columbus, Ohio: Charles Merrill, 1969.

Sue, Eugène. *The Mysteries of Paris*. Trans. Charles H. Town. New York: Harper and Brothers, 1843.

Sumner, William Graham. *Folkways: A Study of the Sociological Importance of Usages, Manners, Customs, Mores, and Morals*. 1906. Boston, New York, etc.: Ginn, 1940.

Susman, Warren, ed. *Culture and Commitment, 1929–1945*. New York: Braziller, 1973.

———. "The Thirties." In *The Development of an American Culture*, ed. Stanley Coben and Lorman Ratner. Englewood Cliffs, N.J.: Prentice-Hall, 1970. 179–218.

Tanselle, G. Thomas. "The Birth and Death of Alknomook." *Newberry Library Bulletin* 6 (May 1979): 389–401.

————. *Royall Tyler*. Cambridge: Harvard University Press, 1967.

Taylor, Edward. *The Poems of Edward Taylor*. Ed. Donald E. Stanford. 4th ed. New Haven: Yale University Press, 1977.

Thernstrom, Stephan, Ann Orlov, and Oscar Handlin, eds. *Harvard Encyclopedia of American Ethnic Groups*. Cambridge, Mass., and London: Harvard University Press, 1980.

Thoreau, Henry David. "A Plea for Captain John Brown." In *Great Short Works of Henry David Thoreau*, ed. Wendell Glick. New York, San Francisco, and London: Harper, 1982. 270–93.

Timrod, Henry. *The Collected Poems of Henry Timrod: A Variorum Edition*. Ed. Edd Winfield Parks and Aileen Wells Parks. Athens: University of Georgia Press, © 1965.

Tocqueville, Alexis de. *Democracy in America*. The Henry Reeve Text. Ed. Phillips Bradley. 2 vols. New York: Knopf, 1951.

Tolson, Melvin B. *Harlem Gallery*. Bk. 1, *The Curator*. Introd. Karl Shapiro. New York: Collier, 1969.

Toomer, Jean. *Essentials*. Chicago: privately printed, 1931.

Trachtenberg, Alan. "Experiments in Another Country: Stephen Crane's *City Sketches*." *Southern Review* 10 (April 1974): 265–85.

Tumin, Melvin M. "The Cult of Gratitude." In *The Ghetto and Beyond*, ed. Peter I. Rose. New York: Random House, 1969. 69–82.

Turner, Frederick Jackson. *The Frontier in American History*. 1920. Introd. Ray Allen Billington. New York: Holt, Rinehart and Winston, 1962.

Twain, Mark. *Life on the Mississippi*. 1883. New York: Bantam, 1963.

Tyler, Royall. *The Contrast*. 1787. In *The Longman Anthology of American Drama*, ed. Lee A. Jacobus. New York and London: Longman, 1982. 5–32.

van den Berghe, Pierre L. *Race and Racism: A Comparative Perspective*. New York: Wiley, 1967.

Van Vechten, Carl. *Nigger Heaven*. New York: Knopf, 1926.

Vauthier, Simone. *Textualité et stéréotypes: Of African Queens and Afro-American Princes and Princesses: Miscegenation in Old Hepsy*. Publication du Conseil Scientifique de la Sorbonne Nouvelle: Paris, [1980].

Veblen, Thorstein. *The Portable Veblen*. Ed. with an introd. by Max Lerner. 1948. New York: Viking Press, 1970.

Vergil. *The Eclogues and Georgics of Virgil*. Trans. C. Day Lewis. Garden City, N.Y. : Doubleday Anchor, 1964.

Villa, José García . *Have Come, Am Here*. New York: Viking Press, 1942.

Wagenknecht, Edward. *William Dean Howells: The Friendly Eye*. New York: Oxford University Press, 1969.

Waldseemüller, Martin. *The Cosmographiae Introductio*. Ed. Charles George Herbermann. New York: United States Catholic Historical Society, 1967.

Wallace, Anthony F. C. Review of David Schneider, *American Kinship*. *American Anthropologist* 71 (February 1969): 100–106.

Wallace, Mac H. In Lee S. McCollester, *A New Emphasis on Some Old American Affirmations: An Address at the Thirteenth Interdenominational Citizens' Thanksgiving Service, Detroit Opera House, Thursday, November 26, 1914*. Detroit: privately published, [n.d.].

Wand, David Hsin-Fu, ed. *Asian-American Heritage: An Anthology of Prose and Poetry*. New York: Washington Square Press, 1974.

Ware, Caroline F. *The Cultural Approach to History*. New York: Columbia University Press, 1940.

Warner, W. Lloyd, and Paul S. Lunt. *The Social Life of a Modern Community*. Yankee City Series, vol. 1. New Haven: Yale University Press, 1941.

————. *The Status System of a Modern Community*. Yankee City Series, vol. 2. New Haven: Yale University Press, 1942.

Washington, Booker T. *Up from Slavery*. 1901. In *Three Negro Classics*, introd. John Hope Franklin. New York: Avon, 1965.

Wendell, Barrett. *Liberty, Union and Democracy: The National Ideals of America*. New York: Scribner's, 1906.

————. *A Literary History of America*. New York: Scribner's, 1900.

Werner, M. R. *Tammany Hall*. Garden City, N.Y.: Doubleday, Doran, 1928.

Westermarck, Edward. *The History of Human Marriage*. London: Macmillan, 1921.

Wilbur, C. Keith. *The New England Indians*. Chester, Conn.: Globe Pequot Press, 1978.

Williamson, Joel. *New People: Miscegenation and Mulattoes in the United States*. New York and London: Macmillan Free Press, © 1980.

Wilson, Woodrow. *The New Democracy: Presidential Messages, Addresses and Other Papers (1913–1917)*. Ed. Ray Stannard Baker and William E. Dodd. Vol. 1. New York and London: Harper, 1926.

Winthrop, John. "A Modell of Christian Charity." 1630. In *Winthrop Papers*, ed. Stewart Mitchell. Vol. 2, *1623–1630*. N.p.: Massachusetts Historical Society, 1931. 282–95.

Winton, Calhoun. "The Theater and Drama." In *American Literature, 1764–1789: The Revolutionary Years*, ed. Everett Emerson. Madison: University of Wisconsin Press, 1977. 87–104.

Wise, Gene. "'Paradigm Dramas' in American Studies: A Cultural and Institutional History of the Movement." *American Quarterly* 31 (Bibliography Issue, 1979): 293–337.

Wohl, R. Richard, and Anselm L. Strauss. "Symbolic Representation and the Urban Milieu." *American Journal of Sociology* 63 (1957–58): 523–32.

Wohlgelernter, Maurice. *Israel Zangwill: A Study*. New York and London: Columbia University Press, 1964.

————, ed. *History, Religion, and Spiritual Democracy: Essays in Honor of Joseph L. Blau*. New York: Columbia University Press, 1980.

Wright, Richard. *Native Son*. 1940. New York: Harper, 1966.

Young, Philip. "The Mother of Us All: Pocahontas Reconsidered." *Kenyon Review* 24 (Summer 1962): 391–415.

Zangwill, Israel. Afterword. 1914. *The Melting-Pot* (1932 edition). New York: Arno Press, 1975.

————. *The Melting-Pot*. 1909. New York: Macmillan, 1910.

————. *The Melting-Pot*. Promptbook, ca. 1909. New York Public Library Theatre Collection.

————. "Three Years of Study." *New York Times* October 24, 1908.

Zelman, Donald L. Review of *The Bracero Experience*: Elitelore versus Folklore. *Journal of American Ethnic History* 1 (Fall 1981): 111–13.

Ziff, Larzer. *Puritanism in America: New Culture in a New World*. New York: Viking, 1973.

Index